A General Register of All the Lodges and Grand Lodges of Freemasons in North America

Also from Westphalia Press
westphaliapress.org

A General Register
of All the
Lodges and Grand Lodges
of Freemasons in
North America

by J. Fletcher Brennan

WESTPHALIA PRESS
An imprint of Policy Studies Organization

A General Register of all the Lodges and Grand Lodges of Freemasons in North America
All Rights Reserved © 2015 by Policy Studies Organization

Westphalia Press
An imprint of Policy Studies Organization
1527 New Hampshire Ave., NW
Washington, D.C. 20036
info@ipsonet.org

ISBN-13: 978-1-63391-259-5
ISBN-10: 1633912590

Cover design by Jeffrey Barnes:
www.jbarnesdesign.com

Daniel Gutierrez-Sandoval, Executive Director
PSO and Westphalia Press

Updated material and comments on this edition
can be found at the Westphalia Press website:
www.westphaliapress.org

A General Register

OF ALL THE

LODGES AND GRAND LODGES

OF

Freemasons in North America

WHICH MAINTAIN MUTUAL CORRESPONDENCE AND RECOGNITION.

COMPILED FROM GRAND LODGE PROCEEDINGS AND DIRECT RETURNS FROM THE SECRE-
TARIES IN OFFICE IN THE LODGES OF THE UNITED STATES AND CANADA,
AND OMISSIONS CORRECTED BY THE GRAND SECRETARIES.

By J. FLETCHER BRENNAN,
*Editor of the American Freemason, and a General History of Freemasonry, trans-
lated from the French of Dr. Rebold, of Paris.*

Light maketh manifest : whatsoever maketh manifest is Light.

Introduction.

WE take the liberty of introducing to the kind regards of the great Fraternity of FREEMASONS in North America this little book, as the product of an earnest effort to place before them a compendious Register of their lodges and grand lodges on this continent, to the extent of all which correspond or recognize each other. As will be seen, those lodges number (8,069) eight thousand and sixtynine, the grand lodges (47) forty-seven, while they mutually represent more than (514,296) five hundred and fourteen thousand, two hundred and ninety-six MEN, all bound, to a certain extent, by similar rites and obligations to assist each other in sickness and in health, and extend each to the other of this vast multitude a brother's hand and a brother's affectionate consideration.

Believing that such a little book would be gratifying as instructive to every Brother Freemason who took that interest in our great Fraternity that is expected of us all, we have, at greater expense and more labor than we anticipated, and with the kind assistance of brethren, the secretaries and grand secretaries, been enabled to present that which we have conscientiously endeavored to make—a correct Register of the information this book presents, and compressed the same into as little space as a due regard for the easy examination and use of it would warrant.

A book of this character, and confined to its subjects, presents a very limited field for literary labor or merit; nevertheless we hope that its contents even in this respect will be satisfactory to those they principally interest. In our notices of grand lodges we have in great measure confined our statements to necessary information, and have presented what we believe to be a correct record as well of their organization as of their standing at this date. Wherever we have exceeded this, we have endeavored to do so not in a spirit of unkind criticism, but fraternally solicitous for the better condition and more truly respectable of those important bodies.

With this, our brief introduction of our GENERAL MASONIC REGISTER to those for whom it has been produced, we bespeak their kind indulgence towards any faults or errors of omission or commission they may discover. With the most careful and pains-taking fidelity in its production, such a book, we respectfully request them to remember, although believed to be nearly perfect, must necessarily be imperfect; and notwithstanding the greatest degree of correctness may be desired and earnestly striven for, where thousands of proper names are presented, incorrectness will inevitably occur.

Cincinnati, Ohio, Oct. 14, 1871.

Summary of Contents.

GENERAL MASONIC REGISTER.

Alabama.

THE Grand Lodge of this State was organized on the 14th June, 1821. Its communications are held in December of each year, at the city of Montgomery. Than this no grand lodge in North America has exercised a manner more paternal and solicitous for their welfare toward the lodges of its jurisdiction. In evidence we can, from personal knowledge, state that in 1858, consequent upon a vote taken in Dec. 1857, there was purchased for and delivered to each lodge in good standing in the State a set of the " Universal Masonic Library," thirty volumes octavo, at a cost to the Grand Lodge of Alabama of about Forty-five Dollars a set ; and on more than one occasion, as we have been informed, when it was ascertained that the treasury exceeded the requirements of the grand lodge, instead of hoarding and putting to interest the excess, as is the manner generally of those organizations, this excess was divided *pro rata* among and returned to the lodges. Engaging in no building operations for any purpose, and keeping expenses at figures designated by the constitution, the revenue, derived from charter fees and fifty cents *per capita* annual dues from the members of the lodges, has always been ample to meet the obligations of this grand lodge. In common with the majority of grand lodges in the Southern States, neither mileage nor per diem is paid by the G. L. of Alabama ; and a proposed change in the constitution, recognizing such payment, was in 1870 voted in the negative by a majority of the lodges. A proposition to assess for the purpose of building a " G. L. Hall " in the city of Montgomery, and under which, though not submitted to the lodges for their rejection or approval, its terms had been by some of them complied with, was, in 1870, repealed by the grand lodge, and a vote passed to return the money received to the lodges which paid it.

During the fifty years this grand lodge has existed there have been 374 lodges set to work by its charters and dispensations, of which 244 were in 1870 returned in good standing, with a membership of 10,985. The Constitution, Sec. 22, of Art. 6, directs that

"Every lodge that shall neglect to make regular return to the G. L., or to pay its dues, or fail to be represented in G. L. for two successive years, or which shall fail to assemble for work for the space of six months, shall be stricken from the books of the G. L., be deprived of the benefits of Masonry, and its charter declared forfeited." Under this provision there were, in 1870, 69 lodges the charters of which were declared forfeited. with 38 reported delinquent for one year, and 19 army numbers extinct, leaving 244 in good standing, and of which 233 were duly represented.

The executive grand officers elected in December, 1870, are—

WM. P. CHILTON, of Montgomery, Grand Master.

JOSEPH H. JOHNSON, of Talladega, Dep. Gr. Master.

WM. H. DINGLEY, of Montgomery, Gr. Treasurer.

DANIEL SAYRE, of Montgomery, Gr. Secretary.

The following information is compiled from the Proceedings of Grand Lodge for 1870, with such corrections made therein as the later information supplied by the lodge Secretaries, in reply to our circulars soliciting the same, afforded.

No.	Name of Lodge.	Members.	Name of Sec'y.	Post Office.
1	Helion,	131	W. H Jarvis,	Huntsville.
3	Alabama,	40	Joseph M. Rothwell.	Claiborne.
4	Rising Virtue,	43	Joshua J. Hausman,	Tuscaloosa.
5	Halo,	18	Myron A. Boynton,	Cahaba.
6	Moulton,	66	Edw. C. M'Donald,	Moulton.
7	Macon,	37	R. C. Dickinson,	Grove Hill.
8	Farrar,	48	W. A. Walker, jr.	Elyton.
9	Gilead.	41	O. C. Ulmer,	Butler.
10	Royal White Hart,	92	J. S. Paullin.	Clayton.
11	Montgomery,	71	Calvin W. Sayre.	Montgomery
12	Marion,	42	Edmund M. Portis,	Suggsville.
14	Florence.	61	Wm. Ragsdale,	Florence.
16	Athens,	80	Samuel Tanner, jr.	Athens.
22	St. Albans,	27	Jas. M. Quinney,	Linden.
24	Geo.Washington,	15	Chas. B. Means,	Clinton.
25	Dale,	67	John T. Cook,	Camden.
26	La Fayette,	55	Wm. N. Knight,	Greensboro.
27	Selma Fraternal,	93	Adolph Jacobson.	Selma.
28	Marengo,	21	Wm. P. Kittrell,	Dayton.
29	Rising Sun,	52	Miles C. Wade,	Decatur.
31	Autoga,	50	Albert W. McNeal,	Autaugaville.
34	Perry,	45	Joseph H. Tyler,	Marion.
36	Washington,	48	Lewis B. Thornton,	Tuscumbia.

No.	Name of Lodge.	Members.	Name of Sec'y.	Post Office.
.37	Courtland,	63	Geo. K. Clopper,	Courtland.
.39	Wetumpka,	62	Wm. S. Penick,	Wetumpka
.40	Mobile,	159	Jas. H. Hampshire,	Mobile.
.41	Livingston,	61	Joseph L. Scruggs,	Livingston.
.42	Hiram,	49	Larkin W. Cannon,	Jacksonville.
.43	Leighton.	23	Parker N. G. Rand,	Leighton.
.44	Gaston.	9	James J. Little,	Warsaw.
.46	Harmony,	110	John C. Thomas,	Eufala.
.47	Warren,	27	Eli T. Sears,	Kingston.
.48	Vienna,	22	Robert E. Mobley,	Pleasant Ridge.
.49	Demopolis,	60	Edward W. Taylor,	Demopolis
.50	Union,	48	B. F. Harwood,	Uniontown.
.51	Jefferson,	21	R. G. Hampton,	Cedar Bluff.
.52	New Market,	45	Geo. D. Norris,	New Market.
.53	Greening,	53	Penick D. Bowles,	Evergreen.
.54	Anuly,	64	James B. Head,	Eutaw.
.55	Mount Moriah,	52	John C. Moorhead,	Pickensville.
.56	Troy,	75	Joel D Murfree,	Troy.
.57	Tuskegee,	56	John C. Smith,	Tuskegee.
.59	Benton.	23	Wm. W. Pruitt,	Benton.
.61	Tompkinsville,	30	Jno. W. Taylor,	Tompkinsville.
.62	St. John	72	Thomas Pullum,	Union Springs.
.63	Social.	37	Joel T. Crawford,	Euon.
.64	Eureka,	97	J. P. Routon,	Greenville.
.65	Liberty,	40	Sam. W. Pegues,	Liberty Hill.
.67	Hamden Sidney.	43	Harper B. Jones,	Montgomery.
.68	Holsey,	46	S. C. Woolfolk,	Glennville.
.69	Howard,	105	J. S. Alexander, Jr.	Mobile.
.70	Central,	55	Geo. W. Rogan,	Montevallo.
.71	Tehopeka,	62	J. J. Shepard, M. D.	Dadeville.
.72	Widow's Son,	35	W. G. W. Albritton,	Snow Hill.
.73	Acacia,	15	C. D. Whitman.	Loundesboro.
.74	Solomon's,	43	J. E. Scarborough,	Chambers C. H.
.76	Auburn,	69	P. H. Swanson,	Anburn.
.77	Uchee,	23	R. P. Scarborough,	Uchee.
.78	Crozier,	27	H. P. Whiteside,	White Pine.
.79	Fredonia,	55	Jas. L. Robinson,	Fredonia.
.80	Wilcox,	45	Jacob Kahn,	Allenton.
.81	St. Stephens	18	T. H. Bailey.	St. Stephens.
.82	Bellfonte.	30	Wm. H. Norwood,	Bellfonte.
.83	Friendship,	53	Jacob D. Kersh,	Centreville.
.88	Meridian Sun,	21	Lloyd Barnes,	Pleasant Hill.
.89	Prattville,	48	Wilbert P. Gholson,	Prattville.
.91	Henry,	52	J. R. L. Grice,	Abbeville.
.94	Philodorian,	32	K. L. Haralson,	Cusseta,
.95	Danville.	90	A. G. Copeland,	Danville,

No.	Name of Lodge.	Members.	Name of Sec'y.	Post Office.
.96.	.Tuckabatchee,	..40	..John W. Hays,	......Crawford........
.97.	.Lozahatchee,	...99	...Wm. W. Little,	.....Cross Plains.....
.98.	.Fulton,	33	..John W. Paul,	.....Orrville........
.99.	.Salem,	54	...Euph. N. Dunn,	.....Salem. ....
100.	.Bridgeville,	...53	..J. A. McKinstry,	....Bridgeville. .....
101.	.Hartwell,	34	..John L. Dodson,	....Oxford..........
102.	.Newbern.	34	..Wm. J. Fain,	......Newburn........
103.	.Benson,	25	..Jas. L. Williams,	...Naplesville .....
104.	.Good Samaritan,	48	..Wm. W. Baird,	......Dudleyville. ....
105.	.Shiloh,	27	..Z. D. Agee,	........Clifton.........
106.	.Herman,	38	..Wm. R. High,	......Sumterville. ....
107.	.Choctaw,	42	..Wm. T. Horn,	......Pushmataha. ....
108.	.Oak Bowery,	...15	..J. S N. Davis,	......Oak Bowery ....
110.	.Forest Hill,	52	..L. A. Lavender,	...Pleasant Grove. .
111.	.Sylvan,	48	..John I. Gray	.......:Fosters.........
115.	.Warrior Stand,	..23	..Richard T. Poole,	...Warrior Stand. ..
116.	.Dekalb,	85	..Joseph C. Bogle,	....Lebanon.........
117.	.Perryville,	43	..S. A. Edward	.......Perryville.......
119.	.Notasulga,	64	..J. A. Dubherby,	.....Notasulga.....
120.	.Waverly,	16	..D. A. Patrick,	......Loachapoka. ....
122.	.Coffeeville,	18	..Andrew J. Pace,	....Coffeeville.......
123.	.Havana,	20	..G. W. Westcott,	.....Havana.........
124.	.Felix	28	..J. W L. Daniel,	.....Midway.........
125.	.Herndon,	49	..James T. Smith	......Union ....
126.	.Tallapoosa,	31	..Henry H. Burnes,	...Loachapoka. ....
127.	.Bolivar,	60	..W. V. Pankey,	.....Stevenson.......
131.	.Yorkville,	37	..W. Pridmore,	...Columbus, Miss. .
132.	.Roanoke,	38	..Wm. A. Handley,	....Roanoke........
133.	.Loachapoka,	62	..Martin W. Smith.	....Loachapoka. ....
134.	.Wiley,	28	..A. Youngblood,	....Farriorville. ....
135.	.Columbia,	......—	..J. A. Coe,	.........Columbia. .....
136.	.Unity,	46	..Geo. Watson,	.....L'w'r Peach Tree
137.	.Rockford,	47	..Wm. J. Peddy,	......Rockford........
138.	.Bradford,	35	..John C. Jones,	......Hanover. ....
139.	.Chilton,	26	..Samson B. Cloud,	...via Shorter's.....
140.	.Shelby,	62	..James T.Leeper,	....Columbiana. ....
142.	.Bldwin,	21	..Geo. W. Robinson,	..Stockton. ....
143.	.Burleson,	35	..Robert J. White,	....Burleson........
144.	.Daleville,	····22	..R. R. Harrell,	......Daleville. ......
146.	.Missouri,	36	..Wm. A. Walker,	....Perote. ....
149.	.Chambers,	28	..F. L. Treadwell,	....Milltown. ....
150.	.Etam,	19	..Wm. Spencer,	......Hamburg Station.
152.	.Mt. Jefferson,	...39	..E. H. Floyd,	........Mt. Jefferson.....
153.	.Monroeville,	52	..John O. Gwynn,	.....Monroeville. ....
154.	.Nixburg,	47	..Fred. K. Oliver,	.....Nixburg.........
155.	.Eastaboga,	41	..A. Montgomery,	....Eastaboga. ......

No.	Name of Lodge.	Members.	Name of Sec'y.	Post Office.
157	Somerville,	48	Chris. A Welsh,	Somerville
158	Maysville,	61	James M. Jones.	Bell Factory.
161	Penick.	59	Benj. T. Smith	Central Institute.
162	Hendrix	27	Abner L. Stokes,	Plantersville
163	Fayetteville,	25	Wm. D. Boaz,	Fayetteville.
164	Chewackla,	9	Otis D. Smith,	Smith's Station.
166	Sumter,	28	Marion E. Tarvin,	Gaston.
168	Mount Hope,	38	Sam. H. Radford,	Mount Hope.
169	Buena Vista.	28	John B. Martin.	Union Springs.
170	Elba.	38	M. G. Stoudemier,	Elba.
171	Clapton.	41	J. M. Williams,	Barns' X Roads.
172	Fellowship.	47	T. G. Williams,	Coal Fire.
173	Andy Jackson,	147	Wm. P. Bell.	Montgomery.
175	Ezel,	16	E. Y. Williams,	Olustee Creek.
176	Davie,	12	Reuben Cope,	Arborvitae.
177	Orion,	25	Duncan Graham,	(not given.)
178	Desotoville,	34	J. C Christopher,	DeSotoville
180	Mount Hilliard,	39	J. W. Hightman,	Mount Hilliard.
181	Aberfoil,	11	Robert A. Bethune,	Arborvitae.
184	Brundige,	53	S. M. Carlton	Brundige.
185	Mount Eagle.	47	B. T. Cohen,	New Site.
186	Catawba,	50	John W. Inzer.	Ashville.
187	Landmark.	17	E. W. Stephens.	Knoxville.
188	Clintonville,	43	Alfred McGee.	Clintonville.
189	Delta.	26	W. D. Campbell,	De Soto. Miss.
190	Tombigbee,	17	J. W. DuBose.	Jefferson
191	Brush Creek,	49	S. W. Blackburn.	Marion.
193	High Log,	26	Archibald Hill,	Fitzpatrick.
195	Opelika.	85	M. F. Echols.	Opelika.
197	Hillabee,	41	Sam. M. Bell.	Pinckneysville.
199	Kiligee,	30	T. J. McDonald,	Chanahatchie.
200	Sylacauga,	37	J. M. Lanning.	Talladega.
201	Helicon.	53	John A. Giddens,	Honorville.
202	Pine Level,	17	Wm. D. Graves,	Pine Level
203	Valley.	16	Wm. Craps.	Smith's Station.
204	Manning Spring.	20	James L. Waugh.	Mt. Meigs.
205	Gainestown,	13	Joseph C. Smith,	Gainestown.
206	Moscow.	78	Arthur T. Young,	Moscow.
207	Pettusville,	43	Thomas B. Daly.	Fort Hampton.
208	Alexandria,	—	A. W. Ledbetter,	Alexandria.
209	Marshall,	46	B. M. Farlane,	Guntersville.
210	Ebenezer,	30	Thomas Swanson.	Cowikee.
212	Putnam,	38	F. A. Murray,	Louina.
213	Euclid.	23	L. R. Wilson.	Fort Browder.
214	Carrollton,	41	Wm. G. Robertson,	Carrollton.
215	Builders,	42	Wm. Baker,	Kymulga.

No.	Name of Lodge.	Members.	Name of Sec'y.	Post Office.
217	Spring Hill,	21	Edward Curtis,	Spring Hill
218	Sam Dixon,	44	T. P. McElrath,	Centre
219	Lineville,	56	J. D. McCann,	Lineville
221	Tensaw,	12	R. W. Slaughter,	Tensaw
222	Western Star,	40	J. J. McElroy,	Cuba Station.
223	Sandy Ridge,	28	Sam. J. Pettus,	Sandy Ridge
224	Newton.	60	B. F. Cassady,	Newton.
225	Louisville,	37	Benj. Jones,	Louisville
226	Santa Fè,	33	T. B. Savage,	Jackson
227	James Penn,	33	J. M. Bethune,	Clopton
228	Dallas.	35	Wm. A. Striplin,	Chulafinne,
229	Lebanon,	44	Wm. H. Mason,	Marion.
230	Bexar,	48	John Arnold.	Bexar.
231	Duck Spring,	42	A. R. Gilbreth,	Greenwood
233	Sepulga,	19	Josiah A. Hicks,	Garland.
235	Harpersville.	42	A. E. McGraw,	Harpersville
236	Gadsden,	109	L. E. Harnlin,	Gadsden
237	Tallassee.	34	I. X. Gaunt,	Tallassee.
238	Fan Mount,	22	David S. Barrow,	Red Level
241	Bowen,	53	John H. McHugh.	Whistler.
242	Coosa;	39	W. A. Humphries,	Sykes Mill.
243	Ramar,	35	C. R. Waller,	Ramar.
244	Dawson,	27	O. H. Crittenden,	Oakey Streak.
245	Millport,	45	John N. Probst.	Millport
246	Harrison,	48	Henry M. Bradley,	Hallsville
247	Cropwell,	46	W. Wadsworth,	Cropwell.
248	Lawrence,	52	N. M. Thornton,	Lawrenceville.
249	Foluca.	21	John M. Howard,	Greenville.
250	Amand.	24	T. M. Vines.	Chestnut Creek.
251	Camp Creek,	37	T. L. Quillain,	Honoroville.
252	Northport,	78	Henry H. Brown,	Northport.
253	Rose Hill,	36	J. J. Richards.	Rose Hill.
254	Quitman.	34	J. H. McDaniel,	Greenville.
256	Gaylesville,	46	A. M. McWhorter,	Gaylesville.
257	Erwin,	40	F. M. Langerd,	Holly Grove.
258	Randolph,	45	Wm. H. Mahan,	Randolph.
259	Magnolia,	83	Charles W. Hooks,	Mobile.
260	Belleville,	41	S. G. Forbes.	Belleville.
261	Talladega,	72	Henry H. Hamill,	Talladega.
262	Highland.	37	David Y. Wyatt,	Hillsboro.
264	Walnut Grove,	58	Wm. A. Murfree,	Walnut Grove.
265	Meridian	49	Green B. Strother,	Huntsville.
266	Mount Pleasant,	19	Wm. M. Ferrell,	Mount Pleasant.
267	Wind Creek,	26	J. R. Johnston,	Melton's Mills.
270	Butler Springs,	30	Thomas H. Barge,	Monterey.
271	Pea River,	47	John E. Bishop,	Victoria.

No.	Name of Lodge.	Members.	Name of Sec'y.	Post Office.
272	Clifton,	28	Theo. H. Watson,	Clifton.
274	Paint Rock,	40	Lafayette Derrick,	Woodville.
277	Larkinsville,	33	Sam. H. M'Mahan,	Larkinsville.
278	Northern,	55	James L. Ledbetter,	New Hope.
279	Flat Creek,	36	Chas. W. Hare,	Monroeville.
280	Springville.	62	Miles M. Fulgham,	Springville
281	Ch. Baskerville,	31	John C. Moore,	Fayette C. H.
282	Richmond,	38	David R. Van Pelt,	Richmond.
283	Daviston,	48	W. W. Williams,	Daviston.
285	Georgiana,	23	J. M. Sims,	Georgiana
286	Walker,	42	Thos. F. S. York,	Arkadelphia.
287	Clinton,	50	J. A. F. Campbell,	Skipperville.
290	Gillespie,	51	Sam. J. Ferguson,	Handy.
291	Fort Deposit,	54	Thomas Blake.	Fort Deposit.
301	Norris,	45	Wm. H. Hawkins,	Pollard.
305	Central City,	66	G. M. M'Connico,	Selma
315	Jonesboro',	43	Thos M'Adory,	Jonesboro'.
317	New Lexington,	26	S. H. Darden,	New'Lexington.
319	Cluttsville,	13	Basil W. O'Neal,	Huntsville
320	Warrenton.	40	T. B. Bayles.	Warrenton
321	Pleasant Hill,	43	Lemuel Burnett.	Pikeville.
323	Holly Grove,	39	Martin A. Clay,	Stevenson.
324	Viola,	22	C. M. Waid.	Chepultepec.
326	Youngsville.	30	Reuben G. Young.	Youngsville.
327	Andrew Chapel,	26	C. M. Graves,	Island Home.
328	Sycamore,	30	M. A. Ray,	Garland.
329	Madison Station,	36	J. T. Lipscomb,	Madison Station.
330	Forkland,	18	P. C. Shumate.	Forkland.
331	Charity,	13	E. M. Carlton,	Six Mile.
332	Blue Eye,	38	E M. Gray,	Lincoln.
334	Oliver,	38	S. M. Gilmore,	Choctaw Corner.
335	Nanafalia,	29	David P. Barr,	Nanafalia.
336	Boligee,	14	J. A. Dunn,	Boligee.
337	Johnson,	28	Henry D. Curtis,	Crenshaw
339	Albert Pike,	61	John F. Craig,	Cherokee.
340	Clear Creek,	38	John A. Thomas,	Larissa.
341	Rogan,	27	G. W. Milam,	Davisville.
343	Summit.	25	T. J. Griffith,	Summit.
344	Pikeville,	24	A. J. Hamilton,	Pikeville.
345	Echo,	35	M. R. Howell,	Echo.
346	Hurtville,	21	E. N. Brown,	Hurtville.
347	Abernathy,	13	J. W. Wigginton,	Kemp's Creek
348	Bienville,	28	T. C. Carter,	Mobile.
349	Ozark,	43	J. W. Dowling,	Ozark.
350	Sipsey,	20	James White.	Sipsey Turnpike.
351	Wilson Williams,	22	Benj. Gifford,	Columbus, (Ga.)

No.	Name of Lodge.	Members.	Name of Sec'y.	Post Office.
353	Rock Mills,	52	T. J. Thomasson,	Rock Mills.......
354	Heaton	27	T. J. Lawler,	Carter's Store....
355	Van Buren,	32	J. B. Appleton,	Collinsville......
356	Ashland	23	Solon W. Hingson,	Ashland.........
357	Rutledge,	30	Wm. R. Houghton,	Rutledge........
358	Barbour	21	John L. Appling,	Carthage........
359	Scottsboro	30	G. D Campbell,	Scottsboro.......
360	Newtonville,	17	Wm. J. Cates	Fayette C. H. ...
362	Collirene,	12	Ed. C. Dunklin,	Benton..........
363	Chester	15	Wm. M. Jack,	Chester.........
364	Pleasant Site,	30	I. J. Rogers,	Pleasant Site....
365	Houston	23	Wm. H. Hyde,	Houston.........
366	Cotaco,	16	Alex. W. Black,	Apple Grove ....
367	Chandler,	27	J. H. Johnson. Jr.	Edwardsville....
368	Cross Plains,	24	Howard A. Hayes,	Cross Plains.....
369	Athelstan,	20	M. L. McCartney,	Mobile..........
370	Goliad,	23	James B. Smith,	Eldridge........
371	Russellville,	8	R. S. Watkins,	Russellville .,...
372	Belmont	14	John J. Tutt,	Demopolis... ..
373	Bell's Landing,	18	A. T. Howard,	Bell's Landing...
374	Lodor,	11	Wm. W. Pitts,	Seale Station.....

Arkansas.

THE Grand Lodge of this State was organized on the 22d of February, 1832. Its communications are held at Little Rock, the capital of the State, in November of each year. It is one of the few grand lodges which recognize Past Masters as regular members, and the only grand lodge extant that devotes the surplus of its revenue to the sustenance of an institution of learning. Each year a Board of Trustees is elected in Grand Lodge to attend to the interests of SAINT JOHN'S COLLEGE, located at Little Rock, and which Board annually, through its secretary, reports the condition of that institution to Grand Lodge. So soon as its liabilities for the current year are ascertained by proper committee, the grand lodge at once votes the residue to be, on the grand treasurer's books, placed to the credit of St. John's College; and this balance, with donations from friends of the college, have thus far proved sufficient to sustain the same in a satisfactory manner. During the year 1870 the college buildings were greatly improved, and are now capable of accomodating over sixty students with sleeping rooms. A suitable boarding-house has also been provided on the grounds, where the students all can be provided with good food at a moderate charge. A president and the necessary professors render this institution a very valuable acquisition to the educational privileges of the whole State. The college is endowed with a lot of valuable land, $35,000 worth of which was, in 1870, sold to persons who agreed to settle upon and improve their purchases, and who, under such contract, and the agreement to pay interest semi-annually for the respective amounts, were allowed ten years within which to pay for their respective purchases.

Neither mileage nor per diem are paid by the G. L. of Arkansas to the representatives or members. In November, 1870, there were enrolled 262 lodges, with a membership of 9,324 master masons. Of those lodges 231 had made returns for the year, and 134 were represented at the communication for that year. The executive grand officers then elected are as follow:

SAM. K. WILLIAMS, of Little Rock, Grand Master.
(This G. L. does not elect a Deputy Grand Master.)
R. L. DODGE, of Little Rock, Grand Treasurer.
LUKE E. BARBER, of Little Rock, Grand Secretary.

The following information is collected from the Proceedings for 1870 of the Grand Lodge, and such later data as we received from the lodge secretaries, in response to our circulars requesting the same :

No.	Name of Lodge.	Members.	Name of Sec'y.	Post Office.
1	Washington,	89	W. C. Roberts,	Fayetteville
2	Western Star,	132	A. J. Thompson,	Little Rock
3	Morning Star,	16	N. C. Neer,	Red Fork
4	Mount Horeb,	—		Washington
5	Liberty,	30	R. B. Sawyer	Mt. Zion Church
6	Van Buren,	69	W. H. H. Shibley,	Van Buren
7	Key	—		Lindsay's Prairie
8	Maxville,	—		Evening Shade
9	Franklin,	118	D. N. Clark,	Clarksville
10	Mount Zion,	70	G. S. Patillo,	Batesville
11	Camden,	60	R. E. Salle	Camden
12	Mount Carmel,	27	H. G. P. Williams,	Pigeon Hill
13	El Dorado,	30	H. O. Tatum,	El Dorado
14	Lewisville,	37	E. A. Wilson,	Lewisville
15	Woodlawn,	45	N. R. Tribble	Woodlawn
16	Manchester,	33	A. S. Russell,	Manchester
17	Dover,	34	R. M Johnson,	Dover
18	Monnt Moriah,	28	J. G. Tanning,	Mount Moriah
19	Arkadelphia,	75	F. M. Green,	Arkadelphia
20	Belle Point,	154	Henry Reutzel,	Fort Smith
21	Jasper,	41	J. J. Hudson,	Jasper
22	Herndon,	22	J. S. Anderson,	Jonesboro
23	Concord,	—		Endora
24	West Point,	41	A. W. Young,	West Point
25	Tulip,	32	W. H. Hunter,	Tulip
26	Polk,	45	J. N. Newton,	Hillsboro
27	Osceola,	54	C. L. Moore,	Osceola
28	Friendship,	20	C. W. Goodwin,	Washington
29	Smithville,	38	G. Thornburgh,	Smithville
30	Pleasant Valley	52	O. P. Anderson,	Nashville
31	Free White,	—		Magnolia
32	Fair Play,	31	A. H. Mitchell,	Benton
33	Warren,	—		Warren
34	Benton,	77	S. M. Sweeten,	Benton
35	Belleville,	43	A. Luther,	Belleville
36	Northwestern,	65	B. G. Lynch,	Maysville

No.	Name of Lodge.	Members.	Name of Sec'y.	Post Office.
.37.	. White River,	...42.	. P. B. Kent,	. . . . Des Arc. . . . .
.38.	. St. John's,	. . . . . 38.	. . W. A. Hartley,	. . . . . . Holly Springs. . .
.39.	. M. O. Hill,	. . . . 27.	. . A. W. Cagle,	. . . . Antoine . . . .
.40.	. Eureka.	. . . . 79.	. . H. Marr,	. . . . Monticello. . . . . .
.41.	. Danville,	. . . . . . 38.	. . J. F. Choate,	. . . . Danville. . . . . . .
.42.	. New Hope,	. . . . . 32.	. . A. Jones,	. . . . Centreville. . . . . .
.43.	. Oakville,	. . . .—	. . . . Three Creeks . . .
.44.	. Odeon.	. . . . 80.	. . A. K. Berry,	. . . . Huntsville. . . . . .
.45.	. Augusta,	. . . . 68.	. . L. M. Ramsaur,	. . . . Augusta. . . . .
.46.	. Lacy,	. . . . 40.	. . B. G. Raymond,	. . . . Lacy. . . . .
.47.	. Poplar Bluff,	. . 32.	. . A. M. Thompson,	. . . Poplar Bluff. . . .
.48.	. Hyperian,	. . . . . . 28.	. . P. E. Lambert,	. . . . . . Long View. . . . . .
.49.	. Searcy,	. . . . 74.	. . W. T. Holloway,	. . . Searcy. . . . .
.50.	. Calhoun.	. . . .—	. . . . Columbia. . . . . . .
.51.	. Brownsville.	. . . . 59.	. . Q. T. Webster,	. . . . . Brownsville . . . . .
.52.	. Titula,	. . . .—	. . . . Clarendon. . . . . . .
.53.	. Southern Star,	. . 36.	. . J. A. Johns,	. . . . Hampton. . . . . . .
.54.	. Evening Star,	. . .43.	. . R. C. Brown,	. . . . . . Russellville. . . . . .
.55.	. Rome,	. . . . 24.	. . W. F. Clark,	. . . . Rome. . . . .
.56.	. Bentonville,	. . . . .—	. . . . Bentonville. . . . .
.57.	. Cave Hill,	. . . . . 52.	. . Wm. B. Brodie,	. . . . Boonsboro . . . . .
.58.	. Rockport,	. . . . . .53.	. . T. J. Thrasher,	. . . . . Rockport. . . . . . .
.59.	. Pilot Hill.	. . . .—	. . . . Salem. . . . .
.60.	. Magnolia,	. . . . 101.	. . B. S. Johnson,	. . . . Little Rock. . . . . .
.61.	. Hamburg,	. . . . . . 48.	. . John Carroll,	. . . . Hamburg. . . . .
.62.	. Hot Springs.	. . .42.	. . G. Belding,	. . . . Hot Springs. . . . .
.63.	. St. Observance,	. 25.	. . J. K. Brodie,	. . . . Plum Bayou. . . . .
.64.	. Yell,	. . . . 58.	. . . . Carollton. . . . . . .
.65.	. El Paso,	. . . . 45.	. . T. D. Wright,	. . . . . . El Paso . . . .
.66.	. Ashland,	. . . . 71.	. . B. Bunch,	. . . . Berryville. . . . . . .
.67.	. Falcon,	. . . . 70.	. . W. R. White,	. . . . . . Magnolia . . . .
.68.	. Champagnolle,	. . 23.	. . W. F. Mayers,	. . . . . Champagnolle. . .
.69.	. Pine Bluff,	. . . . . 48.	. . S. A. Lockhart,	. . . . Pine Bluff. . . . . .
.70.	. Hughey,	. . . .—-	. . . . Hopeville. . . . . . .
.71.	. Randolph,	. . . . . .—	. . . . Pocahontas. . . . . .
.72.	. Powhatan,	. . . . .37.	. . F. M. Wayland,	. . . . Powhatan. . . . . . .
.73.	. Paraclifta,	. . . . . 39.	. . H. H. Cleary,	. . . . Paraclifta. . . . . .
.74.	. Flint,	. . . . 21.	. . W. F. Rasmus.	. . . . . . Flint. . . . .
.75.	. Oak Bluff,	. . . . . 39.	. . L. D. McNiel,	. . . . Oak Bluff. . . . . . .
.76.	. Mars Hill,	. . . . . .—	. . . . Mars Hill. . . . . . .
.77.	. Missouri,	. . . . . . 32.	. . B. T. Powell,	. . . . Mo. Church. . . .
.78.	. Huey. . .	. . . . . . 49.	. . G. M. Marks,	. . . . Eagle Creek . . . . .
.79.	. Ozark,	. . . . 79.	. . J. Moore,	. . . . Ozark. . . . .
.80.	. Moscow,	. . . . . . 80.	. . J. L. W. Gill,	. . . . . Moscow . . . .
.81.	. Byers,	. . . . 48.	. . D. B. Shelton,	. . . . Grand Glaize . . . .
82.	. Columbia,	. . . . . 35.	. . T. M. Thompson,	. . . Magnolia. . . . . . .

No.	Name of Lodge.	Members.	Name of Sec'y.	Post Office.
.83.	.Merrick,	......35.	..J. T. Quin,	........Roseville........
.84.	.Bayless,	........30.	..N. F. Jayner,	......Seminary........
.85.	.Neely,	........28.	..P. H. Norton,	......Copel'd R'ge Set.
.86.	.St. Charles,	.....29.	..N. G. Walton,	.....Silarsville.......
.87.	.Centre Point.	...C5.	..Thomas Lee,	.......Centre Point.....
.88.	.Flanagin,	......39.	..W. J. Spears,	.......Holly Wood.....
.89.	.Sam. Williams,	..22.	..D. D. Barnes,	......Eglantine........
.90.	.Lamartine,	.....—	....	....Lamartine.......
.91.	.Pike,	.........55.	..W. B. Gould.	.......Murfreesboro....
.92.	.Quitman,	.......33.	..J. H. Suddreth,	....Turin........
.93.	.Mate Frammill.	.42.	..C. C Baker.	........Wesley..........
.94.	.Richmond.	.....44.	..G. W. Mayberry,	...Cotton Plant.....
.95.	.Hickory Plains,	.37.	..R. H. Crozier,	·····Hickory Plains..
.96.	.Moore,	........37.	.,M. T. McGee,	......Mount Elba......
.97.	.Lebanon,	......48.	..A. C. Bowen,	.......Trenton. ....
.98.	.Pigeon Hill,	.....26.	..W. S. Finch.	........Pigeon Hill.....
.99.	.Mt. Pleasant.	...75.	..Wm. F. Blackwood...	Pulaski. ....
100.	.Sulphur Spr'gs,	.—	....	...Amity.........
101.	.Leake,	..........35.	..Wm. Parsley,	......Mt. Moriah.......
102.	.Cincinnati,	.....47.	..H. Shields,	........Cincinnati.......
103.	.Bluff Springs,	...61.	..W. F. Pace,	.......Rolling Prairie...
104.	.Carouse.	......—	....	...Lone Grove.....
105.	.Lewisburg,	.....66.	..Wm. Irving,	........Lewisburg.......
106.	.Rob. Morris,	....51.	..S. O. Cloud,	......Oakalona........
107.	.Green Grove,	...40.	..W. C. Watkins,	.....Springfield......
108.	.La Grange,	.....21.	..J. H. Gibson,	.......La Grange......
109.	.Palestine,	......29.	..J. M. Gill,	.........Johnville.......
110.	.Hamilton,	......21.	..H. M. Woodson,	.....Duvall's Bluff....
111.	.Patterson.	......40.	..J. R. Patterson,	.....Clinton..........
112.	.Scottville,	......47.	..C. L. Brewton,	.....Scottville........
113.	.Branson.	......54.	..J. R. Shelton,	......Selma...........
114.	.Centre Hill,	....55.	..B. W. Bolton,	......Centre Hill......
115.	.Campbell,	......48.	..J. H. Gray,	........Searcy..........
116.	.Ouachita,	......18.	..J. H. Callaway,	....Hamburg ......··
117.	.Yellville.	......75.	..A. J. Noe.	..........Yellville........
118.	.Spring Hill,	....50.	..B. F. Arnold,	.......Clarksville.......
119.	.Pea Ridge,	.....66.	..W. B. Dean,	........Pea Ridge.......
120.	.Pleasant Grove,	.18.	..T. H. Baldy,	........Troy............
121.	.Rocky Mount,	..20.	..R. Wallace,	........Falcon........
122.	.White Sulphur,	.33.	..T. Dunnington,	......Wh. Sulph'r Sp'gs.
123.	.Bluffton,	......48.	..L. L. Briggs,	.......Bluffton........
124.	.Elona,	.........44.	..B. Moss,	.., ...Cane Creek. .....
125.	.Brushywood,	...23.	..George Gray,	.......Como...........
126.	.Bayou Dota,	....53.	..G. W. Browning,	....Sulphur Rock....
127.	.Springfield,	....48.	..M. E. Moore.	........Springfield ......
128.	.Dallas,	........35.	..J. N. Lane,	.........Dallas..........

No.	Name of Lodge.	Members.	Name of Sec'y.	Post Office.
129	Jonesboro,	60	Aden Lynch.	Jonesboro.
130	Euclid.	42	J. O. Davis.	Mount Adams
131	Greenwood,	76	W. H. Bell.	Greenwood
132	Waldron,	32	Wm. B. Turman,	Waldron
133	Napoleon,	—		Napoleon.
134	Atlanta,	—		Atlanta.
135	Dedson.	34	J. C. Key.	Mt. Judea.
136	Olive Branch,	67	J. O. Little.	Spring Bank.
137	Philadelphia,	44	H. H. Harris,	La Crosse.
138	Rising Sun,	53	W. H. Huffine.	Blue Mountain
139	Ebenezer,	40	J. W. Moore.	Hempstead.
140	Mount Ida.	35	E. Whittington,	Mount Ida.
141	Lunenburg,	30	B. F. Kimmins,	Lunenburg
142	Crescent.	—		Poplar Bluff.
143	Evening Shade,	61	J. M. Wasson.	Evening Shade.
144	Curia,	43	J. H. Johnson,	Evening Shade.
145	Wooten.	33	J. Martin.	Stony Point
146	Abraham,	37	E. R. Cully,	Rondo.
147	Henderson,	—		Harold.
148	Caledonia,	19	H. B. Cobb,	El Dorado.
149	Putman.	38	H. Carkrum.	Buckskull.
150	Providence,	50	W. C. Roseberry,	Mt. Moriah.
151	Grenade Chapel.	23	R. M. Steel.	Grenade Chapel.
152	Sardis,	15	M. W. Merritt,	Gravel Ridge.
153	Troy.	24	W. S. Smith,	Beech Creek.
154	Elm Springs,	67	T. J. Sherman,	Elm Springs.
155	Charlestown,	43	M. A. Spencer,	Charleston.
156	Acacia,	46	Robert Boas,	Garrettson Land'g.
157	De Witt.	44	H. Halliburton,	De Witt.
158	Holland,	58	J. M. Lay,	Quitman.
159	Ash Flat.	63	L. M. Tucker,	Ash Flat.
160	Jacob Brump,	76	G. Van Valkenburg,	Pine Bluff.
161	Wise.	22	J. Newton,	Palestine.
162	Montongo,	37	A. J. Hall,	Relf's Bluff
163	Reid,	52	J. W. Sorrells,	Black Jack.
164	Adams,	31	C. H. Buercklin,	Pineville.
165	Bellefonte,	91	M. Bristow,	Bellefonte.
166	Mount Holly,	30	J. Hollensworth,	Mount Holly.
167	Madison.	—		Madison.
168	Gainesville,	57	C. Wall.	Gainesville.
169	Dooley's Ferry,	—		Dooley's Ferry.
170	St. Mary's,	28	W. R. Price.	Rosebud.
171	Mariana.	55	J. M. Thomas,	Mariana.
172	Galley Rock,	58	W. A. Ellis,	Galley Rock.
173	Lucy Brandon,	37	F. L. Reid,	Rocky Comfort.
174	Red River,	29	A. J. Mims,	Richmond.

No.	Name of Lodge.	Members.	Name of Sec'y.	Post Office.
175	Evergreen,	28	A. M. Curry	Clayton
176	Reed's Creek,	28	G. W. McLain,	Reed's Creek
177	Tyro,	28	H. Brockman,	Branchville.
178	Mill Creek,	48	H. H. Bibb,	Relf's Bluff.
179	Mine Creek.	57	W. Johnston,	Mineral Springs.
180	Sulphur Rock,	49	H. C. Dye.	Sulphur Rock.
181	Barren Fork,	30	J. M. J. Conyers,	Polk Bayou.
182	Poe,	45	J. B. Whisanant,	Russellville.
183	Arcadia.	60	J. M. Simmons,	Cleburne.
184	Poinsett,	51	J. H. T. Magers,	Harrisburg.
185	Cedar Grove,	43	W. H. Taylor.	Oil Trough.
186	Culpepper,	32	T. P. Blackwell,	Lehi.
187	South Fork,	16	J. Johnson,	South Fork.
188	Walnut Hills,	22	J. G. Morgan,	Walnut Hills.
189	Lafayette,	46	O. F. Russell,	Helena.
190	Colony,	33	J. B. Key,	Deview.
191	Jacksonport,	75	C. Lowe,	Jacksonport.
192	Kirkpatrick,	—		Elgin.
193	Walnut Grove,	—		Pocahontas.
194	Arlington,	47	P. U. Bope,	Camden.
195	Kerr,	34	I. L. Pride,	Clarendon.
196	Kingston,	59	S. B. Grigg,	Kingston.
197	Siloam.	24	J. I. Pond.	Pocahontas.
199	Beech Creek.	30	P. R. Hayes.	Magnolia.
200	Spring Creek.	33	C. B. Thomson,	Edwardsburg.
201	New Boston,	25	E. Turner.	Cass.
202	Blue Mountain,	74	M. C. Cole,	Riggsville.
203	Chicat,	—		Lake Village.
204	Roberta,	37	H. Woodworth,	Princeton
205	Sugar Creek,	32	J. Logan,	Reveille.
206	Taylor.	33	A. A. Williams,	White Oak.
207	Eastern Star,	24	H. Holcomb,	Chalk Bluff
208	Maguire.	35	E. M. Dickinson,	Oil Trough.
209	Bear House.	27	H. W Wade,	Hamburg.
210	Star of the West,	29	O. R. Bryant,	Star of the West.
211	Rising Sun,	29	W. M. Allen,	Forest City
212	Collins.	21	J. S. Welsh,	Cut-Off
213	Bright Star,	45	W. H. Felter,	Dardanelle
214	Meridian,	30	B. L. Watson,	Hamburg.
215	Elizabeth.	38	John L. Cravens,	Shoal Creek
216	Jacinto,	42	W. L. Cook,	Little Rock.
217	Oklahoma.	36	J. J. Phillips,	Boggy Depot.
218	M't'n Meadow,	27	W. S. Stinnell'	Dallas.
219	Osage,	26	Geo. W. Walker,	Osage.
220	Perry,	25	J. Price,	Perryville.
221	Cave Spring,	15	A. Moss,	Cave Spring.

No.	Name of Lodge.	Members.	Name of Sec'y.	Post Office.
222..	Springtown,	....25...	M. Richardson,	.....Hickory.........
223..	Argyle,	........20...	J. M. Peck,	........Philip's Bayou...
224..	Polar Star.	.....29...	M. P. Ray,	........Lead Hill......
225..	Mountain Home,.—			......Mountain Home..
226..	Six Mile,	.......30...	H. F. Watters,	.....Chismsville. ....
227..	Moro,	........20...	W. J. Bunn,	........Hampton........
228..	Mt. Vernon,	....—		.......Lanark.......
229..	Fredonia,	......36...	J G. Robbins,	.....Coldwell........
230..	Little Spring,.	..38...	F. G. Berry,	........Hindsville.......
231..	G. Washington,	.28...	J. T. Kendrick,	....Chambersville...
232..	Bethel,	........18...	J. C. Stephens,	.....Spavinaw. ......
233..	Pleasant Hill,.	..47 ..	.I. Kyle,	............Ozark..........
234..	Pleasant Mound,	54...	John Bennett,	......Ellsworth.......
235..	Cache.	........37...	W. D. Kerr,	.......Clarendon. .....
236..	Prospect Bluff,.	.22...	H. L. Castile,	......Prospect Bluff...
237..	E. H. English,.	..22...	W. H. Kirkley,	.....Des Arc........
238..	Perryville,	.....1...	W. H. Blackwell,	...Perryville........
239..	Whitfield,	......14...	M. Mouser,	........Oak Grove......
240..	Caney,	.........—..	.G. M. Christopher,.	..Caney.. ....
241..	Antioch,	........31...	J. H. Frizell,	........La Crosse.......
242..	Mt. Pisgah,.	....34...	N. H. West,	........Mt. Pisgah Church
243..	Bloomfield,.	....28...	D. Chandler,	.......Double Springs..
244..	Chapel Hill,.	...26...	J. Hodges,	.........Wheelock.......
245..	Dripping Sp'gs,.	19...	W. Deffenbaugh,	....Dripping Springs.
246..	Barber,	........8...	J. V. Clemens,	....
247..	Blocher,	25		.........Booneville.......
248..	Big Bottom,	....15...	M. V. Gautney,	.....Oil Trough......
249..	Du Val,	.........9...	C. E. Goddard,	.....Hartford........
250..	Pisgah,	........16...	H. C. Humphrey,.	...Huddlestons.....
251..	Frenchm's Bayo,	20...	N. B. Lafort,	........Pecan Point.....
252..	Blazing Star..	..50...	C B. Callison,	.....Newburg. ......
253..	Howard,	........23...	G. W. Howard,	.....Howard.........
UD..	Dutchess Creek,.	31...	J. H. Millard,	......Walnut Tree.....
UD..	Lavesque,	24		.:.... ...Wittsburg........
UD..	Bay,	21		.........Moro Bay........
UD..	Vine Grove,.	...33		.................Fayetteville. ....
UD..	Marysville,	......—		.................Lisbon... .. ....
UD..	Golden Rule,	...19		..................Red Bluff........
UD..	Big Creek,	.....—		...................Big Creek.......
UD..	Indian Bay,	10		.................Indian Bay.......
UD..	Canaan,	20		.................Clarksville.......
UD..	Bennet's Bayou,	—..		...................Bennet's Bayou..

California.

THE Grand Lodge of this State was organized on the 18th of April, 1850, by four lodges, working under charters from as many States. Its communications are held in the City of San Francisco, in the new Masonic Temple, in October of each year. Its membership is composed in part of Past ·Masters. The most notable feature about this grand lodge is the running expenses of its grand secretary's office, amounting in 1870 to, including printing, $8,600. For this money, however, the best work is done in the best manner. The revenue of this grand lodge is large, being for an equal number of lodges nearly double the amount levied by the grand lodges of the Atlantic States. With 178 lodges, and a membership of less than 10,000 Master Masons, the revenue for 1870 amounted to $17,500. The representatives are "reimbursed their necessary traveling expenses" from the Representative Fund, (at present 25 cents per member of each lodge in the State paid annually for this fund,) and which payments, in aggregate, amounted in 1870 to the sum of $4,710.25—about equally proportionate with mileage and per diem paid by other grand lodges of like constituency.

The executive officers elect and appointed in October, 1870, are as follow, viz:

     LEONIDAS E. PRATT, of San Francisco, Grand Master.

     ISAAC S. TITUS, of Stockton, Deputy Gr. Master.

     JAMES LAIDLEY, of San Francisco, Gr. Treasurer.

     ALEX. GURDON ABELL, of San Francisco, Gr. Secretary.

     LAWRENCE C. OWEN, of San Francisco, Assistant G. Sec'y.

The following information is collected from the Proceedings for 1870 of the Grand Lodge, and such later data as we received from the lodge secretaries, in response to our circulars requesting the same :

No.	Name of Lodge.	Members.	Name of Sec'y.	Post Office.
..1..	California,	....429...	Robert Riddle,......	San Francisco...
..2..	Western Star,...	57...	A. Dobrowski,......	Shasta..........
..3..	Tehama,........	91...	D. T. Hagedorn,....	Sacramento .....
..5..	Benicia,........	50...	C. E. Holbrook,.....	Benicia..........

No.	Name of Lodge.	Members.	Name of Sec'y.	Post Office.
..8	Tuolumne,	59	T. M. Yausey,	Sonora ....
..9	Maryville,	49	Nelson H. Brown,	Maryville ....
.10	San Jose,	140	Edward Halsey,	San Jose........
.12	Yount,	61	David L. Haas,	Napa...........
.13	Nevada,	123	A. D. Tower,	Nevada.........
.14	Temple,	28	John W. Mast,	Sonoma.........
.16	Eureka,	49	D. W. Shear,	Auburn.........
.17	Parfaite Union	107	A. Bourgoyne,	San Francisco...
.18	Mountain Shade,	50	Wm. Ryan,	Downieville.....
.19	San Joaquin,	63	P. B. Fraser,	Stockton........
.20	Washington,	63	W. C. Felch,	Sacramento..:...
.21	Hawaiian	57	C. T. Gulick,.:	Honolulu,(Sa.Is.)
.22	Occidental	301	W. E. Moody,	San Francisco....
.23	Madison,	124	A. Morehouse,	Grass Valley....
.24	Mariposa,	44	G. S. Miller,	Mariposa.......
.25	Georgetown,	55	I. P. Jackson,	Georgetown.....
.26	El Dorado,	61	Albert J. Lowry,	Placerville......
.27	Trinity,	65	M. F. Griffin,	Weaverville.....
.28	Columbia,	59	John Millington,	Columbia........
.29	Diamond,	30	G. K. Smith,	Diamond Springs.
.30	Golden Gate,	171	A. A. Hobe.	San Francisco....
.31	Mokelumne,	24	Horace M. Stuart,	Mokelumne Hill.
.32	Gold Hill,	42	Isaac Stonecipher,	Lincoln.........
.33	Ophir,	34	E. Burroughs.	Murphy's........
.34	Santa Clara,	66	Wm. Arthur Pitt,	Santa Clara......
.35	San Diego,	52	A. O. Wallace,	San Diego.......
.37	Saint John's	39	Sam. Pellet,	Yreka..........
.38	Santa Cruz,	103	Frank Cooper,	Santa Cruz......
.39	Yuba,	72	J. F. Eastman,	Maryville........
.40	Sacramento,	118	Saml. Sims,	Sacramento......
.41	Martinez,	55	G. A. Sherman,	Martinez........
.42	Los Angeles,	63	H. D. Barrows,	Los Angeles.....
.43	Hiram,	34	R. C. Irvine,	El Dorado.......
.44	Mount Moriah,	233	C. L. Wiggin,	San Francisco...
.45	Crescent,	40	D. S. Sartwell,	Crescent City....
.46	Texas,	63	R. H. Brotherton.	San Juan.......
.47	Michigan City,	40	J. H. Ellsworth,	Michigan Bluffs..
.50	Forbestown,	38	H. S. Maddox,	Forbestown......
.51	Illinoistown,	39	C. Queen,	Colfax...........
.54	Saint James,	25	J. M. Fleming,	Jamestown......
.55	Suisun,	71	W. Owens, Jr	Suisun. ....
.56	Volcano,	53	Benj. Ross...	Volcano.........
.57	Santa Rosa,	50	M. Johnson,	Santa Rosa......
.58	Union,	144	Wm. S. Hunt,	Sacramento......
.59	Gravel Range.	52	C. F. Mausur,	Camptonville....
.60	Plumas,	25	Jno. B. Overton,	Quincy.........

No.	Name of Lodge.	Members.	Name of Sec'y.	Post Office.
.61.	Live Oak,	90	Wm. VanVoorhies	Oakland
.62.	G. Washington,	25	W. J. Beckwith,	Chinese
.64.	Natoma,	51	Geo. M. Comfort,	Folsom
.65.	Amador,	49	C. H. Turner,	Jackson
.66.	Forest,	49	John Kontz,	Alleghany
.68.	Morning Star,	101	M. H. Bond,	Stockton
.69.	Corinthian,	68	Charles Faulkner,	Maryville
.70.	Enterprise,	59	Chas. H. Murphy,	Yuba City
.71.	Nebraska,	30	John D. Perkins,	Michigan Bar
.75.	Mountain Forest,	10	Griffin Meredith,	Eureka North
.76.	Bear Mountain,	30	Thomas J. Deer,	Angels
.77.	Petaluma,	33	W. Emery Cox,	Petaluma
.78.	Calaveras,	30	W. F. Colton,	San Andreas
.79.	Humboldt,	46	David W. Nixon,	Eureka
.80.	Ione,	30	Henry F. Hall,	Ione City
.82.	Yolo,	42	David Shindler,	Cacheville
.83.	Rising Star,	52	A. Huntley,	Forest Hill
.84.	Vesper,	60	G. F. Morris,	Red Bluff
.85.	Indian Diggings,	18	George Goodman,	Mendon
.86.	St. Louis,	66	Joel Eveland,	St. Louis
.87.	Naval,	135	G W. Simonton,	Valleyjo
.88.	Quitman,	37	Wm. C. Clarke,	Moor's Flat
.89.	Rase's Bar,	26	James Dazell,	Smartsville
.91.	North Star,	33	A. P. McCarton,	Fort Jones
.92.	Acacia,	29	Paul Mitchell,	Coloma
.93.	St. Helena,	33	John Cleghorn,	St. Helena
.95.	Henry Clay,	45	Geo. Newman,	Sutler Creek
.96.	Howard,	46	E. W. Potter,	Yreka
.97.	Jefferson,	29	Dixon Brabban,	La Porte
.98.	Hornitos,	41	S. C. B. Bates,	Hornitos
.99.	La Grange,	19	R. T. Davis,	La Grange
100.	Campo Seco,	25	Wm. Woolsey,	Campo Seco
101.	Clay,	42	I. T. Coffin,	Dutch Flat
102.	Manzanita,	74	Jacob Furth,	North San Juan
103.	Oroville,	59	J. M. Vance,	Oroville
104.	Lexington,	52	J. H. Gray,	El Monte
105.	Siskiyou,	14	Albert Blaske,	Henly
106.	Arcata,	25	Joseph Greenbaum,	Arcata
107.	Mount Jefferson,	18	John W. Fuqua,	Garrote
108.	Owen,	27	Joseph B. Leduc,	Scott's Bar
109.	Dibble,	23	Hugh Halligan,	Omega
110.	Pajaro,	53	Andrew Craig,	Watsonville
111.	Chicot,	88	Wm. L. Bradley,	Chico
112.	Summit,	31	W. E. Steuart,	Knight's Ferry
113.	Eden,	51	Chas. H. Haile,	San Leandro
114.	Mount Zion,	14	Wm. Knox,	Grizzly Flat

No.	Name of Lodge.	Members.	Name of Sec'y.	Post Office.
115	Saint Mark's,	19	Alex. B. Horrell,	Fiddletown
117	Concord,	51	Geo. M. Hayton,	Sacramento
119	Clinton,	24	Chas. N. Kingsbury,	Horsetown
120	Fidelity,	132	S. G. Foulkes,	San Francisco
121	Ionic,	35		Iowa Hill
122	Alamo	26	J. J. Slitz,	Alamo
123	Sotoyome,	64	Jos. Albertson,	Healdsburg
124	Table Mountain.	29	Peter Freer,	Oroville
125	Progress,	125	Louis Kaplan,	San Francisco
126	La Fayette,	59	Henry P. Morris,	Sebastopol
127	Hermann,	92	Nicholas Loshe,	San Francisco
128	Visalia,	67	S. O. Creighton,	Visalia
129	Nicolaus,	12	Geo. R. Frye,	Nicolaus
131	Woodbridge,	55	Jno. B. Lillie	Woodbridge
132	Sincerity,	47	Geo. W. Boyden,	Taylorsville
133	Yosemite,	30	Roland C. Chase,	Coulterville
134	Vacaville,	25	Edward W. Day,	Vacaville
135	Valley,	33	John Washley,	Linden
136	Pacific,	168	E. C. Lovell,	San Francisco
138	Violet,	14	Jas N. Steele,	Spanish Flat
139	Crockett,	77	P. C. Miller,	San Francisco
140	Curtis,	24	D. M. Wambold,	Cloverdale
141	Grafton,	31	Hugh Payne,	Hamblin
142	Colusa,	63	J. A. McClain,	Colusa
143	Franklin,	13	J. R. Olsen,	Onisbo
144	Oriental,	144	Wm. H. Loring,	San Francisco
145	Vitruvius,	31	J. C. Hoag,	Bloomfield
146	Abell,	52	C. C. Cummings,	Ukiah
147	Eel River,	35	John W. Cooper,	Rohnerville
149	Lassen,	61	Wm. H. Crane,	Susanville
150	Molino,	34	Chas. Harvey,	Tehama
151	Palmyra,	64	R. O. Turnbull,	Placerville
155	Mt. Carmel,	30	Jos. Beaumont,	Red Dog
156	Woodland,	61	O. B. Westcott,	Woodland
158	Gibsonville,	42	N. H. Stone,	Gibsonville
160	Pilot Hill,	18	C H. Jones,	Pilot Hill
161	Keystone,	24	John M. Baker,	Copperopolis
164	Harmony,	28	W. H. Cunsolus,	Sierra City
166	Excelsior,	108	T. T. Atkinson,	San Francisco
167	Alameda,	52	Geo. W. Bond,	Centreville
168	San Mateo,	39	A. N. Nutting,	Redwood City
169	Mission,	130	Thomas Livesey,	San Francisco
173	Elk Grove,	22	Geo. I. Martin,	Elk Grove
174	Drytown,	25	Wm. Jennings,	Drytown
175	Antioch.	70	Francis Williams,	Antioch
176	Merced,	42	Wm. S. Weed,	Snelling

No.	Name of Lodge.	Members.	Name of Sec'y.	Post Office.
177	Aztlan,	54	Edmund Wells,	Prescott,
178	Phœnix,	42	Joseph Marks,	San Bernardino
179	Mendocino,	52	B. A. Paddleford,	Mendocino
180	Arcturus,	65	Johnson Grover,	Petaluma
181	Russian River,	50	J. J. Lindsay,	Windsor
182	Meridian,	24	P. B. Chamberlain,	Meridian
183	Clear Lake,	35	John R. Cook,	Lower Lake
184	Sierra Valley,	29	A. C. Heineken,	Sierra Valley
185	Claiborne,	26	Saml. Francis,	Punta Arenas
186	Evening Star,	41	J. H. Vogan,	Etna Mills
187	Keith,	71	J. R. Eardley,	Gilroy
188	Oakland,	129	T. W. Bailey,	Oakland
189	Latrobe	17	H. E. Barton,	Latrobe
190	Northern Light,	30	Wm. N. Guptill	Millville
191	Marin,	34	Lewis A. Hinman,	San Rafael
192	Santa Barbara,	39	Geo. P. Teffetts,	Santa Barbara
193	Ferndale,	24	P. F. Hart,	Ferndale
194	Mountain View,	28	G. E. Shore,	Mountain View
195	Buckeye,	24	Jno. W. Lowry,	Buckeye
196	San Simeon,	22	Geo. S Davis	Cambria
197	Paradise,	29	C. U. Thorndike,	Haywood
198	Wilmington,	22	John McCrea,	Wilmington
199	Hartley,	30	Ed. L. Green,	Lakeport
200	Truckee,	45	Jos. H. Ensign,	Truckee
201	Silveyville,	30	James A. Ellis,	Silveyville
202	Pentalpha,	16	J. H. Lander,	Los Angeles
203	Confidence,	23	John R. Norris,	Castroville
204	Salinas,	27	F. M. Jolly,	Salinas
205	Newville,	12	Jas. S. Long,	Newville,
206	Stanislaus,	14	F. Van Matthenesse,	Modesto
207	Anaheim,	19	Bernhard Simon,	Anaheim
208	Rio Vista,	11	Chas. Martell,	Rio Vista
209	King David,	33	Isaac D. Levy,	San Luis Obispo
UD	Rocklin,	17	Ben. F. Smith,	Rocklin
UD	Friendship,	14	S. B. Anderson,	San Jose

Colorado.

The Grand Lodge of this Territory was organized on the 2nd of August, 1861, by the representatives of the three lodges then in the territory, and J. M. Chivington, of Gold Hill, was elected the first grand master. In 1870 15 lodges were in the Territory, with a membership in all of 854 Master Masons. The rejections usually equal the receptions in this jurisdiction, as the population is of a floating character, and mainly unsettled. There has been erected a convenient Masonic Hall at Central City, where the grand lodge meets on the last Tuesday of each Sept'r. Past Masters are not recognized as members of this grand lodge, but past grand and past deputy grand masters are. Mileage and per diem are paid to one representative from each lodge, at rate of 12.5 cents per mile, going and returning, and two dollars per diem for each day in actual attendance.

Among the Resolutions of this grand lodge having the force of law, and styled "Standing Resolutions," is one declaring that the lodge that fails to meet once in six months forfeits its charter. Another is that non-affiliated Masons shall pay grand lodge dues, or be permitted to visit a lodge not more than twice. Another is that no lodge shall grant a demit to any of its members except for one of two purposes : to move out of the jurisdiction or to affiliate in another lodge.

In 1869 this grand lodge reprinted its, proceedings from date of its organization at a cost of $1360. The same is bound in a handsome volume, and for a copy of which the grand secretary is here tendered our fraternal thanks.

The executive officers elected in September, 1870, were—

HENRY M. TELLER, of Central, Grand Master.

C. J. HART, of Pueblo, Deputy Gr. Master.

WM. W. WARE, of Georgetown, Gr. Treasurer.

ED. C. PARMELEE, of Georgetown, Gr. Secretary.

The following information is collected from the Proceedings for 1870 of the Grand Lodge, and such later data as we received from the lodge secretaries, in response to our circulars requesting the same :

No.	Name of Lodge.	Members.	Name of Sec'y.	Post Office.
..1..	Golden City,	....52...	C. C. Carpenter,.	....Golden City.....
..4..	Nevada,	........61...	Aaron M. Jones,	...Nevada.........
..5..	Denver,	.......110...	Geo. W. Howe,	.....Denver.........
..6..	Central,	.......130...	S. I. Lorah,	.........Central City.....
..7..	Union,	.........93...	E. G. Matthews,	.....Denver..........
..8..	Empire,	.... ..31...	D. J. Ball.	..........Empire. ....
.11..	Black Hawk,	...62...	A. B. Clark,	.......Black Hawk.....
.12..	Washington,	....61...	Matt France,	........Georgetown.....
.13.	El Paso,	........40...	Robert Finley,	......Colorado City...
.14..	Columbia,	.......54...	D. A. Robinson,	.....Boulder City....
.15..	Mount Moriah,	..27...	W. H. Thompson,	...Canyon City.....
.16..	Cheyenne,	......58...	J. W. Hutchinson,	...Cheyenne, Wy. T..
.17..	Pueblo,	........50...	Aug. Beach.	........Pueblo..........
.18..	Laramie,	.......40...	J. E. Gates.	........Laramie.........
.19..	Collins,	........20...	J. H. Bradstreet,	....Fort Collins.....

Connecticut.

THE Grand Lodge of this State was organized on the 8th of July 1789, by a convention of delegates from all the lodges in the State, and this was the first independent grand lodge organized in this manner in North America. Delegates from fifteen lodges organized this grand lodge, and elected Pierpont Edwards the first grand master. The business of this grand lodge is conducted in maximum manner at a minimum rate of expense—the grand secretary being paid the stipend of $250 a year for his services. A very low rate of dues is exacted from the lodges, the same being simply a tax of $1.50 per capita for each initiate by the lodges during the year. In 1870 this amounted to $1308. When this tax fails to meet the regular expenses a small assessment is made under a provision of the constitution. The regular communications of this grand lodge are held alternately at Hartford and New Haven on the second Wednesday in May of each year. Past Masters are not recognized as members. No mileage or per diem, nor any other compensation to lodge representatives; while each lodge, under a penalty of $8 for each neglect of such requirement, must be represented, unless at the next grand annual meeting a satisfactory reason for such neglect is tendered. In 1870 there were 99 lodges working under charters, and 4 under dispensation, with a total membership of 14,072, or an average of 136 to each lodge—the highest in North America.

The executive grand officers elected in 1870 were—

ASA SMITH. of Norwalk, Grand Master.

JAMES L. GOULD, of Bridgeport, Deputy Gr. Master

GEORGE LEE, of Hartford, Grand Treasurer.

JOSEPH H. WHEELER, of Hartford, Grand Secretary.

The following information is collected from the Proceedings for 1870 of the Grand Lodge, and such later data as we received from the lodge secretaries, in response to our circulars requesting the same :

No.	Name of Lodge.	Members.	Name of Sec'y.	Post Office.
..1	..Hiram.	688	..W. A. Beers,	New Haven
..2	..St. John's.	181	..F. C. Smith.	Middletown.
..3	..St. John's.	502	..F. H. Ufford.	Bridgeport
..4	..St. John's.	533	..H. R. Morley	Hartford
..5	..Union.	198	..Geo. L. Lownds,	Stamford
..6	..St. John's.	350	..C. M. Gregory,	Norwalk.
..7	..King Solm'n's,	125	..James Huntington,	..Woodbury.
..8	..St, John's,	124	..T. B. Fairchild,	Stratford.
..9	..Compass,	134	..E. S. Morse,	Wallingford.
.10	..Wooster,	155	..H. A. Ransom,	Colchester.
.11	..St. Paul's,	145	..Wm. Demming,	Litchfield.
.12	..King Hiram,.	200	..J. H. Barlow,	Birmingham
.13	..Montgomery,	122	..Eli Ensign.	Lime Rock
.14	..Frederick,	58	..J. P. Trowbridge,	..Plainville.
.15	..Moriah,	217	..C. P. Blackmar,	West Killingly.
.16	..Temple.	78	..Stephen Johns,	Cheshire.
.17	..Federal,	72	..A. T. Blakslee,	Watertown
.18	..Hiram.	58	..C. S. Warner,	Sandy Hook.
.20	..Harmony,.	300	..E. L. Goodwin,	New Britain
.21	..St. Peter's,	105	..Geo. W. Anthony,	..New Milford.
.22	..Trumbull,	31	..E. W. Ensign,	New Haven
.24	..Uriel,	66	..Geo. W. More,	Eagleville.
.25	..Columbia,	71	..Wm. D. Franklin,	..So. Glastonbury.
.26	..Columbia,	73	..E. E. Johnson,	Moodus.
.27	..Rising Sun,	65	..Simeon D. Platt,	..Washington.
.28	..Morning Star,.	106	..Chas. E. Phelps,	..Warehouse Pt.
.29	..Village,	115	..Jos. H. Hough,	Collinsville.
.31	..Union,	623	..Geo. Strong Jr.,	New London.
.32	..Siloam,	—	..E. P. Blague,	Saybrook.
.33	..Friendship,	121	..Chas. N. Hall,	Southington
.34	..Somerset,	359	..John Benson,	Norwich.
.36	..St. Mark's,	129	..Edward Pease,	Tariffville.
.37	..Western Star,.	35	..G. H. Holt,	Norfolk.
.38	..St. Alban's,	76	..R. P. Hutchison,	..Guilford.
.39	..Ark,	27	..David H. Miller,	..Georgetown.
.40	..Union,	293	..G. M. Raymond,	Danbury.
.42	..Harmony,	363	..Dwight Stent.	Waterbury
.43	..Trinity,	75	..Henry M. Smith,	..Deep River.
.44	..Eastern Star,	171	..W. D. Pember,	Willimantic.
.46	..Putnam..	131	..Wyman Towne,	So. Woodstock.
.47	..Morning Star,	138	..G. A. Becker,	Seymour.
.48	..St. Luke's,	51	..E. M. Howland,	Kent.
.49	..Jerusalem,	51	..H. K. Scott.	Ridgefield.
.50	..Warren,	150	..Edmund Rickards,	.South Coventry.
.51	..Warren,	107	..A. C. Goodrich,	Portland.
.52	..Mount Olive,	82	..John G. Hayden,	..Essex.

No.	Name of Lodge.	Members.	Name of Sec'y.	Post Office.
53	Wiow's Son,	63	Chas. P. White,	North Stonington
55	Seneca,	108	N. A. Tuttle,	Wolcottville
56	Franklin,	141	Geo. H. Grant,	Bristol
57	Asylum,	150	E. P. Hubbard,	Stonington
58	Northern Star,	157	J. C Keach,	New Hartford
59	Apollo,	121	E. W. Latham,	Suffield
60	Wolcott,	90	M. C. Kinney,	Staffordville
61	Housatonic,	26	T. F. Watson,	North Canaan
62	Orient,	121	E. W. Hayden,	East Hartford
63	Adelphi,	250	R. C. Smith,	Fair Haven
64	St. Andrew's,	200	C. D. Lincoln,	West Winsted
65	Temple,	71	John S. Jones,	Westport
66	Widow's Son,	116	S. R. Trelease,	Branford
67	Harmony,	67	T. W. Benedict,	New Canaan
68	Charity,	259	John H. Hoxsie,	Mystic Bridge
69	Fayette,	114	Benj. Hirst,	Rockville
70	Washington,	46	Elisha Cobb,	Windsor
71	Relief,	46	E. Morgan,	Mystic Bridge
73	Manchester,	139	H. H. Hollister,	North Manchester
76	Continental,	54	B. F. Neal,	Waterbury
77	Meridian,	306	Lyman T. Lawton,	West Meriden
78	Shepherd's,	141	M. S. Baldwin,	Naugatuck
79	Wooster,	480	H. E. Bushnell,	New Haven
81	Washington,	41	J. D. Allison,	Cromwell
82	G. Washington,	122	John C. Lawton,	Ansonia
83	Eureka,	146	Chas. Bailey,	Bethel
84	Olive Branch,	118	Jno. N. Wilmart,	Westville
85	Acacia,	110	A. D. Finley,	Glenville
86	Daskam,	78	T. H. L. Talcott,	Glastonbury
87	Madison,	76	Geo. C. Dowd,	Madison
88	Hartford,	210	Geo. H. Woolley,	Hartford
89	Ansantawae,	120	Wm. G. Mitchell,	Milford
90	Pawcatuck,	80	D. R. Stillman,	Westerly, R. I.
91	St. Mark,	103	Oscar D. Case,	Granby
92	Conn. Rock,	97	Oswald A. Baehr,	New Haven
93	Monroe,	81	A. D. Eastwood,	Monroe
94	Doric,	83	Jas. L. Arnott,	Thompsonville
95	Jeptha,	69	Chas. H. Taintor,	Clinton
96	Union,	89	Wm. B. Gilbert,	Plymouth
97	Center,	79	John E. Atkins,	Meriden
98	Hiram,	42	E. A. Latimer,	Bloomfield
99	Wyllys,	37	C. A. Bowles,	Hartford
100	La Fayette,	73	A. D. Worthington,	Hartford
101	Evening Star,	32	Amos Oviatt,	Unionville
102	Brainard,	35	P. C. Dunford,	New London
103	Corinthian,	40	Jno. G. Phelan,	Northford

84   GENERAL MASONIC REGISTER.

No.	Name of Lodge.	Members.	Name of Sec'y.	Post Office.
104	Corinthian,	81	I. B. Prindle,	Bridgeport
105	Lyon,	53	A. P. Utley,	Columbia.
106	Quinnebaug,	59	Willard I. Miller,	Putnam.
107	Ivanhoe,	23	James Curzon,	Darien Depot.
108	Old Well,	44	John W. Craw.	South Norwolk.
109	Euclid,	46	Wm. L. Sweetland,	Windsor Locks.
110	Ionic,	57	W. H. Cooley,	Stafford Springs.
UD	Siloam,	19	J. E. Heald.	Saybrook.
UD	Warren,	23	J. R. Sterling,	Hamburg.
UD	Ionic,	17	David H. Miller,	Georgetown.
UD	Relief,	32	John Forsyth,	Mystic Bridge.

Delaware.

THE Grand Lodge of this State was organized on the 6th of June 1806. Its annual communications are held in Wilmington, on the fourth Monday in June. In 1870 there were 18 lodges in the State holding charters from this grand lodge, with a total membership of 967 Master Masons. The most notable act of this grand lodge was the adoption in June, 1867, of a resolution by which it was made an obligation of the Master's degree for every mason in the State to discountenance the making a mason of " any negro, mulatto, or colored person of the United States." In 1869 this resolution was repealed, and one substituted enjoining, under the penalty of expulsion, non-intercourse with any society claiming to be Masonic, unless the same be acknowledged by the Gr. Lodge of Delaware.

The executive grand officers elected in 1870 were—

J. C. McCABE, of Middletown, Grand Master.
W. F. GODWIN, of Milford, Deputy Gr. Master.
J. C. PICKELS, of Wilmington, Grand Treasurer.
JOHN C. ALLMOND, of Wilmington, Grand Secretary.

No.	Name of Lodge.	Members.	Name of Sec'y.	Post Office.
..1..	Washington,	...137	...J. K. Bayles,	........Wilmington. ....
..2..	St. John's,	52	...L. M. Chase,	........New Castle......
..4..	Hope,	15	...Jno. C. Tennant,	....Laurel. ....
..5..	Union,	40	...D. L. Denning,	.....Middletown. ....
..7..	Union,	66	...Isaac C. West,	......Dover ....
..9..	Temple,	49	...Dr. W. F. Godwin,	..Milford. ....
.11..	Temple,	96	...T. J. Lawson	........Wilmington. ....
.12..	Franklin,	27	...Chas. P. Tunnell,	...Georgetown.....
.13..	Harmony,	27	...Jno. W. Flick,	.....Smyrna.........
.14..	Lafayette,	....156.	,..Wm. M. Burk,	......Wilmington......
.15..	Jefferson,	43	...E. D. West,	.......Lewes. ....
.17..	Endeavor,	36	...J. C. Lacy,	.........Milton..........
.19..	Jackson,	43	...Jno. C. Higgins,	....Delaware City...
.20..	Corinthian,	64	...Wm. Marshall,	......Wilmington. ....
.21..	Hiram,	28	...John E. Darbee,	....Seaford. ....
.22..	Felton,	,.......24	...W. J. Reed,	........Felton..........
.23..	Eureka,	52	...Jas. L. Black,	......Wilmington. ....
.24..	Jefferson	12	...Ed. Challenger,	...New Castle......

District of Columbia.

THIS Grand Lodge was organized on the 11th of December, 1810, by lodges in the District working under charters from grand lodges in adjoining States. It holds three regular communications each year: the annual, at which officers are elected, on the first Tuesday in November; the semi-annual on the first Tuesday in May, and the installation of officers on the 27th of December.

Past Masters are recognized as members of this grand lodge. In 1870 there were 19 lodges, with a total membership of 2420 Master Masons. A handsome Masonic Hall has recently been built in Washington City, in which all the lodges, except that at Georgetown, and the grand lodge meet. During 1870 the subject "the Right of Visit" was discussed through a most exhaustive correspondence conducted by the executive of this grand lodge with the other grand lodges of the United States, and the decision arrived at was that it is the right of the W. M. to determine on the reception or rejection of a visitor, *he alone being responsible to the grand lodge.* The executive officers elected in November, 1870, were—

CHAS. F. STANSBURY, Grand Master.
GEO. B. CLARK, Dep. Grand Master.
C. CAMMACK, sr., Grand Treasurer.
NOBLE D. LARNER, Grand Secretary.

The following information is collected from the Proceedings for 1870 of the Grand Lodge, and such later data as we received from the lodge secretaries, in response to our circulars requesting the same:

No.	Name of Lodge.	Members.	Name of Sec'y.	Post Office.
..1..	Federal,	......193...	W. G. Brock.	.......Washington City.
..3..	Columbia,	......63...	M. A. Tappam,	...........do........
..4..	W'sh't'n Naval,	101...	T. B. Cross, Jr.,	...........do........
..5..	Potomac,	.....132...	M. Adler,	..........Georgetown.....
..7..	Lebanon,	.....181...	Chas. W. Darr,	......Washington City.
..9..	New Jerusalem,	126...	Urias Hurst,	.............do........
.10..	Hiram,	........157...	Jno. M. Jewell,	...........do........
.11..	St. John's,	....168...	B. M. Reed,	.............do........
.12..	National,	......102...	J. H. Pilson,	.............do........

No.	Name of Lodge.	Members.	Name of Sec'y.	Post Office.
.14.	.W. Centennial,	.115.	..Thos. Thompson,	......Washington...
.15.	.B. B. French,	..254.	..E. A. McIntire,	..........do........
.16.	.Dawson,	......192.	..G. R. Thompson,	.........do........
.17.	.Harmony,	.....114.	..S. E. Carrington,	.........do........
.18.	.Acacia.	.......102.	..J. B. Cramer.	..............do........
.19.	.Lafayette,	.....226.	..R. J. Blakelock,	..........do........
.20.	.Hope,	.........57.	..R. B. Tompkins,	..........do........
.21.	.Anacosta,	......16.	..C. B. Smith,..	...........do........
.22.	.Geo. C. Whiting,	36.	..F. W. Storch,	..............do........
.23.	.Pentalpha,	.....85.	..J. C. Poynton,	............do........

Florida.

THE Grand Lodge of this State was organized on the 6th of July, 1830, by the delegates from three lodges then in the State, assembled for the purpose at Tallahassee, and John P. Duval, being the senior Past Master present, was elected the first Grand Master. In 1858 this grand lodge voted to purchase, and had delivered to each lodge then existing in the State, a set of the "Universal Masonic Library," at a cost of about $45 each set. In 1859, this grand lodge, under the superintendence of the late Past Grand Master Thomas Brown, reprinted and published its proceedings from its organization to that date, in one large and handsome volume, at a cost of about $1500. In 1870 there were holding under this grand lodge 54 lodges with a total membership of about 2,250. Past Masters are members of this grand lodge ; and its annual communications take place at Tallahassee on the second Monday of January. The executive officers elect in 1870 were—

SAMUEL PASCO, of Monticello. Grand Master.
ALBERT J. RUSSELL, of Jacksonville, Deputy Gr. Master.
T. PRESTON TATUM, of Tallahassee, Grand Treasurer.
DE WITT C. DAWKINS, of Tallahassee, Grand Secretary.

No.	Name of Lodge.	Members.	Name of Sec'y.	Post Office.
1	Jackson,	65	W. M. McIntosh,	Tallahassee.
2	Washington,	27	E. C. Love,	Quincy.
3	Harmony,	38	Theo. West,	Marianna.
4	Coe,	29	W. E. Fulgham,	Greenwood.
5	Hiram.	98	Thos. Simmons,	Monticello
6	Franklin,	28	R. D. Munn,	Appalachicola.
7	Jeff. Davis,	13	C. S. Harley,	Sandy Ford.
9	Barto,	58	Robt. Wilkison,	Barto.
10	Waldo,	42	W. H. Donaldson,	Waldo.
11	Madison.	31	S. H. Bunker,	Madison.
12	Cherry Hill,	33	Jason Truluck,	Ichatucknee
13	Welborn,	31	Thos. A. Carruth,	Welborn.
14	Dade.	79	Geo. F. Ferguson,	Key West.
15	Escambia,	38	W. F. Lee,	Pensacola.
16	Santa Rosa,	64	E. B. Riley,	Milton.
17	York,	17	John P. Morgan,	Houston.

No.	Name of Lodge.	Members	Name of Sec'y.	Post Office.
.18.	.Duval,.........	—..	D. G. Love, ...	Jacksonville.....
.19.	.Marion, ...	13..	J. C. C. Todd,......	Ocala..........
.20.	.Solomon,.......	75...	Samuel W. Fox,...	Jacksonville....
.21.	.Gee............	28...	W. J. Scull........	Chattahoochee...
.22.	.Withlacoochee,	.15...	Rob. J. Beville,....	Belleville. ......
.23.	.Crawfordville,	.21...	W. W. Walker,.....	Crawfordville...
.24.	.Naval..........	70...	A. L. Williams.....	Warrington......
.25.	.Hillsborough...	.36...	J. F. Henderson,...	.Tampa..........
.26.	.Alachua,.......	54...	W. T. Whetstone, ..	.Newnansville....
.27.	.Lake City, ...	47...	Thos. W. Carter, ...	Lake City......
.28.	.Concordia.	94...	E. B. Lane.........	Concord........
.29.	.Micanopi.	57...	J. M. Croxton, ...	Micanopi. ......
.30.	.Suwannee, ...	—....	....	Benton..........
.31.	.Manatee,.......	23...	E. F. Gates,.......	Manatee.........
.32.	.Calahan,.......	—...	J. C. Jones.......	Calahan.........
.33.	.Jefferson, ...	37...	Francis Russell,....	Waukeenah......
.34.	.Palatka, ...	31...	C. Gillis.	Palatka.........
.36.	.Orange,........	—...	M. A. Stewart, ...	Orlando.........
.37.	.Ornan..........	—....	....	Archer.. ....
.38.	.Chipola, ...	23...	J. B. Anderson,....	Greenwood. ....
.40.	.Orion, ...	26...	J. L. Russ.	Vernon.........
.41.	.Gainesville, ...	.54...	H. C. Dozier, ...	Gainesville......
.42.	.Bradford, ...	28...	J. M. Johns, ...	Starke.........
.43.	.Stephen's......	27...	J. R. Kimbrow......	Moseley Hall....
.44.	.Miccosukee, ..	#30....	....	Miccosukee......
.46.	.Providence, ...	.61...	A. J. Weeks, ...	Providence. ....
.47.	.Amelia........	30...	G. Stark...........	Fernandina......
.49.	.Marston, ...	19...	D. H. Wilson,......	Orange Spring...
.50.	.Shiloh.........	42...	J. T. Collins.......	Shiloh.........
.51.	.Brown, ...	45...	Wm. W. Clyatt.	Bronson.........
.52.	.Lake Butler,...	.56...	A. W. Mizell,......	Lake Butler.....
.53.	.Friendship.....	19...	W. H. Geiger, ...	Cotton Plant.....
.54.	.Orange Creek,	.26...	F. M. McKin.	Waldo.........
.55.	.St. John's......	21...	Jno. P. McKay,....	San Augustine...
.56.	.Orange Spring.	28...	Giles Bowers.......	Orange Spring...
.57.	.Campbellton,...	—...	Jas. A. Bowie,.....	Campbellton. ...
.58.	.Leesburg.......	21...	Jno. W. Dyches.	Leesburg. ......
.59.	.Crystal River,	.14..	Edwin B. King,.....	Crystal River....

Georgia.

AN independent Grand Lodge was organized in this State on 16th of December, 1786, the officers being installed on the 27th of the same month, with William Stephens as the first grand master, and Samuel Stirk, grand secretary. No record of the number of lodges participating in this organization seems to have been preserved. The annual communications are held in the City of Macon on the last Wednesday in October. Under the supervision of Dr. Blackshear, the present efficient and painstaking grand secretary, the proceedings of this grand lodge are produced in the best manner. In 1870 there were 272 lodges, with a total membership of about 14,100 Master Masons; and the revenue of the grand lodge for that year $18,324.96. Mileage and per diem to amount of $7,100 was paid in 1869 to the lodge representatives. Past Masters are recognized as members of this grand lodge. There are four deputy grand masters elected yearly, and the supervision of the lodges apportioned among them.

The executive grand officers elected in 1870 were—

SAMUEL LAWRENCE, of Marietta, Grand Master.
DAVIS N. AUSTIN, of Fort Valley, Dep. Gr. Master of District No. 1.
JAMES M. MOBLEY, of Hamilton, Dep. Gr. Master of District No. 2.
JOSIAH J. WRIGHT, of Rome, Deputy Gr. Master of District No. 3.
DAVID E. BUTLER, of Augusta, Dep. Gr. Master of District No. 4.

JOSEPH E. WELLS, of Macon, Grand Treasurer.

J. EMMETT BLACKSHEAR, of Macon, Grand Secretary.

The following information is collected from the Proceedings for 1870 of the Grand Lodge, and such later data as we received from the lodge secretaries, in response to our circulars requesting the same :

No.	Name of Lodge.	Members.	Name of Sec'y.	Post Office.
..1..	Solomon's,	87	J. H. Estill,	Savannah.
..1..	Social,	83	W. H. Crane.	Augusta.
..2..	Stith,	51	John De Witt,	Sparta...
..3..	Benevolent,	99	Geo. D. Case,	Milledgeville....
..4..	Rising Star,	85	Jas. T. Davis,	Eatonton........

No.	Name of Lodge.	Members.	Name of Sec'y.	Post Office.
..5..	Macon,	182...	W. F. Grace,	Macon..........
..6..	Golden Fleece,	.85...	T. L. Anderson,	Covington.......
..7..	Columbian,	...185...	W. B. Jones,	Columbus.......
..8..	Orion.	86...	G. W. Pearce,	Bainbridge......
..9..	Mount Hope,	...82...	L. C. Ryan,	Hawkinsville. ...
.10..	Olive,	59...	Joseph Jackson,	...Talbotton.......
.11..	Franklin,	—...		Warrenton.......
.12..	Cross,	54...	D. G. Stern,	Lumpkin.......
.13..	Americus,	138...	J. E. Sullivan,	Americus.......
.14..	Marion,	37...	W. A. Calaway,	Tazewell........
.15..	Zerubbabel,	...100...	J. A. Sullivan,	Savannah.......
.16..	Hamilton,	48...	T. S. Mitchell,	Hamilton. ......
.17..	Darley,	61...	Chas. Hepburn,	Fort Gaines.....
.18..	Strict Observ.,	.78...	A. A. Turner,	Forsyth.........
.19..	Washington,	101...	H. C Parkerson,	Cuthbert........
.20..	Gen. Warren,	...49...	W. N. Pendergrass,	Monroe........
.21..	Hiram,	29...	A H. Dismukes,	...Florence........
.22..	Mt. Vernon,	....91...	Robt. M. Smith,	Athens..........
.23..	Lafayette,	54...	T. B. Green,	Washington......
.24..	Albany,	138...	W. B. Daniel,	Albany........
.25..	Philomathea,	.150...	R. M. Heard,	Elberton........
.26..	Meridian Sun,	120...	S. W. Mangham,	...Griffin..........
.27..	Morning Star,	..77...	H. T. Jennings,	Thomaston......
.28..	Union,	89...	J. G. Whitfield,	La Grange......
.29..	Madison,	45...	W. H. Bearden,	Madison. ....
.30..	Amity,	32...	Jas· C. Wilson,	Watkinsville.....
.31..	Montgomery,	...26...	J. H. Howell,	Zebulon. ....
.32..	Rising Sun,	67...	M. D. McArthur,	Reidsville......
.33..	Kennesaw,	59...	H. M. Hammett,	...Marietta. ......
.34..	San Marino,	....90...	J. A. Griffin,	Greensboro. ....
.35..	Houston,	86...	Jno. S. Jobson,	Perry............
.36..	Unity,	35...	Henry Newton,	Jefferson........
.37..	Fraternal,	50...	G. G. Weems,	McDonough. ....
.38..	Blue Mountain,	.92...	R. A. Quillian,	Dahlonega.......
.39..	Newburn,	24...	J. M. Beeland,	Newburn. ......
.40..	Ebenezer,	34...	V. M. Moseley,	Ebenezer........
.41..	Pythagoras,	....67...	Jno. N. Pate,	Decatur.......
.42	Concord,	57...	A. J. Monroe,	.. ...Morgan.........
.43..	West Point,	82...	Forney Renfro,	West Point.....
.44..	Lafayette,	84...	Jno. T. Brown,	Cumming. ......
.45..	St. John's,	50...	R. C. Manley,	Jackson........
.46..	Washington,	....54...	W. M. Threlkeld,	Ellaville........
47..	Mizpah,	49...	S. W. Blackshear,	Macon. ....
.48..	Jackson,	37...	Jas. M. Reeves,	Hickory Grove..
.49..	St. Thomas.	...112...	E. S. Remington,	Thomasville.....
.50..	Jasper,	42...	J. H. Holland,	Monticello.......

No.	Name of Lodge.	Members.	Name of Sec'y.	Post Office.
.51.	.Hiram,	43	.W. A. Quinn,	Danbury........
.52.	.W. A. Dove,	39	.M. P. Suber,	Andersonville. ..
.53.	.Mt. Moriah,	46	.L. B. Griggs,	Fayetteville.....
.54.	.Clinton.........	72	.Levi E. Byck,	Savannah. ......
.55.	.Knoxville,	69	.H. C. Saunders,	Knoxville.......
.56.	.Burns,	37	.Allen Perry,	Oak Grove......
.57.	.Greenville,	70	.Wm. T. Revill,	Greenville. .....
.58.	.Hamilton,	153	.Wm. Gallaher,	Sandersville.....
.59.	.Atlanta,	205	.Jno. W. Pierce,	Atlanta.........
.60.	.Coweta,	130	.R. A. Johnson,	Newnan.........
.61.	.Chattahoochee,	.59	.H. B. Lane,	Franklin........
.62.	.Randolph,	19	.R. T. Dozier,	Cuthbert........
.63.	.Georgetown,	58	.W. P. Jordan,	Georgetown.....
.64.	.Mt. Moriah,	46	.Wm. McWhorter,	Woodstock......
.65.	.Traveler's Rest,	63	.W. A. Wicker,	Montezuma......
.66.	.Cherokee,	122	.P. M. Sheibly,	Rome...........
.67.	.Dawson,	66	.J. D. Hammack,	Crawfordville....
.68.	.Dawson,	41	.A. M. Colton,	Social Circle.....
.69.	.Carroll,	26	.W. C. New,	Carrollton.......
.70.	.Erin,	63	.W. K. Hollon,	Erin............
.71.	.Oxford,	30	.J. T. Parker,	Oxford.........
.72.	.Villa Rica,	50	.D. T. Trussell,	Villa Rica......
.73.	.Alcova,	50	.Wm. Pope,	Newton Factory.
.74.	.Unity,	—		Palmetto........
.75.	.Lawrens,	64	.Jas. W. Stanley,	Dublin.........
.76.	.Campbellton,	65	.Wm. B. Swan,	Campbellton.....
.77.	.Canton,	47	.O. W. Putman,	Canton.........
.78.	.Lincoln,	38	.Harvey J. Lang,	Lincolnton......
.79.	Few,	87	.T. B. Lumpkin,	Buena Vista.....
.80.	.Weston,	50	.P. W. Riddick,	Weston.........
.81.	.Oak Bowery,	65	.W. H. Milton,	Ellejay..........
.82.	.W. P. Arnold,	21	.Curtis G. Low,	Wrightsboro.....
.83.	.Zaradatha,	93	.Geo. H. Lester,	Lexington ......
.84.	.Lithonia,	26	.J. C. Johnson,	Lithonia. ....
.85.	.Daniel,	22	.G. G. Smith,	Island Creek.....
.86.	.Magnolia,	56	.H. C. Fryer,	Blakely.........
.87.	.Jonesboro,	87	.J. J. Hanes,	Jonesboro.......
.88.	.Pinta,	115	.H. H. Swatts,	Barnesville......
.89.	.El Dorado,	59	.L. D. Lockhart,	Prattsburg. .....
.90.	.Ringgold,	51	.T. J. Mitchell,	Weldon.........
.91.	.Western,	56	.D. C. Sutton,	Lafayette. ......
.92.	.Casten's,	76	.E. E. Love,	Pleasant Hill....
.93.	.St. Mark's,	32	.W L. Smith,	Hogansville....
.94.	.New River,	50	.L. C. Wisdom,	Corinth.........
.95.	.Eureka,	33	.W. H. Baldy,	Starkville.......
.96.	.Georgia,	47	.D. S. Kellam,	Atlanta.........

No.	Name of Lodge.	Members.	Name of Sec'y.	Post Office.
.97	.Euharlee,	68	W. C. Barber,	Van Wert.
.98	.Houston,	—		Houston.
.99	.Siloam,	45	J. S. Middlebrooks,	Snapping Shoals.
100	.St. John's,	51	John P. Dill,	Clay Hill.
101	.Cartersville,	53	F. M. Johnson,	Cartersville.
102	.Rose,	96	J. A. McCurry,	Whitesville.
103	.Pleasant Ridge,	51	Wm. D. Murray,	Turner Chapel.
104	.Montpelier,	36	Smith Waller,	Russellville.
105	.Dalton.	104	T. L. Caldwell,	Dalton
106	.Quitman,	83	W. J. Whitsitt,	Ringgold.
107	.Thurmond,	—		Hillsboro.
108	.Chapel,	49	W. H. House,	Chapel Hill.
109	.Summerville,	85	J. B. Knowles,	Summerville.
110	.Fort Valley,	100	J. F. Maddox,	Fort Valley.
111	.Stone Mountain,	—		Stone Mountain.
112	.Walton,	33	A. S. Holland,	Shady Dale.
113	.Oostanaula,	16	H. C. Norton,	Rome.
114	.Allegheny,	80	S. A. Major,	Blairsville.
115	.Troup Factory,	43	J. H Traylor,	Troup Factory.
116	.Sincerity,	52	F. S. Johnson, Jr.	Clinton.
117	.Farmer's,	32	W. H. Davies,	Vienna.
118	.Kimbrough,	77	T. J. Wald,	Muscogee.
119	.Muckalee,	36	Jas. Fricker,	Americus
120	.Mackey,	55	Hugh L. Bunn,	Cave Spring.
121	.Caledonia,	39	G. W. Featherston,	Cedar Town.
122	.Williamsville,	31	Jos. Williamson,	Williamsville.
123	.Baber,	34	J. R. Houghton,	White Plains.
124	.Furlow,	39	Jas. T. Cato,	Botsford
125	.Jason Burr,	—		Mountville.
126	.St. Mary's,	22	L. Lippman,	St. Mary's.
127	.Ancient York,	39	T. H. Stallworth,	Sandy Ridge.
128	.Union,	43	G. B. Rollins	Quito.
129	.Fickling,	62	W. O. Russ,	Butler.
130	.Salem,	39	M. G. W. Gordon,	Culloden.
131	.Lawrenceville,	65	J. L. King,	Lawrenceville.
132	.Long Cane,	30	Jno. S. Hill,	Long Cane
133	.Mt. Hickory,	81	H. T. Smith,	Subligna.
134	.Hunter,	62	E M. Newman,	Marshallville.
135	.Fergus,	34	R. S. O'Kelly,	Loganville.
136	.Cassville,	74	A. A. Vincent,	Pine Log.
137	.Live Oak,	14	R. K. Walker,	Darien.
138	.Howard,	48	Jno. F. Smith,	Maxey's.
139	.King David,	44	B. F. Blasingame,	King's Chapel.
140	.Claremont,	76	J. M. Williams,	Liberty Hill.
141	.Charity,	33	B. W. Brown,	Lisbon
142	.Haralson,	40	A. Spier,	Haralson.

44   GENERAL MASONIC REGISTER.

No.	Name of Lodge.	Members.	Name of Sec'y.	Post Office.
143	So. Western,	45	Wm. M. Green,	Aglethorpe
144	Ellerslie,	69	S. M. Brannon,	Ellerslie.
145	Spring Place,	44	W. W. Giddens.	Spring Place.
146	Kiolin,	49	Wm. T. Pike,	Mulberry Grove.
147	Sulphur Spring,	37	R. A. Crawford,	Sulphur Spring.
148	Phi Delta,	73	D. McDonald,	Phi Delta.
149	Woodbury,	46	W. P. Wheless,	Woodbury.
150	Irwinton,	47	Geo. W. Bishop,	Irwinton
151	Wellington,	43	G. B. Bostwick,	Wellington.
152	Sharon Grove,	85	J. W. Ward,	Sharon Grove.
153	Springville,	69	Isaac N. Moon,	Powder Springs.
154	Oothcologa,	93	J. W. Marshall,	Calhoun.
155	Chandler,	72	W. R. Phelts,	Cusseta.
156	Harmony,	40	R. H. Hightower,	McLendon's Store.
157	Pineville,	—		Clarksville
158	Irving,	41	M. A. McNulto,	Chickasawatchee.
159	County Line,	39	J. N. Wilson.	County Line.
160	Trion,	42	G. B. Myers,	Trion Factory.
161	Fallulah,	—		Clarksville
162	Joppa,	52	G. M. Witcher,	Point Peter.
163	Satilla,	44	J. P. Wall,	Kirkland's Store.
164	Twiggs.	76	A. W. Asbell,	Marion.
165	Roswell,	72	F. J. Minhinnett,	Roswell.
166	Webb,	96	Geo. Adams,	Augusta.
167	Floyd,	46	G. W. Fleetwood,	Floyd Springs
168	Adairsville,	41	O. D. Anderson,	Adairsville.
169	Mt. Ebal,	22	Bennet Adams,	Mt. Ebal
170	Rotherwood,	76	A. J. O'Rear,	Rotherwood.
171	Adamsville,	27	Geo. W. Adams,	Adamsville.
172	Ocapilco,	29	D. F. Chapman,	Wade's Store.
173	Patrick Henry,	40	W. G. Redding,	Drayton.
174	Holt.	54	A. J. Williams,	Friendship.
175	Zabud,	51	T. S. Coleman,	New Market.
176	Ackworth,	79	J. R. Humphries,	Ackworth.
177	Pine Grove,	58	R. B. Andrews,	Bear Creek.
178	Philologia,	90	O. Seaman,	Conyers.
179	Trenton,	78	J. C. Taylor,	Trenton.
180	Fairburn,	64	S. G. Johnson,	Fairburn.
181	Milford,	26	J. M. Gatewood,	Milford.
182	Dallas,	52	G. W. Foote,	Dallas.
183	High Falls,	—		High Falls.
184	St. John Baptist,	57	D. R. Stephens,	Valdosta.
185	Cool Springs,	56	Q. L. Harvard,	Cool Springs.
186	Carnesville,	72	Alex. White,	Carnesville.
187	Center,	45	D. F. Scarborough,	Union.
188	Marshall,	49	N. A. Windsor,	Preston.

N..	Name of Lodge.	Members.	Name of Sec'y.	Post Office.
189	Herman,	76	T. J. Holland,	Hartwell
190	Baker,	54	J. T. Roberts,	Newton
191	Rockwell	79	L. Y. Bradbury,	Center Hill
192	Brooksville,	34	J. B. Horsley,	Brooksville
193	Coffee,	44	J. A. Clemens,	Jacksonville
194	Worth.	67	Wm. J. Ford,	Isabella
195	Holmesville.	40	J. H. Moody,	Holmesville
196	Trader's Hill,	33	L. P. Tracy.	Trader's Hill
197	Wells,	54	James Norris,	Calaparchee
198	Millwood.	53	A. J. Cone,	Millwood.
199	Lumber City,	55	T. J. Smith,	Lumber City
200	Eastern Light,	63	Jno. W. Coffee:	Alston Church
201	Ocoee.	21	Jno. C. Logan,	Morganton
202	Tunnel Hill,	70	Wm. L. Headrick,	Tunnel Hill.
203	Ashler,	51	O. R. Belcher, Jr.,	Concord Academy.
204	A. J. Miller.	83	W. C. Worrill,	Thomson.
205	Hickory Flat,	--		Hickory Flat.
206	Bowden.	53	N. Shelnutt.	Bowden.
207	Armonia,	35	T. Jeff. Brown.	Point Peter.
208	Hudson,	39	M. S. Weaver,	Glade's X Roads.
209	Alapaha,	26	J. P. Prescott,	Statenville
210	Brookline,	62	Jno. F. Kirk,	Danielsville
211	Butler,	34	Jas. E. Sharp,	Milltown.
212	Irwin,	--		Irwinville.
213	Ogeechee,:	18	A. W. Stewart,	Ogeechee.
214	Ocean,	58	Wm. T. Jones,	Brunswick.
215	Gaulding,	78	Jas. P. Moore,	Fayetteville
216	Fulton,	94	Chas. S. Cook,	Atlanta
217	Waresboro	47	Wm. Rennie,	Waresboro
218	Simon Holt,	29	J. A. Bean,	Colquit.
219	Gainesville,	60	W. S. Gray,	Gainesville.
220	Pickens Star,	63	W. M. Bearden,	Jasper.
221	Sonora.	64	J. W. Bowles,	Calhoun.
222	Etowah.	63	J. L. Perkins,	Dawsonville.
223	Smith,	49	Chas. Woodard,	Red Hill.
224	Cassia,	75	Eli O'Quin,	Homerville.
225	Attapulgus,	52	N. N. Lester,	Attapulgus.
226	Fort Early,	29	Jas M. Rouse,	Warwick.
227	Altamahah,	31	J. D. McConnell,	Johnson's Station.
228	Yellow River,	45	J. W. Miner,	Yellow River.
229	P. T. Schley,	105	H. S. Bell.	Dawson.
230	Mineral Spring,	20	M. B. Pickett,	Mineral Spring.
231	An't Landmark,	79	B. A. Hart,	Savannah.
232	Mountain,	63	R. A. Johnson,	Good Hope.
233	Ornan,	44	J. G. Rogers,	Kingston.
234	Duncan,	54	J. H. Kirby,	Nashville.

No.	Name of Lodge.	Members.	Name of Sec'y.	Post Office.
235	Alpharetta,	69	O. P. Skelton,	Alpharetta
236	Luthersville,	76	J. W. Taylor,	Luthersville
237	Shalto,	69	M. C. Wade.	Quitman
238	Cassia,	45	G. L. Cain.	Fenn's Bridge
239	Aural,	75	J. A. McMillan,	Mt. Vernon
240	Gordon,	60	Lawrence Butts,	Gordon
241	Camilla,	59	Jno. W. Pearce,	Camilla
242	Groverville,	39	T. B. Whitfield,	Boston.
243	Anderson,	95	M. H. Mason.	Wrightsville
244	Swainsboro,	86	Jno. N. Thompson,	Swainsboro.
245	Lawrence,	56	Jas. B. Manson,	Bethany
246	Little River,	20	Parks Hardman,	Marietta.
247	Austin,	49	E. D. Watson,	Smithville
248	Scriven,	39	S. E. Clark,	Scarboro.
249	Jeffersonville,	40	R. R. Wimberly,	Jeffersonville.
250	Henderson,	20	J. T. Coleman,	Henderson.
251	Stonewall,	56	W. H. H. Stewart,	Louisville
252	Draketown,	44	Jno. Y. Allgood,	Draketown
253	W. P. Haynes,	27	M. S. Medlock,	Rock Factory.
254	Morven,	33	C. W. McRae,	Morven.
255	Raynolds,	36	S. H. Lockett.	Raynolds.
256	Stockton,	30	J. W. Howell,	Stockton
257	Gibson,	50	J. W. Harrison,	Gibson
258	Ivena,	37	J. E. Dickinson,	Steam Mills
259	Youah,	71	J. W. Meeks,	Cleveland
260	Stilesboro.	36	T. Colbert,	Stilesboro.
261	Ophir,	30	J. W. Grogan,	Ophir.
262	Locust Grove,	53	Arch. Brown,	Locust Grove.
263	Damascus,	25	I. B. Douglass,	Damascus.
264	Midville,	26	M. H. Lewis,	Midville
265	Rabun Gap,	59	A. H. McAllister,	Clayton.
266	St. Mary's,	45	W. B. Gray,	Cedar Grove.
267	Unicoie,	40	W. R. McConnell,	Hiawassee
269	St. John's,	41	R. D. Sharpe,	Red Bluff.
270	Blackshear,	32	A. J. Strickland,	Blackshear
271	Hinesville,	29	W. W. Zorn.	Hinesville
273	Moultrie,	25	J. T. J. Cooper,	Moultrie

Idaho.

The Grand Lodge in this Territory was organized 10th December 1867, by three lodges holding under G. L. of Oregon, and one under the G. L. of Washington Territory, and George H Carr was elected the first grand master. In 1870 there were 8 lodges in the jurisdiction, with a total membership of 288 Master Masons. This grand lodge is migratory, holding its annual communications on the first Monday in October, at such place as may be fixed upon at the previous annual session.

The executive grand officers elect in 1870 were—

S. B. CONNELLY, of Pioneerville, Grand Master.

CHAS. HILTON, of Silver City, Deputy Gr. Master.

J. W. GRIFFIN, of Boise City, Grand Treasurer.

H. E. PRICKETT, of Boise City, Grand Secretary.

In reply to our circulars requesting the same, three of the lodges here given furnished the information desired. Otherwise the list is copied from the 1870 Proceedings.

No.	Name of Lodge.	Members.	Name of Sec'y.	Post Office.
1	Idaho,	55	Jonas W. Brown,	Idaho City.
2	Boise,	55	A. L. Richardson,	Boise City
3	Placer	21	M. Eissler	Placerville
4	Pioneer,	34	Ed. A. Stephenson,	Pioneer City
5	Owyhee,	31	Daniel G. Monro,	Silver City
6	War Eagle,	30	P. C. Learned,	Silver City
7	Shoshone,	32	E. C. Sterling,	Boise City
8	Coe,	23	James B. Duke,	Centreville

Illinois.

In 1822 there was a grand lodge organized in this territory, but it succumbed to the anti-masonic excitement which swept the entire country within the subsequent decade. The present Grand Lodge of Illinois was organized at Jackson, on the 6th of April, 1840, by delegates from six lodges, four of those lodges holding under the G. Lodge of Kentucky ; Abraham Jonas was elected first grand master, and Wm. B. Warren the first grand secretary. The annual communications are not fixed, as to place, but had been, until 1870, for many years held in Springfield, in October. Under a change of By-Laws, it is now proposed to permanently locate the grand lodge in Chicago, the principal commercial city of the State. The increase of lodges in Illinois within thirty years has but one parallel in any American State. In 1871 there were 629 lodges, with a total membership of 36,250 Master Masons ; being an increase in the previous ten years of 100 per cent. for the lodges, and 200 per cent. for the membership. A proposition made in grand lodge in October, 1870, to remove the archives to Chicago, was unfortunately not adopted, for they were all destroyed by fire in February 1871, at Springfield, with the office of the Gr. Sec'y. The Proceedings of the 1870 session having, fortunately, been printed at Quincy, were, to extent of about 1500 copies, saved ; those delivered at Springfield having been destroyed. The supervision of this large jurisdiction is at present intrusted to thirty District Deputy Grand Masters, the appointees of the grand master elect. In 1870 the revenue of this grand lodge amounted to $24,570.50, of which the sum of $23,383.17 was disbursed in paying mileage and per diem, appropriations, salaries, printing, postage, &c. for the year—among which $100 only were donated as charity.

The executive grand officers elected in 1870 were—

> DeWitt C. Cregier, of Chicago, Grand Master.
> James A. Hawley, of Dixon, Deputy Grand Master.
> Harrison Dills, of Quincy, Grand Treasurer.
> Orlin H. Miner, of Springfield, Grand Secretary.

Appointed by Gr. Master—

JOHN C. REYNOLDS, of Springfield, Deputy Gr. Sec'y.

The following information is collected from the Proceedings for 1870 of the Grand Lodge, and such later data as we received from the lodge secretaries, in response to our circulars requesting the same :

No.	Name of Lodge.	Members.	Name of Sec'y.	Post Office.
..1..	Bodley,	125	E. M. Broughton,	Quincy.
..2..	Equality,	20	W. H. Crawford	Equality
..3..	Harmony,	115	Jno. W. Craig,	Jacksonville
..4..	Springfield,	119	J. B. Hammond,	Springfield
..7..	Friendship,	142	W. N. Johnson,	Dixon.
..8..	Macon.	157	Nathan L. Krone,	Decatur.
..9..	Rushville,	75	Jno. C. Scripps,	Rushville.
.13..	St. John's,	110	H. M. Gallagher,	Peru.
.14..	Warren,	37	Jas. H. Hart,	Shawneetown
.15..	Peoria,	205	Lewis Keyon,	Peoria.
.16..	Temperance,	66	Joseph Gordon,	Vandalia.
.17..	Macomb,	110	Geo. P. Hall,	Macomb.
.19..	Clinton	83	Auson Thompson,	Petersburg
.20..	Hancock,	54	Jno. D. Hamilton,	Carthage.
.23..	Cass,	54	M. D. Halpin,	Beardstown.
.24..	St. Clair,	58	Alex. B. Russell,	Belleville.
.25..	Franklin,	90	C. W. Leverett,	Upper Alton.
.26..	Hiram,	50	Jos. Davison,	Henderson
.27..	Piasa	87	H. J. Jennison,	Alton.
.28..	Monroe,	35	Wm. Lofink,	Waterloo.
.29..	Pekin,	59	S. G. Puterbough,	Pekin.
.30..	Morning Star,	108	J. C. Brinkerhoff.	Canton.
.31..	Mount Vernon,	53	R. A. D. Wilbanks,	Mount Vernon.
.33..	Oriental,	365	E. N. Tucker,	Chicago.
.34..	Barry,	98	Calvin Jackson,	Barry
.35..	Charleston	85	T. C. Lawrence,	Charleston.
.36..	Kavenaugh,	46	John Bawden,	Elizabeth.
.37..	Monmouth,	131	Richard Wagstaff,	Monmouth.
.38..	Olive Branch,	90	John Mires, Jr.	Danville.
.39..	Herman,	75	M. Wetterhahn,	Quincy.
.40..	Occidental,	165	Wm. S. Easton.	Ottawa.
.42..	Mount Joliet,	154	S. T. Thompson,	Joliet
.43..	Bloomington,	180	Chas. Strehorn,	Bloomington.
.44..	Hardin,	95	G. C. Irvin,	Mount Sterling.
.45..	Griggsville,	79	Wm. H. Clark,	Griggsville
.46..	Temple,	148	N. S. Tucker,	Peoria.
.47..	Caledonia,	40	H. M. Smith,	North Caledonia.
.48..	Unity,	100	G. A. Dunham,	St. Charles.

No.	Name of Lodge.	Members.	Name of Sec'y.	Post Office.
.49.	.Cambridge,	.....59.	..L. H. Patten,	.......Cambridge......
.50.	.Carrollton.	.....87.	..Jas. P. Morrow,	.....Carrollton.......
.51.	.Mt. Moriah,	....96.	..C. M. Wool,	......Hillsboro. ......'
.52.	.Benevolent,	...52.	..D. H. Lollis,	.......Merodosia. .. ...
.53.	.Jackson,	......90.	..W. W. Hall,	........Shelbyville. ....
.54.	.Reclamation,	...56.	..R. M. Parker,	......Nauvoo.........
.55.	.Washington,	....50.	..Darius Greenup,	....Nashville. ......
.56.	.Pittsfield,	.....80.	..W. H. Johnston,	....Pittsfield........
.57.	.Trio,	.........141.	..W. L. Sweeney,	....Rock Island.....
.58.	.Fraternal,	.....89.	..J. A. Hill,	.......Monticello......
.59.	.New Boston,	....68.	..E. S. Benedict,	......New Boston.....
.60.	.Belvidere.	.....127.	..Forrester Clark,	....Belvidere.......
.61.	.Lacon,	.........63.	..T. A. McMorris,	....Lacon..........
.63.	.Saint Marks,	..150.	..G. R. Bassett,	......Woodstock......
.64.	.Benton,	.......70.	..Carroll Moore,	......Benton.......
.65.	.Euclid,	........78.	..E. H. Ditzler,	.......Naperville......
.66.	.Knoxville,	....110.	..Wm. Hester,	........Knoxville.......
.67.	.Acacia,	........84.	..John N. Bedard,	....La Salle.........
.68.	.Naples,	........40.	..Thos. Hollowbush,	..Naples..........
.69.	.Eureka,	.. ..35.	..Jacob Adams,	......Camden Mills....
.70.	.Social,	.........62.	..C. Bodemer,	........Hennepin.......
.71.	.Central,	.......129.	..H. C. Watson,	......Springfield......
.72.	.Chester,	........55.	..A. G. Jones,	......Chester.........
.74.	.Rockton,	.......74.	..E. S. Stiles,	.......Rockton........
.75.	.Roscoe,	........75.	..George G. Smith,	...Roscoe. ....
.76.	.Mount Nebo,	...75.	..Jas. K. Furber,	....Carlinville......
.77.	.Prairie,	.........80.	..John Harris,	.......Paris...........
.78.	.Waukegan,	....138.	..Wm. A. Gray,	.....Waukegan .....
.79.	.Carlisle,	........50.	..H. W. Sprang,	......Carlyle.........
.80.	.White Hall,	....85.	..F. A. Worcester,	....White Hall......
.81.	.Vitruvius,	.....58.	..J. D. Beach,	........Wheeling......
.82.	.Metamora,	....47.	..John J. Perry,	.....Metamora.......
.84.	.De Witt,	.....117.	..Edward De Land,	...Clinton.........
.85.	.Mitchell,	......53.	..G. H. Stempert,	....Mitchell ....
.86.	.Kaskaskia,	.....73.	..J. H. Lindsay,	.....Kaskaskia......
.87.	.Mt. Pulaski,	...53.	..Jacob Yager,	......Mount Pulaski...
.88.	.Havana,	........75.	..Fred. Politz,	......Havana........
.89.	.Fellowship,	.....89.	..John M. Young,	....Marion.........
.90.	.J'r's'l'm T'mple,	185.	..J. C. Sheets,	........Aurora.........
.91.	.Metropolis,	.....80.	..Wm. Kurtz,	......Metropolis......
.92.	.Stewart,	.......81.	..J. Clark Rockwell,	..Geneseo........
.93.	.Toulon,	........56.	..Charles Myers,	.....Toulon....:....
.95.	.Perry,	........70.	..W. A. Reed,	.........Perry ....
.96.	.Sam. H. Davis,	.45.	..O. H. Swingley,	.....Mount Morris...
.97.	.Excelsior,	......94.	..W. W. Lott,	........Freeport........
.98.	.Taylor,	........59.	..E. A. Smith,	........Washington....

No.	Name of Lodge.	Members.	Name of Sec'y.	Post Office.
.99	.Edwardsville	...55	...H. C. Barnsback,	...Edwardsville....
100	.Astoria,	68	...B. C Toler,	........Astoria.........
102,	.Rockford,	165	...W. T. Hyde,	........Rockford..........
103	.Magnolia,	77	..E. R. Manley,	.......Magnolia. ......
104	.Lewistown,	61	..H. C. Abernathy,	...Lewistown......
105	.Winchester,	60	..W. C. Berry,	........Winchester. ....
106	.Lancaster,	39	...Edw. J. Jones,	......Timber.........
107	.Fayette,	43	..R. G. Robertson,	....Fayette.........
108	.Versailles,	52	...John W. Macoy,	....Versailles ......
109	.Trenton,	.....:...50	...H. Cooper,	.........Trenton........
110	.Lebanon,	77	..J. B. Newman,	......Lebanon ....
111	.Jonesboro,	60	...G. W. Williams,	.....Jonesboro......
112	.Bureau,	110	..F. W. Waller,	......Princeton.......
113	.Robert Burns,	..57	..A. F. Glover,	.......Keithsburg....:.
114	.Marcelline,	48	...Wm. Denson,	......Marcelline......
115	.Rising Sun,	60	...Chas. Whitehead,	...Haynesville.....
116	.Vermont,	56	...Wm. Alexander,	....Vermont ....
117	.Elgin,	85	..E. H. Sylla,	.......Elgin............
118	.Waverly,	64	..Henry Watson,	.....Waverly........
119	.Henry,	41	...L. L. Lehman,	......Henry..........
122	.Mound,	95	..B. F Barnes,	......Taylorville......
123	.Oquawka,	70	..W. H. Stockton,	.....Oquawka. ......
124	.Cedar,	95	..Jos. H. Pettit,	......Morris.........
125	.Greenup,	26	...John J. Kellum,	...Greenup........
126	.Empire,	68	...Joseph Baker,	......Pekin.........
127	.Antioch,	56	..H. Pantal,	..........Antioch. ....
128	.Raleigh,	70	...C. P. Burnett.	......Raleigh........
129	.Greenfield,	63	...M. T. Nichols,	.....Greenfield......
130	.Marion,	73	...W. S. Larimer,	.....Salem.........
131	.Golconda,	75	...Theo. Steyer,	.......Golconda.......
132	.Mackinaw,	41	...N. Campbell,	......Mackinaw.......
133	.Marshall,	90	...Young Whitlock,	...Marshall ....
134	.Sycamore,	121	...H. C. Whittemore,	...Sycamore.....
136	.Hutsonville,	38	..J. Racherby,	......Hutsonville.....
137	.Polk,	40	...A. T. Sullinger,	.....M'Leansboro....
138	.Marengo,	95	..F. M. Jewett,	.......Marengo........
139	.Geneva,	96	..H. A. Scott,	.......Geneva.........
140	.Olney,	87	...G. T. Hodges	.....Olney. ....
141	.Garden City,	..175	...C. H. Lillibridge,	...Chicago.........
142	.Ames,	67	..L. R. Craig,	........Sheffield. ....
143	.Richmond,	83	..C. J. Cotting	......Richmond.......
144	.Dekalb,	........86.:	..A. H. Rolph,	......Dekalb. ....
145	.A. W. Rawson,	.54	..D. A. Stitsel,	.......Pecatonica......
146	.Lee Centre,	...52	...Geo. W. Lenn,	....Lee Centre......
147	.Clayton,	61	...T. C. Hatton,	.......Clayton.........
148	.Bloomfield,	80	...James Boles,	.......Bloomfield. ....

No.	Name of Lodge.	Members.	Name of Sec'y.	Post Office.
149	Ewington,	45	D. P. Barr,	Effingham
150	Vienna,	70	T. M. Simpson,	Vienna.
151	Bunker Hill,	59	David Morris,	Bunker Hill.
152	Fidelity,	50	G. W. Harrold,	Fidelity.
153	Clay,	50	J. P. M. Harrison,	Ashley
154	Russell,	47	C. M. Holmes,	Georgetown.
155	Alpha,	170	D. C. Brown,	Galesburg.
156	Delavan,	74	J. M. Evans,	Delavan.
157	Urbana.	89	F. G. Jaques,	Urbana.
158	McHenry,	66	B. N. Wiles,	McHenry.
159	Wethersfield,	82	Robt. Moore,	Kewanee.
160	Wabansia,	197	J. E. Church,	Chicago.
161	Virden,	82	T. A. Rae,	Virden.
162	Hope,	57	Sam. Galt,	Sparta.
163	Westfield,	58	Thomas Teft,	Westfield
164	Ed. Dobbins,	53	J. Birmingham,	Lawrenceville
165	Atlanta.	59	B. Bean,	Atlanta.
166	Star in the East,	180	Wm. Ashworth,	Rockford.
168	Milford,	57	Ira Brown,	Milford.
169	Nunda,	43	Elijah Buck,	Nunan.
170	Evergreen,	142	M. V. Brown,	Freeport.
171	Girard,	63	F. J. Woolley,	Girard.
172	Wayne.	20	Jno. D. Slack,	Waynesville.
173	Cherry Valley,	50	A J. Foster,	Cherry Valley.
174	Lena.	90	C. E. Crain,	Lena.
175	Matteson,	130	C. B. Garnsey,	Joliet.
176	Mendota,	127	P. J. Davis,	Mendota.
177	Staunton,	64	Robert Hoxsey	Staunton.
178	Illinois Central,	125	Wm. Gibson,	Amboy.
179	Wabash,	39	G. W. Cross,	Etna
180	Moweaqua,	60	A. J. Steidly,	Moweaqua.
181	Moultrie,	57	A. N. Smyser,	Sullivan.
182	Germania,	140	E. G. Smith,	Chicago.
183	Meridian,	61	L. B. Payne,	Earlville.
185	Abington,	63	Geo. S. Smith,	Abington.
187	Mystic Tie,	48	C. T. Barber,	Polo.
188	Cyrus,	52	F. H. English,	McCarroll.
189	Fulton City,	102	John Phelps,	Fulton City.
190	Dundee.	65	D. R. Jencks,	Dundee.
191	Xenia,	50	Jas. Portness,	Xenia.
192	Farmington,	56	Jno. J. Elder,	Farmington.
193	Herrick,	30	John Moyes,	Pontoosuc.
194	Freedom,	69	R. S. Woolley,	Freedom.
195	La Harpe,	90	L. S. Cogswell,	La Harpe.
196	Louisville,	52	S. R. Apperson,	Louisville.
197	King Solomon's	48	C. T. Bannister,	Kane.

No.	Name of Lodge.	Members.	Name of Sec'y.	Post Office.
198	Grand View,	46	C. L. Morris,	Grand View.....
199	Homer,	54	J. A. Galusha,	Homer. ....
200	Sheba,	40	W. W. Gray,	Grayville. ......
201	Centralia,	89	C. A. Fletcher,	Centralia........
202	Sterling,	54	Thos. K. Facey,	Sterling.........
203	Lavely,	45	N. R Taylor,	Williamsville. ...
204	Flora,	43	J. F. Wilcox,	Flora...........
205	Corinthian,	38	H. S. Griffith,	East Paw Paw...
206	Fairfield,	47	Wm. W. George,	Fairfield. ....
207	Tamaroa,	45	E. H. Price,	Tamaroa........
208	Wilmington,	113	L. A. Baker,	Wilmington. ....
209	Wm. B.Warren,	180	L. A. Kormandy,	Chicago.........
210	Lincoln,	59	W. G. Starkey,	Lincoln.........
211	Cleveland,	325	Jno. Whitley,	Chicago.........
212	Shipman,	42	W. G. Wallace,	Shipman........
213	Ipava,	59	Isaac David,	Ipava...........
214	Gillespie,	33	T. W. Floyd,	Gillespie........
216	Newton,	58	Sam. B. Brown,	Newton.........
217	Mason,	63	H. T. Hoxsey,	Mason..........
218	New Salem,	41	John Preble,	New Salem.....,
219	Oakland,	40	A. J. Campbell,	Oakland.......
220	Mahomet,	48	W. V. Miller,	Mahomet. ......
221	Leroy.	49	John W. Barley,	Leroy. ....
222	G. Washington,	59	Levi Booth,	Chillicothe......
223	Keeney,	42	J. E. Eby,	Edgington......
224	Mount Pleasant,	53	Henry Funk,	Santa Anna.....
226	Pana,	81	W. H. Trapping,	Pana...........
227	Columbus,	24	Thos. A. Metcalf,	Coatsburg......
228	Lovington,	35	J. H. Dunscombe,	Lovington......
229	Manchester,	38	W. P. Brubaker,	Manchester......
230	New Haven,	20	S. A. Pinney,	New Haven.....
231	Wyanett,	47	W. J. Nichols,	Wyanett ....
232	Farmers,	55	W. B. Warren,	Pellonia.......
233	Blandinville,	40	T. M. Seaton,	Blandinville....
234	Duquoin,	66	J. G. Mangold,	Duquoin.... ...
235	Dallas City,	54	Jonathan Rice,	Dallas City.....
236	Charter Oak,	88	A. J. Wood,	Litchfield.......
237	Cairo,	85	Charles Forest,	Cairo...........
238	Black Hawk,	43	E. C. A. Cushman,	Hamilton. ......
239	Mount Carmel,	48	J. Zimmerman,	Mount Carmel...
240	Western Star,	116	Henry Trevett,	Champaign......
241	Shekinah,	90	S. P. Brush,	Carbondale.....
243	Galva,	95	Nelson Pierce,	Galva..........
244	Horicon,	93	C. C. Bennett,	Rochelle........
245	Greenville,	55	Robert L. Mudd,	Greenville......
246	El Paso,	64	George M. Young,	El Paso........

No.	Name of Lodge.	Members.	Name of Sec'y.	Post Office.
247	Rob Morris,	45	M. L. Newell,	Minouk
248	Golden Gate,	48	G. W. Risely,	Prairie City
249	Hibbard,	67	T. H. Simmons,	Brighton
250	Robinson,	45	E. Callahan,	Robinson
251	Heyworth,	39	O. C. Rutlege,	Heyworth
252	Aledo,	57	John C. Williver,	Aledo
253	Avon Harmony,	72	Royal Bliss,	Avon
254	Aurora,	120	A. G. McDole,	Aurora
255	Donaldson,	49	J. H. Gilmore,	Bear Creek
256	Algonquin	35	W. M. Wilcox,	Algonquin
257	Warsaw,	58	G. B. Heberling,	Warsaw
258	Chemung,	70	J. C. Wooster,	Chemung
259	New Berlin	50	H. B. Williams,	New Berlin
260	Mattoon,	80	William Kemp,	Mattoon
261	Amon,	65	G. H. Mittan,	De Witt
262	Channahon,	44	Ephraim West,	Channahon
263	Illinois,	68	C. A. De Mattos,	Peoria
264	Franklin Grove,	125	Wm. Gibson,	Franklin Grove
265	Vermillion,	59	O. S. Calvert,	Indianola
266	Kingston,	54	Wm. W. Apsley,	Fairweather
267	La Prairie,	55	R. H. Bacon,	La Prairie
268	Paris,	80	J. E. Dyas,	Paris
269	Wheaton,	100	James B. Clark,	Wheaton
270	Levi Lusk,	43	C. A. Pieronnett,	Arlington
271	Blaney,	201	James S. Carter,	Chicago
272	Carmi,	75	T. W. Hay,	Carmi
273	Miners',	70	S. O. Stillman.	Galena
274	Byron,	63	George Kozier,	Byron
275	Milton,	55	Wm. M'Crudden,	Milton
276	Elizabeth,	30	J. H. B. Renfro,	Elizabethtown
277	Accordia,	80	E. Meininger,	Chicago
278	Jo. Daviess,	89	H. C. Gann,	Warren
279	Neoga,	45	W. A. Davis,	Neoga
280	Kansas,	51	H. A. Dodd,	Kansas
282	Brooklyn,	50	John K. Robinson,	Muligan's Grove
283	Meteor,	89	James Forsyth,	Sandwich
284	Alton,	109	John W. Ash,	Alton
285	Catlin,	59	Sam. R. Tilton,	Catlin
286	Plymouth,	49	M. D. Gillis,	Plymouth
287	De Soto,	70	H. H. Smith,	De Soto
288	Genoa,	53	M. W. Cole,	Genoa
290	Cache	65	Geo. E. Lounsberry,	Mound City
291	Wataga,	38	Geo. W. Davis,	Wataga
292	Chenoa,	39	C. S. Elder,	Chenoa
293	Prophetstown,	70	H. R. Kent,	Prophetstown
294	Pontiac,	85	John A. Fellows,	Pontiac

No.	Name of Lodge.	Members.	Name of Sec'y.	Post Office.
295	Dills,	49	John J. Evans,	Hickory Ridge
296	Quincy,	90	B. F. Hoar,	Quincy
297	Benjamin,	48	George W. Cyrus,	Camp Point
298	Wauconda,	75	Wm. Tilmarsh,	Wauconda
299	Mechanicsburg,	28	E. W. Bennett,	Mechanicsburg
300	Hanover,	30	T. E. Moore,	Hanover
301	Courtland,	50	O. B. Ingalls,	Courtland
302	Durand,	86	J. N. Russell,	Durand
303	Raven,	38	J. A. Kenney,	Oswego
304	Cement,	55	C. C. Halliday,	Utica
305	Onargo,	69	Isaac Amerman,	Onargo
306	W. C. Hobbs,	47	Saml. West,	Eureka
307	M. J. Pickett,	105	W. H. Heaton,	Bushnell
308	Ashlar,	72	G. F. Bigelow,	Chicago
309	Harvard,	70	Fletcher Brainard,	Harvard
310	Dearborn,	72	G. F. Bigelow,	Chicago
311	Kilwinning,	240	B. F. De Long,	Chicago
312	Ionic,	61	E. A. Gastman,	Decatur
313	York,	63	Anderson Crough,	York
314	Palatine,	70	F. J. Filbert,	Palatine
315	Irwin,	56	F. W. Joesting.	Alton
316	Abr'm Jonas,	37	A. S. Austin, jr.	Oakalla
317	New Liberty,	35	J. H. Stucker,	New Liberty
318	J. L. Anderson,	66	Joseph Pease,	Augusta
319	Doric,	65	L. E. Hemenway,	Moline
320	Malta,	53	C. B. Safford,	Malta
321	Dunlap,	87	George H. Fay,	Morrison
322	Windsor.	75	M. Montgomery,	Windsor
323	Orient,	18	A. W. Raymond,	Lisbon
325	Harrisburg,	45	T. Y. Reynolds.	Harrisburg
327	Industry,	43	Thos. J. Downer,	Industry
328	Grafton,	45	T. B. Schermerhorn,	Huntley
329	Durham,	38	Wm. Scott,	Durham
330	Altona,	35	G. W. Sawyer,	Walnut Grove
331	Mount Erie,	47	Frank Israel,	Mount Erie
332	Tuscala,	103	Wm. B. Dryer,	Tuskala
333	Tyrian,	95	John B. Saye,	Springfield
334	Sumner,	76	C. C. Lans,	Sumner
335	Schiller,	98	G. Stiehl,	Peoria
336	New Columbia.	59	J. M. Choat,	New Columbia
337	Oneida,	62	W. A. Bell,	Oneida
338	Grand Detour,	43	James Rogers,	Grand Detour
339	Saline,	50	W. A. Humphreys,	Goreville
340	Kedron,	43	Richard Kimble,	Mount Auburn
341	Full Moon,	45	Wm. H. Martin,	Grafton
342	Summerfield,	35	G. W. Tipton,	Summerfield

No.	Name of Lodge.	Members.	Name of Sec'y.	Post Office.
344	Wenona,	63	Wm. Parker,	Wenona
345	Milledgeville,	46	James M'Cready,	Milledgeville
346	N. D Morse,	38	John T. Rush,	Concord.
347	Sidney.	53	Wm. Freeman,	Sidney
348	Russellville,	17	John B. Rich,	Russellville
349	Sublette,	37	Thos. S Angier,	Sublette
350	Fairview,	45	N. M. Downing,	Fairview.
351	Tarbolton,	84	Irvine E. Bliss,	Fairbury.
352	Groveland,	31	D. Sammons,	Groveland.
353	Kinderhook,	41	David Thompson,	Kinderhook.
354	Ark & Anchor,	85	John Piper,	Auburn
355	Marine,	37	J. Sacketts, Jr.,	Marine.
356	Hermitage,	50	A. B. Matthews,	Albion.
357	Kingston Mines,	47	Charles Percy,	Kingston Mines.
358	Orion,	58	J. H. Lucas,	Union.
359	Blackberry,	67	S. S. W. Morrill,	Blackberry Sta'n.
360	Princeville,	32	H. E. Burgess,	Princeville.
361	Douglass,	50	John Wolf,	Mascoutah.
362	Noble,	45	J. C. Leger.	Noble.
363	Horeb,	90	A. L. Schimpff.	Elmwood.
364	Tonica,	48	E. H. Miller.	Tonica
365	Bement,	47	George L. Spear,	Bement.
366	Arcola,	53	Robert L. Warne,	Arcola.
367	Oxford,	79	J. B. McLoughlin,	Oxford.
368	Jefferson,	42	H. Cornelius,	Lynchburg.
369	Newman,	57	D. O. Root,	Newman.
370	Middleton,	40	E. N. Karn,	Middleton.
371	Livingston,	48	R. P. Morgan,	Dwight.
372	Galesburg,	97	A. E. Slater.	Galesburg.
373	Chambersburg,	31	Geo. L. Thompson,	Chambersburg.
374	Shabbona,	55	G. M. Alexander,	Shab'na Grove.
375	Isaac Underhill,	53	E. N. Powell,	Secor.
376	Ash Grove,		No Return.	Ash Grove.
377	Archimedes,	44	Geo. Vondershmitt,	Belleville.
378	Aroma,	33	J. E. White,	Aroma.
379	Payson,	68	Jacob Urech,	Payson.
380	Liberty,	49	R. R. Williams,	Liberty.
381	M. R. Thomson,	67	J. G. S. Best,	Freeport.
382	Gill,	35	Charles Gibbs,	Lynnville.
383	Lamoille,	89	W. B. Howard,	Lamoille.
384	Waltham,	51	James Wylie,	Utica.
385	Mississippi,	42	A. H. Hershey,	Savanna.
386	Bridgeport,	45	Jacob Schlenker,	Bridgeport.
387	Greenbush,	40	A. A. Hoisington,	Greenbush
388	El Dara,	39	J. W. Burke,	El Dara.
389	Kankakee,	100	M. F. Metz,	Kankakee.

No.	Name of Lodge.	Members.	Name of Sec'y.	Post Office.
390	Ashmore,	48	A. T. Robertson,	Ashmore Station.
391	Tolono,	47	Charles H. Bell,	Tolono.
392	Oconee,	32	Milton Lowe,	Oconee.
393	Blair.	210	W. W. Winter,	Chicago.
394	Jerseyville,	73	Morris R. Lock,	Jerseyville.
395	H. G. Reynolds,	39	J. D. Hatfield,	Whitefield.
396	Muddy Point.	52	L. W. Brown,	Mattoon.
397	Shiloh,	40	J. E. Wilkins,	Troy Grove,
398	Kinmundy,	53	A. C. Elder,	Kinmundy.
399	Buda,	46	Benj. Anderson,	Buda.
400	Pacific,	75	E. T. Eads,	Knoxville.
401	Odell.	61	R. Jones.	Odell.
402	Kishwaukee,	35	H. R. Fuller,	Kingston.
403	Mason City,	54	George Young,	Mason City.
404	Batavia,	84	C. C. Stephens,	Batavia.
405	Ramsay,	60	J. F. James,	Ramsay.
406	Bethalto,	47	John V. Richards,	Bethalto.
407	Blue Grass,	45	S. P. Star,	Blue Grass.
408	Stratton,	46	C. M. Pickett,	Vermillion.
409	T. J. Turner,	97	John E. Pettibone,	Chicago,
410	Mithra,	72	Gustav Fisher,	do
411	Hesperia,	144	Charles H. Felton,	do
412	Bollen,	52	Elias Underwood,	Spring Hill.
413	Forreston.	34	D. H. Reynolds,	Forreston.
414	Evening Star,	48	H. H. Bowker,	Davis.
415	Lawn Ridge,	46	Frank E. Stone,	Lawn Ride.
416	Paxton,	67	E. B. Hill,	Paxton.
417	Marseilles,	59	F. L. Butterfield,	Marseilles.
418	Freebourg.	25	Wm. Krauss.	Freebourg.
419	Reynoldsburg,	60	L. W. Fern,	Reynoldsburg.
420	Oregon,	62	M. L. Ettinger,	Oregon.
421	Washburn,	37	James M. Owens,	Washburn.
422	Hyde Park,	67	W. Irving Culver,	Chicago.
423	Lanark,	47	Jesse L. Birch,	Lanark.
424	Exeter,	43	John Alderson,	Exeter.
425	Kaneville.	39	Geo. R. Ross,	Kaneville.
426	Scottville,	41	W. A. Westrope,	Scottville.
427	Red Bud,	35	John Nelson,	Red Bud,
428	Sunbeam,	49	A. Conklin,	Plano.
429	Chebanse,	44	M. A. Swift,	Chebanse.
430	Kendrick,	33	W. C. Manny,	Mound Station.
431	Summit,	35	G. W. Kaine,	Harristown.
432	Murrayville,	46	W. D. Henry,	Murrayville.
433	Annawan,	28	J. C. Blodgett,	Annawan.
434	Makanda,	53	J. S. Hartman,	Makanda.
435	Neponset,	38	W. B. Payne,	Neponset.

No.	Name of Lodge.	Members.	Name of Sec'y.	Post Office.
436	Philo,	42	I. S. Knowles,	Port Byron. ....
437	Chicago,	145	Chas. Cohen,	Chicago.........
438	H. W. Bigelow,	102	Wm. W. Locke,	Chicago.........
439	Luce,	61	Edward T. Eaton,	Quincy. ....
440	Camargo,	48	J. C. Parcel,	Camargo, ...
441	Sparland,	43	W. C. Hewitt,	Sparland. ......
442	Casy,	30	Benj. Bancroft,	Casy. ....
443	Hampshire,	43	H. J. Allen,	Hampshire......
444	Cave-in-Rock,	30	John Tyyer,	Cave-in-Rock....
445	Chesterfield,	35	Edson C. Hall,	Chesterfield. ....
446	Watseka,	70	S. C. Munhall.	Watseka. ....
447	S. D. Monroe,	35	Robt. J. Ford,	Lawrenceville...
448	Yates City,	79	C. B. Rhea.	Yates City......
449	Mendon,	35	Wm. Laughlin,	Mendon.........
450	Loami,	51	J. C. Stansbury,	Loami. ....
452	Grant,	43	R. B. Keyes,	Richview.......
453	New Hartford,	30	Martin Camp,	New Hartford. ..
454	Maroa,	53	J. A. Hood,	Maroa. ....
455	Irving,	43	C. L. Hart,	Irving. ....
456	Nokomis,	40	J. H. Beatty,	Nokomis........
457	Moscow,	46	Wilson Brown,	Moscow.........
458	Blazing Star,	33	M. P. Furlong,	Crab Orchard....
459	Butler,	49	G. W. Brown. Jr.,	Butler.........
460	Jeffersonville,	25	M. S. Banackman,	Jeffersonville....
461	Plainview,	30	Sam. Brown,	Plainview.......
462	Tremont,	29	W. Hayward,	Tremont........
463	Palmyra,	48	R. J. Allmond,	Palmyra........
464	Denver,	37	M. M. Buford.	Denver. ....
465	Huntsville,	30	Wm. G. Denny,	Huntsville......
466	Cobden.	31	John Lambert,	Cobden..........
467	South Macon,	65	George W. Hare,	Macon..........
468	Cheney's Grove,	44	M. C. Young,	Cheney's Grove
469	McLean,	35	E. G. Clark,	McLean ......
470	Rantoul,	39	E. J. Holmes,	Rantoul.........
471	Kendall,	28	Willis Atkins,	Yorkville. ......
472	Amity,	53	H. C. French,	Turner. ....
473	Gordon,	45	A. J. Gulick,	Pocahontas .....
474	Columbia,	35	James L. Gall,	Columbia. ......
475	Walshville,	30	Wm. M. Towle,	Walshville. .....
476	Manito,	31	B. Ruthenburg,	Manito.........
477	New Rutland,	33	Aaron Gove,	New Rutland....
478	Pleiades,	130	H S. De Groodt,	Chicago. ....
479	Wyoming,	50	W. II Butter.	Wyoming. ......
480	Logan,	41	F. S. Selley,	Lincoln......
481	Momence,	48	L. S. Rowell,	Momence. ......
482	Lexington,	39	J. S. Mahan,	Lexington. ......

No.	Name of Lodge.	Members.	Name of Sec'y.	Post Office.
483	Belle City,	35	J. B. Scudamore,	Belle City......
484	Edgewood,	34	Miles Broom,	Edgewood......
485	Oskaloosa,	31	A. H. Porter,	Oskaloosa.......
486	Bowen,	29	M. McNeal,	Bowen.........
487	Andrew Jackson,	30	Joseph Morris,	Locust Grove...
488	Clay City,	30	R. E. Duff,	Clay City......
489	Cooper,	25	John W. Lee,	Willow Hill....
490	Shannon,	34	Jethro Martin,	Shannon. ......
491	Martin,	39	Charles Conrad,	Dunleith........
492	Libertyville,	40	E. W. Parkhurst,	Libertyville.....
493	Tower Hill,	25	John Husband,	Tower Hill......
494	Bath,	43	John S. Duncan,	Bath............
495	Stone Fort,	40	H. A. Wise,	Stone Fort.......
496	Tennessee,	23	W. T. Yates,	Tennessee.......
497	Alma,	32	James P. Campbell,	Alma...........
498	Murphysboro,	65	J. B. Mayham,	Murphysboro....
499	Mount Zion,	29	Wm. C. Wilson,	Zion............
500	St. Paul's,	43	L. W. Shepherd,	Springfield......
501	Stark,	35	T. W. Ross,	Lafayette. ......
502	Woodhull,	45	C. Bunce,	Woodhull.......
503	Odin,	51	S. W. Bird,	Odin. ....
504	East St. Louis,	50	E. W. Weider,	East Saint Louis.
505	Meridian Sun,	48	E. J. Jenks,	White Rock. ....
506	O. H. Miner,	50	Wm. Warrick,	Sheldon. ....
507	Manteno,	45	L. G. Remer,	Manteno........
508	Home.	102	B. B. W. Locke,	Chicago.........
509	Parkersburg,	48	G. W. Parker,	Parkersburg.....
510	J. D. Moody,	30	L. W. Costello,	Iuka. ....
511	Clintonville,	40	John Cox,	Clintonville. ....
512	Wade-Barney,	88	Jabez Brewster,	Bloomington....
513	Cold Spring,	30	John M. Frizzell,	Williamsburg....
514	Bradford,	41	D. A. Blakslee,	Bradford........
515	Dement,	50	E. M. Parsons,	Creston. ....
516	Andalusia,	33	J. W. Ballard,	Andalusia.......
517	Litchfield,	42	C. W. Ward,	Litchfield.......
518	Abr'm Lincoln,	50	Geo. T. McAfee,	Young America..
519	Roseville.	28	R. L. McReynolds,	Roseville. ......
520	Anna,	40	Ford S. Dodds,	Anna...........
521	Illiopolis,	25	A. R. Miller,	Illiopolis. ......
522	Monitor.	53	F. H. Mosely,	Elgin...........
523	Chatham,	50	Thos. M. Moore,	Chatham........
524	Evans,	48	A. B. Bishop,	Evanston. ......
525	Delia,	25	John A. Barr,	Elliottstown.....
526	Covenant,	82	S. G. Pitkin,	Chicago. ....
527	Rossville,	41	A. M. Davis,	Rossville. ......
528	Minooka,	59	H. M. Thayer,	Minooka........

No.	Name of Lodge.	Members.	Name of Sec'y.	Post Office.
529	Adams,	43	Harrison M'Kee,	Stone's Prairie
530	Maquon,	35	L. J. Dawdy,	Maquon
531	Ashton,	37	James Trotter,	Ashton.
532	Seneca,	33	Wm. S. Jackson,	Seneca
533	Freemanton,	25	J. C. Walker,	Freemanton.
534	Cuba,	27	J. K. Welsh,	Cuba.
535	Sherman,	33	Clinton Shaw.	Centre Ridge
536	Plainfield,	44	Guil. Bartholf,	Plainfield
537	J. R. Gorin,	56	W. H. Housel,	Sadorus
538	Lockport,	55	C. L. Stone,	Lockport.
539	Chatsworth,	39	Wm. H. Jones,	Chatsworth
540	Harlem,	40	Andrew T. Vogt,	Harlem
541	Sigel,	20	F. J. Nisewanger,	Hooker.
542	Towanda,	35	E. P. G. Holderness,	Towanda
543	Cordova,	36	H. W. Rathbun,	Cordova.
544	Virginia,	25	James M. Rodney,	Virginia.
545	Elkhart,	33	R. A. Hurt,	Elkhart
546	Nilwood,	30	M. Murphy,	Nilwood.
547	Valley,	29	Thos. Phillips,	Coal Valley
548	Apple River,	40	D. A. Sheffield,	Apple River
549	Newark,	25	C. F. Thunemann,	Newark.
550	Sharon,	40	Jno. I. Wilkins,	Tiskilwa.
551	Darwin,	30	Barus Dixon,	Darwin.
552	Ancona,	30	A. J. Bosserman,	Ancona
553	Kyle.	31	J. W. Hays,	Macomb.
554	Plum River,	25	H. F. Hastings,	Plum River.
555	Humboldt,	22	H. Alschuler,	Ottawa.
556	Dawson,	43	W. W. Judd,	Dawson.
557	Lessing,	38	Louis Blohm,	Chicago
558	Leland,	34	G. J. Monroe,	Leland.
559	Thomson,	44	Will. G. Tate,	Thomson.
560	Madison,	28	G. W. Bentley,	New Douglas
561	Trinity.	53	Geo. R. Barbour,	Monmouth
562	Villa Ridge,	34	J. S. Fombelle,	Villa Ridge.
563	Hamilton,	20	T. W. Anderson,	Otterville.
564	Winslow,	36	Philip Sweely,	Winslow.
565	Pleasant Hill,	29	T. J. Baskett,	Pleasant Hill.
566	Albany,	39	D. S. Effner,	Albany.
567	Frankford,	34	Elijah Estes,	Frankford
568	Delta,	45	Jewett Wilcox,	Cairo.
569	Pomegranate,	25	Robt. H. Griffin,	Time.
570	Jacksonville,	45	Leopold Weil,	Jacksonville.
572	Bardolph,	35	N. H. Jackson,	Bardolph.
573	Gardner,	59	T. J. Huston,	Gardner.
574	Pera,	45	George Head,	Pera
575	Capron,	38	N. H. Wooster,	Capron

No.	Name of Lodge.	Members.	Name of Sec'y.	Post Office.
576	O'Fallon,	45	Levi Simmons,	O'Fallon's.
577	Viola,	36	V. R. Harriott.	Viola.
578	Prairie City,	25	Reuben Bloomfield,	Majority Point.
579	Elbridge.	33	Wm. F. Dinkins,	Elbridge.
580	Hazel Dell,	23	James C. Kelly,	Hazel Dell.
581	Dongala,	40	R. T. Rives,	Dongala.
582	Shirley.	28	L. Furst,	Shirley.
583	Highland,	21	G. Rutz.	Highland.
584	Vesper,	21	John McFarland,	Galesburg.
585	Fisher,	50	Richard Kimble,	Buckhart.
586	Tazewell,	32	Richard Holmes,	Delavan.
587	Princeton,	37	S. G. Paddock,	Princeton.
588	Troy,	20	F. A. Sabin,	Troy.
589	Elwood.	25	F. H. Gray,	Milton Station.
590	Fairmount,	31	S. S. Burke,	Fairmount.
591	Gilman,	25	W. H. Otis,	Gilman.
592	Fieldon.	30	Edward Arkebauer,	Fieldon.
593	Wiley M. Egan,	30	D. B. Fonda,	Jefferson.
594	Lodi,	18	E. B. Robertson,	Lodi.
595	Miles Hart,	30	T. D. P. Henly,	Etna.
596	National,	42	J. D. Colby,	Chicago.
597	Lostant,	37	A. C. Schermerhorn,	Lostant.
598	Dorchester,	21	D. W. Young,	Dorchester.
599	Fowler,	25	A. Y. M'Cormick,	Fowler.
600	Cerro Gordo,	32	John A. Barnes,	Cerro Gordo.
601	Laclede,	20	George Tibbatts,	Laclede.
602	Watson,	20	J. M. Wilhite,	Watson.
603	Clark,	18	Joseph Fulton.	Clark.
604	Hebron,	29	Henry W. Mead.	Hebron.
605	Allin,	19	Geo. A. Wadsworth,	Stanford.
606	Wapella,	31	E. F. Swift.	Wapella.
607	Streator,	33	Geo. W. Cummins,	Streator.
608	Piper,	25	J. F. Finney,	Piper City.
609	Sheldon,	19	Enos T. Soper,	Sheldon.
610	Union Park,	88	G. P. Randall,	Chicago.
611	Lincoln Park,	54	Peter G. Gardner,	do.
612	Rock River,	47	W. S. Peebles,	Sterling.
613	Patoka,	23	Thos. H. Quayle,	Patoka.
614	Forrest,	17	J. B. Dillie,	Forrest Station.
615	Anchor,	19	M. R. La Forge.	Mason City.
616	Wadley,	20	F. M. Wadley,	Franklin.
617	Milan,	23	David Adams,	Good Hope.
618	Basco,	19	D. M'Ginnis,	Basco.
619	Berwick,	32	A. J. A. Smith,	Berwick.
620	New Hope,	39	J. A. Patton,	Livingston.
621	Venice,	18	Preston Bishop,	Venice.

No.	Name of Lodge.	Members.	Name of Sec'y.	Post Office.
622	Hopedale,	23	J. W. Morey,	Hopedale.
623	Locust,	18	Philip Baker,	Owaneco.
624	Du Bois,	16	L. Bunce,	Du Bois.
625	Melrose,	16	S. C. Smith,	Melrose.
626	Putman,	17	C. B. Knapp,	Granville.
627	Union,	14	Stephen Crouder,	Lick Creek.
628	Mosaic,	31	M. D. Holcomb,	Hudson.
629	Old Time,	30	Anson Low,	Havana.
630	Tuscan,	18	Jno. E. Parker,	Griswold.
631	Norton,	21	Chas. W. Fulford,	Caberey.
632	Ridge Farm.	26	A. A. Sulcer,	Ridge Farm.
633	E. F. W. Ellis,	38	S. G. Brownson,	Rockford.
634	Buckley,	40	Jno. W. Riggs,	Buckley.
635	Rochester,	15	Carter Tracy,	Rochester.
636	Peotone,	25	J. M. Tobias,	Peotone
637	Burlington,	28	Franklin Mann,	Burlington.
638	Fortitude,	15	A. S. Swartz,	Sagetown.
639	Keystone.	36	A. L. Miller,	Chicago.
640	Coleta,	27	R. B. Colcord,	Genessee Grove,.
641	Comet.	19		Minier.
642	Apollo,	59	Edwin Greene,	Chicago.
643	D. C. Cregier,	44	A. S. Kenyon,	do.
644	Oblong City,	18	J. G. McKnight,	Oblong City.
645	San Jose,	16	Willis Crabb,	San Jose.
646	Somonauk.	18	John Clark,	Somonauk.
647	Blueville,	24	Jno. L. Culver,	Edinburg.
648	Camden.	15	J. N. Ward,	Camden.
649	Hinsdale,	17		Hinsdale.
650	Irvington,.	16		Irvington
651	Centre Star,	32	J. A. Hawks,	Tuscola.
653	Polar Star,	25	T. K. Means,	Mulkeytown.
653	Greenview,	38	H. K. Rule,	Greenview
654	Woodford,	31	D. C. Smith,	El Paso.
655	Yorktown,	10		Yorktown.
656	Mozart.	10	Jos. Glickselig,	Bloomington.
657	La Fayette.	11		Grand Tower.
658	Rock Island,	26	H. B. Burgh,	Rock Island.
659	Lambert.	30	J. Q. Adams,	Quincy.
660	Grand Chain,	20	Hugh McGee,	Grand Chain.
661	Bethesda,	8		Potosi.

Indiana.

The Grand Lodge in this State was organized at Corydon, then
the capital of the territory, on the 12th of January, 1818, by the
representatives of five lodges. Its annual communications are held
at Indianapolis, the present capital of the State, convening on the
fourth Tuesday of May. In May, 1871, there were 437 lodges, with
a total membership of 23,308 Master Masons. The increase of the
Fraternity in this State corresponds with the increase of population. This grand lodge is possessed of a Hall at Indianapolis, the
value of which has been enhanced by repairs and improvements
put upon it within the past three years. The revenue of this grand
lodge, computed for the year ending May 22, 1871, was $19,259.22,
of which $15,268.12 were expended paying mileage and per diem,
appropriations, salaries, repairs on Hall, printing, postage, etc.,
leaving $9,235.06, the accumulation of two years, as the balance
in the G. T.'s hands. The most notable reform adopted by this
grand lodge occured in 1858, when it was resolved that a lodge
might depose and discipline its W. M., also appeal from his decision
to the members in open lodge. The practice has not become general. Past Masters are not recognized as members of this grand
lodge.

The executive grand officers elected in 1871 were—

MARTIN H. RICE, of Indianapolis, Grand Master.
CHRISTIAN FETTA, of Richmond, Deputy Grand Master
CHARLES FISHER, of Indianapolis, Grand Treasurer.
JOHN M. BRAMWELL, of Indianapolis, Grand Secretary.

For the following information we are indebted to the courtesy
of the Gr. Sec'y, who from the lodge Returns for 1871 kindly supplied the names of such secretaries as had refused or failed to reply
to our circulars, mailed to each, requesting the favor of such reply.
Otherwise, the Proceedings of G. L. for 1871 has been refered to.

No.	Name of Lodge.	Members.	Name of Sec'y.	Post Office.
..1..	Vincennes,	....108...	F. Clarke,..........	Vincennes. .....
..2..	Union,.........	65...	Henry C. Sampson,..	Madison........

No.	Name of Lodge.	Members.	Name of Sec'y.	Post Office.
..3..	Carlisle,	38:..	D. M. Shoemaker,...	Carlisle.........
..4..	Lawrenceburg,	.72...	Myron Haynes,	Lawrenceburg...
..5..	Cambridge,	....151...	Jas. H. Stewart,	....Cambridge City..
..6..	Rising Sun,	....59...	O. H. Miller,	Rising Sun.....
..7..	Versailles,	.....30...	Alf. G. Hunter,	.....Versailles......
..8..	Parke,	.........55...	Jas. H. Baker,	......Rockville.......
..9..	Boone,	........105...	John A. Abbott,	....Lebanon.......
.10..	Napoleon,	.....:.24...	Franklin Houk,	...Napoleon.......
.11..	Harmony,	......55...	Wm. H. James,	.....Brookville......
.12..	Goshen,	...... .88...	E. G. Chamberlain,.	.Goshen....:.....
.13..	Washington,	..72...	Wright Vermelyn,	..Brownstown. ...
.14..	Bedford,	......42...	Thos. C. Williams,	..Bedford.........
.15..	Warren	........100...	Chas. H. Frybarger,	.Connersville. ...
.16..	Golden Rule,	..111...	Geo. W. Hill,	.......Knightstown. ...
.17..	Harrison,	......38...	Daniel Cloud,	.......Logan.......
.18..	Attica,	.........69...	Jonas C. Aylsworth,	.Attica. ....
.19..	Terre Haute,	..204...	Alex. Thomas,	......Terre Haute.....
.20..	St. John's,	......89...	D. C. Hamilton,	.....Columbus.......
.21..	Salem,	........54...	Eli W. Menaugh,	....Salem. ....
.22..	Monroe,	92,	..J. Glass McPheeters,	Bloomington. ...
.23 ..	Centre,	........248.	..Charles Fisher,	.....Indianapolis.....
.24..	Webb,	.........95...	S. C. Byer,	.........Richmond.......
.25..	Wayne,	........117...	Albert H. Cook,	....Fort Wayne.....
.26..	Western Star,	..82...	Wm. H. Nichols,	...Danville. ....
.27..	Florence,	......37...	L. Bledsoe,	.........Florence........
.28..	Shelby,	........86...	Z. B. Wallar,	.......Shelbyville. ....
.29..	Laurel,	........43...	*Charter arrested*..	...Laurel..........
.30..	Charity,	........76...	Edwd. F. Meredith,	.Washington. ....
.31..	Milan,	........66...	Amos W. Crozier,..	.Milan............
.32..	Pisgah,	........41...	Samuel J Wright,	..Corydon. ....
.33..	Tipton,	.......123...	A. H. McDonald,	...Logansport. ....
.34..	Manilla,	.......17...	Wm. T. Emmons,	...Manilla.........
.35..	Marion,	.......159...	John G. Waters,	...Indianapolis. ...
36..	Greensburg,	....96...	C. W. Barker,	......Greensburg.....
.37..	Perry,	........121...	J. Merrill,	.........Lafayette. ......
.38..	Williamsport,	....50...	Justin Rose,	.....Williamsport....
.39..	New Albany,	..118...	Geo. P. Huckeby,	...New Albany....
.40..	Clarke,	........89...	Burditt C. Pile,	.....Jeffersonville.,..
.41..	La Porte,	.......79...	E. G. McCollum.	...La Porte..,....
.43..	Springfield,	.....39...	Matthew R. Shields,	Mt. Carmel.....
.44..	Madison,	......58...	Andrew J. Scott,	...Pendleton.......
.45..	St. Joseph,	....105...	Sam. T. Applegate,	.South Bend.....
.46..	Delaware,	.....132...	Fred. E. Putnam,	...Muncie.........
.47..	Temple,	.........89...	James McD. Hays,	...Greencastle. ....
.48..	Mount Olive,	...54...	John T. Richardson,	.Delphi.........
.49..	Hagerstown,	...65...	Dr S. J. Ford,	.......Hagerstown. ...

No.	Name of Lodge.	Members.	Name of Sec'y.	Post Office.
.50.	.Montgomery,	.163.	..Lucien A. Foote,.	...Crawfordsville...
.51.	.Aurora,.	..96.	..John Walker.	....Aurora.
.52.	.Westport.	...51.	..Geo. W. Cann,	.....Westport.
.53.	.Chesterfield,.	...32.	..W. F. Trueblood,.	..Chesterfield.
.54.	.Clinton,.	...71.	..Wm. H. Hart,.	....Frankfort.
.55.	.Burns,.	..44.	..Alex. Ruble,.	....Manchester.
.56.	.Winchester,	...70.	..Ira Tripp.	...Winchester.
.57.	.Noblesville,	...67.	..E. K. Hall,.	...Noblesville.
.58.	.Liberty,.	..58.	..L. M. Crist,	......Liberty.
.59.	.Jennings,.	..38.	..John S. Silver,	....Vernon.
.60.	.Fountain,	...66.	..Isaac Haupt,	.....Covington.
.61.	.Hanna,	...97.	..Edwin G. Sackett,	..Wabash.
.62.	.Phœnix,.	..51.	..Thos. Poe,	....Rushville.
.63.	.Ashlar,	...32.	..Wm. H. Wilhite,	...Pleasant Hill.
.64.	.Evansville,.	...112.	..A. J. Colburn,.	....Evansville.
.65.	.Belleville,.	...40.	..T. G. Wilson,	.....Belleville.
.66.	.Brookston,	...46.	..John Medaris,	.....Brookston.
.67.	.Miami,.	..87.	..J. Y. Ballou,	......Peru.
.68.	.Friendship,	...36.	..John Roberts,.	...Friendship.
.69.	.Worthington.	...59.	..Obed Mercer,	.....Worthington.
.70.	.Brownsville,.	...53.	..Alex. McDougal,.	...Brownsville.
.71.	.Solomon.	...45.	..Wm. S. Schoonover,.	.Hardinsburg.
.72.	.Lewisville.	....37.	..Abner Ball,	.....Lewisville.
.73.	.Warsaw,	.....128.	..Edward Moon.	....Warsaw.
.74.	.Martinsville,	...93.	..Thomas Mitchell,	...Martinsville.
.75.	.Bainbridge,.	....63.	..S. J. Taylor,.	...Bainbridge.
.76.	.Meridian Sun,.	..75.	..Andrew Eminger,	..La Grange.
.77.	.Mount Moriah,.	.93.	..David M. Kirkwood,	Anderson.
.78.	.Mooresville,.	...64.	..Samuel Shunafelt.	...Mooresville.
.79.	.Fulton,	......102.	..Joseph A. Myers,.	...Rochester.
.80.	.Hopewell,.	...45.	..Wm. B. Suits,.	......Dillsborough...
.81.	.Allensville,.	...80.	..P. S. Sage,	......East Enterprise.
.82.	.Russiaville,	...58.	..Thos. M. Moulder,	..Russiaville.
.83.	.Acme,	......31.	..Benj. F. Sammons,	..Michigan City...
.84.	.Bloomfield,.	...48.	..John. H. Knapp,.	....Bloomfield.
.85.	.Clay.	...76.	..P. J. Geiger,.	....Bowling Green.
.86.	.Social,.	...164.	..Wm. M. McLean,,.	..Terre Haute.
.87.	.Jay, ...,	...88.	..Jno. S. Stanton,.	....Portland.
.88.	.Deming,	......74.	..Wm. F. Daily;	.....North Manchester
.89.	.Montezuma,.	..38.	..Wm. McMasters,	....Montezuma.
.90.	.Portland,	.....44.	..Joseph Moler,	.....Portland Mills...
.91.	.New Castle,	....69.	..W. E. Levezey,	.....New Castle.
.92.	.Gosport,	......85.	..Alva T. Hart,.	....Gosport.
.93.	.Kokomo,.	...74.	..John H. Hull,	.....Kokomo.
.94.	.Milford,.	...44.	..Jas. S. Burney,.	...Clifty.
.95.	.Spencer,.	....70.	..Louis Drescher,.	....Spencer.

No.	Name of Lodge.	Members.	Name of Sec'y.	Post Office.
.96.	.Andersonville,	.35	.Jas. D. Allison,	Andersonville. ..
.97.	.Albion.	48	.Wm. C. Williams,	.Albion. ....
.98.	Fairfield.	78	.E. G. Glidewell,	...Fairfield. ......
.99.	.Jerusalem,	48	.Sam. Bentley,	Clinton. ....
100.	.Edinburg.	64	.C. M. A. Hess,	Edinburg. ......
101	.Hancock.	85	.S. S. Boots,	Greenfield ......
102.	.Economy,	36	.Jas. R. Routh.	Economy. ......
103.	.Dayton,	48	.Jas. D. Long,	Dayton. ....
104.	.Jefferson,	125	.Robt. J. Shaw,	New Albany.....
105.	.Grant,	109	.D. P. Cubberly,	Marion. ....
106.	.Blackford,	55	.Chas. O. Fisher,	Hartford City. ..
107.	.Franklin,	130	.R. T. Taylor.	Franklin........
108.	.Milton,	46	.E. B. Newman,	Milton..........
109.	.Jonesboro,	103	.A. L. Barnard,	Jonesboro.......
110.	.Mystic,	91	.Ulysses D. Cole,	Huntington. ....
111.	.Burlington.	23	.John Egan.	Burlington. .....
112.	.Rockport,	51	.Oliver Morgan,	Rockport. ......
113.	Thorntown,	69	.C. I. Brundage,	Thorntown,.....
114.	.Anderson.	32	.Jno. W. Smith,	Anderson.......
115.	.Westfield.	50	.John M. Kane,	Westfield. ......
116.	.Leatherwood,	44	.H. C. LaForce,	Hiltonville......
117.	.Deerfield,	34	.Thos. N. Pierce,	Deerfield. ......
118.	.Clarksville,	55	.Wm. H. Stearn,	Clarksville. ....
119.	.Paoli,	76	.Abr'm Noblitt,	Paoli...........
120.	.Scott,	48	.J. D. Waters,	Crothersville. ...
121.	.Pike,	62	.Thos. C. Withers,	Petersburg......
122.	.Switzerland,	43	.Julius Black,	Vevay..........
123.	La Fayette,	102	.Jno. C. Tyler,	La Fayette......
124.	.Clarksburg,	59	.John S. Miller.	Clarksburg......
125.	.Prairie,	56	.M. F. Chilcote,	Renssallaer......
126.	.Millersville.	34	.Peter L. Negley,	Castleton. ......
127.	.Annapolis,	53	.John Kelly,	Annapolis.......
128.	.Austin,	53	.D. J. Cauldwell,	Tipton. ....
129.	.Shawnee,	39	.S. A. R. Beach,	Shawneetown. ..
130.	.Mishawaka,	112	.W. H. Judkins,	Mishawaka......
131	.Larrabee.	39	.A. L. Masters,	Stilesville ......
132.	.Cloverdale,	45	.G. E. Baker,	Cloverdale......
133.	.Rome.	54	.Jno. J. Lang,	Rome...........
134.	.Pleasant.	52	.T. G. McCollum,	Acton ....
135.	.Nashville,	47	.E. H. Cox.	Nashville. ......
136.	.Vesta,	41	.Jos. C. Suit,	Jefferson. ......
137.	.Porter,	140	.Geo. W. Hewitt.	Valparaiso......
138.	.Saltillo,	25	.G. A. Rosenbaum,	Saltilloville. ....
139.	.Milroy.	40	.John S. Parker,	Milroy,........
143.	.Oakland,	63	.John W. Combs,	Oaklandon......
141.	.Russellville,	38	.McLeod L. Wasson,	Russellville. ....

No.	Name of Lodge.	Members.	Name of Sec'y.	Post Office.
142	North Salem,	41	Thos. J. Adams,	North Salem.....
143	Tuscan,	60	R. H. Dare,	La Gro.........
144	Alamo,	60	Jas. A. Gilkey,	Alamo.........
145	Bluffton,	61	John D. Hale,	Bluffton.........
146	Jackson.	93	D. A. Kelly.	Seymour.......
147	Farmer's,	50	Benj. J. Peake,	Winterroud....
148	Morning Star,	47	J. A. Humphrey,	Patriot.........
149	Plymouth,	104	C. C. Buck.	Plymouth.......
150	Hope,	38	Jas. G. Weinland,	Hope...........
151	Hartford,	26	Jas. B. Miller.	Hartford........
152	Cannelton,	57	Robt. McCutchon,	Cannelton.......
153	Orleans,	62	John J. Lingle,	Orleans.........
154	Libanus,	67	O. S. Dale.	Monticello......
155	Applegate,	43	Wm. A. Smythe,	Filmore........
156	Metamora,	53	J. J. Rubottom,	Metamora,......
157	Lake,	76	Frank S. Bedell.	Crown Point.....
158	Wilmington,	56	Geo. O. Columbia,	Wilmington.....
159	Whitewater,	44	David M. Vanzant,	Whitewater.....
160	Lawrence.	24	A. W. Bare,	Bryantsville.....
161	Cedar.	24	Wm. H. Smith.	Leesville.......
162	Bridgeport,	27	Wm. Blockwell,	Bridgeport.....
163	Mt. Vernon,	154	Jas. B. Campbell,	Mount Vernon...
164	Ovid,	33	Wm. Carmany,	Ovid...........
165	Allen,	45	Thos. C. Jones,	Moore's Hill.....
166	Newberry.	47	James M. Owen,	Newberry.......
167	New Washingt'n,	38	John C. Fouts,	New Washington.
168	Mt. Pleasant,	56	C. S. Wood,	Loogootee......
169	Bridgeton,	48	R. C. Allen,	Bridgeton.......
170	Summit City,	185	Wm. W. Fisk,	Fort Wayne.....
171	Anthony,	57	Samuel Brenner,	Albany.........
172	Lodiville,	50	Cyrus B. Allen,	Waterman......
173	Stanford,	18	John Breeden,	Stanford........
174	Newburg,	77	Albert Hazen,	Newburg. :.....
175	Greensboro,	44	Cornelius Dille,	Greensboro.....
176	Wooster,	34	Oscar P. Steel,	Everton........
177	Springville,	41	J. H. Gunn,	Springville....
178	Teutonia,	12	Charles Dehne.	Indianapolis....
179	Carthage,	39	Cyrus F. Mullen,	Carthage ......
180	Wolcott,	25	Robertson Fluger,	Wolcott.........
181	Leesburg,	64	J. E. Stephenson,	Leesburg.......
182	Greenwood,	58	Thos. Hardin,	Greenwood.....
183	Kane,	89	Benj. Turnock,	Elkhart........
184	Hermann,	41	Wm. E. Douglass,	Michigantown...
185	Ligonier,	79	J. B. Steelsman,	Ligonier........
186	Darlington,	36	Thos. J. Griffith,	Darlington......
187	Ladoga,	57	W. B. Haskins,	Ladoga.........

No.	Name of Lodge.	Members.	Name of Sec'y.	Post Office.
188	Posey,	52	Geo. A. Andres,	Leavenworth.
189	Columbia City,	99	Theodore Reed,	Columbia City.
190	Oxford.	31	Jacob P. Isley,	Oxford.
191	Grandview,	45	James C. Finch,	Grandview.
192	Westville.	42	N. R. Bowman,	Westville.
193	Morristown,	54	J. L. Dalrymple,	Morristown.
194	Excelsior,	77	Nathaniel S. Paul,	La Porte.
195	Roanoke.	100	Dan. N. Grim,	Roanoke.
196	Richmond,	89	Simon Fox,	Richmond.
197	Zion,	55	A. J. Sanders,	Zionsville.
198	Ripley,	26	W. M. Deeley,	Rei.
199	Cicero,	60	George Good,	Cicero.
200	Hazelrigg,	29	S. G. Hudson.	Jamestown.
201	Rono.	32	Martin L. Stiles.	Rono.
202	Alton,	38	A. N. Peckinpaugh,	Alton.
203	Jerome,	41	Nathan D. Ellis,	Jerome.
204	Terre Coupee.	79	J. H. Service,	New Carlisle.
205	Richland,	57	Alfred Wilson,	Newton.
206	Livonia,	28	Wm. M. Greenslade,	Livonia.
207	Fortville,	52	Wm. R. Rash.	Walpole.
208	Monong,	35	John H. Mallon,	Francisville.
209	Newport,	24	Wm. Collett,	Newport.
210	Northeastern,	52	Eliakim Anderson,	Fremont.
211	Mount Zion,	35	Richard P. Pilling,	Camden.
212	Pennville,	42	E. A. Smith,	Pennville
213	Moorfield,	62	George S. Hulley,	Moorfield.
214	De Kalb,	80	John A. Cowan,	Auburn.
215	Lima,	33	Wellington Forgus,	Lima.
216	Bayless,	18	James F. Noblitt,	Jonesville.
217	Waldron,	18	John W. Haymond,	Conn's Creek.
218	St. Paul.	23	J. F. Scull,	Saint Paul.
219	Butlerville,	57	Joseph Hole,	Butlerville.
220	Advance.	33	R. L. Higginbotham,	Delphi.
221	Paris,	52	James M. Lefebre,	Paris.
222	Kingsbury,	57	Z. Craft,	Kingsbury
223	Linn,	48	Henry D. Nichols,	Lynn.
224	Leo,	44	John Dever,	Leo.
225	Star,	72	Norris S. Bennett.	Orland.
226	Blazing Star,	35	David H. Combs,	Charlestown
227	Bourbon,	54	J. D. Wilkins,	Bourbon.
228	Mitchell,	63	Charles J. Berry,	Mitchell.
229	Whitney,	56	Jos. F. Richardson,	New Burlington.
230	Quincy,	56	Jabez E. Miner.	Elwood.
231	Prince,	72	Wm. B. Kimball,	Princeton.
232	Cornelius,	25	B. D. Bonebrake,	Abington.
233	Downey,	20	Sam. J. Johnston,	Boston.

No.	Name of Lodge.	Members.	Name of Sec'y.	Post Office.
234	Orange	17	Samuel B. Hunt,	Orange
235	Alexandria,	84	Thos. J. Pickard,	Alexandria.
236	Angola,	88	James Jackson,	Angola.
237	Martinsburg,	38	Sam. L. Baker,	Martinsburg.
238	Taylorville,	45	Wm. B. Oard,	Taylorville.
239	Forest,	52	Cyrus S. Stoy	Jarvis.
240	Stranger's Rest,	67	J. A. Brackenridge,	Boonville.
241	Brownsburg,	52	Sam. F. Potts,	Brownsburg.
242	Acacia,	23	Jesse R. Brown,	Greensfork.
243	O'Brian	47	W. M. M'Cormick,	Knox,
244	Galveston,	73	John W. Morgan,	Galveston.
245	Ellettsville,	54	F. E. Wooley,	Ellettsville.
246	King,	64	J. M. Hiltebrand,	Warren.
247	Perkinsville,	58	W. H. Johnson,	Perkinsville.
248	Olive Branch,	24	B. F. Lehew,	Root.
249	Elizabethtown,	56	A. L. Bateman.	Elizabothtown.
250	Bethel,	44	R. W. Anderson,	Bethel.
251	Keystone,	46	John H. Smith,	Castleton.
252	Reynolds,	28	Joseph V. Kenton,	Reynolds.
253	Sardis,	46	A. V. B. Sample,	Charlottesville.
254	Decatur,	109	Seymour Worden,	Decatur.
255	Newpoint,	51	W. E. Barkley,	Rossburg.
256	Troy,	33	Charles A. Sugg,	Troy.
257	Bennington,	38	David C. Gardner,	Bennington.
258	Hudson,	25	L. B. Smith,	Reelsville.
259	Roseville,	43	John Kilburne,	Roseville.
260	Winslow,	36	Byron Brenton,	Winslow.
261	Monrovia,	53	Morris W. Benton,	Monrovia.
262	Winamac,	54	Simon Weyand,	Winamac.
263	Sullivan,	66	Samuel Wall,	Sullivan.
264	Brazil.	130	T. M. Robertson,	Brazil.
265	Mississinawa.	49	John E. Deviney,	Wheeling.
266	North Liberty,	38	E T. Lee.	North Liberty.
267	Xenia,	74	E. R. Robinson,	Xenia.
268	Miller,	38	John B. Crick,	Clark's Hill.
269	Adams,	37	Will. C. M'Coy,	Adams.
270	Southport,	45	Spofford E. Tyler.	Southport.
271	Middletown,	53	Lafayette J. Burr,	Middletown.
272	Orient,	112	Salomon Fisher.	Logansport.
273	Owen	54	Jesse H. Reno,	Quincy.
274	Mound,	53	Austin M. Porter,	State Line.
275	Dunkirk,	74	Richard J. Sutton,	Dunkirk.
276	Kendallville,	110	D. C. Walling,	Kendallville
277	Cadiz.	37	*Charter surrendered,*	Cadiz.
278	Due Guard,	66	W. S. Barber,	Lareville,
279	Sugar Creek.	51	Thos. B. Casey,	Fairland.

No.	Name of Lodge.	Members.	Name of Sec'y.	Post Office.
280	Crescent	59	A. F. Martin,	Miami
281	Independence	21	Andrew Gemmell,	Rigdon
282	Rob Morris,	54	Jno. Huffman,	Campbellsburg
283	New London,	44	Jas. H. Arnett,	New London
284	Geneva	46	Newton Wilkerson,	Scipio
285	Corinthian	48	D. S. Gillespie	Salem Centre
286	Newland,	74	John M. Mitchell,	Salem
287	Plainfield	54	Jas. W. Catterson,	Plainfield
288	Montpelier	33	J. P. A. Leonard,	Montpelier
289	Merom,	53	Thos. Cushman,	Merom
290	Frankton	36	W. H. H. Quick,	Frankton
291	Rolling Prairie,	52	J. D. McMurray,	Rolling Prairie
292	Pimento,	50	P. Bledsoe	Pimento
293	Monroeville,	66	Morris Strass,	Monroeville
294	South Bend,	130	C. Souders	South Bend
295	Lafontaine,	50	Wm. Snyder,	Lafontaine
296	Harlan,	36	J. Stopher	Harlan
297	Ossian,	33	S. C. Goshorn,	Ossian
298	Halfway,	42	John Current,	Halfway
299	Selma	46	W. A. Cecil,	Selma
300	Waveland,	47	Jno. A. Read,	Waveland
301	Germania,	51	Wm. G. Schroeder,	South Bend
302	Waynetown,	56	Jos. S. Henry,	Waynetown
303	Moore	24	Alf. Ragle,	Ragleville
304	Middlefork	34	M. L. Martin,	Middlefork
305	Snow,	42	Wm. H. Smith,	Groves
306	Travel,	75	H. J. Beyorle,	Goshen
307	Waterloo City,	58	E. R. Blattner.	Waterloo City
308	Farmland,	47	Silas H. Moore,	Farmland
309	Fidelity,	35	T. B. Pearson,	Boxley
310	Kinkle,	49	J. M. Haworth,	Denning
311	Wild Cat,	43	Robt. McMahan,	Wild Cat,
312	Capital City,	95	M. D. Stacy	Indianapolis
313	Battle Grove,	49	Wm. H. Randolph,	Battle Grove
314	Harveysburg,	45	P. V. Hockett,	Harveysburg
315	Rainsville,	32	Rufus Jacobs,	Rainsville
316	Reed,	62	E. F. Lawrence,	Evansville
317	Ninevah,	41	T. S. Falkinburg,	Ninevah
318	Rossville,	52	W. A. Gaddis,	Rossville
319	Anci'nt L'mark,	114	Ephraim Hartwell,	Indianapolis
320	Asbury,	26	Winford M. Taylor,	Toronto
321	Hacker,	51	Henry Strieby	Boydston's Mills
322	Harrodsburg,	51	C. R. Stephenson,	Harrodsburg
323	Clear Spring,	69	Daniel B. Dodds,	Mooney
324	Rural,	33	Allen Boram,	Markleville
325	Geo. Washington,	47	C. T. Seibert,	Bristol

No.	Name of Lodge.	Members.	Name of Sec'y.	Post Office.
326	Wm. Hacker,	38	Wm. Seely,	Newville.
327	Belle River,	44	Silas Mead,	Patriot.
328	Vallonia.	25	Andrew J. Burrell,.	Vallonia.
329	Tunnelton,	28	James H. Malott,.	Tunnellton.
330	Sandford,	49	J. W. De Wolfe,	Sandford.
331	Blountsville,	42	Miles M. Holaday,	Blountsville.
332	White River,	42	S. M. Reeve.	Shoals.
333	Mount Etna,	45	W. T. Smith,	Mount Etna.
334	Windfall,	34	Farlow S. Zeck,	Windfall.
335	Galena,	24	Wm. C. Cummins,	La Porte.
336	Vienna,	27	R. M. Ford,	Vienna.
337	Utica,	31	James R. Wilcox.	Utica.
338	De Pauw,	27	Edw. F. Pennington,.	New Albany.
339	Owensburg,	24	John P. Potter,	Owensburg.
340	Jeffersonville,	60	James W. Sweeney,.	Jeffersonville.
341	Greentown,	31	J. R. Lindley,	Greentown
342	Home,	51	John Lillie, jr.	Fort Wayne.
343	Camon,	20	Marshall D. Lee,	Clifford.
344	Unity,	27	Samuel B. Ferguson,	Perrysville.
345	Emmet,	43	Andrew Gelwick,	Bedford.
346	Lexington,	17	C. F. Lanham.	Lexington.
347	Mexico,	28	William Griswold,	Mexico.
348	S'lph'r Sp'g City,	20	L. D. Harvey,	Sulphur Sp. City.
349	Dublin,	43	John W. Scott,	Dublin.
350	London,	39	T. C. Shanklin,	London.
351	Remington,	36	Thos. E. Donnelly,	Remington.
352	West Lebanon,	29	James Kimball,	West Lebanon.
353	Lakeville,	36	Chas. W. Moore,	Lakeville.
354	Gilead,	36	Thos J. Carpenter,.	Gilead.
355	Pythagoras,	19	C. G. Weiss,	New Albany,
356	Walkerton,	40	Wm. A. Dailey,	Walkerton.
357	M. L M'Clelland,	54	Jacob S. Meister,	Hobart.
358	Morgantown,	37	Reuben Griffith,	Morgantown.
359	Sol. D. Bayless,	50	Wm. E. Hood,	Fort Wayne.
360	W. Hacker,	32	W. F. Green,	Shelbyville.
361	Newton,	45	Jno. Z. Johnson,	Alliance.
362	Doric,	32	D. C. Braden,	Ridgeville.
363	Reserve,	20	J. R. Baxter,	Sharpsville.
364	Owensville,	27	Henry Nohny,	Owensville.
365	Kankakee,	19	L. D. Glazebrook,	San Pierre.
366	Wolf Lake,	20	Orlando Krinmell,	Wolf Lake.
367	Huntsville,	24	A. B. Jenkins,	Trenton.
368	Eagle,	43	Jas. K. Gore,	Elkhart.
369	Shelburn,	45	Jas. T. Spencer.	Shelburn.
370	Howard,	38	Lewis W. Leach,	Kokomo.
371	Lake City,	32	C. G. Hossler,	Warsaw.

No.	Name of Lodge.	Members.	Name of Sec'y.	Post Office.
372	Morocco,	30	H. R. Fields.	Morocco.
373	Fairbanks,	24	Nicholas Yeager,	Furman's Creek.
374	York,	28	N. F. Bolton,	Washington.
375	Wheatland,	20	James Dunn,	Wheatland.
376	Newman,	30	Eugene Whitaker,	New Haven.
377	Pierceton,	36	G. B. Lesh,	Pierceton.
378	Colfax,	59	J. A. Clark,	Lowell.
379	Calumet,	32	Wm. B. Carline,	Coffee Creek.
380	Ionic,	56	John N. Strayer,	Wolcottsville.
381	Huron,	16	Asher W. Clark,	Huron.
382	Henry King,	41	F. C. Bacon,	Perry.
383	Somerset,	40	R. Weesner,	Somerset.
384	Osgood,	15	Wm. R. Glasgow,	Osgood.
385	Hillsborough,	24	Thomas C. Barton,	Hillsborough.
386	North Vernon,	34	Jonathan N Jones,	North Vernon.
387	Pittsburgh	23	Wm. H. Harkens,	New Pittsburg.
388	Ireland.	24	Sol. D. Pierce,	Ireland.
389	Naphtali,	22	Samuel M. Patton,	Oakford.
390	Riley.	35	David M. Wallace,	Riley.
391	Samaritan,	37	David H. Sanders,	Marion.
392	Mechanicsburg,	16	Henry Swain,	Mechanicsburg.
393	Canaan,	21	D. H. Demaree,	Canaan.
394	Arctic,	21	Geo. W. Engler,	New Harmony.
395	Alert,	36	John W. Spears,	Alert.
396	Lynnville,	38	J. M. Zimmerman,	Lynnville.
397	Eureka.	22	J. E. Richardson,	Enterprise.
398	Mystic Tie,	60	Wm. S. Cone,	Indianapolis.
399	Argos,	24	Charles D. Chapman,	Argos.
400	Rice,	14	J. M. C. Howe,	College Cor., O.
401	Turpen,	24	Wm. H. Swain,	Union City.
402	Catlin,	21	Price Hawkins,	Catlin.
403	Evergreen,	18	Sidney S. Reed,	Wheeler.
404	New Palestine,	16	Wm. H. Moore,	Sugar Creek.
405	Priam,	25	Robt. Ransom. (W.M.)	Priam.
406	Composite.	28	A. Applewhite,	Madison.
407	Green Castle,	15	George E. Blake,	Green Castle.
408	Schmidlapp,	14	Isaac C. Earhart,	Kent.
409	Knightsville,	25	W. J. Dixon,	Knightsville.
410	Antioch,	17	Henry Kantz,	Antioch.
411	Solsberry,	19	R. D. Mavis,	Solsberry.
412	Six Mile,	14	Wm. B. Whitcomb,	Six Mile.
413	Trafalgar,	14	Elzy B. Willan,	Trafalgar.
414	Bremen.	19	Moses Keyser,	Bremen.
415	Dover Hill,	25	A. W. Porter,	Dover Hill.
416	Greenville,	16	Samuel W. Waltz,	Greenville.
417	Hiram,	16	Dr. John Pritchet,	Centreville.

No.	Name of Lodge.	Members.	Name of Sec'y.	Post Office.
418	Kosciusko,	21	Thomas Cammack,	Milford
419	Dupont,	17	Geo. W. Williams,	Dupont
420	Goodwin,	53	I. D. Nixon,	Hazelton.
421	Carmel,	21	Sylvanus Comer,	Carmel.
422	Pleasant Home,	16	A. H. Williamson,	Koutt's Station
423	Walton,	14	W. P. Beall,	Walton.
424	Gentryville,	24	Wm. M. Jones,	Gentryville.
425	Transitville,	10	M. F. Johnson,	Transitville.
426	Olive,	10	Wm. G. Bundy,	Winchester
427	Arcana,	18	Martin F. Skinner,	Arcana.
428	Pittsboro,	14	Daniel F. Hill,	Pittsboro.
429	Edwardsport,	9	J. T. Finley,	Edwardsport.
430	Cadiz,	20	Simon C. Vanwinkle,	Cadiz.
431	Mauckport,	14	John W. McIntire,	Mauckport.
432	Newton Stewart,	16	James N. Marlett,	Newton Stewart.
433	Muncie,	10	Wm. M. Little,	Muncie.
434	Thomas Newby,	12	David N. Berg.	Cambridge City.
42	Humboldt,	26	John Kuppenheimer,	Terre Haute,
439	New Garden,	11	B. F. Bailey,	Newport.
440	Eminence,	21	Solomon Dorsett,	Eminence.
UD	Columbia,	17	W. S. Hargrove,	Patoka.

Jowa.

The Grand Lodge in this State was organized on 3d of January, 1844, by the representatives of three lodges in convention at Iowa City, Oliver Cock being elected the first grand master. The annual communications are convened on the first Monday of June. The place of meeting has been changeable, and but recently fixed for the next four years at Davenport, where Dr. Burtis of that city has tendered gratis the use of suitable apartments in his Opera House to the Grand Lodge of Iowa. In 1860 there were 150 lodges in the State. In 1871 there were 280 lodges chartered, and 4 under dispensation, with a total membership of 12,548. In ten years, as in Illinois, the lodges in Iowa have doubled, and the membership trebled, and in this condition have but kept pace proportionately with the increase of population in that period in those States. Hereafter this grand lodge will pay mileage and per diem to its members. The proposition to do so was adopted in June, 1871, and the first payments then made. The business of this body is performed in the best manner, at a moderate expense. The Proceedings are admirably printed, and the work of the Gr. Sec'y unexcelled. This grand lodge has reprinted and published its Proceedings since its organization. and the same, bound in three handsome volumes, are purchaseable at a moderate price. The library of this grand lodge, at present located in one of the Burtis Opera House rooms. at Davenport, is a desirable collection of Masonic books and periodicals.

The executive grand officers elected in 1871 were—

O. P. WATERS, of Muscatine, Grand Master.

T. J. COPP, of Burlington, Grand Treasurer.

THEO. S. PARVIN, of Iowa City, Grand Secretary.

This grand lodge does not elect but the Gr. Master appoints the Deputy Grand Master. For the information following we are principally indebted to the Proceedings of G. L. for 1870, and the Gr. Sec'y, and also to the Bro. Secretaries who have responded to our circulars soliciting later information.

No.	Name of Lodge.	Members.	Name of Sec'y.	Post Office.
..1	Des Moines,	...90	C. P. DeHaas,	Burlington
..2	Iowa,	78	Wm. Leffingwell	Muscatine.
..3	Dubuque,	103	Wm. E. Wiehe,	Dubuque.
..4	Iowa City,	115	Albert S. Bixby,	Iowa City
..5	Wapello,	39	A. M. Williams,	Wapello.
..6	Marion,	71	T. C. Ovington,	Marion.
..7	Hiram.	16	M. Thompson,	Augusta.
..8	Mt. Pleasant.	109	H. J. Howard	Mt. Pleasant.
..9	Keosauqua,	...77	Johnson Russell,	Keosauqua
.11	Cedar.	60	S. E. Welzer.	Tipeton.
.12	Eagle.	118	S. W. Johnson,	Keokuk.
.13	Clay Pool,	...44	W. O. Hoover,	Fort Madison.
.14	Franklin,	106	R· Van Beuthusen,	Bloomfield.
.15	Clinton,	70	N. Steel,	Fairfield.
.16	Ottumwa,	98	Moses B. Walker,	Ottumwa.
.17	Salem.	58	J. B. Rose,	Salem.
.18	Triluminar,	120	Geo. T. Craig.	Oskaloosa.
.20	Burlington,	69	Wm. E Woodward,	Burlington.
.21	Olive Branch,	56	A. R. Wier,	Agency City.
.22	Pioneer.	165	C. B. Worthington,	Des Moines.
.24	Golden Rule,	23	L. P. Atkins,	Rochester.
.25	Crescent.	81	G. F. Bennett,	Cedar Rapids.
.26	Washington,	87	H. E. Stone.	Washington.
.27	Mt. Moriah,	...49	Jas. A. Bateman,	Farmington.
.28	New London,	64	Wm. Cabeen,	New London.
.29	Hardin,	74	Robt. Southerland,	Keokuk.
.30	Hawkeye,	76	P. A. Brumfield,	Muscatine.
.31	Zion,	58	Saml. Welch,	Iowa City.
.33	Winchester,	19	W. A. Jones,	Winchester.
.34	De Witt,	77	A. W. Jack,	De Witt.
.36	Helion.	68	U. S. Belden,	Maquoketa.
.37	Davenport,	156	M. D. Snyder,	Davenport.
.38	Richland,	45	Wm. Turner,	Richland.
.40	Troy,	40	C. W. Stevenson,	Troy.
.42	Jackson,	76	J. K. Boyles,	Centreville.
.43	Evening,	69	O. A. Moser,	Winterset.
.44	Snow,	36	Wm. Sanderson,	Le Claire.
.45	Crawfordsville,	41	H. Schwaebe,	Crawfordsville.
.46	Anamosa.	70	Robert Dott.	Anamosa.
.47	Bentonsport,	44	J. H. Easter,	Bentonsport.
.48	Danville.	34	W. H. Stewart,	Danville.
.49	Metropolitan,	97	Thos. Hardy,	Dubuque.
.50	Aurora,	54	Onias Hale,	Milton.
.51	Bellevue,	42	H. W. Ray,	Bellevue.
.52	Lafayette,	89	M. A. Molere,	Montezuma.
53	Warren,	77	E. W. Perry,	Indianola.

No.	Name of Lodge.	Members.	Name of Sec'y.	Post Office.
.55	Pella,	70	R. H. Lacy,	Pella.
.56	Birmingham,	22	F. G. Torrance,	Birmingham.
.58	Glenwood	67	H. J. Rockwell,	Glenwood
.59	Newton,	107	Jesse Rickman,	Newton
.60	Camanche,	41	O. B. Lawton,	Camanche.
.61	Oriental,	69	E. A. Parsons,	Knoxville.
.62	Vinton,'	75	James Wood,	Vinton.
.63	Chariton,	100	Dell Stuart,	Chariton.
.64	Brighton,	36	Jas. H. Auld,	Brighton
.65	Black Hawk,	77	J. F. Whitney,	Cedar Falls.
.66	Union,	56	H. R. Allen,	Frankville.
.67	Constellation,	29	P. C. Blossinger,	Colesburg.
.68	Glasgow,	44	C. Herkrich,	Glasgow.
.69	West Union,	70	C. H. Talmadge,	West Union.
.70	Clayton,	51	P. B. Mason.	Monona.
.71	Bluff City,	80	John J. Monell,	Council Bluffs.
.72	Elkader,	56	W. B. Hunt,	Elkader.
.73	Buonaparte,	46	G. F. Smith,	Buonaparte.
.74	Eddyville,	87	R. W. Boyd,	Eddyville.
.75	West Point,	23	J. Evringham,	West Point.
.76	Albia,	74	S. T. Craig,	Albia.
.77	Osceola,	66	D. D. Wilson,	Osceola.
.78	Grand River,	68	A. Frazier,	Leon.
.79	Mount Olive,	71	J. W. Augsburg,	Boonsboro.
.80	Adel,	—	N. G. Long.	Adel.
.81	Benton City	58	Geo. F. Jones,	Shellsburg.
.83	Hartford,	42	A. J. Duncan,	Hartford.
.84	Epworth,	27	E. Starger,	Epworth.
.86	Jefferson,	68	J. P. Gaston,	Drakeville
.87	Independence,	73	D. S. Deering,	Independence.
.90	Garnavillo,	33	G. W. Beach,	Garnavillo.
.91	Corydon,	80	J. S. Whittaker	Corydon.
.93	Lyons,	60	T. R. Beers,	Lyons.
.94	Butler,	38	J. J. Eichar,	Clarksville
.95	Mount Calvary,	90	Geo. C. Shipman,	West Liberty.
.96	Richmond,	42	A. D. Stinson,	Richmond.
.99	Nevada,	79	S. S. Stratton,	Nevada.
100	Western Star,	93	Robert Drought.	Clinton.
102	Osage,	123	D. B. Cotton,	Osage.
103	Sioux City,	79	J. H. Bolton,	Sioux City.
104	Abingdon,	46	F. M. Trobee,	Abingdon.
105	Waterloo,	118	C. W Mutton,	Waterloo.
106	Martinsburg,	44	A. C. Romig,	Martinsburg.
107	Columbus City,	50	W. H. Neal,	Columbus City.
108	Marshall,	127	George Neill,	Marshalltown.
109	Decatur,	44	Thomas Ward,	Decatur.

No.	Name of Lodge.	Members.	Name of Sec'y.	Post Office.
110	Capital,	94		Des Moines
111	Ashlar	68	F. L. Kirke,	Fort Dodge
112	Mount Vernon,	79	R. Rose.	Mount Vernon
113	Polar Star,	49	D. S. Glidden.	Indian Town
114	Marengo,	72	H. E. Goldthwaite,	Marengo
115	Star,	37	M. Eirth,	Swede Point
116	Tyrrell,	122	L. L. Lusk,	Waverly
117	Montague,	46	J. K. Buck,	Eldora
118	Toledo,	57	L. B. Nelson,	Toledo
119	Unionville,	38	J. B. Morrison,	Unionville
120	Adoniram,	25	W. J. Williams,	Marshall
121	Panora,	49	C. W. Hill,	Panora
122	Ionic,	17	G. W. Neff,	Atalissa
123	Orange,	17		Guthrie Centre
124	Lovilia,	32	Solomon Williams,	Lovilia
125	Mosaic,	75	H. Tuttle,	Dubuque
126	Magnolia,	62	W. H. Eaton,	Magnolia
127	Cascade,	35	W. W. Bolton,	Cascade
128	Pleasant,	63	D. C. Davis,	Pleasantville
129	Bradford,	39	E. R. Dickerson,	Bradford
130	Strawberry Pt.	52	J. E. Baird,	Strawberry Point
131	Equity,	49	F. J. Pattee.	Jaynesville.
132	Orion,	25	Chas. E. Lane,	Dyersville.
133	Bellair,	42	H. S. Rogers.	Bellair.
134	Harmony.	32	Joseph Cotey,	West Mitchell.
135	Bezer,	104	Rob. Grant,	M'Gregor
136	Joppa,	27	E. J. Aldrich,	Montrose.
137	Lewis,	49	L. O. Reinig,	Lewis
138	Fontanelle,	29	H. R. Campbell,	Fontanelle
139	Springville,	60	E. D. Jones.	Springville.
140	Nodaway,	107	W. M. Alexander,	Clarinda.
141	St. Charles,	78	E. A. Brown.	Charles City.
142	Vienna,	44	S. W. Newland,	Center Point.
144	Evergreen,	69	S. H. Hazleton,	Lansing.
145	Benevolence,	47	O. Dennison,	Mason City
146	Talleyrand.	48	F. H. Farley,.	Talleyrand.
147	Prairie la Porte,	41	Jacob Luther,	Guttenburg
148	Fairbank,	34	C. E. Redfield,	Fairbank.
149	Dayton,	35	E. G. Whitstine,	Dayton.
150	Cresco,	54	W. C. Patterson,	Cresco.
151	Afton,	41	E. C. Wilcox,	Afton.
152	Newburn.	31	J. W. Whitlock,	Newbern.
153	Nishnebotany,	78	H. F. Gagnebin,	Sidney.
154	Waukon,	65	J. W. Pratt,	Waukon.
155	Patmos,	50	A. B. Oakley,	Mechanicsville.
156	Taylor,	78	W. F. Walker,	Bedford.

No.	Name of Lodge.	Members.	Name of Sec'y.	Post Office.
157	Adams,	58	J. P. Cummings,	Quincy
158	Wiscotta,	52	W. E. Alumbaugh,	Redfield
159	Morning Star,	80	Andrew Watts,	Jefferson
160	Clermont,	46	C. W. D. Lathrop,	Clermont
162	Red Oak,	55	Z. M. P. Shank,	Red Oak
163	Bellefontaine,	—		Bellefontaine
164	St. Clair,	40	W. L. Harper,	Florence
165	Manchester,	83	W. B. Jewell,	Manchester
166	St. John,	51	C. E. Bramble,	Yankton
167	Wilton,	50	J. B. Mulford,	Wilton
168	Farmers',	29	J. C. Clarke,	Foote
169	Resurgam,	40	J. E. Sugg,	Sabula
170	Temple,	30	A. C. Northrop,	Garden Grove
171	Doric,	37		Morning Sun
172	National,	39	P. Scholler,	National
173	Burns,	84	Sam. L. Gardner,	Monticello
174	Corinthian,	42	W. H. Price,	Brooklyn
175	Hope,	60	J. Dayton,	Belle Plaine
176	Acacia,	55	J. P. Williams,	Webster City
177	Euclid,	53	S. W. Lord,	Clarence
178	Occidental,	43	B. W. Trout,	Sac City
179	Faith,	47	John Carman,	Mount Ayr
180	Pythagoras,	28	Wm. Walker,	Lancaster
181	Great Lights,	79	O. H. Lucken,	Decorah
182	Webb,	54	J. P. Mathos,	Sigourney
183	Hiram Abiff,	60	Henry S. Martin,	Lineville
184	Zeradatha,	54	H. C Babcock,	Wheatland
185	Tyre,	29	Wm. H. Lindsay,	Gossport
186	Amity,	40	J. H. Duglass,	Oskaloosa
187	Rising Sun,	32	J. G. Quackenbush,	Worthington
188	Napthali,	37	D. S. Burson,	South English
189	Emblem,	32	P. F. Poole,	Pleasant Plain
190	Attentive Ear,	42	C. H. Carpenter,	Sandyville
191	Anchor,	37	Wm. N. Davidson,	Hampton
192	Mason's Home,	42		Iowa Falls
193	Clay,	23	J. M. Gwinn,	Lewisburg
194	Fairview,	47	E. D. Martin,	Monroe
195	Eastern Star,	21	C. Bergk,	Dakotah
196	Mystic Tie,	25	A. Lyons,	Murray
197	Charity,	17	H. T. Wood,	Carrollton
198	Kilwinning,	40	A. Lauback,	Batavia
199	Lincoln,	42	A. F. Allen,	Blairstown
200	Anc't L'dmark,	36	J. Fletcher Scoles,	Walnut Fork
201	Jeptha,	18	J. A. Underwood,	Grant City
202	York,	23	J. Hutchinson,	Taylorville
203	Hiram of Tyre,	58	R. W. Wells,	Tama City

No.	Name of Lodge.	Members.	Name of Sec'y.	Post Office.
204.	Brotherly Love,	36	A. R. Prescott,	Postville........
205.	Prudence,	36	J. H. Warren,	Algona. ....
206.	Keystone,	47	D. L Blakeslee,	Wyoming.......
207.	Xenium,	45	S. N. Thompson,	Mt. Pleasant.....
208.	Trinity, . :	56	W. D. Middleton,	Davenport......
209.	Composite,	59	L. Burgus,	Montana........
211.	Relief.	34	Wm. C. Moss,	Brownville......
212.	Unity.	23	G. R. Turner,	Ottawa. ....
213.	Truth.	29	J. C. Harwood,	Forest City.....
214.	Howard,	40	James Greenleaf.	Lime Spr'g Sta'n.
215.	Concordia,	30	R. Bates,	Hopeville.......
216.	Trowel,	37	W. H. Brinkerhoff.	La Porte City. ..
217.	Quitman,	23	C. D. Randall.	Stilesville.......
218.	Preston.	56	H. J. Hills,	Prairie City.....
219.	Fountain,	48	C. Guy Hays,	Ackley. ....
220.	Yosemite,	30	C. W Nation,	Morrisburg. ....
221.	Fraternal,	56	E. S. Carl.	Davenport. .....
222.	Sylvan,	38	T. F. Kenyon,	Jessup..........
223.	Vesper,	28	J. A. Goodrich,	Onawa. ....
224.	Cassia,	29	O. H. Maryatt,	Farley. ....
225.	Tadmor.	21	C. S. Taylor,	Greeley.........
226.	Progress,	21	Geo. Wright,	Kossuth.........
227.	Lebanon,	40	D. Zimmerman,	Lynnville.......
228.	Fidelity,	18	S. B. Delk,	Smyrna.........
229.	Gavel.	20	J. W. Kitch,	Marysville......
230.	Justice,	28	S. Rogers,	Iuka. ....
231.	Social,	30	Eli Sweet,	Millersburg.....
232.	Valley,	25	P. S. Tood,	Missouri Valley..
233.	Champion.	20	J. Kern,	Norwalk........
234.	Silver Urn,	11	.	Silver Creek.....
235.	Good Faith,	16	H. R. Lyons,	Winfield. ....
236.	Toleration,	31	G. B. McFall,	Tremont........
237.	Arcturus.	36	A. M. Johnson,	Ossian..........
238.	White Marble,	17		North Liberty. ..
239.	Compass.	25	D. W. Schoolcraft.	Parkersburg.....
240.	Zerubbabel,	33	J. J. Hutchison,	Lake City.......
241.	Kedron,	27	H. C. Clark,	Maysville.......
242.	Universe,	15		Coal Creek......
243	Concord,	23	H. C. Cook,	St. Ausgar......
244.	Hospitable,	62	C. H Tyler,	Dunlap. ....
245.	Triangular,	45	R. F. Newell,	Fredonia. ......
246.	Good Will,	31	J. H. Vantasee,	Chickasaw. .....
247.	Shiloh,	42	W. Hildreth,	Winthrop.......
248.	Pleiades,	44	J. Sanborn,	Fayette.........
249.	Arcadia,	25		Ames...........
250.	Verity,	24	G. E. Frost,	Clear Lake......

No.	Name of Lodge.	Members.	Name of Sec'y.	Post Office.
251	Corner Stone,	20	W. Bucklin,	Marble Rock....
252	Antiquity,	26		Moravia.........
253	Jerusalem,	44	Wm. Harris,	Hamburg. ......
254	Lilly,	22		Malcolm. ....
255	Emulation,	23	A. Reynolds,	Clinton.........
256	Fortitude,	27	A. Smart,	De Soto.........
257	Incense,	19	I. M. Malcombe,	Vermillion......
258	Jordan,	40	F. D. Kendall,	Moingona.......
259	Excelsior,	45	R. J. Finch,	Council Bluffs...
260	Industry,	13	C. Moore,	Springfield......
261	Escallop,	23	O. L. Eastman,	Shell Rock......
262	Equality,	28	C. C. Read,	Steamboat Rock.
263	Mt. Herman,	27	A. V. Eastman,	Cedar Rapids....
264	Signet,	20	F. E. Dennett,	Carroll. ....
265	Cedar Beam,	34	F. W. Ballou,	Nashua. ....
266	Northern Light,	16	B. H. Beckett,	Northwood......
267	Palmyra,	—	*Charter surrendered,*	Palmyra. ....
268	Damascus,	37	D. Burkhart,	Albion.......
269	Empire,	24	C. G Graves,	Ottumwa. ......
270	Montgomery,	16	J. C. Robb,	Villisca.........
271	Pymosa,	28	Wm. Waddell,	Atlantic. ....
272	Landmark,	8	E. G. Burkham,	Sioux City. .....
273	Hermon,	34	C. N. Perry,	Grinnell. ......
274	Arcana,	22	G. Bailey,	New Hampton...
275	Instruction,	16	Geo. A. Morris,	Corning.........
276	Terrestrial,	19	E. M. Pierce,	State Center. ...
277	Perfect Union	16	Thomas Harris,	Dresden........
278	Bethlehem,	11	R. D. Blakesly,	Bethlehem. .....
279	Mountain Shade,	11	Jno. J. Freeman,	Volga City. ....
280	Meridian,	9	W. R. Reynolds,	Jasper City.....
281	Right Hand,	—	D. C. Butterfield,	De Witt.........
282	Devotion,	—		Denison.........
283	Purity,	8	H. R. Marshall,	Casey...........
284	Level,	15	George J. Wright,	Central City.....
285	Plumb,	12	E. McFarland,	Siam..........
286	Square,	23	A. S. R. Reynolds,	Earlville........
287	Sharon,	19	E. P. Hall,	Victor..........
288	Elk Point,	22	John Lawrence,	Elk Point, Da. Ter.
289	Amicable,	29	Daniel Thomas,	Smithland.......
290	Canopy,	18	J. H. McFarland,	Oxford, ...
291	Archimedes,	13	Levi Whistler,	Baden..........
292	Columbia,	13	Jona. H. Voorhies,	Colo...........
293	Mount Tabor,	25	C. T. B. Bass,	Dexter.........
294	Rock,	25	Z. C. Trask,	Nora Springs. ...
295	Mount Carmel,	12	J. W. Barnett,	Freedom........
296	Victory,	18	R. A. Whittaker,	Waterloo. ......

No.	Name of Lodge.	Members.	Name of Sec'y.	Post Office.
297	Mount Nebo,	25	Daniel Hunt,	Avoca
298	Hermitage,	19	C. H. O'Brien,	Andrew
299	Otley,	22		
300	Tri-Centum,	21		Shenandoah
UD	Token,			
UD	Bunker Hill,			
UD	Neophite,			
UD	Rhodes,			

Kansas.

THE Grand Lodge in this State was organized on the 27th November, 1855, by delegates from two lodges. The proceedings having been pronounced illegal, another convention of delegates from all the lodges in the territory met, on the 17th March, 1856, ratified the proceedings of the previous convention, and thereupon opened a grand lodge for the territory, with Richard R. Rees the first grand master. The increase of lodges and brethren in Kansas since that date has kept pace with the population. In 1870 there were 96 lodges, and 3,761 members. This grand lodge has no abiding place at which to hold its annual communications, neither does it pay mileage or per diem to its members, among which Past Masters are recognized. The treasury is small, and grand lodge dues kept at a figure sufficient to meet current expenses only, or about $2000 per annum.

The executive grand officers elect in 1870 were—

JOHN H. BROWN, of Leavenworth, Grand Master.
JOHN M. PRICE, of Atchison, Deputy Gr. Master.
CHRISTIAN BECK, of Leavenworth, Grand Treasurer.
E. F. CARR, of Leavenworth, Grand Secretary.

Following the example set by the G. L. of Iowa, some years ago, but abrogated in 1871, this grand lodge elects three "Custodians of the Work," who serve a term of years, and whose traveling expenses, unless paid by the lodges which they visit, are paid by the Grand Lodge. In both States the object of this arrangement was to teach in the lodges a system of work and lectures adopted by the respective grand lodges as the most correct and satisfactory— a result that in Iowa is believed to have been accomplished.

The following information is collected from the Proceedings for 1870 of the Grand Lodge, and such later data as we received from the lodge secretaries, in response to our circulars requesting the same :

No.	Name of Lodge.	Members.	Name of Sec'y.	Post Office.
..1..	Smithton,	33	B. N. Forbes,	Iowa Point......
..2..	Leavenworth,	.114	O. C. Beeler,	Leavenworth....
..3..	Wyandotte,	57	Gus. J. Neubert,	Wyandotte......
..4..	Kickapoo,	38	D. H. Sprong,	Round Prairie...
..5..	Washington,	.144	S. A. Frazier,	Atchison........
..6..	Lawrence,	71	B. McAllaster,	Lawrence.......
..7..	Union,	71	H. H. Snyder,	Junction City...
..8..	Bourbon,	61	D. A. Pritchard,	Fort Scott.......
..9..	Acacia,	48	J. M. Bartholow,	Lawrence........
.10..	King Solomon,	.78	H. C. Ganz,	Leavenworth...
.11..	Ottumwa,	22	H. C. Dewitt.	Ottumwa.......
.12..	Emporia,	.67	E. P. Bancroft,	Emporia,........
.13..	Nemaha,	17	Jos. Fulton,	American City...
.14..	Oskaloosa,	73	Thos. C. Dick,	Oskaloosa.......
.15..	Tecumseh,	17	Wm. Lambuth,	Tecumseh.......
.16..	Lafayette,	84	Sam. G. Hoyt,	Manhattan.......
.17..	Topeka,	112	W. F. Baker,	Topeka.........
.18..	Franklin,	80	W. D. Walsh,	Ottawa.........
.19..	Olathe,	55	W. A. Ocheltree,	Olathe.........
.20..	Circleville,	27	J. Telfer.	Circleville. .....
.21..	Grasshopper F's,	62	A. J. Gunn,	Grasshopper F'lls
.22..	Paris,	44	J. H. Barlow,	Paris. ....
.23..	Palmyra,	40	H. M. Scott,	Baldwin City....
.24..	Osage Valley,	.33	D. M. Martin,	Ossawatomie. ...
.25..	High Prairie,	28	Wm. Wilson,	High Prairie.....
.26..	St. John's,	--	R. Beiga	Leavenworth....
.27..	Neosho,	62	D. H. Tuler,	Leroy. ....
.28..	Eldora,	42	John Cross,	Mapleton. ......
.29..	Pacific,	62	J. C. Redfield,	Humboldt.......
.30..	Valley,	32	W. L. Plowman,	Lawrence. ......
.31..	Arcana,	63	M. T. Landon,	Doniphan. ......
.32..	Auburn,	57	Reuben Stees,	Auburn.........
.33..	Mound City,	58	F. C. Bacon,	Mound City.....
.34..	Great Light,	35	John J. Oliver,	Silver Lake. ....
.35..	Hiawatha,	66	A. L. Ellis,	Hiawatha. ......
.36..	Council Grove,	.35	T. P. Nichols,	Council Grove...
.37..	Paola,	100	J. B. Hobson	Paola...........
.48..	Iola,	45	C. Gillihan,	Iola............
.39..	Seneca,	40	Leopold Coben,	Seneca. ....
.40..	Desoto,	24	B. Taylor,	Desoto..........
.41..	Bl'ming Grove,	.28	Frank Colpetzer,	Blooming Grove.
.42..	Holton,	44	James O'Brien,	Holton. ..:.....
.43..	Monticello,	25	M. D. Stapleton,	Monticello. .....ℓ
.44..	Delphian,	67	G. M. Everline,	Garnett.........
.45..	Easton,	31	P. C. Thornton,	Easton.........
.46..	Rising Sun,	60	H. H. Henderson,	Fort Scott ......

No.	Name of Lodge.	Members.	Name of Sec'y.	Post Office.
.47.	.Xenia,	.48.	.A. L. Selig,	.Xenia.
.48.	.Monrovia,	.25.	.B. F. Wallack,	.Monrovia.
.49.	.Nine Mile,	.19.	.D. R. Churchill.	.Delaware.
.50.	.Calvary,	.58.	.D. A. Comstock,	.Leavenworth.
.51.	.Orient,	.70.	.Sam. K. Lakin,	.Topeka.
.52.	.Perry,	.38.	.W. B. Spurlock,	.Perry.
.53.	.Granada,	.33.	.George K. Hatch,	.Capioma,
.54.	.Shawnee,	.38.	.W. F. Hollenback,	.Shawnee.
.55.	.Troy,	.59.	.D. W. Brown,	.Troy.
.56.	.Spring Hill,	.38.	.W. G. Davidson,	.Spring Hill.
.57.	.Coyville,	.29.	.Thos. C. Craig,	.Coyville.
.58.	.Mt. Pleasant,	.25.	.P. W. Hull.	.Mt. Pleasant.
.59.	.Dick Rees,	.22.	.Jas. McGinniss,	.Leavenworth.
.60.	.Salina.	.60.	.John B. Groger,	.Salina.
.61.	.Twin Springs,	.—.	.A. G. Seaman,	.Twin Springs.
.62.	.Americus,	.—.	.Charter revoked.	
.63.	.Adams,	.70.	.A. B. Close,	.Oswego.
.64.	.Wathena,	.43.	.G. W. Barr,	.Wathena.
.65.	.Gardner,	.21.	.J. B. Uhl,	.Gardner.
.66.	.Burlington,	.38.	.F. R. Stratton,	.Burlington.
.67.	.Frankfort,	.47.	.E. J. Rothrick,	.Frankfort.
.68.	.Hiram,	.30.	.R. Beiga,	.Leavenworth.
.69.	.Centre,	.10.	.Charter surrendered.	
.70.	.Mt. Moriah,	.32.	.Christopher Diehl,	.Salt Lake, U. T.
.71.	.Baxter,	.70.	.John M. Cooper,	.Baxter Springs.
.72.	.Huron,	.13.	.J. J. Sloan,	.Huron.
.73.	.Chetopa;	.55.	.A. A. Case,	.Chetopa.
.74.	.Mystic Tie,	.—.		.Augusta.
.75.	.Wamego,	.30.	.C. E. Chandler,	.Wamego.
.76.	.Erie,	.30.	.Jos. A. Wells,	.Erie.
.77.	.Ionic.	.11.	.T. M. Gruwell,	.Neosho Rapids.
.78.	.White Cloud,	.25.	.D. C. Taylor,	.White Cloud.
.79.	.Corinthian,	.27.	.C. D. Waldo,	.Burlingame.
.80.	.Zaredatha,	.20.		.Cottonwood Falls
.81.	.New Albany,	.20.	.J. M. Edmiston,	.New Albany.
.82.	.Tuscan,	.20.	.R. Slavens,	.Neosho Falls.
.83.	.Doric,	.11.	.J. B. Smith,	.Endora
.84.	.Jefferson,	.12.	.John A. Gorham,	.Winchester.
.85.	.Sutton,	.25.	.G. B. Vroom,	.Waterville.
.86.	.Evergreen,	.21.	.D. M. Watson,	.Montana.
.87.	.Ashler,	.17.	.M. A. Payne,	.Clinton.
.88.	.Eureka,	.18.	.H. H. Cox,	.Pleasanton.
.89.	.Home,	.13.		.Centralia.
.90.	.Goldeh Rule,	.31.	.R. H. Waterman,	.North Topeka.
.91.	.Marysville,	.17.	.James S. M'Gill,	.Marysville.
92.	.Mission,	.22.	.Wm. Rouse,	.Osage Mission.

No.	Name of Lodge.	Members.	Name of Sec'y.	Post Office.
.93.	.Girard.	........16...	Stephen A. Atwood,	.Girard..........
.94.	.Harmony.	......26...	J. N. Sutherland,..	..Neodosha.......
.95.	.Constellation,..	.13...	Wm. Spencer.	Fredonia. ......
.96.	.Delaware,	......12...	John C. Grinter,....	White Church....
UD.	.Euclid.			.Lyndon........
UD.	.Polar Star,			.Netawaka.......
UD.	.Fortitude,			.Independence...
UD.	.Fidelity.			.Eureka.........
UD.	.Benevolent,			.Abylene........
UD.	.Unity,.			.Wichita........
UD.	.Western Star,			.Solomon........
UD.	.Keystone,			.Parker. ....
UD.	.Prudence,			.Columbus.......
UD.	.Cedar,			.New Chicago....
UD.	.Frontier,			.Washington.....

Kentucky.

The Grand Lodge in this State was organized on 16th October, 1800, by a convention of delegates from the lodges then in the State holding under the Grand Lodge of Virginia, after receiving the consent of that body, in reply to a memorial addressed to it a month previously, and William Murray was elected the first grand master. Until 1858 the annual communications of this grand lodge were held in the Masonic Hall at Lexington, and since that year in the Masonic Temple at Louisville, in October. Neither mileage nor per diem were paid its members, until 1869, in which year the grand lodge dues having been increased 25 per cent. per capita of the total membership, the payment was begun, and has since been continued. This grand lodge has at present a treasury of $100,000 invested in Stocks, Bonds. and Mortgages of various designations. of which $75,000 are invested in the Masonic Temple building in the City of Louisville. Among the sources of this grand lodge's revenue there is one which, in this day of general denunciation of the business it is derived from, may be regarded as of very questionable character. In 1802 the then State Legislature of Kentucky to this grand lodge granted a Lottery privilege, for the purpose of thereby raising money to build a Masonic Hall at Lexington, and which privilege, from lack of knowledge as to the profitable manner of working it. was for some years subsequently exploited by the grand lodge "Lottery Trustees" at a loss, until finally and for the past sixty years farmed out to regular Lottery practitioners. In view of the fact that this grant, albeit the object of it was duly accomplished more than fifty years ago, was never abrogated, while the annual revenue derived from it in this past half century has never subserved any educational, moral, or charitable purpose, it is believed that the Grand Lodge of Kentucky Freemasons is now quite rich enough to forego all further receipt of or benefit to be derived from it ; nevertheless, so far, and up to the present time, no action tending to such result has been moved in this grand lodge, and the revenue from this source, at present $500, appears annually in the grand treasurer's account. Except in the case of the G. L. of Maryland, to which a few years previously by the Maryland Legislature a similar privilege was granted for a like purpose, no other State legislature has ever granted a grand lodge of Freemasons such a privilege. By the Maryland grand lodge, however, its Lottery privilege was annulled many years ago.

In 1870 there were holding under the G. L. of Ky. about 413 lodges, with the total membership 20,338, the dues of whom to the grand lodge are $1 each per annum. The executive grand-officers elect in 1870 were—

> CHARLES EGINTON, of Covington, Grand Master.
> E. B. JONES, of Paducah, Deputy Grand Master.
> ALBERT G. HODGES, of Frankfort, Grand Treasurer.
> JOHN M. S. M'CORKLE, of Louisville, Grand Secretary.

For thirty years the Proceedings of this grand lodge have been printed by one person — at present and for that whole period the grand treasurer,— and the result is that at the present time they are printed in no better style than that of thirty years ago, while the price is equal to that charged for the finest work done in the most expensive printing houses in America. It is believed that a change in this particular will result in obtaining work corresponding with the improved typography and style of hodiernal book-making, and creditable to this large and wealthy grand lodge jurisdiction. From those Proceedings for 1870, and the later data supplied by such Bro. Secretaries as responded to our circulars, we collect the following information.

No.	Name of Lodge.	Members.	Name of Sec'y.	Post Office.
..1..	Lexington,	....87..	Joseph G. Chinn,	...Lexington......
..4..	Hiram........	116...	H. J. Hyde,	........Frankfort.......
..5..	Solomon's,	....81..	George Petry,	......Shelbyville......
..8..	Abraham's,	....125..	James McBirnie,	....Louisville.......
..9..	Jerusalem,	.....95..	P. H. King,	.... Henderson......
.14..	Mount Vernon,	..50...	Chas. O. Kenney,	...Georgetown.....
.16..	Paris Union,	....75..	Humphrey F. Logan,	Paris ....
.17..	Russellville,	....78..	W. M. F. Caldwell,	..Russellville.....
.18..	St. Andrews,	..101...	Edmund J. Peckover,	Cynthiana......
.20..	Winchester,	....59...	Robert Moore,	.......Winchester......
.22..	Daviess,..:.......	*No Returns*............	...Lexington.......
.23..	Montgomery,	...76...	Lewis Apperson,	....Mount Sterling..

No.	Name of Lodge.	Members.	Name of Sec'y.	Post Office.
.24	Allen,	104	W. A. Williams,	Glasgow
.25	Richmond,	86	S. S. Parkes,	Richmond
.28	Franklin,	77	Chas. H. Lucas	Danville.
.37	Hopkinsville,	58	Jas. C. Campbell,	Hopkinsville.
.40	Amity,	25	Alex. M'Clintock,	Millersburg.
.41	Landmark,	66	Jos. C. Bailey,	Versailles.
.47	Fortitude,	33	Wm. Manby,	La Grange
.50	Springfield,	55	Jas. S. Ray,	Springfield
.51	Clarke,	204	Wm. E. Woodruff,	Louisville.
.52	Confidence,	51	John. B. Gibson,	Maysville.
.53	Warren,	66	J. C. Ewing,	Harrodsburg.
.54	Greensburg,	54	Drury Hudson,	Greensburg.
.55	Bath,	56	Benj. F. Perry,	Owingsville
.57	Bloomfield,	54	Arch. C. Thomas,	Bloomfield.
.58	Benevolent,	32	Andrew H. Calvin,	Centreville
.60	Lincoln,	50	L. R. Yates,	Stanford
.61	Hart.	26	G. C. Richardson,	Nicholasville.
.65	Dougherty,	93	Wash. F. Conway,	Carlisle
.66	Morganfield,	56	J. V. Cromwell,	Morganfield.
.67	Breckenridge,	50	Williamson Cox,	Hardinsburg.
.71	Vespers,	34	Jas. D. Russell.	Elkton
.73	Bowlinggreen,	132	Jno. J. Hilburn,	Bowlinggreen.
.76	Morrison,	71	Virgil Hewitt,	Elizabethtown.
.78	Jonathan,	43	W. D. Stone,	Liberty
.79	Washington,	34	O. H. Peters,	Nor. Middletown.
.80	Augusta,	46	Jacob P. Reese	Augusta,
.81	Salem,	61	Randolph Noe.	Salem.
.82	Princeton,	89	Jas. E. Barnes,	Princeton.
.85	Grant.	62	J. H. Webb,	Williamston
.86	Dewitt Clinton,	28	Isaac Smith,	Clintonville.
.87	Lebanon,	63	Jas. W. Hopper,	Lebanon
.88	Green River,	41	J. Mitt. Brents,	Munfordville.
.89	Greenup,	114	K. B. Graham,	Greenupsburg
.90	Anderson,	23	Isaac Hoffman,	Lawrenceburg.
.95	Good Faith,	45	H. Ashley.	Florence.
.96	Columbia,	39	David Griffith,	Columbia.
.99	Duvall,	63	Wm. B. Carothers,	Bardstown.
104	Lancaster,	93	Robt Kinnaird,	Lancaster
105	Murray,	81	P. M. Ellison,	Murray.
106	Mt. Moriah,	86	Geo. W. Earnest,	Louisville.
108	Tadmor,	62	Jno. D. Pulliam,	Warsaw.
109	Covington,	63	W. H. Maybery,	Covington.
110	Warren,	39	J. B. Cummins,	Leesburg.
111	Somerset,	75	C. A. Zachary,	Somerset.
112	Fleming,	83	Saml. W. Cox,	Flemingsburg.
113	Antiquity,	41	Wm. F. Alexander,	Louisville.

No.	Name of Lodge.	Members.	Name of Sec'y.	Post Office.
115	Hancock,	57	J. D. Powers, jr.,	Hawesville.
116	Minerva,	30	J. J. Perham,	Minerva.
117	Sharpsburg,	42	Chas. D. Armstrong,	Sharpsburg.
118	Big Spring,	48	A. R. Morris,	Big Spring.
120	Hickman,	55	Robt. W. Davis,	Hickman.
121	Cadiz,	46	Robt. D. Baker,	Cadiz.
122	Harrison,	25	Abraham Ditto,	Brandenburg.
123	Bradford,	44	L. S. White,	Independence.
124	Pittman,	85	F. R. Wright,	Campbellsville.
125	St. John's,	53	J. R. Graham,	Salvisa.
127	Paducah,	72	Jay C. Small,	Paducah.
128	Owen,	41	Solomon Klein,	Owenton.
129	Barker,	28	D. T. Applegate, sr.,	West Point.
130	Owensboro,	70	John Wandling,	Owensboro.
131	Hickman.	87	Rich. C. Scott,	Clinton.
132	B. R. Young,	59	Luke Kennady,	Hodgenville.
133	Cloverport,	38	D. R. Murray, jr.,	Cloverport.
134	Carrollton,	38	Orson Britton, jr.,	Carrollton.
136	Marion,	44	L. D. Knott.	Bradfordsville.
137	Irvine,	83	Weeden M. Witt,	Irvine.
138	Smithland,	39	Harvey Briggs,	Smithland.
140	Paint Lick,	55	Allen Conn,	Paint Lick.
142	Blandville.	66	Geo. W. Reeves,	Blandville.
143	Madisonville,	70	J. N. Taliaferro,	Madisonville.
144	M'Kee,	65	C. Pitman.	London
145	Trimble,	42	J. T. Shepherd,	Grayson.
147	Mount Zion,	121	F. C. Abbott,	Louisville.
148	Providence,	68	J. K. Givens,	Providence.
150	Crittenden,	—		Crittenden.
151	La Fayette,	29	Robert J. Cooper,	La Fayette.
152	Alexandria,	35	John S. Ducker,	Alexandria.
153	Holloway,	65	John Roby.	Sherburne.
154	Brooksville,	51	James W. Staton.	Brooksville
155	Bullitt,	65	Joseph M. Abbott,	Shepherdsville.
156	Hartford,	66	Sam. E. Hill,	Hartford.
157	Lovelaceville,	52	Jas. C. Benedict,	Lovelaceville.
158	Bedford,	63	Jacob Zeager,	Bedford.
159	Col. Clay,	83	Rich'd H. Ramsay,	Covington.
160	Devotion,	57	John L. Gilmore,	Lexington.
161	Wingate.	47	Thos. M. Elston,	Simpsonville.
163	Robert Burns,	139	P. H. Jeffries,	Newport.
164	Taylor,	44	Wesley Howard,	Colemansville.
165	Westport,	39	D. Johnston,	Westport.
167	Joppa,	40	Thos. B. Leonard,	Emp. Iron Works
168	Caseyville,	47	James D. Ames,	Caseyville.
169	Oldham,	46		Brownsboro.

No.	Name of Lodge.	Members.	Name of Sec'y.	Post Office.
170	Millburne,	59	J. B. Quigley,	Millburne
172	Roberts,	62	J. A. Roberts,	Fulton Station...
173	Columbus	39	Wm. F. Donaldson,	Columbus
174	Good Samaritan,	49	Wm. H. Marquam,	Lexington.
176	Oxford,	23	Harvey S. Parks,	Oxford.
177	S'pson B'volent.	168	John B. Montague,	Franklin
178	Tompkins	44	H. C. Reid,	Edmonton
179	Adam's Fork,	—		Fordsville
180	Salt River,	63	Chas. Hough,	Mt. Washington.
182	Allensville,	24	W. W. Frazer,	Allensville.
183	Madison,	71	S. E. Higgins,	Kirksville.
184	Hustonville,	66	R. W. Bradley,	Hustonville.
186	Livermore,	54	H. L. Freeman,	Livermore.
187	Mountain,	73	Jas. H. Tinsley,	Barboursville.
188	Concord,	58	Peter M. Gurrant,	New Concord...
189	Simpson,	51	Chas. T. Chilton	Newcastle.
190	Suwanee,	64	L. E. Lester,	Eddyville.
191	Lewis.	39	Charles W. Parsons,	Portland,
192	Neatsville	50	J. L. Carter,	Neatsville.
193	Harry Hudson,	38	S. O. Weatherbee,	Middleton.
194	Butler,	50	Thos. J. Hargau,	Pitt's Point.
195	Apperson	101	Thos. D. Marcum,	Louisa.
196	Sardis,	56	Thos. J. Dobyns,	Sardis.
197	Bryantsville,	58	Chas. S. Welsh,	Bryantsville.
198	Mayo,	24	John B. Otten	Flag Spring.
199	Zerubbabel,	44	Wm. P. Dirickson,	Aaron's Run.
200	Model,	60	W. H. Luten,	Moscow.
201	Magnolia,	48	Gordon Schooling,	Mackville.
202	Walton,	40	Wm. F. Norman,	Walton.
203	Scott,	46	Alex. M. Ferguson,	Stamping Ground
204	Bethel,	26	Elisha M. Flack,	Trenton.
205	Benton,	87	W. H. Holland,	Benton.
206	Albany,	70	James E. Chilton,	Albany
207	Germantown,	29	J. E. M'Clean,	Germantown
208	Graham,	77	John W. Ham,	Scottsville
209	Harvey Maguire,	97	John Barker,	Perryville.
210	Taylorsville,	105	Charles B. Stilwell,	Taylorsville.
211	Wintersmith,	62	Ben. W. Payne,	Garnettsville.
212	Stephensburg,	33	Wm. H. Gardner,	Stephensburg
213	Proctor,	59	Elias M. Price,	Beattyville.
214	Fairview,	67	Ed. S. Stuart,	Fairview,
215	New Haven,	47	Geo. Whitehead,	New Haven.
216	Napoleon,	41	Elijah Hogan,	Napoleon.
217	Gordonsville,	51	Benj. N. Kennedy,	Gordonsville.
218	Philip Swigert.	62	Wm. Driskill,	Fisherville
219	Union,	55	Wm. S. Phillips,	Uniontown.

No.	Name of Lodge.	Members.	Name of Sec'y.	Post Office.
220	De Moss,	51	F. Pfanstiel,	De Mossville....
221	Roaring Spring,	47	Wm. G. Davenport,	Roaring Spring..
222	Orlon,	54	John B. Applegate,	Falmouth. ......
223	Compass,	71	H. H. Littell,	Louisville.: ....'.
224	Willis Stewart,	80	Henry Miller,	Louisville.......
226	Mitchell.	17	F. S. Wilson,	Keene. ....
228	Bewleyville.	43	E. R. Pennington,	Bewleyville.....
229	McAfee.	53	Wm. G. Daniel,	Cornishville.....
230	James Moore,	38	Robt. F. Ferguson,	Lindsay's Mills..
231	Bear Wallow,	56	B. M. Parrish,	Caverna. ....
232	Dycusburg	43	E. M. Marshall,	Dycusburg......
233	Red Riv. I.W'ks,	63	R. F. Cooper,	Ruckerville. ....
234	Nolin,	43	Andrew M'Candless,	Uptonville. .....
235	Hampton,	91	H. C. Ferguson,	Catlettsburg.....
236	Litchfield	85	Thos. R. McBeath,	Litchfield. ......
238	Adairville,	54	Edwin R. Moore,	Adairville. ......
239	St. George,	80	Chas. Plohn,	Louisville.......
240	St. Mary's,	27	John T. Wood,	Concord.. ......
242	Canton.	53	Thos. N. Ingram.	Canton..........
244	Pond River,	70	W. W. Hancock.	Greenville. .....
245	Carroll,	32	David M. Reveal,	Lower B. L. Sp'gs
246	Hope,	34	W. F. Horton,	Flat Rock......
247	Fredonia,	68	James A. Maxwell,	Fredonia........
248	Ashbysburg,	29	J. H. Weir,	Ashbysburg.....
249	Henry,	56	Jas. T. McAlister,	Campbellsburg..
251	Gradyville,	58	Benj. F. Hunter,	Milltown. ......
252	Hoffmansville,	41	R. J. Laughlin,	Nebo...........
253	Ceralvo,	39	J. H. Kimmel,	Ceralvo........
254	Morse,	38	J. W. Parkes,	Kingston........
255	Mt. Gilead,	34	J. W. Bobbitt,	Adam's Mills....
256	Bigham,	—		Marion..........
258	Excelsior,	135	W. Broster Kennedy,	Louisville. .....
260	Sparta.	52	Wm. Bond,	Sparta..........
261	Trumbo,	31	Marcus W. Bailey,	Wyoming. ......
262	Hudsonville,	90	Ralph E. Cox,	Hudsonville.. ..
263	Mt. Eden.	—		Mount Eden.....
264	Burlington,	29	S. B, Huey,	Burlington......
265	West Union,	24	John W. Penn,	Dry Run........
266	Robinson,	81	John D. Sheppard,	Louisville.......
268	Wm. B. Allen,	66	Wm. A. Elkin,	Greensburg. ....
271	Hillsboro,	51	Mathew G. Jones,	Hillsboro. ......
272	Cassia,	25	James R. Read.	Logansport. ....
273	Zebulon,	19	Joseph M. Davidson,	Prestonburg.....
274	Foster,	53	W. H. R. Markley,	Foster..........
275	Ausonia,	25	Wm. M. Browder,	Olmsted Station.
276	Temple Hill,	57	Ben. C. Keys,	Shiloh..........

No.	Name of Lodge.	Members.	Name of Sec'y.	Post Office.
278	Meridian,	23	J. M. Roby,	Poplar Plains....
279	Charity,	57	Walter Matthews,	Mayslick...
280	Woodbūry	—		Woodbury.
281	Preston,	129	J. Allen Porter,	Louisville.
282	Eminence	55	Wm. P. Thorn	Eminence
283	New Retreat,	46	R. B. Stubblefield,	Kansas
284	Russell	79	G. T. Isbell.	Jamestown
285	Oak Grove,	44	Sam. A. Miller,	Murray.
286	Newton,	37	J. M. Gossett,	Bethel
287	J. M. Bullock.	53	Virgil A. Lewis,	Christiansburg...
288	Pembroke,	41	W. W. Garnett	Pembroke.
290	Birmingham,	39	Martin H. Haven,	Birmingham.
291	Mt. Olivet,	112	W. M. Chandler,	Mount Olivet....
292	Donavan,	28	W. S. B. Hill,	Boston
293	Yelvington,	33	W. W. Morrison,	Yelvington
294	Johnson,	36	Sam. J. Parks,	Webster
296	Mullen,	41	John N Rainey,	Rutland
297	Hodges,	44	S. M. Cain,	Whitesville.
298	J. Speed Smith.	41	James A. Seay,	Willsburg.
299	Raywick.	29	W. M. Holt,	Raywick.
300	Jamestown,	51	G. W. Shivell,	Woodville
301	Ion,	46	E. Schneider,	Little Hickman..
302	Harmony,	70	W. H. Miller	Mayfield.
303	Lewisport,	23	Jos. G. Smith,	Lewisport.
304	Boone Union,	—		Union.
306	Garrard,	39	Alex. Collier,	Buckeye.
307	Forsythe,	34	G. D. Jones,	Ruddle's Mills...
308	Forrest.	26	A. G. Moore,	Beverly.
309	E. S. Fitch,	53	Geo. Neff,	Howe's Valley...
310	Calhoun,	25	Jas. W. Overstreet,	Calhoun
311	Highland,	38	Oliver W. Burnes,	West Liberty. ...
312	Paradise.	32	David Duncan,	Paradise.
313	Faithful Friend,	30	Francis Gross,	Lockport
314	Carlow,	54	Peter Countzler,	Dixon.
315	Kingston,	45	John W. Parkes,	Kingston.
316	Manchester,	44	H. L. Ward,	Manchester.
318	Marks.	36	John D. Williams,	Knottsville.
319	Mark Tyler,	59	Chas. J. Watkins,	Cadiz.
320	James F. Keel,	56	Wm. O. Pace.	Center.
321	Tompkinsville,	47	Sam. J. Hunter,	Tompkinsville. ..
322	Alma.	68	Wm. A. Cockrell,	Mount Sterling..
323	Loving.	66	H. C. Franklin,	Fountain Run...
324	Henryville,	51	Wm. E. Price.	Henryville.
325	Poage,	60	J. C. Miller, jr.	Ashland
327	L. M. Cox,	75	Rice Dulin,	Wooldridge's...
328	Waynesburg,	54	S. McMullin,	Waynesburg....

No.	Name of Lodge.	Members.	Name of Sec'y.	Post Office.
329	Woodsonville,	20	Thos. M. Williams,	Woodsonville....
330	Middleton,	56	Wm. H. Read,	Franklin........
331	Thos. M. Lillard,	61	B. Q. Roberts,	Verona........
332	Antioch,	59	W. W. Jenkins,	Hinkleville. ....
333	Preachersville,	36	W. H. Miller,	Lancaster.......
335	Beaver Creek,	77	E. R. M'Ginnis,	Johnsonville. ...
336	A. W. Graham,	61	R. S. Knowles,	Smith's Grove. ..
337	Helena,	24	H. Green Campbell,	Helena. ....
338	Waco,	52	Rich. M. Johnson,	Waco...........
339	Crotona,	42	And. J. Reynolds,	Fulton Station...
340	Thomas Ware,	46	John A. Clarke,	Claysville.......
341	Miles,	33	Alonzo Rawlings,	River View......
342	Mason,	41	James K. Lloyd,	Maysville. ......
343	Harney,	95	G. B. Sloss,	Woodburn.......
344	Ghent,	69	Sam. Howard, jr.	Ghent. ....
345	Golden Rule,	144		Covington.......
346	Sacramento,	46	Benj. Plain,	Sacramento. ....
347	Pratherville,	61	R. D. Reynolds,	Slaughtersville ..
348	Pleasant Grove,	48	E. E. Wright,	Monticello......
349	Thos. N. Wise,	36	Leonard H. See,	Duncan.........
350	Marrow Bone,	34	D. B. Williams,	Marrow Bone. ...
351	Winfield,	38	T. S. Gabbart,	Bohon. ....
352	Stanton,	50	N. M. Rice,	Stanton........
354	Hamilton,	30	Thos. B. Johnson,	Hamilton. ......
355	M'Corkle,	22	J. A. Smith,	Brownsville. ....
357	Pellville,	33	Wm. Huff,	Pellville. ....
358	Newport,	89	S. C. Goshorn,	Newport. ....
359	Sugar Grove,	45	James A. Causey,	Sugar Grove. ...
360	Haywood,	52	R. J. Jordan,	Massack.........
361	Baltimore,	47	Wm. H. Moss,	Wingo's Station.
362	Wilmington,	46	John Ellis,	Northcott's Store.
363	Polar Star,	66	Joseph A. Sparks,	Vanceburg......
365	Pythagoras,	28	A. S. Newton,	Goshen. ....
366	Pleasant Grove,	60	John J. Erwin,	Crossland ......
367	Ark,	45	Warren Watkins,	Millerstown. ....
368	Bibb,	42	T. C. Reed,	Miller's Creek. ..
369	Hinton,	45	N. A. Coulter,	Mayfield. ....
370	Ashland,	87	Wm. M. Weber,	Mount Vernon...
371	Zion Hill,	60	Chesley Nunn,	Westonburg.....
372	Hico,	80	Reuben N. Hatcher,	Hico. ....
373	Trowel,	33	L. W. Gee.	Pace's..........
374	Auburn,	60	James C. Vick,	Auburn.........
375	Thomas C. Cecil,	37	Rich. M. Ferrell,	Piketon........
376	Falls City,	122	J. J. Hayes,	Louisville......
377	Elijah Upton,	41	Sam. M. Kinnaird,	Greencastle. ....
378	Melone,	54	N. P. Wells,	Jeffersontown. ..

No.	Name of Lodge.	Members.	Name of Sec'y.	Post Office.
379	Montsarrat,	39	Sam. B. Robertson,	Calhoun.
380	Reliance,	17	B. C. Hunter,	Keysburg.
381	Paintsville,	48	J. W. Walker,	Paintsville.
382	Farmington	53	James T. Bell,	Farmington.
383	Cannonsburg,	64	Wm. Gard.	Ashland.
384	Olive Branch,	52	Addison F. Mayo,	Falls of Rough.
385	Cairo,	65	Robert B. Butte,	Cairo.
386	Fox,	31	Chas. J. Fox.	Dover.
387	Carrsville.	45	James N. Clemens,	Carrsville.
388	Rio Verde.	58	Paul A. Savage.	Omega.
389	John J. Daviess,	26	B. L. Johnson,	Masonville.
390	Bordley.	34	Richard A. Mart,	Bordley.
391	Gasper River,	57	P. L. Hutcheson,	Rabbittsville.
392	Mintonville,	43	M. G. M'Clure,	Mintonville.
393	West M'Cracken,			Woodville
394	Deaver.	40	Henry H. Reynerson,	Liberty.
395	Hiram Bassett,	20	D. E. Bullock,	North Fork.
396	Danville,	55	John Waters,	Danville.
397	Aspen Grove,	30	W. W. Pettit,	Flower Creek.
398	Dick Barnes,	48	W. B. Rogers,	Bainbridge.
399	Beech Grove,	46	W. S. Buckner.	Greensburg.
400	Louisville.	139	Rich'd B. Caldwell,	Louisville.
401	Briensburg,	35	Tho's T. Grubbs,	Briensburg.
402	Shearer.	27	Urban V. Williams,	Bridgeport.
403	Pleasant Valley,	50	Rob't Church,	Henderson
404	Union Grove,	79	Vance Smith,	Rockfield.
405	Sullivan.	19	Enoch A. Johnson,	Trenton.
406	Stephensport,	24	H. B. B M'Coy,	Stephensport.
407	East M'Cracken,	28	Thomas C. Davidson,	Florence Station.
408	Lynnville.	37	Wm. B. Cook,	Lynnville.
409	M. J. Williams,	51	Albert Toon,	New Liberty.
410	Pleasureville,	45	Geo. M. Hill,	Pleasureville.
411	East Owen,	50	A. B. Acree,	Owenton.
412	Cuba,	36	R. N. P. Fields,	Cuba.
413	Cumberland,	36	Lewis A. Waggoner,	Burksville.
414	T. F. Rees,	32	W. W. Clubb,	Franklinton.
415	Muhlenburg,	34	S. J. Rhoads,	South Carrollton.
416	Longview,	18	James A. M'Kenzie,	Long View.
417	Three Springs,	39	A. T. Snoddy,	Three Springs.
418	Cave City,	56	Geo. D. Mentz.	Cave City.
419	Tampico,	16	G. J. Cundiff,	Campbellsville.
420	Cromwell,	80	J. H. Leach,	Cromwell.
421	Consolation,	44	J. Milton Clark,	Hopkinsville
422	Hebardsville,	33	J. Fielding Lewis,	Hebardsville
423	Mason's Creek,	37	L. L. Howard,	Mason's Creek.
424	Casey,	24	A. Williams,	Williams' Store.

No.	Name of Lodge.	Members.	Name of Sec'y.	Post Office.
425	Booneville,	44	A. H. Clark,	Booneville
426	Panther Creek,	29	G. W. Hall,	Curdville
427	Marshall	66	A. B. Dawkins,	Port Royal
429	Thomas Todd,	37	Calvin F. Sanders,	Clay Village
430	T. W. Wash,	36		Aliceton
431	Monticello,	65	W. T. Francis,	Monticello.
•432	Crab Orchard,	57	Wm. G. Welch,	Crab Orchard.
433	Chaplin	40	John H. Duncan,	Chaplin
434	Oakland	28	J. J. Raulinson,	Oakland
435	Southville.	25	H. Clay Carriss,	Southville
436	Jos. H. Branham,	29	Jasper B. Karn,	Owensboro
437	O. D. Henderson.	31	Lewis C. Gabbard,	Irvin.
438	Reedyville,	30	Wm. J. J. Nash,	Reedyville.
439	Eldorado,	49	W. A. Holman,	McAfee
440	Sympsonia,	40	James L. Wallace,	Sympsonia.
441	Fairfield,	34	Harrison Wells,	Fairfield.
442	Newburg.	39	Geo. W. Seebolt,	Newburg.
443	B. F. Reynolds,	32	Wm. T. Sears,	Moorfield.
444	Four Mile,	47	Wm. P. Owen,	Winchester
445	Athens	27	S. L. Parker,	Athens.
446	Short Creek,	29	Virgil Wilson,	Short Creek.
447	Corydon	35	Geo. T. Baldwin,	Corydon.
448	Landrum,	30	J. C. Owen,	Wingo's Station.
449	Plain City,	70	W. M. Greenwood,	Paducah.
450	Mystic Tie,	33	Robt. S. Winlock,	Campbellville
451	Bethlehem,	20	J. Burney Matt,	Walnut Grove
452	Wesley,	39	David P. Johns,	Wesley
453	Shiloh	32	Fielding Jones,	Caseyville
454	Daniel Boone.	38	Sanford Oldham,	White Hall
455	Walton's Creek,	28	E. R. Ashley,	Hartford ◊.
456	Harrod's Creek,	26	Clarence Bate,	St. Mathews.
457	J. D. Crandell,	46	W. A. Armstrong,	⌐ Earl's P. O
458	Carter	26	W. T. Mozee	Cordova.
459	I. T. Martin,	35	T. H. Daugherty,	Stonewall
460	Perseverance,	30	Jno. C. Hannon,	Smithfield.
461	Milton,	27	R. H. Strother,	Milton.
462	New Salem,	49	B. J. Herrington.	Mt. Temperance.
463	King,	34	S. F. Kirksey,	Murray.
464	Cox,	56	Sam. M. Spradling,	Campton
465	Evergreen,	17	Wm. N. Boaz,	Boaz Station
466	W. M. Winstead,	30	John B. Elder,	Owensboro
467	Dixon,	31	P. D. Clayton.	Dixon
468	Stonewall,	15	John H. McIntire,	Loretto
469	Estill,	35	Jos. P. Wright.	Red Riv. I. W'ks.
470	Keystone,	50	Rev. L. H. Salin,	Pleasant Home.
471	Ruscoe,	34	W. R. M'Chesney,	Princeton

No.	Name of Lodge.	Members.	Name of Sec'y.	Post Office.
472	W. G. Simpson,	73	E. T. Calvert,	Monterey.
473	Joe Ellis.	38	Marion Yates,	Buford.
474	Friendship	31	Elijah Roy	Jamestown.
475	Bratton's Mill,	24	John K. Hester,	Bratton's Mills.
476	Milford	23	George Green,	Milford.
477	Caney Fork,	27	W. B. Davis.	Berry's Lick.
478	Samuel Reed,	23	Arthur Rose.	Ludlow.
479	Robert Mallory,	28	Jno. H. Caplinger,	Ballardsville.
480	Star.	27	R. H. Parent,	Rough & Ready.
481	Palestine,	35	D. S. Robertson,	Lovelaceville.
482	Phelps.	27	Jas. E. Clarke,	Moorhead.
483	Monument,	18	Isaac W. Lambert,	Knottsville
484	Parkersville,	33	Sol. J. Howard,	Eddyville.
485	Elk Creek,	37	B. F. Sloan,	Elk Creek,
486	Rising Sun,	24	Jas. E. Terry,	Hiseville
487	J. C. Whitlock,	20	J. B. Carloss,	Cadiz.
488	Argus,	21	Robt. C. Mayers,	Fancy Farm.
489	Hazlewood,	24	J. T. Wilson,	Barlow City.
490	Eginton,	27	Jno. C. Watkins,	Williamsburg.
491	Sievers,	19	C. J. Sievers,	Waterloo.
492	Stanford,	43	A. A. M'Kinney,	Stanford.
493	Jeptha,	15	J. F. Parr,	Wolf Creek.
494	Buford.	23	R. A. Broadhurst,	Midway.
495	Low'r Blue L'ks,	54	Robt. Sadler,	Blue Lick Springs
496	New Providence,	22	W. R. Allbritton,	Murray.
497	Hale Spring,	23	Jos. D. McElrath,	Brewer's Mills.
498	Glencoe.	26	R. E. Foster,	Glencoe.
499	South Ballard,	29	W. T. Western,	Blandville.
UD.	Orient,	15		Head Quarters.
UD.	Ash,	8		Mt. Eden.
UD.	Texas,	9		Texas.
UD.	Gainesville	7		Scottsville.
UD.	Duncan,	7		Duncan.

Louisiana.

The Grand Lodge in this State was organized on 11th of July, 1812, by the representatives of five lodges then in the State holding under four different grand lodges, one of them being that of Marseilles in France, and P. Francis Du Bourg was elected the first grand master. In 1848-'49 there were two grand lodges, which, in 1850 united and formed that which now exists, and the annual communications of which are held in February. In 1871 there were in the jurisdiction of this grand lodge 148 lodges, with a total membership of 7,307 Master Masons. Lodges work in any Rite they may prefer, but no lodge works in two or more Rites. In 1869 this grand lodge issued its bonds for $75,000, bearing 8 per cent. interest; otherwise its liabilities did not in 1871 exceed $2,500, while its assets were in that year estimated at $269,215.60, of which $125,000 is the estimated value of the Grand Lodge Hall, and the unsold "Masonic Temple Property," near that part of the city known as Tivoli Circle, is estimated at $70,000. These estimates for the property in question, in ordinary times, are believed to be not excessive. A proposition, however, to enhance the value of those assets, by the erection of a new Masonic Temple, is under earnest consideration. Neither mileage nor per diem are paid its members by this grand lodge. Its printed Proceedings compose a large and handsome annual, and offer the reader, to some extent in French as well as in the English language, all the information concerning this jurisdiction and Masonry in general that is necessary in such a volume.

The executive grand officers elect in 1871 were—

> SAM. MANNING TODD, of New Orleans, Grand Master.
> AMOS KENT, of Tangipaho, Deputy Grand Master.
> H. RUFUS SWASEY, of New Orleans, Grand Treasurer.
> JAMES C. BATCHELOR, of New Orleans, Grand Secretary.

The following information we collect from the Proceedings of G. L. for 1871, with such changes made therein as the later data supplied by the lodge secretaries enabled us to make.

No.	Name of Lodge.	Members.	Name of Sec'y.	Post Office.
..1..	Perfect Union,	..54...	Paul F. Laborde,	...New Orleans....
..2..	Polar Star,	.....45...	F. Levasseur,	............do ....
..3..	Concorde,	......47...	E. A. Devron,	............do........
..4..	Perseverance,	..49...J.	Magendie,	.............do........
..5..	St. Andrew,	....46...	R. Lafontaine,	...........do........
..5..	Los Amigos d'Or.	65...M.	Blanco,	...............do........
..9..	Silencio,	.......54...	F. Gelbert,	..............do........
.19..	Humble Cottage,	75...K. H.	Bodemuller,	..Opelousas. .....
.24..	Western Star,	...62...J. A.	M'Guire,	......Monroe.........
.28..	St. Albans,	.....54...	E. C. Kiblinger,	....Jackson..........
.31..	Feliciana,	......45...	E. D. Remondet,	....St. Francisville..
.38..	Phœnix,	.......46...	Ed. Phillips,	........Natchitoches. ...
.44..	Foyer Maçonniq.	87...P.	Brugier, jr.	.....New Orleans. ...
.45..	Jackson.	........44...J. A.	McRady,	......Greenwood. .....
.46..	Germania,	.....102...	Ed. Ehrhard,	......New Orleans. ...
.47..	St. James,	......72...	M. Granary.	........Baton Rouge. ...
.50..	Providence,	....45...	G. A. Smith,	.......Lake Providence.
.51..	Minden,	.......89...	W. E. Paxton,	......Minden.........
.52..	Olive,	.........93...	C. O. Gayle,	........Clinton. ....
.53..	Union Fraternal,	33...T. C.	Lawrence,	....Farmerville.....
.54..	Mount Gerizim,	.73...S. W.	Riley,	........Bastrop.........
.55..	De Soto,	.......82...J. J.	Yarborough,	...Mansfield.......
.56..	Lafayette.	......53...H. W.	Sherrard,	....Vernon.........
.57..	Franklin.	.......83...	A. J. Frere,	........Franklin........
.58..	Fr'nds Harm'ny,	79...H.	Marks,	.........New Orleans. ...
.59..	Mount Moriah,	.212...J.	Furneaux,	............do........
.63..	Tunica,	.........19...J. Q.	Keller,	......Tunica..........
.65..	Geo.Washington.	93...	F. A. Dentzel,	......New Orleans....
.66..	Dudley,	.......115...J. B.	Fox.	...............do........
.68..	Marion,	.......152...	Thos. Cripps,	............do........
.70..	Hiram,	.......88...	W D. Taylor,	...........do........
.72..	Alpha Home,	...79...J. P. G.	Sumner,	.........do........
.75..	Sabine,	........21...	R. A. Forbis,	.......Fort Jessup.....
.76..	Quitman,	.....168...J. D.	Tilden,	.....New Orleans. ...
.78..	Orleans,	.......123...	A. Queant,	...........do.........
.80..	DeWitt Clinton,	.27...	W. T. Hollis,	........Marion. ....
.83..	Mount Vernon,	.23...	James R. Pipes,	...Logansport. ....
.84..	Oliver,	........67...	Algernon Hilton,	...Alexandria......
.86..	Pleasant Hill,	...40...R. W.	Freeman,	....Pleasant Hill....
.87..	Lafayette,	.....41...T.	Bellisain,	........Petersonville....
.88..	Many.	.........30...J. J.	Horton,	.......Many ....
.89..	Cypress,	.......49...T. W.	Woodruff,	....Benton. ....
.90..	Benevolent,	....37...	I. D. Moore,	.......Thibodeaux.....
.92..	Monticello,	.....36...J. M.	Gaddis,	......Floyd..........
.94..	Napoleon,	......37...	C. C. Norman,	......Ouchita City.....
95..	Bellevue,	......28...	Wm. C. Hill,	........Bellevue:.......

No.	Name of Lodge.	Members.	Name of Sec'y.	Post Office.
.96.	.St. Helena,	....77...	S. R. Parker,	.......Greensburg. ....
.98.	.Hermitage,	.....85...	P. L. Boulocq,	......New Orleans....
101.	.Franklinton,	....64...	Chas. D. Ott,	......Franklinton.....
102.	.Louisiana.	....145...	A. Waugh,	........New Orleans....
103.	.Cloutierville,	..24...	W. L. Richardson,..	.M'th Cane River.
104.	.Mt. Lebanon,	..25...	J. D. Duke	.........Mt. Lebanon....
105.	.Trinity,	........49...	R. B. Walters,	.....Trinity. ....
106.	.Vienna,	........70...	R. E. Russ,	.........Vienna. ....
108.	.Sparta,	........61...	R. K. Thompson,	...Sparta..........
109.	.Castor.	........24...	Joel Tatum,	........Castor Landing..
110.	.Harrisonburg.	..63...	A. Conn,	.........Harrisonburg. ..
111.	.Urim	..........41...	Thos. L. Simpson,	...Forksville.......
112.	.Bartholemew,	..27...	W. M. Washburn,	...Plantersville.....
113.	.Thos. Jefferson,	.38...	W. D. Henderson,..	.Spearsville......
115.	.Shreveport,	....70...	J. H. Hecox,	......Shreveport......
116.	.Acacia,	........38...	Henry Desorby,	.....Plaquemine. ....
117.	.Milford,	........—		....................Manchac Settl'm't
118.	.Terryville,	.....28...	L. J. L. Dark,	.....Terryville.......
120.	.Deerfield,	.....47...	C. R. Slider,	........Delhi........
121.	.Lisbon.	........53...	J. F. Ford,	........Lisbon. ....
122.	.Mackey,	.......52..	Alex. J. Kolb,	......Ringgold. ......
123.	.Liberty,	.......53...	Chas. Hungerford,..	.Keachi. ....
124.	.Kellertown,	....41...	A. J. Norwood,	.....Kellertown.......
125.	.Pearl River,	....44...	J. E. Ford,	........Line Academy...
126.	.Arcadia.	.......56...	Jno. N. Ryant,	......Arcadia.........
127.	.Spring Hill,	....33...	J. W. Hopkins,	....Spring Hill Ch...
129.	.Dawson,	.......—		...............Scottsville,......
131.	.Shiloh,	........67...	J. B. Hamilton,	.....Shiloh. ....
133.	.Gordy,	........29...	J. Warren Jackson,.	.Cheneyville.....
135.	.Plains.	.........38...	R. S. Troth,	........Plains Store.....
136.	.Athens,	.........36...	J. H. Simmons,	.....Athens. ....
138.	.Jeffersonian,	....23...	Buck Lacy,	........Kingston. ......
139.	.Houma,	........34...	A. W. Connelly,	....Houma. ....
140.	.Cool Spring,	...39...	Geo. W. Tignor,	...Colquette.......
143.	.Downsville,	....62...	E. S. Pipes,	........Downsville. ....
144.	.Ocean,	.........77...	J. A. Litten.	........New Orleans. ...
145.	.Hope.	..........35...	W. Brandt.	........Vermilionville..
146.	.S. Brotherhood,	.57...	D. H. Hayes,	......Springville......
147.	.Anacoco,	.......27...	Thos. Richardson,..	.Anacoco.........
148.	.Red Land,	......37...	Rufus H. Allen,	....Red Land......
149.	.Darlington,	.....37...	John L Nettles,	....Darlington......
150.	.Perkins.	........23...	H. W. Miller,	.....Donaldsonville..
151.	.Eastern Star.	..107...	Sol. M. Brian,	......Winfield........
152.	.Homer,	........55...	J. R. Ramsay,	......Homer..........
153.	.SS. John,	........78...	W. H. Martin,	......Algiers.........
154.	.Fillmore,	.......32...	W. H. Bledsoe,	.....Fillmore.......

No.	Name of Lodge.	Members.	Name of Sec'y.	Post Office.
155	Cherry Ridge,	18	M. L. McFarland,	Farmersville
156	Kisatchie,	24	D. W. Self,	Kisatchie
158	Rapides,	30	Joseph T. Hatch,	Huddleston.
159	Morganza,	30	T. S. Denson,	Morganza
160	Livingston,	37	C. I. Bradley,	Ponchitula
161	Brookville,	52	A. Fort Sharp,	Port Jefferson
162	Burnsville,	48	C. Marshall,	Shangaloo
163	Atchafalaya,	50	J. Ben. Kirk,	Simsport.
164	Columbia,	55	R. S. Slemens,	Columbia.
165	Lake Charles,	32	J. W. Bryan,	Lake Charles.
166	Excelsior,	100	W. Star,	New Orleans
167	Linnwood.	160	Henry Abel,	do
168	Montgomery,	48	D. Hardy,	Montgomery
169	Haynesville,	78	T. Price,	Haynesville.
170	Orus,	56	L. Jolissaint,	New Orleans.
171	Kosmos,	48	B. Ambrustor,	do
172	Union,	69	Herman Meister,	do
173	Orient,	92	V. Meilly,	do
174	Dante,	68	S. Delfini,	do
175	Amite City,	48	J. W. Addison,	Amite City
176	Perf't Harmony,	74	L. L. Miller,	New Orleans.
177	Eureka,	27	J. W. Mallory,	Bonner
178	Tulip,	29	W. A. Watson,	Tulip.
179	Caddo,	85	R. Kahn,	Shrevesport.
180	Little Flock,	26	M. K. Speight,	Muny.
182	Sam. Todd,	48	J. B. Ashley,	Sugartown.
183	Longwood,	36	T. M. Mooring,	Hoss's Mills.
184	Spring Creek,	25	J. P. Wall,	Sp. Cr'k Church,
185	Orphan's Friend,	53	J. J. Smith,	Big Cave.
186	Kisatchie Union,	25	A. Dowden,	Kile's Mills.
187	Flat Lick,	32	F. H. K. Lane,	Flat Lick Bayou.
188	Covington,	29	S. Joseph,	Covington.
189	Evergreen,	41	W. A. Stewart,	Evergreen.
190	Corinthian,	27	Thos. D. Clarke,	New Orleans.
191	Jefferson,	41	H. P. Phillips,	do
192	Abbeville,	24	A. Bernard,	Abbeville.
193	Aurora,	37	Felix Ehrman,	New Iberia.
194	Mt. Olivet,	11	A. Stagg,	Bayou Boeuff,
195	Trenton,	28	R. J. Wheaton,	Trenton.
196	Saline,	30	H. H. Hathorn	Saline.
197	Magnolia,	35	G. Dreyfus,	Washington.
198	Brookline,	23	W. S. Robinson,	Hood's Mills,
199	Mallet Woods,	35	C. W. Forman,	Prudhomme City.
200	Oak Grove,	27	T. B. Reneau,	Oak Grove.
201	Summerfield.	17	Chas. J. Cargile,	Summerfield.
202	Holly Springs,	14	J. Murrell,	Holly Springs.

No.	Name of Lodge.	Members.	Name of Sec'y.	Post Office.
203	Assumption,	26	L. U. Folse,	Napoleonville.
204	Corner Stone,	17	A. G. Satcher,	Lewisville
205	Doric,	22	A. Ehrman,	Brashear City
206	Tyrian,	22	P. J. Wheatley,	Williamsport
207	Howard,	10	W. S. Rounds,	Springfield
208	N H. Bray,	17	M. H. Stanley,	Walnut Hill
209	R. F. McGuire,	9	W. A. Scott,	Rayville
UD	Missionary,	11	W. H. Holloman	Missionary Ridge.
UD	Beacon,	13	J. D. Pennington,	Arizona
UD	Blazing Star,	10	E. M. Dubroca,	West Baton Rouge

Maine.

The Grand Lodge in this State was organized on the 1st of June 1820, by delegates from the several lodges then assembled at Portland for that purpose, and the Hon. Wm. King, governor of Maine, and which in that year was separated from the Commonwealth of Massachusetts, was elected the first grand master. The annual communications of this grand lodge occur in May in the Hall owned by the several Masonic 'bodies at Portland. In 1870 there were 153 chartered lodges, and six holding under dispensation, with a total membership of 14,820. The jurisdiction is divided into nineteen districts, and each put in charge of a D. D. G. M. appointed by the G. M. elect. These officers are paid their traveling expenses; they report annually, and also collect from the several lodges in their respective districts the G. L. annual dues, and pay the same to the grand treasurer. This grand lodge has a "Charity Fund," of $15,000, not sunk in a grand temple, but carefully invested in U. S. Bonds and Bank Stocks, the interest of which is devoted to the relief of worthy applicants for Masonic charity, 87 of whom were, in 1870, reported as having been relieved to extent in all of $1,420. The revenue of this grand lodge is but slightly in excess of a very low rate of current expenses, or about $5,000 per annum. Neither mileage nor per diem is paid to its members.

The executive grand officers elect in 1870 were—

> John H. Lynde, of Bangor, Grand Master.
> David Cargill, of Augusta, Deputy Grand Master.
> Moses Dodge, of Portland, Grand Treasurer.
> Ira Berry, of Portland, Grand Secretary.

The following information we collect from the Proceedings of G. L. for 1870, with such changes made therein as the later data supplied by the grand secretary and the lodge secretaries enabled us to make.

No.	Name of Lodge.	Members.	Name of Sec'y.	Post Office.
..1.	Portland,	362	Eben. Wentworth,	Portland........
..2.	Warren,	100	Austin F. Kingsley,	.East Machias....
..3.	Lincoln,	126	Chas. H. Blagdon....	Wiscasset......
..4.	Hancock,	87	Isaac L. Shepherd,	.Castine. ....
..5.	Kennebec,	144	J. Edwin Nye,	Hallowell. ......
..6.	Amity,	89	L. M. Kenniston,	Camden.........
..7.	Eastern,	169	N. B. Nutt,	Eastport........
..8.	United,	123	Ira P. Booker,	Brunswick......
..9.	Saco,	170	C. C. Temple	Saco............
.10.	Rising Virtue,	.220	Jonathan Burbank,	.Bangor. ....
.11.	Pythagorèan,	...63	Seth W. Fyfe,	Fryeburg. .....
.12.	Cumberland,	...76	David W. Merrill,	New Gloucester..
.13.	Oriental,	157	F. J. Littlefield,	Bridgeton.......
.14.	Solar,	178	W. D. Hill,	Bath...........
.15.	Orient,	132	E. L. Dillingham.	Thomaston. ....
.16.	St. George,	68	Judson M'Callum,	Warren.........
.17.	An't L'dmark,	.311	Wm. Ross, jr.	Portland........
.18.	Oxford,	101	A. Oscar Noyes,	Norway.........
.19.	Felicity,	155	W. H. Pilsbury	Bucksport.......
.20.	Maine,	135	Clifford Belcher,	Farmington .....
.21.	Oriental Star,	.164	Hiram A. Ellis,	Livermore ......
.22.	York,	63	Mark H. Ford,	Kennebunk. ....
.23.	Freeport,	44	Jas. M. Smythe,	Freeport........
.24.	Phœnix,	181	Wm. H. Fogler,	Belfast. ....
.25.	Temple,	85	Wm. V. Harmon,	Winthrop. ......
.26.	Village,	94	Benj. F. Higgins,	Bowdoinham ....
.27.	Adoniram.	66	W. G. Lord,	Limington......
.28.	Northern Star,	..94	James Collins,	North Anson,....
.29.	Tranquil,	147	Geo. S. Woodman.	Auburn.........
.30.	Blazing Star,	..73	John Larrabee,	Dixfield.........
.31.	Union,	85	J. A. Walker,	Union..........
.32.	Hermon,	121	W. Benjamin,	Gardiner........
.33.	Waterville,	124	N. Stiles,	Waterville. .....
.34.	Somerset,	171	N. Woodbury,	Skowhegan :....
.35.	Bethleham,	165	Oliver B. Quinby,	.Augusta. ....
.36.	Casco,	160	Jos. R. Curtis,	Yarmouth.......
.37.	Washington,	96	Jas. B. Neagle,	Lubec. ....
.88.	Harmony,	108	J. C. Summersides,	.Gorham.........
.39.	Penobscot,	111	Newell H. Bates,	Dexter..........
.40.	Lygonia,	183	Aug. T. Somerby,	Ellsworth. ......
.41.	Morning Star,	.50	Jas. E. Chase,	Litchfield.......
.42.	Freedom,	97	James Mills,	Limerick........
.43.	Alna,	116	C. F. Philbrick,	Damariscotta. ...
.44.	Piscataquis,	82	Saml. V. Millett,:	Milo...........
.45.	Central,	110	E. E. Wiggin,	China..........
.46.	St. Croix.	169	Levi L. Lowell,	Calais..........

No.	Name of Lodge.	Members.	Name of Sec'y.	Post Office.
.47.	.Dunlap,	150.	Geo. S. West.	Biddeford
.48.	.Lafayette	67.	Geo. A. Russell,	Readfield.
.49.	M'r'd'n Spl'nd'r,	105.	A. P. Smith,	Newport.
.50.	.Aurora.	164.	Enoch Davies,	Rockland.
.51.	.St John's,	111.	Albert Goodwin,	South Berwick.
.52.	.Mosaic,	153.	E. B. Averill,	Foxcroft.
.53.	.Rural.	48.	A. H. Bailey,	Sidney.
.54.	.Vassalboro,	110.	Stephen Frye,	Vassalboro.
.55.	.Fraternal,	59.	Luke H. Roberts,	Alfred.
.56.	.Mt. Moriah,	51.	D. G. Tarbox,	Denmark
.58.	.Unity,	51.	Chas. A. Dorman.	Freedom.
.59.	.Mount Hope,	32.	Thaddeus Hastings,	South Hope
.60.	.Star in the East,	177.	Edward A. Pond,	Oldtown.
.61.	.King Solomon's,	92.	D. D. Kennedy,	Waldoboro.
.62.	.King David's,	82.	David Howe.	Lincolnville.
.63.	.Richmond.	115.	David S. Richards,	Richmond.
.64.	.Pacific,	79.	John Whitney,	Exeter.
.65.	.Mystic,	128.	F. G. Rogers,	Hampden.
.66.	.Mechanics,	114.	A. J. Durgin,	Orono.
.67.	.Blue Mountain,	40.	Harry P. Dill,	Phillips.
.68.	.Mariner's,	140.	E. Y. Gilmore,	Searsport.
.69.	.Howard,	101.	L. D. Curtis,	Winterport.
.70.	.Standish,	53.	Chas. F. Swasey,	Standish.
.71.	.Ri-ing Sun,	109.	Jas. C. Saunders,	Orland
.72.	.Pioneer,	50.	Jarvis Hayward,	Dalton
.73.	.Tyrian,	130.	F. C. Whitehouse,	Mechanic Falls.
.74.	.Bristol.	140.	James Varney.	Bristol.
.75.	.Plymouth,	91.	Clarendon Butman,	Plymouth
.76.	.Arundel,	71.	S. E. Bryant.	Kennebunksport.
.77.	.Tremont,	121.	Jno. T. R. Freeman,	Tremont.
.78.	.Crescent.	139.	Henry Scurrah,	Pembroke.
.79.	.Rockland,	242.	Edgar A. Burpee,	Rockland
.80.	.Keystone,	90.	Gilson C. Jones,	Solon.
.81.	.Atlantic,	265.	Alfred M. Burton,	Portland.
.82.	.St. Paul's,	89.	J. L. Fuller.	Rockland.
.83.	.St. Andrew's,	229.	A. B. Marston,	Bangor.
.84.	.Eureka,	88.	W. Long,	St. George
.85.	.Star in the West,	85.	L. B. Fogg,	Unity.
.86.	.Temple.	175.	Wm. V. Harman.	Saccarappa
.87.	.Benevolent.	70.	I. W. Johnson,	Carmel.
.88	.Narraguagas,	116.	C. J. Milliken,	Cherryfield
.89	.Island,	71.	Daniel A. Hatch,	Islesboro
.91	.Harwood,	121.	John L. Pierce,	Machias.
.92.	.Siloam,	107.	E. F. Tukey,	Kendall's Mills.
.93	.Horeb,	79.	Wm. H. Chesley,	Lincoln Centre.
.94.	.Paris,	108.	F. H. Skillings,	South Paris

No.	Name of Lodge.	Members.	Name of Sec'y.	Post Office
.95.	.Corinthian,	.....70.	..G. A. Towle,	.......Hartland........
.96.	.Monument,	....103.	..J. H. Bradford,	......Houlton........
.97.	.Bethel.......	.90.	..L. T. Barker,	......Bethel..........
.98.	.Katahdin,	......58.	..A. T. Coburn,	......Patten..........
.99.	.Vernon Valley,	101.	..Marcellus Tozer,	....Mount Vernon...
100.	.Jefforson,	.....66.	..Chas. R. Houghton,.	.Bryant's Pond...
101.	.Nezinscott,	.....73.	..S. D. Andrews.	.....Turner.........
102.	.Marsh River,	...83.	..John H. Gordon,.	.. Marsh River.....
103.	.Dresden,	....	...No Returns.	.......Dresden........
104.	.Dirigo,	.........77.	..C. K. Evans,	......China..........
105.	.Ashlar,	.......136.	..John F. Putnam,.	...Lewiston........
106	Tuscan.	......181.	..A. D. Tracy,	......Addison Point...
107.	.Day Spring.	....56.	..Stephen Adams.	....West Newfield...
108.	.Relief, ..	.....60.	..Arthur A. Holmes,.	.Belgrade.........
109.	.Mount Kineo,	...90.	....	.......Mt. Kineo.......
110.	.Monmouth,	.....71.	..L. Pettingill,	......North Monmouth
111.	.Liberty......	.126.	..J. C. Knowlton,	...South Montville.
112.	.East'n Frontier,.	60.	..Jno. B. Trafton,	.....Fort Fairfield...
113.	.Messalonskee,	..63.	..J. W. Gilman,	......West Waterville.
114.	.Polar Star,	....131.	..L. M. Plummer,	.....Bath..........
115.	.Moderation,	...72.	..James Meserve,	.....West Buxston...
116.	.Lebanon......	..75.	..Albert G. Emery,	....Norridgewock...
117.	.Greenleaf,	......85.	..Roscoe G. Smith,	....Cornish........
118.	.Drummond,	.....60.	..E. A. Sadler,	......East Parsonsfield
119.	.Pownal,	.......84.	..F. W. Fowler,	......Stockton........
120.	.Meduncook,	....43.	..I. W. Collamore,	....Friendship......
121.	.Acacia,	......78.	..Wm. D. Roak,	.....Durham........
122.	.Marine.	......151.	..F. B. Ferguson,	..).Deer Isle........
123.	.Franklin,	......72.	..Luther Curtis,	......New Sharon.....
124.	.Olive Branch,.	..92.	..John Johnston,	... Charleston......
125.	.Meridian,	.....71.	..Dennison Walker,.	..Pittsfield........
126.	.Timothy Chase,	100.	..John W. Harnden,	..Belfast.........
127.	.Presumpscot,	...79.	..V. C. Hall,	........Windham......
128.	.Eggemoggin,	...86.	..E. T. Fuller,	........Sedgwick......
129.	.Quantabacook,.	.50.	..Nathan P. Bean,	....Searsmont ......
130.	.Trinity.	........49.	..Amasa Howe,	....Presque Isle.....
131.	.Lookout,	......37.	..Ellery D. Perkins,.	..Cutler..........
132.	.Mount Tire'm,	..66.	..Sylvanus W. Cobb,.	..Waterford......
133.	.Asylum,	.......45.	..J. W. Maxim,	......Wayne. ....
134.	.Trojan.........	.40.	..J. L. Merrick,	.....:.Troy........
135.	.Riverside,	......59.	..J. J. A. Hofses,	......Jefferson........
136.	.Ionic,	.........52.	..G. O. Bailey,	........Gardiner. ......
137.	.Kenduskeag,	....72.	..Rich'd M. Dolliver,	..Kenduskeag.....
138.	.Lewy's Island,.	.61.	..Charles A. Rolf,	.....Princeton.......
139.	.Archon.........	.69.	..Amos Whitney,	.....East Dixmont...
140.	**.Mount Desert,**	..77.	..E. M. Hamor,	......Mount Desert...

No.	Name of Lodge.	Members.	Name of Sec'y.	Post Office.
141	Augusta,	46	E. F. Blackman,	Augusta
142	Ocean,	54	Jos. Curtis,	Wells
143	Preble,	53	Edwin J. Reed,	Spring Vale
144	Seaside	42	Alden Blossom,	Boothbay
145	Moses Webster,	66	E. H. Lyford,	Vinalhaven
146	Sebasticook,	33	A. Rowell,	Clinton
147	Evening Star,	29	Jas. H. Decaster,	Buckfield
148	Forest,	36	Jno. A. Larrabee,	Springfield
149	Doric,	22	E. R. Haynes,	Monson
150	Rabboni,	55	Chas. A Coombs,	Lewiston
151	Excelsior,	28	Mark L. Sylvester,	Northport
152	Crooked River,	48	A. B. Lovewell,	Bolster's Mills
153	Delta,	35	Marshall Walker,	Lovell
154	Mystic Tie,	19	Geo. N. Coburn,	Weld
156	Wilton,	50	J. D. Storer,	Wilton
UD	Ancient York,			
UD	Cambridge,	40	Sands Bailey,	Cambridge Vil
UD	Anchor,			South Bristol
UD	Esoteric,			Ellsworth
UD	Fisher,			Corinna
UD	Carrabassett,			Canaan

Maryland.

The Grand Lodge in this State was informally organized at Talbot C. H., on the 31st of July, 1783, by the representatives of five lodges all situate on the Eastern shore, and holding charters from the Provincial grand lodge of Pennsylvania ; the lodge at Annapolis, holding its charter since 1750 from the Massachusetts Provincial grand lodge, taking no part in the organization. Subsequently on the 17th of April, 1787, this 1783 grand lodge was reorganized, by representatives from all the lodges in the State, who assembled at Baltimore for that purpose. In the same year this grand lodge was, by the then Maryland Legislature, granted a Lottery privilege to enable it build a Masonic Hall in the City of Baltimore, and by which privilege such building was, in the course of several years, erected, and remained the property of the grand lodge until 1869, when the present Masonic Temple was completed, and which latter, as a Masonic building speculation is not considered an unquestionable success. This grand lodge has a " Charity Fund " of at present about $75,000. but, like that of the G. L. of Mass., it is all invested in the new Temple, upon which a large amount is about to be raised by an issue of G. L. Bonds, with which to clear that property entirely of outside debt. This grand lodge pays neither mileage nor per diem to its members. In 1870 there were 76 chartered lodges with a total membership of 5,161 Master Masons. This grand lodge holds its annual meeting in November in the Temple at Baltimore. There is what is called a Grand Steward's Lodge, which meets when occasion requires.

The executive grand officers elect in 1870 were—

> JOHN H. B. LATROBE, of Baltimore, Grand Master.
> FRANCIS BURNS, of Baltimore, Deputy Grand Master.
> FRED. K. FICKEY, of Baltimore, Grand Treasurer.
> J. H. MEDAIRY, of Baltimore, Grand Secretary.

From the Proceedings of the G. L. for 1870, with omissions courteously supplied by the grand Sec'y, the following information has been arranged.

No.	Name of Lodge.	Members.	Name of Sec'y.	Post Office.
..3..	Washington,....	83...	H. I. Irwin, ...	Baltimore.......
.13..	Concordia, ...	144...	Chas. E. Needles, ...	do.........
.25..	Amicable,.....	130...	A. Wilson, jr., ...	do..........
.34..	St. John's, ...	195...	M. H. Kerner, ...	do..........
.44..	Mt. Ararat,....	100...	W. S. Richardson,...	Bel Air.........
.45..	Cassia,........	84...	Elias Taylor, ...	Baltimore......
.46..	Door to Virtue,	.62...	S. A. Leister........	Westminster.....
.48..	Union,........	63...	J. H. Crawford,.....	Baltimore. ......
.51..	Warren, ...	305...	H. B. Jones, ...	do.........
.53..	Harmony,.....	69...	Jno. H. Price, jr., ...	Port Deposit.....
.58..	Columbia,.....	108...	H. Goldenburg.,....	Frederick. ......
.60..	Union........	250...	H. C. Showacre,....	Baltimore.......
.66..	Cambridge, ...	.51...	Jno. R. Rosse, ...	Cambridge......
.68..	King David's,	.137...	Jas. W. Booze,......	Baltimore......
.70..	Patmos, .•......	42...	S. W. Hazeltine, ...	Ellicott's City....
.84..	Friendship,....	91...	J. W. Cook,.......	Hagerstown. ....
.87..	Burns.........	62...	Hatch Turner, ...	St. Michaels.....
.88..	Adherence,....	146...	W. A. Wentz, ...	Baltimore.......
.89..	Annapolis, ...	67...	Geo. M. Taylor,....	Annapolis.......
.91..	Wicomico, ...	70...	A. J. Benjamin,.....	Salisbury.......
.93..	Cornthian.	74...	Jas. D. Cassard,....	Baltimore.......
.94.	Geo. Washington.	35...	Thos. I. Hood,......	Westminster.....
.95..	Nottingham,:..	.28...	M. R. Stamp,.......	Nottingham. ....
.96..	Monumental. ..	179...	Wm. H. Clark,.....	Baltimore.......
.97..	Ben. Franklin,.	112...	Francis Spavin, ...	do........
.98..	Eureka.........	36...	Henry Tonkin,......	Millington ......
.99..	Mountain,.....	40 ..	R. R. Sanner,.......	Frostburg.......
100..	Potomac.......	70...	S. F. McBride,......	Cumberland. ....
101..	Howard, ...	67...	James Earp,.......	Elk Ridge Land'g
102..	Coates,........	73...	R. J. Trippe, ...	Caston.........
103..	Hiram..........	59...	Maurice Miller, ...	Westernport ....
104..	Lebanon, ...	42...	Adam Shower,......	Manchester. ....
105..	Eureka,........	54...	J. M. Beckenbaugh,	.Sharpsburg. ....
106..	Manokin, ...	78...	T. S. Sadler,.......	Princess Anne...
107..	Hiram,........	83...	Wm. D. Jones,......	Baltimore.......
108..	Centre, ...	174...	J. W. Meakin,.......	do.......
109..	Mystic Circle,	.158...	Jno. Turner, jr., ...	do.......
110..	Arcana,.......	198...	R. M. Hart, ...	do.......
111..	Lafayette,.....	105...	E. C. Bosworth, ...	do.......
112..	Freedom,......	57...	Dr. J. W. Steel,.....	Freedom........
115..	Chester,.......	42...	W. T. Urie,........	Chestertown ....
116..	Mt. Moriah, ...	56...	John F. Conrey,....	Towsontown ....
118..	Corsica,.......	54...	Jas. Wooters,......	Centreville.....
119..	Howard,.......	20...	Jas. Massey,.......	Greensborough. .
120..	Maryland......	115...	Wm. E. Clark, ...	Baltimore.......
121..	Solomon's, ...	36...	Thos. Jeff. Pitt,....	Savage.........

No.	Name of Lodge.	Members.	Name of Sec'y.	Post Office.
122	St. Mary's,	32	J. R. T. Reeves,	Mechanicsville...
123	Pythagoras.	45	Saml. Mansfield,	Baltimore.
124	Doric.	48	J. Wilson Brown,	do.
125	Cecil.	35	Wm. Lindsey,	Chesapeake City.
127	Landmark,	44	D. Maxwell,	Baltimore.
128	Temple,	44	R. J. W. Garey,	Denton.
129	Calvert,	12	Geo. E. Weiden,	Owensville
130	Susquehanna,	53	T. M. Sumption,	Havre de Grace.
131	Ohr,	34	H. Swartzweider,	Cumberland.
132	Joppa,	48	Henry Helwig,	Baltimore.
133	Oakland,	15	S. L. Townshend,	Oakland.
134	Bentley Springs,	38	S. W. Mackey,	Bentley Springs.
135	Stevenson,	31	W. W. Verdin, jr.,	Lapidum.
136	Fidelity,	27	Jos. Dorsey,	Baltimore.
137	Linganore,	21	P. Lugenbeel,	Unionville.
138	Choptank,	16	Geo. P. Jones,	East Newmarket.
139	Phœnix,	30	John T. Gorsuch,	Baltimore.
140	Medairy,	33	G. W. Lantman,	Williamsport.
141	Olney,	18	H. Ridgeley,	Olney
142	Prince Frederick,	28	S. Sollers,	Prince Frederick.
143	Plymouth,	21	I. Lightner,	Union Bridge ...
144	Mizpah,	21	C. D. Luckett.	Rockville.
145	Ionic.	14	Andrew Banks,	Reisterstown.
146	Pickering.	27	David Bell,	Woodberry.
147	Chesapeake,	35	Thos, H. Bock,	Crisfield
148	Kedron.	21	M. L. Dudley,	Baltimore.
149	Laurel Wreath,	33	Wm. H Harrison,	Laurel
150	St. Columbo,	20	S. Cox, jr.,	Port Tobacco.
151	Mt. Vernon,	26	Geo. Evans,	Baltimore.
152	Waverly,	13	I. E. Loughridge,	Waverly.

Massachusetts.

The Grand Lodge in this State was organized on the 9th of June, 1792, by two bodies representing all the lodges at that time in the State, each of which had exercised grand lodge privileges during many years previously, and John Cutler was elected the first grand master. Its annual communications are held 14th of December, with quarterly communications in March, June and September, also a communication on the 27th Dec. for the installation of the officers elected at the annual on the 14th of that month. The lodges in this State are not numbered, but are listed in alphabetical order, numbering in 1870, in all, 182. of which there were 3 in South America, 1 in China, and 1 in Peru, and containing in all 20,253 Master Masons. This grand lodge pays neither mileage nor per diem to its members. Its treasury and Charity Fund—the latter $75,000— are invested in the Boston Masonic Temple, a building that represents over half a million of dollars, and in which nearly all the Masonic bodies in that city meet. Except sufficient to meet very moderate current expenses, the regular revenue of this grand lodge, with the gross amount of a tax of $1 for each affiliated Mason in the State, payable yearly for thirteen years, or commuted to a single payment of a less gross amount, constitute a " Sinking Fund for " the purpose of paying the indebtedness of the G. L., removing " the incumbrance of liabilities upon the Temple, and placing the " Charity Fund upon an independent basis." The liabilities on the Temple are, by this arrangement, in course of liquidation at the rate of $20,000 a year. The State is divided into 16 Masonic districts, and each put in charge of a District D. G. M., who visits each lodge in his district, receives the dues and taxes therein, and pays the same to the grand treasurer, making an annual report to the grand master. Each operative lodge is represented by its three first officers elect, each of whom has a voice, and either of whom the vote of his lodge. Since first election of the present grand master the business has been made manifest through its printed Proceedings in the fullest and most satisfactory manner, with nothing suppressed that should be made known—the publication for 1871 being a noble volume of nearly 600 pages, printed in the best style, and presenting to the reader every item of interest that during the previous year in any manner affected this grand lodge.

The executive grand officers re-elected in 1870 were—

WILLIAM SEWALL GARDNER, of Boston, Grand Master.
JOHN M'CLELLAN, of Boston, Grand Treasurer.
SOLON THORNTON, of Boston, Grand Secretary.

The following information we collect from the Proceedings of G. L. for 1871. with such changes made therein as the later data supplied by Breth'n lodge secretaries enabled us to make.

Name of Lodge.	Members.	Name of Sec'y.	Post Office.
Aberdour,	77	Warren G. Monk,	Boston
Acacia,	91	Abner L. Steele,	Gloucester
Adam's,	76	Geo. T. Wyer,	Wellfleet
Adelphi,	70	John H. Locke	South Boston
Alfred Baylies,	91	Edwin S. Staples,	Taunton
Amicable,	203	Charles Tufts,	Cambridgeport
Amity,	150	T. C. Everett,	Danvers
Ancient York,	190	Rich. W. Baker,	Lowell.
Ancient Landmark,	.59	J. E. L. Voseler,	Shanghai, China.
Artisan,	46	David A. Allen,	Winchendon
Ashlar,	126	Wm. G. Davis,	Rockport.
Athelstane,	129	Courtland T. Webb.	Worcester.
Aurora,	125	Chas. A. Morgan,	Fitchburg.
Baalbec,	160	Albert Hurl.	East Boston
Belmont,	52	Geo. V. Butterfield,	Belmont.
Berkshire,	70	Daniel Lapham	South Adams.
Bethel,	54	Charles Richards,	Enfield
Bethany,	53	M. Perry Sargent,	West Amesburg .
Bethesda,	88	J. T. Needham,	Brighton.
Bethesda,	98	(Not reported,)	Valparaiso, S. A.
Blackstone River,	102	Geo. H. Bates,	Blackstone
Blue Hill,	51	H. S. Messinger,	Canton.
Bristol,	130	John T. Bates,	Attleboro
Caleb Butler,	80	Henry C. Sherwin,	Ayer.
Charity,	34	Alonzo R. Smith,.	North Cambridge
Charles C. Dame,	94	Robt. A. Coker,	Georgetown
Charles W. Moore,	50	Henry Allison,	Fitchburg.
Chicopee,	212	M. C. Hadley,	Chicopee
Cincinnatus,	142	Herbert C. Joyner,	Great Barrington.

Name of Lodge.	Members.	Name of Sec'y.	Post Office.
Columbian...........	325	Wm. Martin,.......	Boston...........
Corinthian...........	85	S. J. Ballou.........	Concord.......
Corner Stone, ...	75	John S. Loring.....	Duxbury........
Dalhousie...........	156	H. F. Allen,........	Newtonville.....
Day Spring, ...	52	E. F. Morris,........	Monson.........
Delta, ...	57	Chas. G. Thompson,	Weymouth ......
De Witt Clinton,.....	59	James Cox,.......	Sandwich.......
Doric, ...	107	H. L. Snow,........	Hudson.........
Eden,...............	54	Addison Sanford, ...	Ware...........
Eliot...............	63	C. H. Smith.........	Jamaica Plains...
Eleusis,.............	52	Wm. C. Ireland....	Boston..........
Essex.	182	Joseph Swasey,....	Salem..........
Eureka,.............	195	H. W. Emerson,....	New Bedford....
Evening Star,........	—	N. W. Shores, ...	Lee ....
Excelsior,..........	60	W. A. Wyckoff,....	Franklin.......
Faith..............	49	James W. Poor,....	Charlestown.....
Franklin, ...	80	Geo. R. Newton....	Grafton.........
Fraternal,..........	150	Oliver C. Hoxsie, ...	Hyannis ....
Fellowship, ...	124	Warren K. Churchill,	Joppa Village...
Gate of the Temple, .	146	Alban S. Green, ...	South Boston....
Germania, ...	109	Fred. Blocklinger, .	Boston..........
Globe,.............	25	Arthur F. Curtis,....	Hinsdale........
Golden Fleece, ...	104	Wm. B. Phillips,....	Lynn...........
Grecian, ...	240	Jos. H. Safford,....	Lawrence......
Hammatt,...	85	Saml. L. Fowle, ...	East Boston, ...
Hampden,...... ...	212	P. S. Bailey,.......	Springfield......
Harmony,..........	61	J. A. Barber,.......	Northfield.......
Hayden.	93	David Clapp. jr.,....	Brookfield .....
Henry Price, ...	179	Elijah S. Waitt,.....	Charlestown ....
Hiram.............	181	G. H. Lancaster,....	Arlington......
Hiram,.............	—	(Not working.)....	Caldera. Chili,S.A.
Hope,.............	82	Jas. H. Greenwood,.	Gardner ....
Howard.	—	W. F. Kinney,.....	South Yarmouth.
Huntington, ...	36	Wm. S Tinker,....	Huntington. ....
Hyde Park, ...	77	Henry S Buntoñ,...	Hyde Park......
Ionic,.............	85	Geo. S. Clark, ...	East Hampton...
Ionic,.............	89	I. C. Howland,....	Taunton ....
Isaac Parker,.......	60	Lorenzo Noble, ...	Waltham. ......
James Otis,.........	69	O. M. Hinckley, ...	Barnstable ......
Jerusalem,.........	241	Egbert I. Clapp, ...	Northampton....
J. L. Hutchinson, ...	—	(No return,)	Arica, Peru, S. A.
John Abbott,.......	171	Aaron Sargent, ...	North Somerville.
John Cutler,........	125	E. M. Nash,........	Abington. ......
John Hancock, ...	93	Jas. O. Emerson,...	Methuen........
John T. Heard, ...	88	Chas. H. Howe,.....	Ipswich ....
Joseph Warren,.....	360	I. H. Pope,........	Boston ... .

Name of Lodge.	Members.	Name of Sec'y.	Post Office.
Jordan	120	E. C. Spofford,	Peabody
John Warren,	69	Henry Whittemore,	Hopkinston.
Kilwnning,	43	O. F. Osgood,	Lowell
King David,	191	Harry A. Cushman,	Taunton.
King Hiram,	170	Albert Sweetser,	Provincetown.
King Phillip,	117	James Brady. jr.,	Fall River.
King Solomon's,	239	Geo. H. Marden,	Charlestown
Konohassett,	77	Geo. W. Merritt,	Cohassett.
Lafayette,	71	John D. Willard,	Boston Highlands
Lafayette,	116	Robert King,	North Adams.
Liberty,	144	James H. Kendall,	Beverly.
Marine,	47	W. H. Hewins,	Falmouth.
Massachusetts,	219	Wm. H. Hawker,	Boston.
Martha's Vineyard,	59	A. W. Smith,	Tisbury.
May Flower,	94	Jacob B. Shaw,	Middleboro.
Meridian,	139	Edix T. Turner	Natick
Merrimack,	180	Francis Stevens,	Haverhill.
Middlesex,	65	C. J. Frost,	Framingham.
Mizpah,	85	Wm. Page,	Cambridgeport
Monitor.	152	Thos. Kirke,	Waltham
Mountain,	73	J. L. Newell,	Shelburne Falls.
Morning Star,	271	Lewis S. Carpenter,	Worcester.
Morning Sun,	--	Henry W. Billings,	Conway.
Mount Carmel,	195	Timothy Stevens.	Lynn.
Mount Herman,	140	P. R. Litchfield,	Medford.
Mount Hope,	211	A. B. Leonard,	Fall River
Mount Horeb,	100	Sparrow Horton,	Woburn
Mount Horeb,	235	Chas. H. Kelly,	West Harwich
Mount Holyoke,	30		So. Hadley Falls.
Mount Hollis,	77	Wm. H. Brown,	Holliston.
Mount Lebanon.	304	Thos. Waterman,	Boston.
Mount Moriah,	187	Jas. R. Gladwin,	Westfield.
Mount Olivet,	100	Chas. L. Fuller,	Cambridge.
Mount Tabor,	257	J. H. S. Pearson,	East Boston.
Mount Tom,	163	L. C. Browning,	Holyoke.
Mount Vernon.	165	H. E. Twiner, jr.,	Malden.
Mount Zion,	82	John O. Rice.	Barre.
Montague,	255	Henry D. Barber,	Worcester
Montgomery,	101	Lewis Faler,	Milford.
Mystic,	130	H. S. Russell,	Pittsfield.
Norfolk Union,	72	Hiram Alden,	Randolph.
North Star,	78	B. W. Houghton,	Ashland.
Old Colony,	90	Lincoln Fearing,	Hingham.
Olive Branch,	110	E. A. Sumner,	Millbury.
Orange,	114	Geo. A. Drake,	Orange.
Orient,	118	W. C. Shapleigh,	South Dedham.

Name of Lodge.	Members.	Name of Sec'y.	Post Office.
Oriental,	46	Tristram H. Holly,	Edgartown
Orphan's Hope,	149	C. H. Pratt,	East Weymouth
Oxford,	54	J. E. Hammond,	Oxford
Pacific.	120	Edward B. Sears,	Amherst
Palestine,	45	James P. Stewart,	Everett.
Paul Dean,	52	John T. Kimball,	North Easton
Paul Revere,	153	Jonas. R. Perkins,	No. Bridgewater.
Pentucket.	300	Eliphalet Hills,	Lowell.
Pequosette,	101	Chas. H. Bradley	Watertown
Philanthropic,	105	S. P. Hathaway,	Marblehead.
Pilgrim,	149	Darius F. Weeks,	Harwich.
Pioneer,	92	Abel Bealkey.	Somerset.
Plymouth,	110	Josiah R. Drew,	Plymouth
Putnam,	110	Luther L. Parker,	East Cambridge.
Pythagorean,	61	Isaiah P. Atsatt,	Marion.
Quaboag,	85	John Wetherbee,	Warren
Quinnebaug,	100	Thomas Cocroft,	Globe Village.
Rabboni,	25	Geo. S. Carpenter,	South Boston
Republican,	180	W. F. Harding,	Greenfield.
Revere	171	Wm. W. Baker,	Boston.
Rising Star,	95	S. Aug. Bowdlear.	Stoughton.
Robert Lash,	40	Benj. F. Dodge,	Chelsea
Roswell Lee,	217	John A. Hall,	Springfield
Rural,	134	S. Dewing, jr.,	Quincy
Saggahew,	120	J. H. L. Bosquet,	Haverhill.
St. Alban's.	130	Edwin W. Clarke,	Foxborough.
St. Andrew's,	40	A. A. Wellington,	Boston.
St. Bernard	35	Franklin Este,	Southborough.
St. James',	78	Ellis Fanbanks,	Mansfield.
St. John's,	343	Solon Thornton,	Boston.
St. John's,	73	N. Greeley,	Newburyport
St. Mark's,	59	Daniel P. Pike,	Newburyport.
St. Matthew's,	88	Jos. A. Smart,	Andover.
St. Paul's,	199	Horace Smith,	South Boston.
St. Paul's,	45	A. S. Lawrence,	Groton.
Siloam,	74	F. W. Kimball,	Westboro.
Social Harmony,	73		Wareham.
Solomon's Temple,	120	Daniel W. Taft,	Uxbridge.
Star,	85	E. T. Lewis,	Athol
Star in the East.	335	Jas. C. Hitch,	New Bedford
Star of Bethlehem,	213	C. A. Blanchard,	Chelsea
Starr King,	105	Wm. B. Upton,	Salem
Thomas,	62	A. H. Willis,	Palmer.
Trinity,	129	H. J. Brown,	Clinton.
Tuscan,	190	P. B. Robinson,	Lawrence.
Tyrian,	167	Addison Center,	Gloucester.

Name of Lodge.	Members.	Name of Sec'y.	Post Office.
Upton,.....	—	John R. Cole,.......	Cheshire. ....
Union,.............	101	Charles P. Swain,...	Nantucket.......
Union,.............	172	George A. Jones, ...	Dorchester. .....
United Brethren,....	108	Joseph W. Barnes, ..	Marlboro. ......
Warren,...........	126	Sam. F. Merrill,.....	Amesbury. . . .
Washington, ...	252	George F. Davis, ...	Boston Highlands
Webster,..........	101	F. L. Mixer, ...	Webster. ....
Wilder,............	93	Samuel Whittier,....	Leominster......
Winslow Lewis, ...	67	George L. Andrews, .	Boston..........
William North, ...	80	G. Winf. Knowlton, .	Lowell. ....
William Parkman, ...	65	Thos. W. Ayer, ...	Winchester. ....
William Sutton,......	58	Benj. F. Colley, ...	Saugus. ....
Wisdom, ...	50	Hiram N. Cooke,....	West Stockbridge
Wyoming,...........	202	G. C. Stantial, ...	Melrose.........
Zetland,.............	51	Henry T. Parker,...	Boston..........

Michigan.

The Grand Lodge in this State was organized "by a constitutional number of lodges in 1841," such lodges being of those which had not dissolved pursuant to the resolution adopted by the convention in 1829. suspending in that territory all Masonic labor.—This convention was composed of members of the first grand lodge organized at Detroit in 1826, and of which Gen. Lewis Cass was elected the first grand master. The annual communications of the present grand lodge occur in January, at the City of Detroit. In 1860 there were 122 lodges, with a total membership of 5,816. In 1870 there were 286 lodges, with a total membership of 22,172. The annual revenue of this grand lodge is about $9.000, of which the larger part is disbursed in paying mileage and per diem to its members. A balance of about $10,000 in 1871 constituted the entire treasury of this grand lodge. A proposition, made in 1869, to tax the whole membership for the purpose of building a Masonic Temple at Detroit did not meet a favorable reception, and was consequently abandoned.

The executive grand officers elect in 1871 were—

JOHN W. CHAMPLIN, of Grand Rapids, Grand Master.

HENRY CHAMBERLAIN, of Three Oaks, Deputy Gr. Master.

RUFUS W. LANDON, of Niles, Grand Treasurer.

JAMES FENTON, of Detroit, Grand Secretary.

For the following information we are indebted to the courtesy of the Gr. Sec'y, who from the lodge Returns for 1871 kindly supplied the names of such secretaries as had refused or failed to reply to our circulars, mailed to each, requesting the favor of such reply. Otherwise, the Proceedings of G. L. for 1871 has been refered to.

No.	Name of Lodge.	Members.	Name of Sec'y.	Post Office.
1	Zion,	328		Detroit.
2	Detroit,	393	W. H. Smith	do
3	Union of St.Obs.	278	Geo. A. Winslow,	do
4	St. Jo Valley,	112	W. R. Taggart,	Niles.
5	Rochester,	81	N. M. Price,	Rochester.
6	Mt. Clemens,	71	Wm. S. Robinson,	Mt. Clemens
7	Washington,	74	J. S. Paterson,	Tekonsha.

No.	Name of Lodge.	Members.	Name of Sec'y.	Post Office.
.8.	Trenton.	84	Wm. S. Anders, jr.,	Trenton.........
.9.	Evergreen,	119	Geo. J. Ward,	St. Clair........
.10.	Dowagiac.	88	J. J. Vansiper,	Dowagiac.......
.11.	Pine Grove.	153	Robert Yates,	Port Huron .....
.12.	Battle Creek,	152	Thos. G. Knox.	Battle Creek ....
.13.	Phœnix,	155	W. G. Shipman,	Ypsilanti. ......
.14.	Murat.:	117	Geo. L. McGregor,	Albion. ....
.16.	Lafayette,	132	J. W. Storm........	Jonesville......
.17.	Jackson,	144	J. B. Tomlinson,	Jackson.........
.18.	Tyre.	249	Geo. M. Dumon,	Coldwater ......
.19.	Adrian,	208	Henry Clay.........	Adrian ....
.20.	St. Albans,	150	Watson B. Mead,	Marshall........
.21.	Pontiac,	262	A. S. Matthews,	Pontiac. ....
.22.	Kalamazoo,	215	T. F. Giddings.	Kalamazoo......
.23.	Flint.	205	Chas. S. Brown,.	Flint. ....
.24.	Mt. Hermon,	65	Wm. Frankish.......	Centerville. ....
.25.	Paw Paw,	126	A. Sortore..........	Paw Paw. ......
.26.	Maxson,	138.	John R. Wirts,	Hudson ....
.27.	Monroe,	115	Lewis Grant.	Monroe.........
.28.	Union.	83	E. McDonald	Union City......
.29.	Humanity.	60	Chas. D. Beert......	Homer. ....
.30.	Concord,	102	H. C. Hodge,	Concord ....
.31.	Portland,	105	Thos. Steel, ...	Portland ....
.32.	Fidelity,	147	A. F. Warrener,	Hillsdale. ......
.33.	Lansing.	125	H. H. Larned......	Lansing ....
.34.	Grand River,	222	Arthur Wood.	Grand Rapids....
.35.	Siloam,	128	D. R. Hibbard,	Constantine. ....
.36.	Ionia,	166	Hiram A. Chapman,	Ionia...........
.37.	Lyons,	120	David C. Spalding,	Lyons. ....
.38.	Howell,	108	E. A. Young,	Howell. ....
.39.	Western Star,	60	D. H. Reiter,	Berrien Springs.
.40.	Franklin,	—	Geo. E. Mills,	Litchfield. ......
.41.	Romeo.	70	M. J. Brabb, ...	Romeo..........
.44.	Birmingham,	143	R. G. Mitbee.......	Birmingham.....
.46.	Orion,	67	J. W. Marsh........	Orion...........
.47.	Plymouth Rock,	114	A. G. Laraway,	Plymouth.......
.48.	Austin,	44	D. A. Wright, ...	Austin,.........
.49.	Meridian Sun,	128	W. G. Cummins,	Sturgis. ....
.50.	Michigan.	135	C W. Stowell,	Jackson.... ..' ...
.51.	Almont.	79	James T. Ferguson,	Almont.........
.52.	Hastings.	120	Geo. W. Slade,	Hastings.... :....
.54.	Lapeer,	90	Wm. Graham,	Lapeer.... ....
.55.	Backus,	82	C. C. Allison.	Cassapolis......
.56.	Occidental.	95	J. W. Brewer,	St. Joseph.......
.57.	Three Rivers,	146	J. F. Bateman,	Three Rivers....
.58.	Port Huron,	100	H. Reemals,	Port Huron. ....

No.	Name of Lodge.	Members.	Name of Sec'y.	Post Office.
.59	.Climax,	.68	.Moses Hodgeman,	.Climax.
.60	.Cedar,	.84	.H. C. Gridley,	.Clarkston.
.61	.Lexington,	.147	.Bernard Miller,	.Lexington.
.62	.S. Ward.	.63	.F. H. Ward	.Marine City.
.63	.Eaton Rapids,	.108	.Alanson Osborn,	.Eaton Rapids.
.64	.Macomb,	.68	.Oran Freeman,	.Washington.
.65	.Washtenaw,	.84	.H. P. Ludden,	.Dexter.
.66	.Capital of S. O.,	.125	.Henry F. Conely,	.Lansing
.67	.Ontonagon,	.44	.Stephen Lwanger,	.Ontonagon.
.68	.Buchanan,	.100	.Seth Smith,	.Buchanan.
.69	.Tecumseh,	.176	.Thomas Cummins,	.Tecumseh.
.70	.Mason,	.109	.S. A. Paddock,	.Mason.
.73	.Colon,	.85	.Edwin R. Hill,	.Colon.
.74	.Dundee,	.65	.Jas. Parker,	.Dundee.
.75	.Utica,	.94	.E. W. Lawrence,	.Utica.
.76	.Livingston,	.104	.Geo. W. Teeple,	.Pinckney.
.77	.Saginaw,	.172	.John H. Miller,	.East Saginaw.
.78	.Otsego,	.71	.Geo. B. Norton,	.Otsego.
.79	.Germania,	.43	.F. W. Moyer,	.Saginaw City.
.80	.Byron,	.54	.E. B. Welsh,	.Byron.
.81	.Owasso,	.78	.Emory L. Brewer,	.Owasso.
.82	.Lake St. Clair,	.60	.G. M. Wilson,	.North Baltimore
.83	.Bellevue,	.80	.J. A. Birchard,	.Bellevue.
.84	.Oxford.	.76	.J. T. Stanton,	.Oxford.
.86	.Valley City,	.163	.James N. Davis,	.Grand Rapids.
.87	.Anchor of S. O.	.50	.W. J. Handy,	.Kalamazoo
.88	.Butler,	.40	.A. J. Shook.	.Quincy.
.89	.Myrtle,	.92	.Wm. A. Hack,	.Martinville.
.90	.Lowell,	.135	.H. S. West.	.Lowell.
.91	.Ashlar,	.242	.Alfred F. May.	.Detroit.
.92	.Prairie,	.74	.E. T. Cogswell,	.Galesburg
.93	.Star,	.66	.W. W. Green, jr.,	.Osseo
.95	.Morenci,	.72	.N. D. Todd,	.Morenci
.96	.Greenville,	.87	.J. Griffith,	.Greenville
.97	.Niles,	.107	.John A. Allan,	.Niles.
.98	.Waterford,	.59	.Solon Cooley,	.Waterford
.99	.Decatur,	.82	.C. S. Cockett,	.Decatur.
100	.Oakwood,	.60	.Henry Giddings,	.Oakwood
101	.Marquette,	.—	.A B. Taylor,	.Marquette
102	.Blanchard,	.57	.H. Camburn,	.Petersburg.
103	.Greenly,	.218	.R. H. Robinson,	.Adrain.
104	.White Pigeon,	.102	.G. G. De Pucy,	.White Pigeon
105	.St. John's,	.137	.Sylvester Hoyt,	.St. Johns.
106	.St. Peter's,	.67	.D. A. Hewitt.	.Edwardsburg
107	.Eureka,	.48	.Geo. B. De Long,	.Monroe.
108	.Rockland,	.—	.M P. Anderson,	.Rockland.

No.	Name of Lodge.	Members.	Name of Sec'y.	Post Office.
109	Fenton,	208	J. E. Vreeland,	Fentonville.
110	Hiram,	87	H. H. Peters,	Newport.
111	Allegan	82	J. D. Follett, jr.,	Allegan.
112	Wayne,	93	W. R. Corlet,	Wayne
113	Hamilton,	84	Isaac Hopser,	Moscow.
114	Blissfield,	81	S. L. Foster,	Blissfield.
115	Corunna,	95	Orton Williams,	Corunna.
116	Excelsior,	103	John Anderson,	Grass Lake.
117	Reading,	96	G. S. Bartholomew,	Reading
118	Schoolcraft,	85	Wm. H. Fox,	Schoolcraft.
119	Rising Sun,	83	John Buckley,	Lawrence.
120	Charlotte.	141	Randolph Buck,	Charlotte.
121	Commerce,	66	J. T. Fleming,	Four Towns.
122	Ottawa,	63	Thos. Welbon,	Eastmanville.
123	Ithaca,	57	Alanson Jeffery,	Ithaca.
124	Eagle.	90	M. F. Soule,	Burr Oak.
125	Fairfield,	108	W. L. Winchip,	Fairfield.
126	Forest,	54	H. Reed,	Capac.
127	Ovid,	88	A. H. Haight.	Ovid.
128	Ypsilanti,	108,	F. C. Wheeler,	Ypsilanti.
129	Bay City	124	Milo H. Foster,	Bay City.
130	Stockbridge,	89	James Shepard,	Stockbridge.
131	Newaygo,	66	W. Persons,	Newaygo.
132	Linden.	86	L. D. Cook,	Linden.
133	Saline,	71	Jacob Sturm,	Saline.
134	Holly,	91	Richard Howchin,	Holly.
135	Quincy,	72	Joseph Snell,	Hancock.
136	Pokagon,	51	Henry Calverly,	Pokagon.
137	Mendon,	85	Abram H. Voorhees,	Mendon.
138	Port Hope.	105	George Drury,	Port Hope.
139	Grand Haven.	96	Luke Wright,	Grand Haven.
140	Muskegon,	164	A. A. Buhlock,	Muskegon.
141	Mystic,	116	A. M. Shepard,	Bronson's Prairie
142	Memphis,	75	George Peck,	Memphis.
143	Harmony,	68	W. H. Clark, jr.	Armada.
144	Russell,	47	A. E. Dunbar,	Erie....!
145	Maple Rapids,	69	W. F. Pettey,	Maple Rapids.
146	Boston,	81	Abner F. Noyes,	Savanac.
147	Warren,	80	E. Dewey,	Hudson.
148	Manchester,	54	O. Frank Hall,	Manchester.
149	United.	78	John Albertson,	Cooper.
150	Dryden,	72	Jacob C. Lamb,	Dryden.
151	Farmington,	70	H. G. Sexton,	Farmington.
152	Redford,	90	John M. Lee.	Redford.
153	Williamston,	58	J. M. Tompkins,	Williamston.
154	Saginaw Valley,	116	Racine Piermont,	Saginaw.

No.	Name of Lodge.	Members.	Name of Sec'y.	Post Office.
155	Salina,	77	S. S. Linton,	South Saginaw...
156	Olive,	58	Wm Martin,	Chelsea.
157	Addison,	83	J. B. Osborn,	Addison.
158	Star of the Lake.	118	B F. Hayes,	South Haven. ...
159	Golden Rule,	109	S. M. Webster,	Ann Arbor
160	Dansville,	71	Z Ransom,	Dansville.
161	North Newbury,	76	Geo. C. Lemon,	North Newbury..
162	Coloma,	40	C. C. Perry,	Coloma.
163	Vassar,	45	J. E. North,	Vassar.
164	Fowlerville,	86	D. W. Dinterff.	Howell.
165	Milford,	90	Edwin Habble,	Milford.
166	Mt. Vernon,	102	F. E. Marsh,	Quincy.
167	Tracy.	55	Lewis Smith,	Deerfield.
168	Temple,	125	Jos. Wesley,	Adrian.
169	Brooklyn,	121	H. Woodward,	Brooklyn.
170	Wyandotte,	69	G. W. Bryon,	Wyandotte
171	Big Rapids,	89	Wm. Whalin,	Big Rapids
172	Dearborn,	65	John Crosbey,	Dearborn.
173	Evening Star,	64	Alex. Keer,	Medina.
174	Genessee,	103	H. L. Young,	Flint.
175	Clinton,	81	J. E. Gravis,	Clinton.
176	Hillsdale,	52	W. H. Tillman,	Hillsdale.
177	Croton,	38	J. G. Van Leuven,	Croton.
178	Tu can,	79	W. Crosset,	Hubbardston.
179	Grand Ledge,	91	Saml. Chaderick,	Grand Ledge.
180	Pilgrim,	58	J. R. Odell,	Fremont Centre..
181	Orangeville,	52	Eli Nichols,	Orangeville.
182	Lovell Moore,	82	S. Bedford,	Muskegon
183	Parma,	77	L. H. Ludlow,	Parma.
184	Palmyra,	60	F. P. Barlow,	Palmyra
185	Pleasant Lake,	51	A. Southwick,	Leslie
186	Northville,	63	W. F. Huges,	Northville
187	Richmond,	60	S M. Stone,	Richmond
188	St. Louis,	44	Chas. Beil,	St. Louis
189	Adams,	53	Franklin Noyse,	North Adams.
190	Portsmouth,	68	C. L. Watrous,	Portsmouth.
191	Unity,	42	H. Barendreght,	Holland
192	Summit,	58	D. E. Hinman,	Buchanan
193	Dutcher,	83	Homer Mauvel,	Saugatuck
194	Chesaning,	58	J. F. McIntyre,	Chesaning
195	Delta,	38	H. Fletcher,	Escanaba.
196	Gratlan.	62	Geo. D. Wood,	Gratlan,
197	Winfield,	37	Henry S. Willis,	Onondaga
198	Montague,	59	Henry P. Dowling,	Montague.
199	Alpena,	94	Henry S. Seage,	Alpena.
200	Oceana,	67	C. M. Baker,	Pentwater

No.	Name of Lodge.	Members.	Name of Sec'y.	Post Office.
201	Algonac,	37	C. H. Weeks.	Algonac.
202	Negaunee,	63	A. M. Sutherland,	Negaunee
203	Palo,	55	A. B. Barnes,	Palo.
204	Coffinberry,	38	E. B. Ferguson	Bangor.
205	Vienna,	68	John K. Frost,	Pine River
206	Park.	48	Geo. Campbell,	Parkville.
207	Bedford,	48	O. A. Nichols,	Bedford.
208	Brady,	64	M. Hill,	Brady.
209	Liberty,	53	S. H. Holmes,	Liberty.
210	Hadley..	39	A. D. Mills,	Hadley.
211	Hartland,	53	Sam. Mapes,	Hartland.
212	Leslie,	83	Wm. H. Rice,	Leslie.
213	Cedar Springs,	68	R. Kromer,	Cedar Springs
214	Peninsular,	60	E. L. Jones,	Dowagiac.
215	Cato,	33	A. Bedford,	Forestville.
216	Lawton,	54	Albert Jennings,	Lawton
217	Richland,	62	C. W. Jones,	Yorkville.
218	Houghton,	99	C. E. Raymond.	Houghton.
219	Cass,	43	James McDonald,	Port Austin.
220	Athens,	51	J. T. H. Cave,	Athens.
221	Bloomingdale.	35	Wm. Kilheffer.	Lake Mills.
222	Traverse City,	30	J. N. Bradfoot.	Traverse City.
223	Flushing,	70	H. L. Williams.	Flushing.
224	James Fenton.	80	Darwin E. White.	Wayland.
225	Augusta.	50	George Rorabeck,	Augusta.
226	Mount Moriah,	60	Geo. S. Gage,	Cairo.
227	Violinia,	31	Milton J. Gard,	Violinia.
228	Manistee,	76	N. W. Nelson,	Manistee.
229	Lisbon,	62	S. Atherton,	Lisbon.
230	Laingsburg,	41	H. P. Dodge,	Laingsburg.
231	Middleville.	51	S. G. Webster,	Middleville.
232	Vermontville,	59	C. E. Hammond,	Vermontville.
233	Salathiel,	34	Richard Holmes,	Keeler.
234	Spring Lake,	28	Henry Cliff,	Spring Lake.
235	Plainwell,	56	C. J. Poor,	Plainwell.
236	Goodrich,	38	E. A. Rockafellow,	Atlas.
237	Sanilac,	46	Wm. Thomson, jr.	Port Sanilac.
238	Elsie,	36	S. E. Gillam,	Elsie.
239	Three Oaks,	100	Rob. D. Cross,	Three Oaks.
240	Oriental,	92	Jos. McLeod.	Detroit.
241	Corinthian,	42	H. T. Burdick,	St. John's.
242	Keeweenaw,	35	William Walls.	Eagle Harbor.
243	Au Sable,	56	John F. Allros,	Au Sable.
244	Alma,	27	James Hall,	Alma.
245	Camden,	51	James C. Bradley,	Camden
246	Rockford,	71	D. W. C. Burch,	Rockford.

No.	Name of Lodge.	Members.	Name of Sec'y.	Post Office.
247	Brighton,	43	E. F. Allright,	Brighton.
248	Berlin,	48	J. W. Chappell,	Berlin.
249	Gaines,	46	John Roper,	Gaines.
250	Stanton Star,	51	J. M. Dickerson.	Stanton.
251	Wigton,	37	Warren M. Wigton,	Hart.
252	Okemos,	35	Conrad Helwig,	Okemos.
253	Allen,	58	L. R. Walkins,	Allen.
254	Wakeshma,	46	H. J. Daniels,	Fulton.
255	Nashville,	43	E. R. White.	Nashville.
256	Wenona,	42	E. T. Carrington,	Wenona.
257	Sumner,	41	Thomas Patterson,	Alma.
258	Bridgeport,	21	S. Hill,	Bridgeport.
259	Cambria,	36	Orange Porter,	Cambria Mills.
260	Cold Water,	49	A. G. Stevens,	Cold Water.
261	Covenant,	43	Harvey K. Lane,	North Lansing.
262	Fraternity,	58	W. S. Corsedine,	Ann Arbor.
263	Schiller,	32	Herman Rohus.	Detroit.
264	East Bay,	15	E. Hill,	Acme.
265	Northport,	26	George N. Smith,	Northport.
266	Leonard,	26	W. M. Ball,	Ransom.
267	Olivett,	27	Chas. W. Stow,	Olivett.
268	Mattawan,	45	C. W. Bassett,	Mattawan.
269	Menominee,	32	Edward Leake,	Menominee.
270	Crystal,	32	Geo. B. Farley,	Frankfort.
271	Calumet,	51	James Loranger,	Calumet.
272	De Witt,	40	J. A. Street,	De Witt.
273	Center,	41	Daniel Cromwell,	Midland City.
274	Baldwin,	32	Hugh McDonald,	East Tawas.
275	Elk Rapids,	17	R. W. Bagot,	Elk Rapids.
276	Humboldt.	21	Wm. Rossner.	Grand Rapids.
277	Northern Star,	13	John C. Senter,	Unionville.
278	Clayton,	46	John M. Rothrock,	Clayton.
279	Vernon.	30	Arthur Garrison,	Vernon.
280	Ada,	19	Martin Remington,	Ada.
281	Pomona.	—	T. C. Jordon,	St. Joseph.
282	Charlevoix,	16	Jackson Ingorsol,	Charlevoix.
283	Cheboygan,	24	Geo. W. Bell,	Cheboygan.
284	Springport,	11	O. F. Smith,	Springport.
285	Mt. Gilead,	30	A. L. Smith,	Crystal.
286	Washtenong,	—	F. S. Freeman,	Ionia,
287	Bailey,	17	R. Baker,	Breedsville.
288	Salt River,	16	J. G. Ziegler,	Salt River
289	Benona,	8	Henry Hoffman,	Benona.
290	Vandalia.	—	J. B. Slutis,	Vandalia.
291	Marcellus,	—	Chas. Ovose,	Marcellus.
292	Alcona,	—	Geo. L. Colville,	Harrisville.

Minnesota.

The Grand Lodge in this State was organized at the City of St. Paul, Feb. 23, 1853, by the representatives of the three lodges in the State, chartered respectively by the grand lodges of Ohio, Wisconsin, and Illinois, and Dr. A. E. Ames was elected the first grand master. Its annual communications are held in the City of St. Paul in January. The increase of lodges since 1853 has kept pace with the increase of population. In 1871 there were 80 lodges, with a total membership of 4,588. During previous years a fund of $3,000 had been invested for benevolent, which, in 1870, was nearly all spent for business purposes, and of which the principal amount was expended in publishing a reprint of the Proceedings of this grand lodge from 1853 to 1869, inclusive. A fine volume, bound in cloth, has been produced, the sales of which are expected to reimburse the expenditure involved in the production of this book. The revenue for 1870 was $3,237.50, one half which was expended paying mileage and per diem to the officers and members of the G. L., after paying which the G. T. reported the entire treasury, including all funds, at less than $2,000.

The executive grand officers re-elected in 1871 were—

C. W. Nash, of St. Paul. Grand Master.

G. Griswold, of St. Charles, Deputy Grand Master.

George L. Otis, of St. Paul, Grand Treasurer.

William S. Combs. of St. Paul, Grand Secretary.

The following information we collect from the Proceedings of G. L. for 1871, with such changes made therein as the later data supplied by Breth'n lodge secretaries enabled us to make.

No.	Name of Lodge.	Members.	Name of Sec'y.	Post Office.
..1..	St. John's,	86	Leonard Clark,	Stillwater
..2..	Cataract,	180	Chas. F. Smith,	St. Anthony's F'ls
..3..	St. Paul.	107	John Moulton,	St. Paul
..4..	Hennepin.	250	H. Tannatt.	Minneapolis
..5.	Ancient L'dm'k,	137	Jos. C. P. Ordway,	St. Paul

No.	Name of Lodge.	Members.	Name of Sec'y.	Post Office.
..7..	Dakota,.....,...	75...	A. J. W. Thompson,.	Hastings........
..8..	Red Wing.....	118...	Andrew Allen,......	Red Wing .....
..9..	Faribault.......	87...	H. P. Sine.........	Faribault.......
.11..	Mantorville,....	71...	Geo. B. Arnold,.....	Mantorville.....
.12..	Mankota......	120...	Hugh McMurtrie....	Mankota........
.14..	Wapahasa,.....	76 .	Francis Talbot,.....	Wabasha........
.16..	Monticello,.⌣..55		Sam. E. Adams,....	Monticello......
.17..	Hokah,........	62...	Neil Currie,........	Hokah..........
.18..	Winona,......	169...	Walter G. Dye, ...	Winona.........
.19..	Minneapolis, .	139...	E. W. Storer,......	Minneapolis.....
.20..	Caledonia, ...	42...	J. J. Beldin, ...	Caledonia.......
.21..	Rochester, ...	174...	Chas. Rush, ...	Rochester.......
.22..	Pleasant Grove,.	63...	R. D. Hathaway,....	Pleasant Grove..
.23..	North Star,.....	95...	John. H. Denton,....	St. Cloud. ......
.14..	Wilton,........	32...	James B. Hill,......	Wilton..........
.26..	Western Star. .	40...	Robt. B. Skinner,....	Albert Lea......
.27..	Blue Earth Val..	41...	E. A. Hotchkiss,....	Winnebago City..
.28..	Clear Water. ...	39...	H. J. Ranney, ...	Clear Water.....
.29..	Morning Star, .	35...	H. D. Gurney, ...	La Crescent.....
.30..	Anoka.	90...	O. L. Clewelle, ...	Anoka..........
.31..	King Hiram,....	21...	C. B. Tyler,......	Belle Plains.....
.32..	Sakatah,......	39...	M. S. Kimball,......	Waterville ......
.33..	Star in the East,	86...	A. C. Hickman,.....	Owatonna.......
.34..	Oriental,.......	29...	John Jennings, ...	Cannon Falls....
.35..	Mt. Moriah, ...	69...	A. H. Truax,......	Hastings........
.36..	Preston.	118...	J. B. Veall, ...	Preston..........
.37..	Mystic Tie,....	62...	M. A. Robinson, ...	Pine Island .....
.38..	Washington,....	34...	F. E. Barrett,......	Waseja. ....
.39..	Fidelity,......	128...	C. L. West,........	Austin. ....
.40..	Carnelian,......	80...	H. E. Humphrey, ...	Lake City......
.41..	Hermon,.......	38...	A. Tappan,........	Zumbrota. ......
.42..	Hope, ...	45...	F. B. Dean.........	Glencoe ....
.43..	Harmony,......	46...	R. M. Elliott,.......	Lewiston. ......
.44..	King Solomon, .	62...	Chas. H. Lord,.....	Shakopee. ......
.45..	Union,........	55...	J. E. Risedorph,....	Le Sueur. ......
.46..	Evergreen,.....	41...	H. H. Heydon,.....	Saratoga........
.47..	Concord,.......	34...	Wm. Lancaster,.....	Cleveland.......
.48..	Social,.........	69...	Geo. E. Bates, ...	Northfield......
.49..	Rising Sun,.....	92...	H. H. Stern,........	St. Charles.....
.50..	Watertown, ...	72...	Josephus Allen,.....	Watertown......
.51..	Acacia, ...	29...	J. S. Norris,........	Cottage Grove...
.52..	Cannon River,.	54...	Isaac Hand.........	Morristown. ....
.54..	Nicollet, ...	64...	Geo. W. Dryer, ...	St. Peters.......
.55..	Zion, ...	29...	J. L. Bullard,.......	Taylor's Falls. ..
.56..	Meridian, ...	78...	S. S. M'Kenny, ...	Chatfield.......
.57..	Blue Earth City,	36...	R. B. Johnson,.:	Blue Earth City..

No.	Name of Lodge.	Members.	Name of Sec'y.	Post Office.
.58.	Spring Valley,	.39	A. M. Alden,	Spring Valley. ..
.59.	Temple.	30	David A. Adams,	Hutchinson. ....
.60.	Star in the West,	41	P. F. Fargusen,	Sauk Center.....
.61.	Ashlar.	48	C. L. Webber,	Eyota ....
.62.	Star.	33	Jas. S. Hillyer.	Rockland. ......
.63.	Illustrion,	65	Alfred D. Perkins,	Plainview. .....
.64.	Chain Lake,	29	Frank S. Livermore,	Fairmont. ......
.65.	Golden Rule,	27	T. W. Palmer,	Lakeland ....
.66.	Madelia.	10	W. W. Murphy,	Madelia ....
.67.	Corinthian,	15		Farmington. ....
.69.	Mystic Star,	27	H. E. Crandell,	Rushford ....
.70.	Forest City,	28	F. V. De Costa,	Forest City .....
.71.	Paynesville,	23	John W. Derby,	Paynesville. ....
.72.	Lansing.	22	T. B. Morrill,	Lansing. ....
.73.	Brownsville,	20	Chas. Mehl,	Brownsville. ....
.74.	Minneiska,	21	L. R. Brooks,	Minneiska. ......
.75.	Eureka,	41	W. G. Telfer,	La Roy.........
.76.	Joppa,	40	Benj. F. Weber,	Garden City.....
.77.	Tuscan,	22	H. J. Wadsworth,	Waseca. ....
.78.	Mystic Circle,	15		Houston ....
.79.	Palestine,	40	Albert N. Seip,	Duluth...... ...
.80.	Henderson.	19	John C. Stoever,	Henderson. .....
.81.	Constellation,	27	Joseph Gilpin,	Alexandria .....
.82.	Howard,	18	J. A. Johnson,	Howard Lake. ..
.83.	Huram Abi,	45	Hiram Hatch,	Kasson.........
.84.	Orient,	—	Wm. E. Barber,	Money Creek....
.85.	High Forest,	—	E. S. Wooldridge,	High Forest.....
.86.	Tyrian,	—	Edward W. Robie,	Mazeppa........
.87.	Doric,	—	H. A. Park,	Wells ....

Missouri.

The Grand Lodge in this State was organized on the 24th of April, 1821, at St. Louis, by representatives from the three lodges then in the territory, all holding charters from the G. L. of Tenn., the earliest of such charters being dated in October, 1816, and the latest in February, 1821, and Thos. F. Rennick was elected the first grand master. On the 4th of the following May at the installation instead of T. F. Renick, the grand master first installed was Nathaniel B. Tucker. In 1825 Gen. Lafayette and his son, Geo. Washington Lafayette, were elected by acclamation honorary members of this grand lodge, and being introduced, were received by the grand loge standing, an address being delivered by the Gr. Tr., to which Gen. Lafayette replied. In 1831 this grand lodge refused to adopt a proposition to dissolve, in view of the anti-masonic feeling then extant. In 1841 it purchased about 1350 acres of land, with the improvements thereon, with which to establish a Masonic College, and which College was dedicated on the 24th June, 1845. In 1847 this College was located at Lexington, the citizens of that town having subscribed $33,000 for the erection of necessary buildings, of which the corner-stone was laid on the 18th May, 1847, the grand master G. H. C. Melody presiding. An endowment fund of $53,000 was announced as the sale of scholarships, and the grand lodge made provision, up to 1860, for the board, clothing, and education of one orphan from each Masonic District into which the State was then divided. In 1861 the College property was presented to the State of Missouri, on the single condition that the State establish it as a first class Normal School, but, instead, it was during the subsequent four years converted into a Military School, then gradually abandoned, and on the 22d of March, 1870, the State reconveyed the property to the G. L., and in October of that year, a committee of that body was appointed to advertise for sale, and deed the whole property to the best bidder for it.

This grand lodge holds its annual communications in October. in St. Louis. Past Masters are recognized as members. It pays neither mileage, nor per diem. Its attempt in 1869 to tax the membership of the lodges $1 a year for a series of years, to buy a Masonic Temple in St. Louis, was not favorably regarded, and the project being abandoned, the funds collected under the first year's levy were returned to the lodges. In 1870 there were 388 lodges, with a total membership of 18,493. The business of the grand secretary is most efficiently performed by the present officer, and he is liberally paid: The G. L. Proceedings are printed on the finest paper, and in the best manner ; and this grand lodge, while not possessed of any treasury worthy of mention, is in easy circumstances, and, without lowering its self-respect by discussing at length the merits of the object can and does donate of its means to charity as occasion demands. There are at present 38 Masonic Districts, for each of which a District D. G. M. is appointed.

The executive grand officers elected in 1870 were—

> THOMAS E. GARRETT of St. Louis, Grand Master
> RUFUS E. ANDERSON, of Palmyra, Deputy Gr. Master.
> WILLIAM N. LOKER, of St. Louis, Grand Treasurer.
> GEO. FRANK GOULEY, of St. Louis, Grand Secretary.

The following information we collect from the Proceedings of G. L. for 1871. with such changes made therein as the later data supplied by Breth'n lodge secretaries enabled us to make.

No.	Name of Lodge.	Members.	Name of Sec'y.	Post Office.
..1..	Missouri,	......119...	Chas. F. Vogel,	.....St. Louis. ....
..3..	Beacon,...	...102...	Milton H. Wash,	......do...........
..4..	Howard,	......55...	Henry M'Kinley,	...New Franklin. ..
..5..	United,	.......77...	E. D. Ott,	.........Springfield......
..6..	Ark,	.........32...	J. M. Cardwell,	.....Newark. ....
..7..	O'Sullivan,	.....47...	J. D. Van Bibber,	...Walnut Grove...
..8..	Williamsburg,	..63...	Jas. G. Crane,	......Williamsburg....
.9..	G. Washington,	177...	J. H. Wyeth,	.......St. Louis. ....
.10..	Agency,	.......54...	Lem. Poter,	.. ..Agency.........
.11..	Pauldingville,	..53...	Wm. A. Kabler,	....Wright City.....
.12..	Tyro,	.........46...	F. P. Morrow,	......Caledonia.......
.13	.Rising Sun,	....75...	M. T. Samuel,	......Barry..........
.14..	Auburn,	.......33...	Isaac N. Ellis,	......Auburn.........
.15..	Western Star,	..56...	Silas A. Riggs,	......Victoria. ....
.16..	Memphis,	......86...	Chas. S. Martin,	...Memphis. ....
.17..	Clarksville,	....72...	F. M. Reynolds,	.....Clarksville......
.18..	Palmyra,	......132...	John M. Dresher,	...Palmyra... ....

No.	Name of Lodge.	Members.	Name of Sec'y.	Post Office.
.19.	Paris Union,	81	...A. H. Carver,	......Paris. ....
.20.	St. Louis,	117	...Ed. Popper,	........St. Louis. ......
.21.	Greencastle,	35	...Thos. B. McNeal,	...Greencastle, ...
.22.	Willington,	77	...F. W. Hoglestein,	...Dekalb. ....
.23.	Florida.	30	...J. B. Herndon,	.....Florida. ....
.24.	Wyaconda.	61	...T. O. Towels,	.......Lagrange. ......
.25.	Napthtali,	141	...John Decker.	......St. Louis ....
.26.	Mexico,	82	...James Carroll,	.....Mexico ....
.27.	Evergreen,	44	...Chas. R. Curtis,	.....New Haven. ....
.28.	St. John's,	144	...Wm. H. Hall,	......Hannibal. ......
.29.	Windsor.	47	...R. T. Taylor,	......Windsor. ....
.30.	Huntsville,	50	...T. B. Minor,	......Huntsville ....
.31.	Liberty,	80	...D. Hughes,	.........Liberty. ....
.32.	Lafayette.	42	...W. P. Boulware,	...Lexington ......
.33.	Ralls,	61	...Jas. G. Wylie,	.....Madisonville. ...
.34.	Troy,	69	...Jas. M. McLellan,	...Troy. ....
.35.	Mercer,	42	...Wm. B. Ballew,	.....Princeton.......
.36.	Cooper,	87	...John Russell,	......Booneville. ......
.37.	Cedar,	28	...G W. Fitzgerald,	...Shotwell........
.38.	Callao,	47	...E. E. Richardson,	...Callao. ....
.39.	Modena,	39	...H. C. Thompson,	....Modena........
.40.	Mt. Moriah,	66	...Thos. Hayward,	.....St. Louis. ......
.41.	Ætna,	30	...S. J. Pulliam,	.......Ætna. ....
.42.	Middle Grove,	..16	...J. B. Quisenberry,	..Middle Grove. ..
.43.	Jefferson,	83	...Edmund S. Woog...	.Jefferson City. ..
.44.	Jacksonville,	...51	...R. F. Polson,	......Jacksonville ....
.45.	Bonhomme,	..........(Not reported,)	...Manchester. ....
.46.	Wentzville,	58	...Levi L. Keller,	.....Wentzville......
.47.	Fayette,	74	...John M. Reid,	.....Fayette........
.48.	Fulton,	96	...Sam. L. Dedman,	....Fulton..........
.49.	Haynesville,	60	...W. S. Marsh,	......Holt..........
.50.	Xenia,	23	...John P. Downing,	...Xenia...........
.51.	Livingston,	61	...W. I. Pritchett,	......Glasgow.......
.52.	Wakanda,	126	...Jas. H. Moore,	......Carrollton.......
.53.	Weston,	96	...C. P. Gilbert,	......Weston. ......
.54.	Douglas,	18	...John Northcutt,	....Marthasville.....
.55.	Arrow Rock,	...57	...Wm. Potch,	......Arrow Rock.....
.56.	Tipton,	58	...W. V. Van Ostern,	..Tipton.........
.57.	Richmond,	116	...W. D. Fortune,	....Richmond.......
.58.	Monticello,	109	...J. H. Leeper,	.......Monticello......
.59.	Centralia,	52	...Harvey Hulin,	.....Centralia.......
.60.	New Bloomfield,	76	...B. O. Austin,	.......New Bloomfield..
.61.	Waverly,	61	...H. J. Galbreath,	....Waverly........
.62.	Vincil,	45	...John Nelson,	.......Cameron........
.63.	Cambridge,	33	...Wm. T. Nock,	......Cambridge......
.64.	Monroe,	53	...Charles Swift,	......Monroe City.....

No.	Name of Lodge.	Members.	Name of Sec'y.	Post Office.
.65	Pattonsburg,	...50	G. F. Woodward,	...Pattonsburg.....
.66	Linn.	...53	J. J. McDaniel,	....Linn............
.67	Rocheport,	57	Mort. A. Boyd,	....Rocheport......
.68	Tebo,	130	James Parks,	......Clinton. ....
.69	Sullivan,	57	E A. Solf,	.........Sullivan ....
.70	Roanoke,	84	E. W. Shores,	......Roanoke........
.71	Savannah,	48	Henry Grobe,	.....Savannah. ......
.72	Danville,	39	W. D. Bush,	.......Danville.........
.73	Eureka,	83	Jas. L. Applegate,	..Brunswick. .....
.74	Warren,	......—	No Returns.	........Keytesville. ....
.75	Ashley.	28	Alfred Oden.	.......Ashley. ....
.76	Independence,	..90	James Lucas,	......Independence. ..
.77	Lebanon,	77	Newton Jones,	......Steelville ....
.78	St. Joseph,	164	A. B. Fraser,	.......St. Joseph......
.79	Polar Star,	160	D. W. Sadler,	.......St. Louis. ......
.80	Bridgeton,	43	J. D. Parsons,	.....Bridgeton.......
.81	Hickory Grove,	48	Robt. Wade.	.........Hallville........
.82	Jackson.	70	S. D. Sandusky,	....Linnaeus. ......
.83	Laclede,	47	Ben. B. Harrison,	...Lebanon........
.84	Potter.	57	Isaac Oppenheimer,	.Longwood......
.85	Miami,	61	Danl. F. Bell,	......Miami.........:..
.86	Brookfield	81	J. E. Kelley,	.......Brookfield.......
.87	Washington,	89	D. A. DeArmond,	...Greenfield.......
.88	Dresden.	38	P. D. VanDyke,	....Dresden. ....
.89	Friendship,	92	W. W. Thornton,	...Chillicothe. .....
.90	King Solomon,	..35	Patrick Hagerty,	....St. Catharine. ...
.91	Madison,	31	R. M. Ragland,	.....Madison........
.92	Perseverance,	..67	C. G. Hunter,	.....Louisiana. ......
.93	St. Marks.	60	Alex. Ross.	.........Cape Girardeau..
.94	Evening Star,	.30	J. B. Vance,	........Cuba........
.95	Chapman,	54	Chas. Elfeld.	........Las Vegas, N. M.
.96	St. Andrew's,	...46	C. M. Shackleford,	..Shelbyville. ....
.97	Bethany,	67	Wm. P. Robinson,	..Bethany.........
.98	Webster,	100	J. A. Bingaman,	....Marshfield.......
.99	Mt. Vernon,	34	Wyatt Harris.	.......Mt. Vernon. ....
100	Canton,	67	W. B. Henton, jr.,	...Canton. ....
101	Easton.	44	W. C. Benight,	......Easton. ....
102	Bloomington,	...71,	S. W. Rhodes,	....:...Bloomington.....
103	West View,	34	Thos. F. Bast,	......Millersville. ....
104	Heroine.	92	E. B. Cravens,	......Kansas City....
105	Kirksville,	83	J. L Porter,	........Kirksville. ......
106	Macon,	113	A. L. Knight.	......Macon..........
107	Golden Square,	.83	Edward W. Dill,	....Westport. ......
108	Aztec.	32	Edwin J. Orn,	.......Las Cruces. N. M.
109	Montezuma,	66	David J. Miller,	....Santa Fè, N. M...
110	Marcus,	82	Dr. G. H. Leach,	...Fredericktown ..

No.	Name of Lodge.	Members.	Name of Sec'y.	Post Office.
111	Trenton,	67	A. H. Blackholder,	Trenton
112	Graham,	51	J. R. Welch,	Graham
113	Plattsburg,	51	Virgil R. Porter,	Plattsburg.
114	Twilight,	97	Thilo Fyfer,	Columbia.
116	Daviess,	70	Henry C. McDougal.	Gallatin
117	Versailles,	71	Mat. C. White,	Versailles.
118	Kingston,	42	N. M. Smith,	Kingston.
119	De Soto,	—	(No returns,)	De Soto.
120	Compass,	27	F. M. McDonald,	Parkville.
121	Erwin,	101	Ed. Westner,	St. Louis.
122	Dover,	33	W. A. La Bertew,	Dover
123	Herman,	24	Gustav. Mertens,	Herman
124	Dardenne,	24	R. E. Gamble.	O'Fallon.
125	Gentryville,	84	R. M. M'Cammon.	Gentryville.
126	Seaman,	70	John P. Butter,	Milan.
127	Athens,	61	S. W. Clark,	Albany.
128	Live Oak,	—	(No returns.)	Pleasant Hill.
129	Constantine,	84	J. M. Brown,	Charleston.
130	West Prairie,	53	F. M. Wilkins,	Clarkton.
131	Potosi,	73	Wm. T. Hunter,	Potosi.
132	Farmington,	92	A. Parkhurst,	Farmington.
133	Star of West,	83	Eli D. Ake,	Ironton.
134	Pleasant Mount,	46	A. E. Whitney,	Pleasant Mount.
135	Warrensburg,	60	J. R. Heath,	Warrensburg.
136	Phœnix,	44	D. L. Caldwell.	Bowling Green.
137	Prairieville,	53	Robt. H. Wright,	Prairieville.
138	Lincoln,	31	Robt. Maskland,	Fillmore.
139	Oregon,	47	T. C. Dungan,	Oregon.
140	Papinville,	39	L. Culbertson,	Papinville
141	Middlebury,	38	Jacob Ashbrook,	Middlebury
142	Pleasant Grove,	54	J. J. Wharton,	Otterville.
143	Irondale,	52	Calland Arnold,	Irondale.
144	Modern,	50	John Lopp,	Humansville.
145	Rising Star,	49	M. L. Abernathy,	Ebenezer.
146	McGee,	57	Jehu Teter,	College Mound.
147	Cass,	86	M. W. Garrison,	Harrisonville.
148	Yancey,	29	M. N. Lamance.	Pineville.
149	Lexington,	92	B. R. Ireland,	Lexington
150	Birming,	82	E. Y. Kirkman,	Halleck
151	Milton,	55	Wm. L. T. Evans,	Milton.
152	Bloomfield,	81	Robt. W. Christy,	Bloomfield.
153	Linn Creek,	17	J. O. Morrison,	Linn Creek
154	Concord,	54	Jas. W. Pledge,	Concord
155	Spring Hill,	41	S. J. Dewey,	Spring Hill
156	Ashland,	—	(No returns.)	Ashland.
157	North Star,	66	Malcolm M'Killop,	Rockport.

No.	Name of Lodge.	Members.	Name of Sec'y.	Post Office.
158	Johnson,	74	Geo. M'Creath,	Greenville
159	Pacific,	60	John E. York,	Pacific
160	Pleasant,	39	B. W. Mitchell,	Morrisville
161	Clifton Hill,	49	J. M. Graves,	Clifton
162	Whitesville,	57	J. W. Popplewell	Whitesville
163	Occidental,	215	D. J. Mauge,	St. Louis
164	Joachim,	50	W. H. H. Thomas,	Hillsboro.
165	Maryville,	68	Thomas H. Brown,	Maryville.
166	Mirabile	29	T. G. Klepper,	Mirabile
267	Orient Français,	43	Aug. Willermuth,	St. Louis
168	Colony,	38	J. W. Conley,	Colony.
169	Camden Point,	—	(*No returns*,)	Camden Point.
170	Benevolence,	40	Orville Wilcox,	Utica
171	Hartford,	29	Thos. H. Moss,	Hartford
172	Wolf Island,	—	(*No returns*.)	Wolf Island.
173	Union,	37	Fred. C. Mehl,	Union
174	Sturgeon,	75	D. Mayer,	Sturgeon.
175	Newton,	49	W. B. Roark.	Newtonia.
176	Point Pleasant,	53	F. W. Maulsley,	Williams Landing
177	Texas,	74	J. H. Steffens,	Houston
178	Griswold,	38	Chas. Wilson,	Price's Branch
179	Pride of West	128	Samuel Davis,	St. Louis.
180	Des Moines,	32	John M. Hiller,	Athens.
181	Novelty,	66	R. Rhodes,	Novelty
182	Stewartsville,	44	Jas. C. Ritchie,	Stewartsville.
183	California,	56	Albert G. Byler,	California.
184	Calhoun,	48	Wm. E. Grisham,	Calhoun.
185	Chamois,	31	Henry Marquand,	Chamois.
186	Morality,	37	S. W. Downing,	Renick
187	Henry Clay,	47	John W. Martin.	Millersburg.
188	Hannibal,	82	J. F. E. Phillips,	Hannibal.
189	Zeradatha,	122	D. M. McDonald,	St. Joseph
190	Putnam.	60	T. H. Jones,	Newton
191	Zerubbabel,	91	Wm. C. Wells,	Platte City
192	Frankfort,	85	G. Phillips,	Frankfort.
193	Augerona,	50	J. A. Posey,	Missouri City
194	Wellsville,	38	J. M. Barker,	Wellsville
195	Bolivar,	47	E. P. S. Roberts,	Bolivar.
196	Quitman,	51	W. H. Frankum,	Quitman
197	Carthage,	91	M. M. James,	Carthage..
198	Allenville,	36	Wm. Anthony,	Allendale.
199	New Hope,	46	R. F. Sanders,	New Hope.
200	Sonora,	27	A. H. Humiston,	Sonora.
201	Jamesport,	43	W. K. P. Allen,	Jamesport
202	Westville.	31	W. H. Kallison,	Bucklin.
203	Green Ridge,	31	J. Frank Tomlin,	Green Ridge.

No.	Name of Lodge.	Members.	Name of Sec'y.	Post Office.
204	Rowley,	47	Ed. R. George,	Arnoldville.
205	Triluminia,	51	G. W. Colbert,	Marshall
206	Somerset,	53	Geo. Randle,	St. Johns.
207	Clay,	68	W. H. Wears,	Haynesville.
208	Salisbury,	61	John E. Weber,	Salisbury.
209	Poplar Bluffs,	41	Jas. S. Ferguson,	Poplar Bluff.
210	Unionville,	48	Chas. T. Triplett,	Unionville
211	Hickory Hill,	32	A. G. Templeton,	Hickory Hill.
212	Four Mile,	26	N. J. McBride,	Four Mile.
213	Rolla,	112	A. H. Orchard,	Rolla.
214	Forest City,	49	J. A. Gooch,	Forest City.
215	Hoonersville,	43	W. M. Satterfield,	Cotton Plant.
216	Granby,	43	Wm. S. Mesplay,	Granby
217	Barbee,	42	R. L. Ferguson,	Brownsville.
218	Good Hope,	90	A. E. Gusching,	Carondelet.
219	New Boston,	24	D. Y. Howard,	New Boston.
220	Kansas City,	130	Julius E. Levy,	Kansas City.
221	Mystic Tie,	52	G. C. Pepper,	Oak Ridge.
222	Farmer's,	26	Wm. R. Allen,	La Belle.
223	Woodlawn,	34	John C. Rodes,	Woodlawn
224	Hamilton,	57	Wm. Wilmot,	Hamilton.
225	Salem,	56	W. McDonald,	Salem
226	Saline,	19	A. W. Thomson,	St. Genevieve.
227	Cypress,	29	G. W. Freeman,	La Clede.
228	Shelbina,	73	J. W. Townsen,	Shelbina.
229	Nevada,	20	Jas. P. Thomas,	Alpha
230	St. James,	67	R. C. Valker,	St. James
231	Warrenton,	—	(No returns,)	Warrenton
232	Lone Jack,	23	Thos. B. Benton,	Lone Jack
233	Bucklin,	—	(No returns,)	Bucklin.
234	St. François,	46	Andrew H. Baker,	Libertyville.
235	Ionic,	31	Wm. Carson,	Van Rensellaer.
236	Sedalia,	119	L. B. Jackson,	Sedalia.
237	La Plata,	80	S. C. Davidson,	La Plata.
238	Rushville,	46	S. B. Wells,	Rushville.
239	Spencersburg,	29	John L. Tribble,	Spencersburg.
240	Granville,	33	M. D. Blakey,	Granville.
241	Palestine,	52	R. A. Harris,	St. Charles.
242	Portland,	29	Alfred Ries,	Portland.
243	Keystone,	94	A. R. Strain,	Saint Louis.
244	Middle Fabius,	38	W. A. Coffey,	Middle Fabius.
245	Knob Noster,	68	Alonzo Case,	Knob Noster.
246	Montgomery,	37	Joseph Schnessler,	Montgomery City
247	Neosho,	59	A. Mass,	Neosho.
248	Rochester,	47	M. G. Ruby,	Rochester.
249	Carroll,	39	Wm. H. Adams,	Miles Point.

No.	Name of Lodge.	Members.	Name of Sec'y.	Post Office.
250	High Hill,	27	T. J. Clyce,	High Hill.
251	Hope,	33	Arch. S. Bryan,	Washington.
252	Alanthus,	23	Josiah W. Osborn,	Alanthus.
253	Lindley,	25	Chas. H. Cook,	Lindley.
254	Butler,	60	V. B. Vandyke,	Butler.
255	Alton,	37	M G. Norman,	Alton.
256	Shekinah,	31	Chas. G. Warne,	Hanover.
257	Lodge of Light,	29	James Ewart,	Eagleville.
258	Ravenna,	29	W. H. McKinley,	Ravenna.
259	Lodge of Love,	28	H. D. B. Cutler,	Lancaster.
260	Mechanicsville,	29	John N. Snider,	Mechanicsville.
261	Florence,	26	P. P. Ellis,	New Florence.
262	Holden,	57	John H. Hughes,	Holden.
263	Summit,	45	T. R. Thornton,	Lee's Summit.
264	Fayetteville,	40	W. N. Thornbuckle,	Fayetteville.
265	Corinthian,	69	N. H. Conklin,	Warrensburg,
266	Social,	27	A. C. Wells,	Martinsburg.
267	Aurora,	80	Wm. H. Callendar,	Saint Louis.
268	Lodge of Truth,	28	A. M. Attebery,	Atlanta.
269	Rock Prairie,	38	Thos. J. Ingraham,	Union Hall.
270	New Salem,	36	S. H. Thompson,	New Salem.
271	Solomon,	52	John H. Payne,	Springfield.
272	Granite,	58	A. C. Stenett,	Sedalia.
273	Saint Clair,	48	J. E. Lewis,	Osceola.
274	Newmarket,	31	James R. Ferrill,	Newmarket.
275	Tranquillity,	23	B. J. O'Rear,	Arrow Rock.
276	Grand River,	29	Thos. Crawford.	Morristown.
277	Index,	26	Lysander West,	Index.
278	Avilla,	48	H. T. Dunleavy,	Avilla.
279	Hogle's Creek,	30	James B. Brent,	Quincy.
280	Lodge of Peace,	36	W. W. Cover,	Chilhowee.
281	Fenton,	26	M. C. Mamelan,	Fenton.
282	Cosmos,	34	Robert Lyle,	St. Louis.
283	Stockton,	53	James A. Cogbe,	Stockton.
284	Lily,	23	L. J. Yates,	Grant City.
285	Earl,	31	B. M. McFetridge,	Coffeesburg.
286	Hesperian,	47	A. Barter,	Virgil City.
287	Craft,	27	J. W. Barrett,	Canton.
288	Hermitage,	27	Charles Kroff,	Hermitage.
289	Acacia,	34	James H. Stout,	Paradise.
290	Fairmount,	28	G. S. Stafford,	Fairmount.
291	Edina,	47	Benj. Bowen,	Edina.
292	Lamar,	49	G. F. Burkhardt,	Lamar,
293	Sarcoxie,	36	David T. Dodson,	Sarcoxie.
294	Mound City,	33	John Serantz,	Mound City.
295	Moniteau,	36	Lewis Reed,	Jamestown.

No.	Name of Lodge.	Members.	Name of Sec'y.	Post Office.
296	Grove,	23	A. B. M. Thompson,	Webster Grove..
297	Ozark,	38	John Beagle.	Fair Grove......
298	Marble Hill,	24	John M. Roberts,	Marble Hill.....
299	Temple,	40	D. A. M. Grover,	Kansas City.....
300	Doric..	40	Aug. Hoeting,	Faulkner's Hill..
301	White Hall,	46	C. M. Myers,	Barnard.........
302	Lick Creek,	20	T. F. Gill,	Perry..........
303	Osage,	87	Robert McNeil,	Nevada City.....
304	Faithful,	25	James D. Dennis,	Little Black.....
305	Clarence,	47	Jacob E. Mann,	Clarence........
306	Ashlar,	24	J. L. Bowman,	Commerce......
307	New London,	27	Geo. E. Mayhall,..	New London. ....
308	Parrott,	44	Isaac Wilson,	Maysville. ......
309	King Hiram,	45	D. D. Gant..	Knoxville.......
310	Sikeston,	18	Henry A. Smith,	Sikeston ....
311	Kearney..	27	G. H. Plitt.	Kearney ....
312	Mt. Pleasant,	45	Geo. T. Kenyon,	Mt. Pleasant ....
313	Kingsville,	31	Wm P. Hunt,	Kingsville ......
314	St. Aubert,	21	E. W. Hopkins,	St. Aubert ......
315	Altona,	23	Oscar Reeder,	Altona ....
316	Rural,	13	J. E. Jackson.	Kansas City. ....
317	Osborn,	22	Freeman Patten,	Osborn. ....
318	El Dorado,	23	J. F. Murphy,	Luray ....
319	Paulville,	23	Chas. Patterson,	Paulville ....
320	Chapel Hill,	19	John W. Bledsoe,	Chapel Hill. ....
321	Jonathan,	35	C. R. Dawson,	Grant's Hill.....
322	Hardin,	19	S. K. Crispin,	Hardin ....
323	Corner Stone,	31	J. Furth.	St. Louis........
324	McDonald,	54	J. C. Randall,	Independence ...
325	Dockery,	17	J. M. Thompson,	Bottsville.......
326	Kit Carson,	21	Geo. P. Hayslip,	Elizabethtown...
327	Mount Zion,	33	Thos. A. Collins,	West Plains. ....
328	Cainsville,	32	A. B. Montgomery,	Cainsville.......
329	Kennedy,	28	J. W. Lamar,	Lamar Station...
330	Lathrop,	34	B. J. Burk,	Lathrop ....
331	Charity,	—		St. Joseph ......
332	Clark City,	—		Clark City ......
333	Chillicothe.	69	J. R. Middleton,	Chillicothe......
334	Breckenridge,	31	N. L. Trosper,	Breckenridge....
336	Oak Grove,	37	A. L. Jacobs,	Oak Grove......
338	Myrtle,	32	A. A. M'Cuistian,	Millville........
339	Fidelity,	22	Henry Meads,	Farley..........
340	Amity,	21	C. Ringen,	Smith City ......
341	Relief,	14	M. L. M'Clure,	Springfield......
342	Circle,	30	J. R. Fox,	Roscoe. ....
343	Agricola,	36	A. R. Chitwood,	Norris Fork. ...

No.	Name of Lodge.	Members.	Name of Sec'y.	Post Office.
344	Moberly....	...45	...Chester Adams,.....	Moberly ....
345	Fellowship,.....	13	...Jas. A. Bolen, ...	Fidelity. ......
346	Arlington,......	12	...Rob. M. Tuttle,.....	Arlington ......
347	Landmark.	20	...Elias Small,........	Kennett.........
348	Ash Grove,.....	21	...J. F. G. Bentley, ...	Ash Grove......
349	Lone Star,......	—	...Edward Baldwin, ..	Mount Vernon...
350	Tyrian, ...	—	...G. M. Vandyke,.....	Johnstown......
351	Mosaic, ...	22	...E. H. Mathews.	Belleview.......
352	Friend.	31	...John W. Walker, ...	Ozark, ...
353	Ben Franklin, ..	29	...James Brackenridge,	Savannah. ......
354	Hebron.........	17	...Jos. E Moore,......	Mexico. ....
355	Adelphi, ...	12	...B. Mitchell,........	Union Mills. ....
357	Phelps, ...	17	...L. H. Ruland,......	Phelps City. .....
358	Comfort.	25	....	Rocky Comfort...
359	Garrett,........	25	...John L. Thurman,...	White Hare.....
360	Tuscan, ...	63	...John F. Randall,....	St. Louis........
362	Hiram..........	9	...Benj. H. Ballard,....	Kahoka.........
363	Fraternal......	13	...John W. Peinplin,..	Catawissa.......
364	King David, ...	18	...Joseph W. Churns, ..	Kansas City.....
365	Warsaw.	30	...Peter S. Hay.......	Warsaw. ......
366	Unanimity, ...	25	...James L. M'Cluer, ..	Weston.........
367	Barry,..........	24	...Winter Frost.......	Washburn.......
370	Williamstown, ..	19	...Manson Bowen, ..	Williamstown. ..
371	Craig...........	27	...Wm. H. Davis,......	Craig ....
UD	Medoc,.........	15	....	Medoc..........
UD	Mitchell, ...	24	....	Columbus.......
UD	Malta, ...	14	....	Malta Bend. ....
UD	Crescent Hill, ...		....	Crescent Hill....
UD	Composite, ...	15	....	Doniphan. ......
UD	Louisville,.....	11	....	Louisville.......
UD	Mandeville, ...	15	....	Mandeville......
UD	West Point,.....		....	West Point. ....
UD	Plumb,..........		....	Middletown.....
UD	Ancient Craft,..		....	King City.......
UD	Kilwinning,.....		....	Uniontown......
UD	Coatesville,......	7	...John F. James,...	.Coatesville......
UD	Queen City, ...	16	...Geo. W. Wilson, ..	.Queen City.....
UD	Richland,.......		....	Richland. ......
UD	Ancient Landmark,......		....	Landmark.......
UD	Harmony, ...	23	...J. L. Metcalf,......	Vibbard........
UD	Alexander, ...		....	Bedford ....
UD	Dayton.		....	Dayton.........
UD	Woodside,......	14	...J. R. Woodside, ...	Thomasville.....
UD	Border.		....	Elk Mills. ......
UD	Arcana. ..		....	Winterville. ....
UD	Marionville, ...	12	...Elijah Clark,......	Marionville.....

Mississippi.

The Grand Lodge in this State was informally organized by the representatives of three lodges in the State on the 27th July, 1818. Those lodges held charters respectively from the grand lodges of Kentucky and Tennessee. On the 25th of the following August a second convention was held, when this grand lodge was regularly organized, Henry Tooley being elected the first grand master. The annual communications are held in January at such place as may at the previous session be selected. That for 1871 was held at Vicksburg. when it appeared that there were 278 lodges with a total membership of 11.254 Master Masons. This grand lodge pays mileage and per diem to its members, among which Past Masters are recognized. The revenue reported in January, 1871, was suf-sufficient to pay $8,200 mileage, &c., and, after paying other allowances, the G. T. reported $56.75 on hand, with $162.28 due him for his commissions account. Since 1860 the lodges have decreased in this State 50 in number, while in membership those remaining have increased about ten per cent. The jurisdiction is divided into ten districts, with a District D. G. M. who is appointed by the G. M. elect, in charge of each. In April, 1871, this grand lodge was incorporated by the State legislature.

The executive grand officers nearly all re-elected in 1871 were—

GEORGE R. FEARN, of Canton, Grand Master.
E. T. HENRY, of Vicksburg, Deputy Gr. Master.
GEO. H. GRAY, Sr., of Clinton, Grand Treasurer.
J. L. POWER, of Jackson, Grand Secretary.

The following information we collect from the Proceedings of G. L. for 1871, with such changes made therein as the later data supplied by Breth'n lodge secretaries enabled us to make.

No.	Name of Lodge.	Members.	Name of Sec'y.	Post Office.
..1..	Harmony,	......56...	W. H. Stewart,......	Natchez ......:
..2..	And'w Jackson,	46...	C. C. Nauck, ...	do............
..3..	Washington,....	43...	Julian L. Foote, ...	Port Gibson.....
..5..	Columbus, ...	.74...	Jos. H. Stevens,.....	Columbus.......

No.	Name of Lodge.	Members.	Name of Sec'y.	Post Office.
.16.	.Clinton.	29	.Geo. H. Gray, sr.	.Clinton.
.17.	.P. B. Tutt.	55	.R. M. Middleton,	.Benton
.19.	.Leaf River,	26	.W. S. Granberry,	.Monroe.
.21.	.Raymond,	39	.B. S. Davis,	.Raymond.
.23.	.Pearl.	57	.C. Johnson.	.Jackson
.24.	.Lexington,	57	.Joseph Marlow,	.Lexington
.25.	.Gallatin,	42	.James L. Ard,	.Gallatin.
.26.	.Vicksburg,.	.78	.C. E. Thomas.	.Vicksburg
.28.	.Canton,	71	.Leon Bailey,	.Canton.
.29.	.Coleman,	46	.Sam. R. Collier,	.Brandon.
.31.	.Grenada,	63	.S. S. Angevine,	.Grenada.
.32.	.Aberdeen,	62	.Myer Gattman,	.Aberdeen.
.33.	.Oxford,	56	.G. W. Smith,	.Oxford.
.34.	.Olive Branch,	.58	.A. Manguin,	.Williamsburg.
.35.	.Holly Springs,	.93	.Henry C. Corey,	.Holly Springs.
.36.	.Carrollton,	70	.Benj. Roach,	.Carrollton.
.37.	.Liberty,	74	.Chas. E. Davis,	.Liberty.
.40.	.Macon,	69	.B. F. Howell,	.Macon.
.42.	.Yazoo.	69	.W. C. Williams,	.Yazoo City
.43.	.Shady Grove,	.81	.J. F. Alford,	.Crystal Springs.
.45.	.Salem,	24	.G. N. Dickerson,	.Salem
.47.	.Ripley,	56	.W. W. Robinson,	.Ripley
.48.	.Pythagorean,	48	.J. J. Campbell,	.Winona.
.49.	.Greensboro,	.39	.R. Nolen,	.Greensboro.
.51.	.Hernando,	61	.J. T. Moseley,	.Hernando.
.53.	.Lafayette,	23	.C. R. Bailey,	.Quitman.
.54.	.Sterling,	37	.W. M. Brame,	.Paulding
.55.	.Chulahoma,	.77	.J. H. Alexander,	.Chulahoma.
.56.	.Mississippi,	.45	.F. B. Harwood,	.Rodney.
.57.	.Harrison,	.37	.J. M. Williams,	.Garlandsville
.58.	.Thos. Hinds,	.53	.B. B. Paddock,	.Fayette.
.59.	.Tappan,	54	.J. B. Robertson,	.Goodman.
.61.	.Eureka,	52	.C. M. Ashley,	.Goodman.
.63.	.Asylum,	90	.H. W. Keller.	.Woodville.
.64.	.DeKalb,	51	.H. J. Gully.	.DeKalb.
.65.	.Silas Brown,	56	.Wm. J. Brown, jr.	.Jackson..
.66.	.Panola,	57	.L. J. Ballard,	.Panola
.67.	.Houston,	.38	.A. F. Hiller,	.Houston.
.68.	.Vanetta,	43	.R. Fraker,	.Raleigh.
.70.	.Evening Star,	.36	.J. B. Lewis,	.Sinai Church.
.71.	.Joseph Warren,	.63	.J. A. Hearne,	.New Albany.
.72.	.Wilson,	52	.A. G. Levy,	.Enterprise.
.73.	.Madison,	21	.J. J. Robertson,	.Vernon.
.74.	.Camden,	38	.J. C. Russell,	.Camden.
.75.	.Louisville,	56	.D. N. Oakley,	.Louisville.
.76.	.Ebenezer,	53	.T. L. Yancey,	.Senatobia.

No.	Name of Lodge.	Members.	Name of Sec'y.	Post Office.
.77.	. Evergreen,	. . . . . 26.	. . H. Cooper,	. . . . Decatur. . . . .
.79.	. Eastern Star,	. . . 35.	. . Wm. Vannerson,	. . . . Monticello. . . . . .
.80.	. Scott,	 29	. . W. M. Chambers,	. . . Hillsboro. . . . . . .
.81.	. Pontotoc,	. . . . . . 56.	. . J. J. Slack,	. . . . Pontotoc. . . . .
.82.	. Oakland,	. . . . 44.	. . James Moore,	. . . . . . Oakland. . . . .
.83.	. Coffeeville,	. . . . . 46.	. . F. P. Tempel,	. . . . . . Coffeeville. . . . . .
.84.	. De Witt Clinton,	57.	. . J. L. Cain,	. . . . Vaiden. . . . .
.85.	. Pikeville,	. . . . . . 25.	. . Sam. J. Cox.	. . . . Buena Vista. . . . .
.86.	. Mount Moriah,	. 49.	. . J. M. Johnson,	. . . . . . Black Hawk. . . .
.87.	. Prairie,	. . . . 53.	. . Geo. M. Scott,	. . . . . . Okalona. . . . . . .
.88.	. Trinity,	. . . . 60.	. . James M. Lewis,	. . . . Kosciusko. . . . . . .
.89.	. Abert,	. . . . 57.	. . John A. Jacobs,	. . . Starkville. . . . . . .
.90.	. Spring Port,	. . . 53.	. . J. T. Harmon,	. . . . . . Springport. . . . . .
.91.	. United Friends,	. 32.	. . Thos H. Johns,	. . . . . Leoto. . . . .
.92.	. Willis,	. . . . 38.	. . S. S. Henson,	. . . . . . Polkville. . . . . . .
.93.	. Philadelphia,	. . . —.	. . J. C. Wilson,	. . . . Philadelphia. . . .
.94.	. Iuka,	. . . . 65.	. . S. N. Dewoody,	. . . . Iuka. . . . .
.95.	. Emory,	. . . . 29.	. . Henry Gilliam.	. . . . . Emory. . . . .
.97.	. Richmond,	. . . . . 45.	. . Jo. P. Morgan,	. . . . Richmond. . . . . . .
.98.	. Utica,	. . . . 46.	. . C. J. Broom,	. . . . Utica. . . . .
.99.	. No. Mt. Pleasant,	21.	. . F. M. Davis,	. . . . No. Mt. Pleasant.
100.	. De Soto,	. . . . 57.	. . J. W. Lyde,	. . . . Cockrum. . . . . . .
101.	. Malone,	. . . . 22.	. . C. C. Stout,	. . . . Palo Alto. . . . . .
102.	. Wayne,	. . . . 39.	. . W. H. Patton,	. . . . . . Shubuta . . . . . .
103.	. Sharon	. . . . 24.	. . J. T. Hicks.	. . . . Sharon. . . . .
104.	. Coahoma,	. . . . . . 33.	. . Geo. R. Alcorn,	. . . . Friar's Point. . . .
105.	. Pearl River,	. . . 30.	. . O. H. P. Davis,	. . . . Carthage. . . . . . .
106.	. Union,	. . . . 33.	. . W. J. Bass,	. . . . Mt. Carmel, ...
107.	. Bethel,	. . . . 37.	. . W. F. Skinner,	. . . . . . Kosciusko. . . . . .
108.	. Baldwyn,	. . . . . . 74.	. . Jno. E. Williams,	. . . Baldwyn. . . . .
110.	. Claiborne,	. . . . . . 22.	. . Geo. W. Allen,	. . . . Rocky Spring . . .
111.	. Moses Cook,	. . . 41.	. . S. Gause,	. . . . Gainesville. . . . . .
112.	. Bovina,	. . . . 55.	. . W. Bell,	. . . . Bovina. . . . .
113.	. Hyland,	. . . . 38.	. . J. D. Laughlin,	. . . . . . Warrenton. . . . . .
114.	. Lowndes,	. . . . . . 54.	. . C. Lee Lincoln,	. . . . Columbus. . . . . . .
115.	. Byhalia,	. . . . 52.	. . D. C. C. Rodgers,	. . . Byhalia. . . . .
116.	. Corinth,	. . . . 97.	. . C. F. Sawyers,	. . . . . . Corinth. . . . .
117.	. Unity,	. . . . 27.	. . W. D. Smith,	. . . . Edward's Depot.
118.	. Camargo,	. . . . . . 33.	. . W. Mullins,	. . . . Shannon. . . . .
120.	. Biloxi,	. . . . 37.	. . Lyman B. Holly,	. . Biloxi. . . . .
121.	. Vicksburg,	 84	. . W. M. Chamberlin,	. . Vicksburg. . . . . .
124.	. Thomastown,	. . . 28.	. . John T. Donald,	. . . . Thomastown . . . .
125.	. Center Hill,	. . . . 49.	. . A. G. Perry,	. . . . Olive Branch. . . .
126.	. Solomon,	. . . . . . 52.	. . J. T. Harry,	. . . . Independence. . .
127.	. Friendship,	. . . . 28.	. . W. G. Boardman,	. . . Como. . . . .
129.	. Patton,	. . . . 34.	. . R. M'Kinley,	. . . . Lauderdale Sta'n

No.	Name of Lodge.	Members.	Name of Sec'y.	Post Office.
130	Toomsuba,	44	J. G. Knox,	Toomsuba.
131	Fulton,	50	N. Davis,	Fulton.
132	Water Valley,	129	J. O. Hendricks,	Water Valley
133	Summerville,	38	John E. Burrage,	Summerville.
134	Lodi,	31	Wm. H. Allen,	Lodi.
135	Greenwood,	31	Wm. A. Gillespie,	Greenwood.
136	Charles Scott,	42	A. B. Guynes,	Crystal Springs.
137	Falconer,	29	Daniel M'Call,	Shubuta.
138	Mellen,	51	T. Jeff. Reynolds,	Chunkey Station.
139	Castilian,	56	J. R. Hefflin,	Durant.
140	Benela,	34	W. B. Enochs,	Benela.
141	Waterford,	39	John Hogg.	Waterford.
144	Dabney Lipscomb,	38	R. M. Smith,	Crawfordsville
145	Looxahoma,	25	J. R. Puryear,	Looxahoma.
146	Jefferson,	38	A. M. Moore,	Scooba.
148	Lamar,	26	Robt. A. Baird,	Early Grove.
149	Orizaba,	72	R. I. Hill	Orizaba.
150	Center Ridge,	41	J. S. Ross,	Lauderdale.
151	Daleville,	34	J. M. Keeton,	Daleville
152	Palmetto,	33	N. A. Lankford,	Verona.
153	Pine Bluff,	25	S. G. Jenkins,	Pine Bluff.
154	Polar Star,	44	H. F. Folwell,	Handsboro.
155	Pittsboro,	29	J. S Ryan,	Pittsboro
156	R. E. Lee,	37	N. A. Hood,	Chesterville.
157	G. Washington,	59	R. Riddick,	Charleston.
158	Jeremiah,	47	J. W. Rutland,	Horn Lake.
159	Cannon,	73	B. T. Palmer,	West Point.
162	St. John,	21	J. E. Hogg,	Byron.
163	Vinton,	19	T. C. Cogdell,	Vinton.
164	Carson,	26	H. J. Casey,	Snow Creek.
165	Smithville,	44	A Thompson,	Smithville.
166	Auburn,	29	R. L. Lowry,	Auburn.
167	Bay Springs,	50	R. J. Moore,	Bay Springs.
168	Homestead,	27	Reuben Warren,	Deasonville.
169	Tallebonela,	49	D. W. Fowler,	Tallebonela.
170	Benj. Franklin,	38	C. R. Webb,	Meadville.
171	Good Hope,	32	F. M. Stubbs,	Good Hope
172	Rienzi,	54	B. F. Williams,	Rienzi.
173	Bahala,	55	T. C. Collins,	Beauregard
174	Adelphian,	38	S. N. Berryhill,	Bellefontaine.
175	Howry,	75	J. R. Sparkman,	Cooksville
176	Satartia,	56	Dent H. Miles,	Satartia.
177	Rob. Burns,	46	Willis Barfield,	Winona.
178	Speight,	36	J. H. Montgomery,	Cotton Gin Port.
179	Tuscumbia,	49	Wm. F. Wallace,	Tuscumbia.
180	Chapel,	50	C. G. Harris,	Well's.

No.	Name of Lodge.	Members.	Name of Sec'y.	Post Office.
181	Concord	88	Isaac G. Clark	Union Church
182	Theodosia	47	E. C. Hunter	Sarepta
184	Eldorado	52	T. J. Douglas	Hohenlinden
185	Rocky Ford	71	J. Baker	Rocky Ford
186	Meridian	38	H. C. Fallon	Meridian
188	Marietta	35	E. H. Tyra	Marietta
189	Long Creek	52	B. F. Crowell	Eureka
190	Center	48	W. J. Lowe	Kosciusko
191	White Plains	46	A. G. Ames	Damascus
193	South Union	26	W. T. Youngblood	Homewood
194	Walnut Hills	54	R. E. Charles	Vicksburg
195	Laurel Hill	51	Sam. Houston	Laurel Hill
196	Bluff Springs	45	F. M. Glass	Durant
197	Dover	25	W. H. Collins	Dover
198	Oak Bowery	41	R. L. Donald	Claiborne
199	Enon	47	W. W. Carter	Augusta
201	Yockena	36	Jas. E. Cooper	Panola
202	Pascagoula	36	Moses Graff	Moss Point
203	Fair River	26	Z. J. Summers	Brookhaven
204	Big Creek	54	Peter Quinn	Whitefield
205	Webster	64	P. G. McMakin	Webster
206	Greenville	21	L. Meyer	Greenville
209	D. Mitchell	33	J. L. Power	French Camp
210	Bolivar	35	A. D. Leech	Beulah
211	Vienna	25	E. W. Carr	Forest
213	Huntsville	17	W. L. D. White	Huntsville
214	Sincerity	29	Jonas Hiller	Magnolia
215	Rising Glory	33	Moses Herman	Osyka
217	W. P. Mellen	30	D. W. Denson	Goshen Springs
218	Mooresville	31	G. M. Phillips	Mooresville
219	Canaan	30	W. D. Hicks	Saulsbury
220	Sparta	48	J. A. Wilkinson	Sparta
222	S. B. Stampley	33	G. C. Armstrong	Fayette
223	Sunflower	40	L. L. Casey	McNutt
224	New Hope	38	J. W. Holland	Spring Valley
226	Sylvarena	15	B. Y. Statham	Raleigh
227	Chapel Hill	39	T. L. Beadles	Big Creek
228	Campbellton	42	T. C. Kelly	Guntown
229	Western Star	40	Robt. W. Boydston	Water Valley
230	Cato	60	F. M. Martin	Cato
231	Summit	39	W. T. Tyler	Summit
232	Pattona	24	A. K. Jones	Port Gibson
233	Burnsville	36	Louis Hilman	Burnsville
234	Chickasahay	34	John E. Johnson	De Soto
235	Wm. R. Lackey	59	J. E. Harman	Goodman
236	Mount Moriah	21	D. R. Longins	Silver Creek

No.	Name of Lodge.	Members.	Name of Sec'y.	Post Office.
237	Pleasant Hill,	34	W. N. Nabers,	Yockny
238	G. M Hillyer,	28	D. T. Guyton,	West Station
239	C. T Bond.	30	M. Ayers,	Hickory Flat
240	Pass Christian.	33	Thos. Bond. jr.,	Pass Christian.
241	Brookhaven.	83	J. H Stewart,	Brookhaven
242	Walnut Grove,	31	David Henderson,	Walnut Grove.
244	Jno. A. Quitman,	23	P. L. Marsalis,	Smithdale
245	Hazlehurst,	60	J. C. Pitts,	Hazelhurst.
246	Acacia,	32	A. J. Cassity,	Terry
248	Eulogy,	26	A. H. Harding,	Lexington
249	Waynesboro,	50	W. S. Davis,	Waynesboro
250	Jonesborough,	43	W. R. Walker,	Jonesborough.
251	Double Springs,	32	J. L. Sherman,	Double Springs.
253	New Ireland,	47	W. A. Germany,	Union
254	Morton,	55	James D. Jones,	Morton.
257	Tunica,	29	T. W. L. Askew,	Austin
259	John S. Cain,	39	T. J. Crawford,	Red Land
260	Bogue Chitto,	30	James Hall,	Bogue Chitto
260	Brooks,	25	A. S. Lyde.	Choctaw Agency.
261	Oktibbeha,	20	B. E. Petty,	Tampico
263	Verona,	39	W. M. Burdene,	Verona.
264	Mt. Olive,	33	Alex. Fairly,	Jaynesville.
268	Longstreet,	32	J. McLemore,	Meridian
274	Lafayette Spr's,	47	Thos. Wood,	Lafayette Springs
276	B. F. Comfort,	28	J. West Cathon,	Pelahatchie
277	Winstonville,	22	Geo. E Hayne,	Fearn Springs
278	Cadaretta,	30	C. K. Holland,	Cadaretta
280	Caledonia,	32	Jas. E. Carter.	Caledonia
282	Mace's Creek,	21	H. B. Baddon,	Holmersville.
283	S. C. Conly,	28	W. A. Coleman,	Prospect.
284	Cornersville,	43	E. J. Marett,	Cornersville.
285	Stonewall,	26	H. J. Hanks,	Picken's Station.
286	Shufordville.	19	C. J. Bobo,	Friar's Point
287	Arkabutla,	39	W. W. Haley,	Arkabutla
288	China Grove,	36	B. J. Stewart,	Lake Station
289	Graysport.	34	J. R. Williams,	Graysport.
290	Tippah,	24	J. J. Hicks,	Hickory Flat.
291	Slate Springs.	37	J. J. Fox.	Cadaretta.
292	Crook's Hill,	21	H. B. Ormand,	Brandon.
293	Oak Grove,	38	J. T. Bailey,	Oak Grove
294	Saltillo,	56	Walker Lynn,	Saltillo
295	Slaughter,	29	S. S. Field,	Shuqualak
297	Henderson Ray,	42	M. H. Tharpe,	Post Oak
298	Lake,	30	W. Lee Wilkins,	Lake
300	T. N. Martin.	43	J. W. Winter,	Cherry Hill
301	Scott Thompson.	36	J. W. Faires,	Brooksville

142 GENERAL MASONIC REGISTER.

No.	Name of Lodge.	Members.	Name of Sec'y.	Post Office.
302	Currie,	26	J. M. Swiggart.	Trenton
303	Dixon,	19	W. F. Kirkland,	Dixon
304	Fairfield,	20	J. P. Robinson,	Ellistown
305	Booneville,	51	John R. Moore,	Booneville
307	Sardis,	39	Jas. N. Waddey,	Sardis
308	Lauderdale.	31	J. R. Smith,	Meridian
309	Breckenridge,	23	H. C. Smith.	Erata
310	Tokopola.	28	B. D. Ferrill.	Tocopola
311	Bunker Hill,	19	T. J. H. Sullivan,	Bunker Hill
312	Belmont,	11	Charter surrendered,	Winona
313	Pinckney Mills,	20	J. Watts.	Decatur
314	Homochitto,	43	L. B. McLaurin,	Caseyville.
315	Lambert,	22	J. H. Worley,	Saulsbury
316	State Line,	25	Joseph Grisham,	Line
317	J. M. Wesson,	21	Jas. M. Wesson, jr.	Wesson
318	Tupelo,	23	J. M. Williams,	Tupelo.
319	Dallas,	35	Charles Powell,	Tocopola.
320	Abbeville.	28	A. A. Houston,	Abbeville
321	Dry Grove,	25	A. Parsons.	Dry Grove
322	Center Star.	36	W. H. Leigh.	Guntown
323	Golden Grove,	17	J. H. Fiske,	Union
324	B Springer,	24	J. Adler.	Vicksburg.
325	Stonewall.	15	J. R. Morris,	Westville.
326	Bolton.	30	S. O. Smith.	Bolton.
327	Duck Hill,	27	Jos. R. Binford,	Duck Hill
328	McDonald,	20	S. D. Bookout,	Ashland
329	Banner,	26	M. W. Folkes,	Banner.
330	Woodlawn,	24	A. P. Pressly,	Columbus.
331	Perkinsville,	13	D. M. Perkins,	Buck Horn
332	Stonewall Jackson.	24	B. T. Hurt..	Long Creek.
333	King Solomon,	23	G. H. Lesser,	Meridian
334	J. A. Galbreath,	15	S. S. Starnes,	Brandywine Spr.
335	Greenleaf,	14	J. W. Sanders,	Pleasant Church.
336	W. S. Ritnor,	31	J. M. Parker,	Crystal Springs.
337	Green,	15	F. W. Backstrom,	Augusta
338	D. W. Allen.	12	L. C. Underwood,	Cold Water
339	Cherry Creek,	9	N. M. Berry,	Cherry Creek.
340	Tabernacle,	21	W. H. Thornton,	Pine Valley
341	J. T. Lamkin,	17	A. Cothey,	Thyatira.
342	Evansville,	15	T. B. Brigham,	Senatobia.
343	Hickory,	—	J. D. Bolton.	Hickory.
344	Lockhart,	10	W. A. Kelley,	Lockhart
345	Sidon,	10	J. E. Hitsch,	Sidon
346	J. S. Swofford,	16	Wm. P. Smith,	Lafayette Springs

Montana.

The Grand Lodge in this Territory, was organized at Virginia
City on the 24th January 1866, and John J. Hull, was elected the
first grand master. Its annual communications occur in October,
at such place as may at the previous session have been elected.
In 1870 there were in the territory 14 lodges, with a total membership of about 500. This grand lodge recognizes Past Masters as
members and voters, and pays all its officers and members mileage
and per diem. Its revenues are barely sufficient to do so and meet
necessary current expenses, at present ; but time will correct this.

The executive grand.officers elected in 1870 were—

N. P. LANGFORD, of Helena, Grand Master.

J. R. WESTON, of Diamond City, Deputy Gr Master.

HENRY ELLING, of Virginia, Grand Treasurer.

SOL. STAR, of Helena, Grand Secretary.

From the Proceedings of the G. L. for 1870, with omissions courteously supplied by the grand Sec'y, the following information has
been arranged.

No.	Name of Lodge.	Members.	Name of Sec'y.	Post Office.
..1..	Virginia City,	..66...	Thos. Muffly, ...	Virginia City....
..2..	Montana,	......42...	W. I. Marshall, ...	. .do.........
..3..	Helena,	......78...	John Moffitt,........	Helena ....
..4..	Nevada,	......49...	J. W. Van Brocklin,	.Nevada.\.......
..5..	Morning Star,	.. 62...	E. M. Carpenter,....	Helena ....
..6..	Gallatine,	......23...	R. P. Menefee, ...	Bozeman........
..7..	Diamond City,	..47...	Wm. Parr..........	Diamond City...
..8..	Wasatch	........40...	John Cummington, .	.Salt Lake. U. T..
..9..	King Solomon's.	48...	Ph. Kœnigsberger, .	.Helena.........
.10.	Summit	........19...	Chas. St. Clair, .,..	.Summit City....
.11.	Flint Creek.	.... 28..	....	......Phillipsburg ....
.12.	Red Mountain,	..25...	J. W. Beck, ...	Red Mt City....
.13.	Missoula,	......14...	J. W. Menesinger,..	.Missoula Mills...
.14.	Deer,	..........—.	.W. B. Dance, W. M.	.Deer Lodge City.

Nebraska.

The Grand Lodge in this State was organized at Omaha City, on the 14th of September, 1857, by the representatives of three lodges in the State, the third of which had been chartered but in the previous month of June, and each of which had been chartered by a different grand lodge. R. C. Jordan was chosen as the first grand master. Its annual communications occur in June, at such place as may at the previous session be elected. An annual tax of fifty cents per capita is levied upon the membership at large to create an "Orphan's Educational Fund." In 1870 this fund amounted to $2.634.21, and placed by its Trustees at 12 per cent. interest. The annual revenue of this grand lodge is sufficient to meet current expenses, and also to pay mileage and per diem to its officers and members, the amount of the latter, in 1870, being $377.20. In that year there were in the jurisdiction 31 lodges, with a total membership of 1379. The business of this grand lodge, as is apparent from the well-arranged and printed Proceedings for 1870, is by the present grand officers conducted in the best manner, and at a moderate charge for current expenses. As an efficient officer the present grand secretary is duly recognized from the fact that, after serving four years in that office, he was elected successively D. G. M. and G. M., to which latter office he was re-elected in 1866, and, in 1869, again re-elected to the office of Gr. Sec'y.

The executive grand officers, all re-elected in 1870, were—

H. P. Deuel, of Omaha City, Grand Master.
W. E. Hill, of Nebraska City, Deputy Gr. Master.
Geo. B. Graff, of Omaha City, Grand Treasurer.
R. W. Furnas, of Brownsville, Grand Secretary.

The following information we collect from the Proceedings of G. L. for 1870, with such changes made therein as the later data supplied by Breth'n lodge secretaries enabled us to make.

No.	Name of Lodge.	Members.	Name of Sec'y.	Post Office.
..1..	Nebraska,	45	Wm. Robinson,	Belleview
..2..	Western Star,	129	Albert Tuxbury,	Nebraska City
..3..	Capitol,	156	W. R. Bowen,	Omaha
..4..	Nemaha Valley,	78	S. French,	Brownville
..5..	Omadi,	49	J. P. Bayha,	Dakotah City
..6..	Plattsmouth,	45	P. E. Ruffner,	Plattsmouth
..7..	Decatur,	30	Alfred Schroter,	Decatur
..8..	Falls City,	44	H. O. Hanna,	Falls City.
.10..	Solomon,	29	E. H. Clark,	Fort Calhoun
.11..	Covert.	114	G. M. Bartlett,	Omaha
.12..	Nebraska City,	50	E. R. Richardson,	Nebraska City
.13..	Orient,	16	D. Randolph,	Rulo
.14..	Peru,	35	D. C. Cole,	Peru
.15..	Fremont,	55	J. M. Davis,	Fremont
.16..	Eureka,	17	F. W. Burchardt,	Arago
.17..	Tecumseh,	32	Alex. Bivens,	Tecumseh
.18..	Ashland,	35	C. N. Folsom,	Ashland
.19	Lincoln,	18	C. H. Gere.	Lincoln
.20..	Rock Bluffs,	24	J. D. Patterson,	Rock Bluffs
.21..	Washington,	39	V. G. Lantry,	Blair
.22..	Macoy,	14	G. L. Seybolt,	Plattsmouth.
.23..	Pawnee,	21	R. A. Kennedy,	Pawnee City.
.24..	Lafayette,	12	Lewis Dunn,	Grant
.25..	St. John's,	45	J. Bultmann.	Omaha
.26..	Beatrice,	16	H. M. Reynolds,	Beatrice
.27..	Jordan,	15	John E. Douglas,	West Point
.28..	Wyoming,	14	F. Gilman,	South Pass City.
.29..	Hope.	21	H. W. Shubert,	Hillsdale.
.30..	Blue River,	25	Geo. B. France,	Milford.
.31..	Tekama.	16	A. T. Conklin,	Tekama
.32..	Platte Valley,	30	Henry Bricken,	Cottonwood Sp's

New Hampshire.

The Grand Lodge in this State was organized at Dartmouth, on the 8th of July, 1789, by delegates from *all* the lodges in the State at that time, and consequently this must be regarded as the first independent grand lodge that was thus regularly constituted in all North America. Hon. John Sullivan, then President of the State of N. H., (before the title " Governor ") was the first grand master. This grand lodge has annual and semi-annual communications, the first occuring on the 18th and 19th of May, and the last on the 28th of December. In 1870 there were 71 lodges in the jurisdiction, and a total membership of 6,612 Master Masons. This grand lodge derives its revenue but from dispensations, charters, diplomas, and a tax on initiations ; and as the increase of membership is necessarily slow in a State whose population is decreasing, the revenue of this grand lodge is therefore very limited, and barely sufficient to meet current expenses.

The executive grand officers elected in 1870 were—

JOHN R. HOLBROOK, of Portsmouth, Grand Master.
N. M. CUMNER, of Manchester, Deputy Gr. Master.
DANIEL R. BARRET, of Nashua, Grand Treasurer.
ABEL HUTCHINS, of Concord, Grand Secretary.

From the well-printed Proceedings of this grand lodge for 1870 we present the following list of the lodges in this State. Wherein it differs the information has been more recently supplied by the lodge secretaries, in response to our circulars.

No.	Name of Lodge.	Members.	Name of Sec'y.	Post Office.
..1..	St. John's,	309	Geo. P. Edny,	Portsmouth
..6..	Franklin,	193	Geo. E. Durant,	Lebanon
..7..	Benevolent,	75	Wm. P. Parmelee,	Milford.
..8..	North Star,	115	Geo. H. Emerson,	Lancaster.
..9..	Hiram,	—	Albert W. Hawkes,	Claremont
.10..	Mt. Cube,	49	Jesse K. Carr,	Orford.
.11..	Blazing Star,	210	John A. Harris,	Concord
.12..	Faithful,	47	Geo. Olcott,	Charlestown
.14..	King Solomon's,	47	Albert Sanborn,	Wilmot.

No.	Name of Lodge.	Members.	Name of Sec'y.	Post Office.
.15.	.Mt. Vernon,	....—..	.D. P. Quimby,	......Newport. ....
.16.	.Olive Branch,	..81..	.Frank C. Green,	....Plymouth. ....
.17.	.Morning Star,	.102..	.Thomas Rust,	.....Wolfeboro .....
.18.	.Charity,	......61..	.L. S. Jaquith,	......Jaffrey. ....
.19.	.Sullivan,	.......—..	.Wm. L. Plumer,	...Epping ....
.21.	.Humane.	.....152..	.Chas. W. Brown,	....Rochester.......
.22.	.Mt. Moriah,	....28..	.Jas. W. Kilton,	...Grafton. ....
.23.	.Cheshire,	...105..	.Jos. I. Shallies,	.....Cornish. ....
.26.	.Bethel,	.......23..	.Danl. G. Murphy,	...New Ipswich....
.26.	.Altemont,	....117..	.J. H. Steele,	....Peterborough ...
.29.	.Strafford,	....184..	.Amasa Roberts,	....Dover ....
.30.	.St. Paul's.	.....93..	.Jas. A. Dickey,	....Alstead.........
.31.	.St. Peter's.	.....84..	.Danl. M. Perkins,	..Bradford........
.32.	.Mt. Lebanon,	.150..	.Geo. B. Lane,	......Laconia.........
.37.	.Evening Star,	..45..	.W. Wentworth.	.....Colebrook ......
.38.	.Harmony,	....104..	.DeWitt C. Newman,	.Hillsborough....
.39.	.Rising Sun,	...230..	.Jacob D. March,	....Nashua ....
.40.	.Philesian,	.....88..	.S M. Kendrick,	....Winchester......
.41.	.Lafayette,	....264..	.Thos. W. Lane,	.....Manchester .....
.42.	.Social Friend's,	151..	.Daniel K. Healey,	...Keene ....
.43.	.Aurora.	........78..	.Gawn Wilkins,	......Henniker. ......
.44.	.St Mark's,	.....70..	.Lewis S. Morris,	...Derry (East.)....
.45.	.Pacific,	........34..	.L. F. Attwood.	......Francestown ...
.46.	.Grafton.	......94..	.Thos. M. Stevens,	...Haverhill.......
.47.	.Rising Star,	...116..	.Jona. F. Garland,	...Newmarket .....
.49.	.Libanus,	.....181..	.E. A. Crawford,	....Somersworth. ...
.50.	.Social,	.........97..	.W. C. Clough,	...Enfield.........
.52.	.Clinton,	......41..	.Jos. P. Chandler,	....Wilton..........
.53.	.Columbian,	.....55..	.Chas. W. Kendall,	...Walpole........
.56.	.St. Andrews,	..238..	.Fred. E. Willis,	.....Portsmouth. ....
.57.	.Carroll.	......98..	.Charles H. Andrews,	Freedom. ......
.58.	.Charter Oak,	...90..	.Cyrus K. Moore,	....Effingham.......
.59.	.Star in the East,	114..	.Geo. E. Lane.	.......Exeter. ....
.60.	.Meridian,	.....115..	.John P. Jewell,	....Franklin........
.61.	.Washington,	...196..	.Chas. G. Blake,	.....Manchester. ....
.62.	.Unity,	........75..	.B. B. Plummer,	...Wakefield.....
.63.	.Moose Hillook,	..56..	.Sam. G Currier,	....Wentworth......
.64.	.Kane.	.......166..	.M. C. Parker,	......Lisbon. ....
.65.	.Granite,	.......86..	.Chas. D. Allen,	.....Rollinsford......
.66.	.Burns,	........109..	.L. D. Sanborn,	....Littleton........
.67.	.Souhegan,	......34..	.Chas. P. Richardson,	Mason.........
.68.	.Red Mountain,	..60..	.S. B. Wiggin.	.......Sandwich......
.69.	.Mt. Prospect,	..55..	.Geo. B. Stevens,	....Ashland........
.70.	.Eureka,	........86..	.Edgar H. Woodman,	.Concord........
.71.	.Fraternal,	.....153..	.Josiah B. Edgerly,	...Farmington.....
.72.	.Horace Chase,	.86..	.Loren M. Currier,	...Fisherville.....

No.	Name of Lodge.	Members.	Name of Sec'y.	Post Office.
.73	Gorham.	90	John E. Willis,	Gorham
.74	Ossipee Valley,	48	F. II. Lord	Ossipee
.75	Winnipisaukee,	81	Chas. Hayes.	Alton
.76	Rockingham,	106	John H. Nutting,	Candia.
.77	Golden Rule,	67	N. E. Pratt,	Hinsdale
.78	Doric,	68	Geó. W. Balcom,	Tilton.
.79	Union	74	Chas. B. Dow	Bristol
.80	Monadnock,	51	Alb. G. Hurlbutt,	Troy.
.81	Kearsarge,	46	N. Woodbury, jr.	Andover
.82	Corinthian,	40	S. G. Blaisdell,	Pittsfield
.83	Chocarua,	36	J. H. Prescott,	Meredith
.84	Gideon,	66	Sam'l E. Woodman,	Kingston
.85	Spickett,	42	Chas. M. Vittum,	Salem
.86	White Mountain.	40	Ira S. M. Gove,	Whitefield
.87	Mount Wash't'n,	35	Hiram H. Dow,	North Conway
.88	Of the Temple,	36	Samuel Nims,	Keene

Nevada.

———

The Grand Lodge of this State was organized on the 12th October, 1865, at Virginia City, being the year in which the State of Nevada was cut off mainly from California, and at which time there were in the former eight lodges, all chartered by the G. L. of the latter State. Its annual communications occur in September, at Virginia City. It pays neither mileage nor per diem to officers or members. Its revenue, equal in 1870 to $2.20 per capita from its total membership, was but sufficient to meet current expenses. In that year there were in the State 14 lodges, with 992 members.

The executive grand officers elected in 1870 were—

GEORGE ROBINSON, of Washoe City, Grand Master.
M. A. SAWTELLE, of Austin, Deputy Grand Master.
SAMUEL W. CHUBBUCK, of Gold Hill, Grand Treasurer.
WM. A. M. VAN BOKKELEN, of Virginia, Grand Secretary.

From the G. L. Proceedings for 1870, printed in San Francisco, we present the following list of lodges in the State.

No.	Name of Lodge.	Members.	Name of Sec'y.	Post Office.
1	Carson,	105	Benjamin Edson,	Carson.
2	Washoe,	39	Chas. N. Harris,	Washoe.
3	Virginia,	141	Chas. H. Fish.	Virginia
4	Amity	61	A. J. Hutchinson,	Silver City
5	Silver Star,	122	S. W. Chubbuck,	Gold Hill.
6	Esmeralda,	24	Chas. E. Baldwin,	Aurora
7	Escurial,	136	Joseph Gruss,	Virginia
8	Lander,	100	D. M. Godwin,	Austin
9	Valley.	34	John C. Hazlett,	Dayton.
10	Austin,	46	Wm A. Cheney.	Austin
11	Oasis,	22	Geo. R. Williams,	Belmont
12	Douglass,	42		Genoa
13	Reno,	68	W. S. Bender.	Reno.
14	White Pine,	52	D. St. Clair Stevens,	Hamilton

New Jersey.

According to the latest history of the matter—that published by the grand secretary in 1870— the Grand Lodge in this State was organized at the town of New Brunswick, on the 18th December, 1786, by an assembly of Master Masons, hailing indifferently from lodges in that and other States. It was a singular affair and unique in the manner of it. Beyond the choice in some way expressed (it does not appear that they were elected by ballot,) of seven grand officers, this "association" at that time proceeded not. Of those officers Hon. David Brearley, then the Chief Justice of New Jersey, was chosen the first grand master. Of what lodge he was a member. if of any in that State or any other, does not appear ; and the same can be remarked of his deputy. On the 30th of the following January those seven officers, being the usual six elect with the addition of a deputy grand secretary, were installed, and thereupon this grand lodge immediately began to exercise the functions of such a body, by chartering lodges, &c. After July, 1789, Hon. D. Brearley, however, no more appears as grand master, although in the subsequent January he was "re-appointed" grand master, and installed by proxy, nor is there any reason assigned for his disappearance. After the July session, in 1790. the endorsement of the new "Rules and Regulations" then adopted shows that there were at this time 8 lodges in the State, numbered from 1 to 8, inclusive, all of which had been originally dispensated and subsequently warranted (chartered) by this grand lodge ; and thus proving that in the State of New Jersey there existed but one lodge on the 18th Dec. 1786. viz. St. John's, (location not given but believed to be the then town of Newark,) of which Moses Ogden, then present, signed himself a member. In his introductory remarks Bro. Hough, it is true, asserts that "Lodge. No. 10" was in 1786 located at Bedminster, and "Lodge, No. 32" at Burlington ; but he subsequently renders the fact clear that both of those lodges had ceased to work for some years previous, that in consequence their warrants had been called in by the G. L. in Pennsylvania, on whose registry they had

[150]

stood, and that they were entirely extinct by 1786. Hence it is evident that those who hailed from either of them at the assembly of Dec. 18, 1786, did so simply as *quondam* officers and members, and in no wise as delegates ; particularly so was this the case with regard to those of " No. 10," for in the latter part of the minutes, written 13th January, 1787, "No. 10, *Pennsylvania*," follows the names of all but one of those who attached their signatures on that occasion, as endorsers of the previous (Dec. 18) movement. It may be added that of those endorsers, sixteen in all, twelve hailed from lodges in Pennsylvania, (including those from "No. 10,") and three respectively from Albany, N. Y., Boston, Mass., and Liverpool, England.

From the year 1790 this grand lodge seems to have been conducted in a carefully circumspect manner. In January, 1791, new officers were chosen, among which, of the original officers, only appear the grand master elect and deputy grand secretary. That the organization was entirely satisfactory is evident, as no subsequent attempt to organize a grand lodge in what is to-day considered the regular manner seems to have been at any time even suggested ; and this is certainly a pungent sarcasm on those hodiernal Masonic jurisconsults, who decide as incorrect and the organization irregular, if not clandestine, any movement not in accord with their dicta having for its object the establishment of a grand lodge of Ancient Free and Accepted Masons.

The annual communications of this grand lodge occur in January, usually at Trenton. In 1871 there were in the jurisdiction 118 lodges with 9,164 members. Unlike other grand lodges, in this the first six elective officers attend to their official duties during the year, and report at the annual session ; consequently, instead of but four, there are six executive grand officers elect, and who for 1871 were—

    Wm. E. Pine, of Cresskill, Grand Master.
    Wm. W. Goodwin, of Camden, Deputy Gr. Master.
    ·Nathan Haines, of Burlington, Senior Gr. Warden.
    James V. Bentley, of Morristown, Junior Gr. Warden.
    Wm. R. Clapp, of Trenton, Grand Treasurer.
    Joseph H. Hough, of Trenton, Grand Secretary.

This grand lodge has nothing invested in real estate. It pays neither mileage nor per diem to officers or members. It appoints a deputy grand secretary, who is paid his expenses only, also a grand lecturer, whose services being continuous he is paid a fair recompense. The revenue is modest, and but sufficient to meet current expenses.

The following information we collect from the Proceedings of G. L. for 1871. with such changes made therein as the later data supplied by the lodge secretaries enabled us to make.

No.	Name of Lodge.	Members.	Name of Sec'y.	Post Office.
1	St. John's,	171	Frank Hodson,	Newark
2	Brearley,	107	John H. Stiles,	Bridgeton
3	Cincinnati,	84	John M. Moore,	Morristown
4	Tuckerton,	50	Edwin A. Bragg,	Tuckerton
5	Trenton,	223	Geo. M. Mitchell,	Trenton
6	Lebanon,	17	R. W. Taylor,	Clarksville
7	Newark,	249	D. J. Camfield,	Newark
8	Clinton,	65	Saml. S. Adamson,	Baskingridge
9	Washington,	79	Arthur Wilson,	Eatontown
10	Franklin,	50	D. Pateman Berry,	Irvington
11	Union,	86	Chas. W. Monroe,	Orange
12	Amwell,	128	Chas. Roberts,	Lambertville
13	Warren,	175	Richard T. Drake,	Belvidere
14	Mt. Holly,	104	Chas. W. Heisler,	Mt. Holly
15	Camden,	180	Jas. M. Cassady,	Camden
16	Olive Branch,	75	Thos. C. Swift,	Freehold
17	Hiram,	260	Jno. A. Shawda,	Jersey City
18	Harmony,	63	J. A. Noble,	Tom's River
19	Union,	148	Robt. W. Helm,	New Brunswick
20	Acacia,	80	Warren Segur,	Dover
21	Mystic Br'hood,	90	John E. Norris,	Red Bank
22	Diogenes,	119	Henry Becker,	Newark
23	Harmony,	183	Hiram C. Clark,	Newton
24	Prospect,	27	Jas. H. Day,	Mendham
25	Northern,	165	Jno. N. Kumerle,	Newark
26	Jerusalem,	82	D. S. Campbell,	Plainfield
27	Lafayette,	76	Danl. G. Urmston,	Rahway
28	Mt. Moriah,	123	Robt. Julian,	Bordentown
29	Joppa,	124	A. T. Secor,	Patterson
30	Cape Island,	81	Geo. H. White,	Cape Island
31	Varick,	191	Wm. P. Ayers,	Jersey City
32	Burlington,	80	Ellwood Conner,	Burlington
33	Washington,	149	Jos. E. Busby.	Elizabeth
34	Stewart,	71	C. H. Bonnell,	Clinton Station
35	Hoboken,	183	John T. Seymour,	Hoboken
36	Mansfield,	99	Jacob C. Wandling,	Washington

No.	Name of Lodge.	Members.	Name of Sec'y.	Post Office.
.37	.Darcy,	78	Geo. Hanson,	Flemington ....
.38	.Princeton	54	Rich. Runyan,	Princeton.......
.39	.Excelsior	203	Chas. B. Thurston,	Newark.........
.40	.Bloomfield,	65	Fred. A. Pressler,	Bloomfield......
.41	.Hightstown	59	Thos. C. Pierce,	Hightstown ....
.42	.Independence.	130	R. S. Price,	Hackettstown ...
.43	.Paterson Orange,	112	Aug. Wiskeman,	Paterson........
.44	.Central	42	Sam. O. Ross,	Vincentown.....
.45	.Benevolent,	120	Alfred N. Horton,	Paterson........
.46	.Solomon's,	86	B. M. Polhemus,	Somerville......
.47	.Bergen,	161	Thos. P. Rockett,	Bergen ....
.48	.Enterprise,	133	Robt. F. Laird,	Jersey City ....
.49	.Essex,	106	Geo. N. Sanborn,	Elizabethport ...
.50	.Mercer,	101	Henry E. Finch.	Trenton ....
.51	.Oriental,	191	Andrew M. Clark,	Newark.........
.52	.Delaware,	125	James E. Moon.	Phillipsburg.....
.53	.Eagle.	148	Theodore Tasheira,	Jersey City......
.54	.Excelsior,	72	Joseph Miller.	Salem..........
.55	.Kane,	109	Sam'l D. Aspinwall,	Newark.........
.56	.Orion.	103	Thos. Palmer.	Frenchtown.....
.57	.Corinthian,	70	John R. Long.	Orange. ....
.58	.Shekinah,	125	Saml. Steinmetz,	Millville........
.59	.Caldwell,	49	Chas. P. Harrison,	Caldwell........
.60	.Arcana,	82	Wm. L. Teush,	Boonton ....
.61	.Raritan,	42	Moses Martin,	Perth Amboy ...
.62	.Fraternité Franç.	29	Charles Pieters,	Newark.........
.63	.St. Stephen's,	55	Jos. H. Murphy,	South Amboy. ..
.64	.Cesaræa,	57	Asbury F. Wallings,	Keyport........
.65	.Star,	53	Chas. R. Rowell,	Tuckahoe. ......
.66	.Schiller,	59	W. J. Bohler,	Newark.........
.67	.Passaic,	61	Leonard L. Grear,	Passaic. ....
.68	.St. Alban's,	132	Geo. G. Trelease,	Newark.........
.69	.Vineland,	91	W. A. E. Tompkins,	Vineland ....
.70	.Pioneer,	61	Wm. H. De Wolfe,	Hackensack.....
.71	.Hudson.	62	Wm. Hartung,	Hoboken ....
.72	.Teutonia,	86	Robert Ehrlich,	Jersey City......
.73	.Wall,	44	Robert Laird,	Squan Village...
.74	.Jersey City,	122	Geo. A. Lacas,	Jersey City ....
.75	.Neptune,	41	Wm. T. Cobb,	Mauricetown. ...
.76	.Ashler,	60	Isaac N. Snider,	Trenton ....
.77	.Alpine,	35	George Driggs,	Closter ....
.78	.Long Branch,	60	Edmond H. Clark,	Long Branch....
.79	.Trinity,	62	Henry Wootton,	Absecom ....
.80	.Highland,	62	Chas. H. Hall,	Hudson City ....
.81	.Herman,	45	Henry Strauss,	Elizabeth ....
.82	.Falls City,	43	Will Hague,	Paterson........

No.	Name of Lodge.	Members.	Name of Sec'y.	Post Office.
.83.	.Americus,	.....25.	..Chas. S. Demarest,	..Woodbridge ....
.84.	.Palisade,	.......50.	..A. F. Vanderlieth,	..Union Hill......
.85.	.Glassboro,	.....48.:.	.Geo. S. Moffett,	.....Glassboro.......
.86.	.Doric,	.........45.	..Henry Morgan.	.....West Hoboken...
.87.	.Florence,	.......34.	..H. B. Vanneman,	....Woodbury ......
.88.	.Ivanhoe,	.......60.	..Vernon Royle,	.....Paterson ......
.89.	.Ocean,	.......·25.	..Geo. B. Bernard,	....Bricksburg......
.90.	.Aberdeen,	.....22.	..Josiah P. Gerau,	....Matawan ....
.91.	.Forest Grove,	..34.	..Jas. A. Pearson,	....Franklinville....
.92.	.Pyramid,	.......44.	..A. J. Allen,	.......New Egypt......
.93.	.Madison,	.......45.	..Wilbur F. Morrow,	..Madison. ....
.94.	.Ionic,	.........:101.	..Thos. G. Rowand,	..Camden ....
.95.	.Mantua,	.........41.	..C. J. Martel,	.......Mantua. ....
.96.	.Unity,	.........24.	..Geo. R. Greene,	.....May's Landing..
.97.	.Evening Star,	....40.	..Jos. S. Miner,	.....Bridgeton. .....
.98.	.Samaritan,	.....42.	..A. Howell,	..........Deckertown. ....
.99.	.Bayonne,	......43.	..Eben. C. Earl.	......Bergen Point....
100.	.Century,	.......20.	..Lewis H. Smith,	....South Orange....
101.	.Cloud,	.........37.	..Thos. Hallam.	......Gloucester City..
102.	.Friendship,	.....17.	..B. A. Bartholf.	.......Pascack ....
103.	.Amity,	.........41.	..A. W. Hatfield,	.....Lafayette ....
104.	.Cannon,	.........55.	..Remington Corson,	..Seaville ....
105.	.Eastern Star,	...33.	..George Creed,	.....Bound Brook....
106.	.Cosmos.	........58.	..Albert Delano,	.....Newark.........
107.	.Beverly.	.......23.	..Jos. R. Praul.	.......Beverly ....
108.	.Belleville,	......24.	..Edwd. P. Snowden,	..Belleville. ......
109.	.Rising Star,	....30.	..James N. Davis,	....Jersey City.....
110.	.Of the Temple,	..22.	..Wm. Muirheid.	..........do.........
111.	.Palestine,	......31.	..James C. Harra.	....New Brunswick..
112.	.Triluminar,	....27.	..Chas. G. Pitcher,	....Newark ....
113.	.Fidelity.	.........7.	..L. H. Kendall,	.....Hohokus. ....
114.	.Humboldt,	.....15.	..John J. Volhaar,	....Paterson........
115.	.Tuscan,	.........10.	..Alex. Cass,	....Englewood......
116.	.Alpha,	.........9.	..Saml. Morrow, jr..	..Newark.........
117.	.Trimble.	.......14.	..J. G. Milligan,	......Camden ....
118.	.Pythagoras,	....11.	..Geo. Nevill,	.......Newark.........

New York.

The Grand Lodge in this State has been organized at various times. As early as 1782 a Provincial Grand Lodge was chartered by that London grand lodge of which Laurence Dermott was grand secretary, which became independent in 1783 by resignation of the original officers and their departure with the British troops when they evacuated New York City ; but for many years this body was not recognized as having jurisdiction over the brethren within the whole State. Subsequently there were extant for some years a " City " grand lodge and a " Country " grand lodge, which, in 1827, united for more effective resistance to the anti-masonic excitement, which at that time had attained considerable force. Until 1836 this united grand lodge was supreme, but, in that year, a body styled " St. John's Grand Lodge " was organized by brethren who considered themselves harshly treated and unduly punished by the G. L. endorsing the action of a " Grand Steward's Lodge ;" and for thirteen years this " St. John's Grand Lodge " performed all the functions of such an organization, and until 1850, when it coalesced with what for one year had then been known as the " Willard," or generally recognized grand lodge, in contradistinction to a third body organized in 1849, and known as the irregular, or " Phillips" grand lodge, and which for nine years performed all the functions of a grand lodge until, in 1858, it amalgamated with the other, on terms satisfactory to both ; and since which time there has been but one grand lodge in the State of New York—the largest Masonic grand lodge jurisdiction at present in North America.

The annual sessions of this grand lodge are held in the City of New York, commencing on the first Tuesday of June. In 1871 there were holding under this grand lodge 656 lodges, with a total membership of 77,079 Master Masons—an average of 102 members to each lodge. Those lodges are divided into 25 districts, with each in charge of a Dist. D. G. M., who is appointed by the grand master elect, and reports annually. The annual revenue received from the lodges by this grand lodge amounts to about $65,000, one-third of which, taxed on initiations, is passed to the credit of the " Hall and Asylum Fund," and subsequent to 1871 this amount will be increased by 25 cents per capita of the total membership in the State, or equal at present to about $20,000 more. To the various " Relief Lodges " in the State this grand lodge pays annually about $6,500, and about $1000 to especially deserving objects of its charity, a few of whom may be regarded as pensioners upon its bounty. The balance of its annual revenue is expended paying mileage and per diem to members, salaries to its officers, and the necessary current expenses. Within the past few years every lesser consideration has been merged in the erection of a grand temple, for which the " Hall and Asylum Fund,"— the accumulation of many years and various combinations — has been appropriated. With $340,000 invested in the land upon which this temple is in course of erection, in the City of New York, and, to May 1871, about $100,000 expended in construction, &c., with the earnest efforts of the Trustees to keep out of debt, the certain completion of this temple is in no wise doubtful. Those Trustees are the first five officers elect of the grand lodge, and hence the re-election of those officers during the construction of the temple becomes necessary, to the end that they be allowed to execute the trust confided to them in manner satisfactory to themselves and the large and wealthy constituency they represent.

These officers, therefore, re-elected in 1871 were—

> JOHN H. ANTHON, of New York City, Grand Master.
> CHRISTOPHER G. FOX, of Buffalo, Deputy Gr Master.
> EDMUND L. JUDSON, of Albany, Senior Gr. Warden.
> JAMES W. HUSTED, of Peekskill, Junior Gr. Warden.
> JOHN W. SIMONS, of N. Y. City, Grand Treasurer.
> JAMES M. AUSTIN, of N. Y. City, Grand Secretary.

For the following information we are indebted to the courtesy of the Gr. Sec'y, who from the lodge Returns for 1871 kindly supplied the names of such secretaries as had refused or failed to reply to our circulars, mailed to each, requesting the favor of such reply, and carefully corrected the whole list, including the membership column, wherever our manuscript was incorrect. Otherwise, the uniformly well-arranged and printed Transactions of G. L. for 1871 has been refered to.

No.	Name of Lodge.	Members.	Name of Sec'y.	Post Office.
..1..	St. John's	180..	Stephen E. Gardner,	New York City..
..2..	Ind. Roy. Arch,	136...	W. D. Everit,	............do.......
..3..	Mount Vernon.	166...	C. Van Allen,	......Albany........
..4..	St. Patrick's.	124	..Jerry Keck.	........Johnstown......
..5..	Master's,	227	..Cornelius Glen,	.....Albany.........
..6..	St. George's,	..276...	Thompson Dealtry,	..Schenectady.....
..7..	Hudson,	186...	W. H. W. Loop,	....Hudson.........
..8..	Holland,	190...	A. W. King,	.... New York City..
..9..	Unity,	69...	Hampton C. Bull,	...New Lebanon Sp.
.10..	Kingston.	325...	H. D. Baldwin,	.....Kingston........
.11..	Of Antiquity,	114...	J. D. Totten.	........New York City ..
.12..	Trinity,	126...	F. J. Miller,	............do........
.13..	Apollo,	342...	C. H. Hitchcock,	....Troy ....
.14..	Temple,	290...	Thos. P. Way,	.....Albany.........
.15..	Western Star.	...65...	W. E. Foote,	........Bridgewater.....
.16..	Pr. of Orange,	...75...	A. S. Gardiner,	......New York City..
.17..	L'Union Franç.	.31...	Edward Allison,	...........do........
.19..	Fortitude,	301...	Jas. P. Eastmead,	...Brooklyn ....
.20..	Abram's.	117...	Aug. Summers,	......New York City...
.21..	Washington,	...125...	R. B. Coppins,	...........do........
.22..	St. John's,	....69...	S. B. Ingham,	.......Greenfield Center
.23..	Adelphi.	186...	M J. Bennett.	......New York City ..
.26..	Albion.	...92...	Jas. A. Harriott,	.........do........
.27..	Mount Moriah,	125...	Maurice De Vries,	........do........
.28..	Benevolent,	...167...	Wm. J. Surre,	.............do........
.30..	Dirigo,	114...	Isaac Harlem,	.............do........
.31..	Mechanic,	......84...	Jas. A. Slavin,	...........do........
.32..	Warren.	104...	Dewitt Van Vliet,	...Schultzville .....
.33..	Ark.	121...	Willard N. Smith,	...Geneva. ....
.35	Howard,	120...	Alfred B. Price,	....New York City..
.39..	Olive Branch,	.209...	W. H. Anderson,	....Le Roy.........
.40..	Olive Branch,	...50...	F. B. Parkhurst,	......Frankfort. ......
.41..	Sylvan,	113...	M. E. Kenyon,	......Moravia ....
.44..	Evening Star,	...75...	C. Cadsgan,	........Hornellsville. ...
.45..	Union,	88...	J. S. Galentine.	.....Lima ....
.47..	Utica.	202...	W. E. Hopkins,	.....Utica............
.48..	Ark.	187,,	Wm. K. Reed,	......Coxsackie ......
.49..	Watertown,	...264...	S. T. Woolworth,	....Watertown......
.50..	Concord,	81...	John McMahon.	.....New York City..
.51..	Fidelity,	181...	Horace H. Eldred,	..Ithaca...........
.53..	Brownville,	...79...	Horace Skinner,	...Brownville.. ..
.54..	German Union,	139...	Hermann Conrad,	...New York City..
.55..	Granville,	66...	John W. Potter,	....Middle Granville.
.57..	Hohenlinden,	..323...	J. W. Osborn,	.......Brooklyn ....
.58..	Phœnix,	......176...	John A. Jones,	......Lansingburg ....
.62..	Manhattan,	363...	Henry V. Myers,	....New York City..

No.	Name of Lodge.	Members.	Name of Sec'y.	Post Office.
.63.	.Morton,	89	.Ebenezer Kellum,	.Hempstead
.64.	.Lafayette,	177	.W. Irving Adams,	.New York City.
.65.	.Morning Star,	.102	.Matthew Hart,	.Canisteo.
.66.	.Richmond,	.124.	.Fred. Groshen,	.Port Richmond.
.67.	.Mariner's,	118	.R. W. Pain,	.New York City.
.68.	.Montgomery,	.63	.Chas. V. Vagler,	.do
.69.	.Naval	181	.J. T. Couenhoven,	.do
.70.	.John Hancock,	159	.John H. Simpson,	.do
.73.	.Lockport.	210	.W. H. M'Cay,	.Lockport
.75.	.Evening Star,	.183.	.E. A. Learned,	.West Troy
.79.	.Hamilton,	103	.Jos. White, M. D.	.Canajoharie.
.82.	.Phœbus,	77	.Warren Reynolds,	.New Berlin
.83.	.Newark,	112	.D. F. Wilcox,	.Newark.
.84.	.Artizan,	166	.D. Deforest. jr.,	.Amsterdam
.85.	.Washington,	111	.Wheeler B. Melins,	.Albany
.86.	.Pythagoras,	77	.J. F. Poggenburg,	.New York City.
.87.	.Schodack Union,	79	.David Becker,	.Schodack Centre.
.90.	.Franklin,	105	.John J. Lee,	.Ballston Spa
.91.	.King Solomon's.	294	.H. Stowell,	.Troy
.93.	.Military,	96	.G. T. Ewers,	.Manlius
.94.	Of Strict Observ.	109	.S. M. Underhill,	.New York City.
.95.	.Union,	312	.H. W. McIntire,	.Elmira
.96.	.Phœnix,	121	.Henry M. Allen,	.Whitehall.
.97.	.Renovation,	118	.S. A. Rivenburgh,	.Albion
.98.	.Columbia,	116	.Chas. H. Bell,	.Chatham 4 cor's.
103.	.Rising Sun,	147	.H. W. Hays,	.Saratoga Springs.
104.	.Lewis,	67	.Byron Bennet,	.Howard
105.	.Hiram,	302	.W. A. Jarrett,	.Buffalo
106.	.Manitou,	113	.Chas. Huggins,	.New York City.
107.	.North Star,	62	.M. V. B. Meeker,	.Moira
108.	.Milo,	54	.M. H. Rose.	.Penn Yan
109.	.Valley,	369	.Clifton C. Gifford,	.Rochester
110.	.Scipio,	53	.Chas. S. Robinson,	.Aurora.
111.	.St. Lawrence,	.190	.J. F. Simmons,	.Canton
112.	.Steuben,	141	.V. Brother,	.Bath
113.	.Seneca,	141	.Michael Moore,	.Waterloo
114.	.Union,	72	.J. M. Chadwick,	.Ovid
115.	.Phœnix,	141	.G. H. Tousey,	.Dansville
116.	.Cohoes,	151	.D. M. Adams,	.Cohoes
117.	.Painted Post.	.219	.J. H. Wolcott,	.Corning
118.	.Addison Union,	.84	.R. P. Brown,	.Addison
119.	.Oasis.	73	.Theodore Rudolph,	.Prattsville
120.	.Hamilton.	176	.G. T. Burn,	.Hamilton
121.	Glen's Falls,	.120	.H. B. Bates,	.Glen's Falls.
122.	.Mount Morris.	.122	. Moses Camp,	.Mount Morris.
123.	.Dundee,	133	.W. Benedict,	.Dundee.

No.	Name of Lodge.	Members.	Name of Sec'y.	Post Office.
124	Saint Paul's,	204	Henry B. Fitch,	Auburn
126	Eastern Light,	129	C. F. G. Cunningham,	Greene
127	Oswego,	196	Chas. L. Clark,	Oswego
128	Ogdensburg,	142	R. E. Gordon,	Ogdensburg
129	Sanger,	109	C. E. Hewitt,	Waterville
130	Port Byron,	72	E. Homel,	Port Byron
131	Myrtle,	125	H. E Dunham,	Havana
132	Niag'a Frontier,	124	William Pool,	Niagara Falls
133	Naples,	64	Thos. J. Clement,	Naples
134	Lowville,	135	W. H. Lawton,	Lowville
135	Sackett's Harb.	114	N. E. Bacon,	Sackett's Harbor.
136	Mexico,	101	N. H. Dobson,	Mexico
137	Anglo Saxon,	171	Wm. Conklin	Brooklyn
138	Otsego	192	Theo. S. Sayles.	Cooperstown
139	Milnor,	87	Theo. M. Norton,	Victor
140	Clinton,	207	A. J. Goffe,	Waterford
141	Cato,	101	W. Hapeman,	Cato
142	Morning Sun,	103	J. C. Douglass.	Port Henry
143	Concordia,	164	Daniel Wander,	Buffalo
144	Hiram,	193	H. E. Nichols,	Fulton
145	Mount Moriah,	176	Alex. M. Lowry,	Jamestown
146	Western Union,	76	R. M. Willis,	Belfast
147	Warren,	91	I. J. Mersman,	Union Springs
148	Sullivan,	74	Otto I. Hintermister,	Chittenango
149	Au Sable River,	80	N. C. Boynton,	Keeseville
150	Sauquoit,	94	Wm. Knight,	Sauquoit
151	Sentinel,	35	Valentine Reimann,	Greenwood
152	Hanover,	124	Julius A. Parsons,	Forestville
153	Friendship,	251	G. W. Buffum,	Owego
154	Penfield Union,	88	A. F. Church,	Penfield
155	Clinton,	130	J. A. Martin,	Plattsburg
156	Ocean,	159	Henry C. Velvin,	New York City
157	Trumansburg,	141	V. R. Burlew,	Trumansburg
158	Carthage,	167	G. T. Happ.	Carthage
159	Pultneyville,	73	Geo. B. Cady,	Pultneyville
160	Seneca River,	122	Geo. D. Alden,	Baldwinsville
161	Erie,	252	Matthew Thielen,	Buffalo
162	Schuyler's Lake,	122	J. Chappell,	Schuyler's Lake.
163	Yonnondio,	299	A. M. Ostrander,	Rochester
164	Philanthropic,	110	H. H. Richardson,	Camden
165	Booneville,	84	H. M'Cluskey.	Booneville
166	Forest,	150	John C. Mullett,	Fredonia
167	Susquehanna,	70	N. D. Card.	Bainbridge
168	Mentour,	95	A. H. Erwin,	Painted Post.
169	Clinton,	86	Leroy Smith,	Clinton
171	Lafargeville,	80	H. B. Edmonds,	Lafargeville

No.	Name of Lodge.	Members.	Name of Sec'y.	Post Office.
172.	Chaumont,	103.	O. S. Wilcox,	Chaumont
173.	Monroe,	116.	S B. Northrop,	Brockport
174.	Theresa,	187.	Geo. Cornwall,	Theresa
175.	Oxford,	139.	L. A. Knott,	Oxford
176.	Montezuma,	62.	Charles Higgins,	Montezuma
177.	Binghampton,	197.	Geo. L. Lawyer,	Binghampton.
178.	Atlantic,	206.	Charles W. Sy,	New York City.
179.	German Pilgrim.	121.	John B. Kaiser,	do
180.	Westchester,	140.	Geo. Williamson,	Sing Sing.
181.	Little Falls.	184.	A. L. Burt,	Little Falls
182.	Germania.	167.	Joseph Hammerle,	New York City.
183.	Farmersville,	84.	Wm. V. Bruyn,	Farmersville.
184.	Turin,	80.	J. E Stuher,	Turin
185	Independent,	153.	John Rush, jr.,	New York City.
187.	Darcy,	137.	Ephraim Japha.	do
188.	Marsh,	165.	Joseph Bedell,	Brooklyn, E. D.
189.	Cortlandt,	121.	Thos. C. Herrington,	Peekskill.
190.	Munn,	144.	Jas. Fairbairn,	New York City.
191.	Lebanon,	167.	W. S. Smith.	do
193.	Ulster.	172.	John Kearney.	Saugerties
194.	Piatt.	123.	Wm. J. Jessup,	New York City.
195.	Excelsior,	218.	Josiah Parkin.	do
196.	Solomon's,	106.	Morgan Purdy,	Greenburgh.
197.	York.	167.	Jacob Ritchy,	New York City.
198.	Silentia.	203.	Thos. K. Durham,	do
199.	Harmony,	130.	F. Walter.	do
200.	Sincerity,	117.	H. Underwood,	Phelps.
201.	Joppa,	313.	Richard Sharp.	Brooklyn
202.	Zschokke,	98.	Francis de Malignon,	New York City.
203.	Templar,	192.	J. S. Still,	do
204.	Palestine,	140.	G. G. Bonington,	do
205.	Hyatt.	179.	Geo. P. Hamilton,	Brooklyn
206.	Empire City.	171.	Jos. P. Jardine,	New York City.
207.	United States,	149.	W. S. Thompson,	do
208.	Cyrus,	195.	A. J. Burton,	do
209.	National,	150.	E. Percival.	do
210.	Worth,	172.	John W. Timson,	do
211.	Pocahontas,	137.	Thos. H. Kerr,	Seneca Falls
213.	Racquette Riv.	135.	S. A. Redway,	Potsdam.
214.	Geneseo,	87.	H. Johnson,	Geneseo
216.	Franklin,	66.	Guy W. Hollister,	Westville
217.	Governeur,	149.	Jas. W. Ormiston,	Governeur
218.	Hartland,	81.	H. J. Harrington,	Johnson's Creek.
219.	Summit.	152.	R. M. Mateer,	Westfield
221.	Cayuga,	89.	Thos. Cushman,	Scipio Centre
223.	Roman,	177.	Geo. P. Russ,	Rome

No.	Name of Lodge.	Members.	Name of Sec'y.	Post Office.
224	Oriental,	259	J. P. Tapping,	Utica
225	Allegheny,	96	L. B. Scott,	Friendship
226	Antwerp.	98	John Muir. M. D.	Antwerp
227	Eastern Star,	166	Thos. A. Granger,	New York City
228	Enterprise,	124	Chas. C. Alford.	do
229	Pike.	82	Orson Beardsley,	Hume
230	Wellsville,	110	Saml. F. Hanks,	Wellsville
231	Canastota,	89	E. H. Rose.	Canastota
232	Navigator,	136	Aaron Wiener,	New York City
233	Pacific,	211	Horace Forbush,	do
234	Rising Sun,	193	Milo B. Randall,	Adams
235	Keystone.	229	Anthony Walsh,	New York City
236	Philipstown,	143	Thomas Edwards,	Cold Spring
237	Champlain,	79	A. N. Merchant,	Champlain
238	Orient,	75	P. H. Sage,	Copenhagen
239	Cattarangus,	81	John Manley,	Little Valley
240	Washington,	188	John E. Rogers,	Buffalo
241	Constitution,	260	Henry C. Parke,	New York City
243	Eureka,	268	Jos. A. Cook.	do
244	Hope,	299	Thos. G. Wilson,	do
245	Polar Star,	260	Malcolm Stewart,	do
246	Arcana,	93	J. Edmund Banks,	do
247	Tonawanda,	107	G. R. McEuen,	Tonawanda.
248	Palmyra.	144	E. W. Cummings,	Palmyra
249	Charter Oak,	160	Wm. B. Smeeton,	New York City
250	Jno D. Willard,	174	Thos. J. Drew,	do
252	Olean,	161	R. H. Ranwick,	Olean
253	Old Oak,	108	Dexter White,	Millport.
254	Walworth,	45	H. G. C. Rose.	Walworth.
255	Livingstone,	60	Mark Whiting,	Colden
256	Fort Brewerton,	57	Q. F. Cushing,	Brewerton.
257	Mount Nebo,	286	H. Steiner,	New York City
258	Macedonia,	48	L. Daniels,	Bolivar.
259	Sisco,	91	John Ross,	Westport
260	Mount Hope,	70	J. D. Earle,	Fort Ann
261	Evans,	123	Warren K. Russell,	Angola.
262	Phœnix.	117	C. W. Blackney,	Gowanda
264	Baron Steuben,	85	Chas. F. King,	Stokes
265	Speedsville.	81	W. S Lawrence,	Speedsville
266	Poughkeepsie,	212	Isaac Tompkins,	Poughkeepsie
267	Fort Edward,	137	Henry Willard,	Fort Edward.
268	Herman,	252	Wm. Drechsler,	New York City
270	Oneida.	149	W. Hector Gale,	Oneida Depot
271	Ch'r Walworth,	139	Fred. W. Herring,	New York City
272	Mystic Tie.	118	Julius Fuld,	do
273	Metropolitan.	98	Wm. Johnston,	do

7²

No.	Name of Lodge.	Members.	Name of Sec'y.	Post Office.
274	Arcturus.	95	James Barton,	New York City..
275	Sylvan Grove,	259	Wesley B. Church,	do
276	Mohawk Val.,	109	Wm. H. Schall,	Mohawk
277	Henry Clay,	187	Ezra J. Ferry,	New York City..
278	Marion	78	James T. Wilson,	West Farms.
279	King Solomon's,	158	Philip Michaelson,	New York City..
280	Doric,	225	Wm. Borman,	do
281	Peru,	47	W. T. Warner,	Peru
282	Otego Union,	52	E. E. Bowen,	Otego
283	Beacon,	127	R. Carver	Matteawan
284	Baltic,	162	R. Van Valkenburg,	Brooklyn. E. D...
285	G. Washington,	252	Wm. W. Warner,	New York City..
286	Montauk,	113	Nevin W. Butter,	Brooklyn
287	Continental,	151	Jas. B. Smith.	New York City..
288	Brooklyn,	94	James A. Palmer,	Brooklyn
289	St. Andrew's,	84	Henry Grant,	Hobart.
290	Spencer,	73	Ira M. Howell,	Spencer
291	N. Constellation,	136	Fred. A Lewis,	Malone.
292	Parish.	84	Chas. W. Chase,	North Buffalo
293	Cape Vincent,	72	W. E. Ingalls,	Cape Vincent
294	Canandaigua,	164	J. J. Stebbins,	Canandaigua
295	Cataract,	90	Geo. R M'Chesney,	Reynale's Basin..
296	Clayton.	84	Chas. M. Marshall,	Clayton.
297	Alexandria,	141	A. C. Cornwall,	Alexandria Bay.
298	Fish House,	133	Erskine A. Tanner,	Northampton
299	Keshequa,	90	Sidney S. Morris,	Nunda
300	Garoga,	69	Wm. H. Jeffers,	Rockwood
301	Irondequoit,	167	Otis N. Shelton.	Dunkirk
302	Norwich,	202	Walton D. Wicks,	Norwich
303	Sylvan,	103	A. A. Stone,	Sinclairville
304	Schiller.	90	C. A. F. Hanstein,	Brooklyn, E. D...
305	Central City,	307	R. M. Beecher,	Syracuse.
306	Cuba.	111	Geo. H Swift,	Cuba.
307	Ellicottville,	88	Edwin S. King,	Ellicottville.
308	Seneca Lake,	61	Henry Bickett,	West Dresden
309	Newburgh,	175	G. W. Decker,	Newburgh
310	Lexington,	307	Wm. Manley,	Brooklyn
311	Mount Zion,	234	J. G. Patton.	Troy
312	Grass River,	43	R. Lovegrove,	Madrid
313	Stony Point,	115	Wm. N. Secor,	Haverstraw
315	Wawayanda,	138	S. A. Jessup,	Piermont
316	Atlas,	280	Geo. W. Duryee,	New York City..
317	Neptune,	152	John Nixon,	do
318	Joseph Enas,	60	James L. Adams,	Rushford
319	Black Lake,	81	Geo. F. Rawland,	Morristown
320	Union Star,	83	L. N. Allen,	Honeoye Falls

No.	Name of Lodge.	Members.	Name of Sec'y.	Post Office.
321	St. Nicholas.	121	Edwd. A. Rogers,	New York City
322	Star of Bethlehem.	129	John Taylor,	Brooklyn
323	Amity	187	John J. Tindale,	New York City
324	Freedom.	55	Geo. B. Fellows,	Unadilla
325	Republican	78	J. A. Slawson	Parish
326	Salem Town,	46	John M. Frees,	Cayuga.
327	Acacia.	128	C. W. Taylor,	New York City
328	Port Jarvis,	246	L. L. Adams,	Port Jarvis
329	Zerubbabel,	145	David Ackerson,	New York City
330	New York,	292	Frank E. Moran.	do
331	Hornellsville,	184	A. G. Howard,	Hornellsville.
332	Jefferson.	174	C. M. Woodward,	Watkins
333	Westbrook.	108	G. P. Cady.	Nicholas
334	Cherry Valley,	82	Jas. Hetherington.	Cherry Valley
335	Widow's Son,	49	A. L. Martin.	Clermont
336	Medina,	121	Rufus M. Grummon,	Medina.
337	Greenbush,	158	Oliver Herbert,	Greenbush
338	Putnam,	206	Geo. F. Forman,	New York City
339	Puritan,	155	Oliver Green,	do
340	Modestia,	120	Ph. Pfeil.	Buffalo
341	Clyde,	101	J. N. Arnold, M. D.	Clyde
342	Lily,	127	Thos. W. Timpson,	Morrisania.
343	Rondout,	266	G. Webster.	Rondout
345	Lodi,	75	Geo. C. Gibbs.	Lodi
346	Whitesville,	—	*Charter surrendered,*	Whitesville.
347	Hampton,	77	H. S. Kellogg.	Westmoreland
348	Adelphic,	173	Benj. F. Howe.	New York City
349	Peconic,	132	Geo. E. Post,	Greenport
350	Chemung Val.,	89	W. C Buck,	Chemung
351	Springville,	55	*(No Returns.)*	Springville
352	Homer.	121	W. B. Coggerhall,	Homer
353	Woodhull.	31	P. Masten,	Woodhull.
354	Progressive,	288	Geo. T. Crane,	Brooklyn. E. D.
355	Jerusalem.	138	John B. Icke,	Lansingburg
356	United Bro's,	217	Edward Hein.	New York City
357	Caneadea,	59	Henry Burleson.	Caneadea.
358	Queen City.	124	Christopher G. Fox,	Buffalo.
359	Elm Creek,	120	Hiram Fosdick,	Randolph.
360	Afton.	109	J. Farnsworth,	Afton
361	Central,	151	Chas. O. Mann.	Brooklyn
362	Valatie.	70	Rev. J. C. S. Weills,	Valatie.
363	Evergreen,	71	S. R. Stewart.	Springfield Cent'r
364	Horse Heads,	96	Chas. W. McNish,	Horse Heads.
365	Goshen,	72	Asa S. Strong,	Goshen.
367	Corner Stone,	219	Jos. L. Hasbrouck,	Brooklyn, E. D.
368	Croton,	148	Jas. R. Ostrander,	Croton Falls

No.	Name of Lodge.	Members.	Name of Sec'y.	Post Office.
369	Callimachus,	103	H. M. Sponenbergh,	Phœnix
371	Sagamore,	131	E. M. Tomlinson,	New York City
372	Sandy Hill,	89	J. W. Wait,	Sandy Hill
373	La Sincérité,	67	P. Huot,	New York City
374	Monumental,	53	T. H. Hoffman,	Red Hook
375	Niagara,	191	C. P. T. La Roche,	Lockport
376	Ontario,	109	Reuben F. Wilson,	Wilson
377	Rushville,	84	E. R. Breck,	Rushville
378	Big Flatts,	60	W. H. Fiarr,	Big Flatts
379	Oakland,	97	F. C. Spellman,	Castile
380	Murray,	106	S. E. Howard,	Holly
381	Huguenot,	115	H. R. Yetman,	Tottenville
382	Long Island,	381	E. F. Van Orden,	Brooklyn
383	Aurora,	59	S. V. R. Tuthill,	Fort Covington
384	Cherry Creek,	94	Darwin L. Carl,	Cherry Creek
385	Weedsport,	102	G. A. Benedict,	Weedsport
386	Jordan,	120	Alex. Van Vleck,	Jordan
387	La Fraternidad,	45	F. Lothes,	New York City
388	Upper Lisle,	79	R. O. Williams,	Upper Lisle
389	Margaretsville,	68	J. B. Ackerly,	Margaretsville
391	Salem,	100	Joseph Oliver,	Salem
392	Sodus,	108	F. W. Belden,	Sodus
393	Waddington,	46	William Hatch,	Waddington
394	Cobbleskill,	151	J. L. Pindar,	Cobbleskill
395	Amber,	56	Leander Perkins,	Parishville
396	Deposit,	127	Ellicott Evans,	Deposit
397	Ivy,	247	F. D. Ramsdell,	Elmira
398	Home,	77	Abraham Marshall,	Northumberland
399	Maine,	59	O. Holden,	Maine
400	Van Rensallaer,	116	L. U. Davis,	Hoosick Falls
401	Suffolk,	141	John B. Post,	Port Jefferson
402	Crescent,	158	Wm. Y. Taft,	New York City
403	Green Point,	166	Jas. H. Whitehorne,	Green Point
406	Humanity,	102	A. F. Gillette,	Lyons
407	Waverly,	148	W. P. Stone,	Waverly
408	City,	141	C. H. Bass,	New York City
409	Commonwealth,	561	Jonathan Jones,	Brooklyn
410	La C. A. Cosm.,	47	J. J. Burnier,	New York City
411	Candor,	95	E. R. Brundage,	Candor Centre
412	Hoffman,	203	Charles J. Boyd,	Middleton
413	West Star,	82	E. H. Wilder,	Varysburg
414	Scriba,	44	William Sheldon,	Constantia
415	Pulaski,	164	Benj. Snow,	Pulaski
416	Wayne,	44	P. B. Quinly,	Ontario
417	Wadsworth,	231	John R. Stewart,	Albany
418	Mosaic,	183	A. Pennal,	New York City

No.	Name of Lodge.	Members.	Name of Sec'y.	Post Office.
419	Arcade,	122	J. N. Woodworth,	China
420	New London,	44	O. W. Hines,	New London
421	Genoa,	76	H. W. Atwater,	Genoa
422	Frontier City,	138	E. Nichols,	Oswego
423	Herkimer,	83	H. W. Quackenbush,	Herkimer
425	Warrensburg,	81	Geo. W. Gleason,	Warrensburg
426	Northfield,	67	Henry Parry,	Pittsford
427	Cascade,	138	H. O. Graham,	Oak Hill
428	High Falls,	70	Orson Holden,	Colton
429	Gloversville,	179	John L. Getman,	Gloversville
430	Star of Hope,	110	Geo G. Sickles,	Brooklyn
431	Auburn,	119	H. V. Quick,	Auburn
432	Rhinebeck,	99	James L. Letten,	Rhinebeck
433	Fort Plain,	146	Adam Hix,	Fort Plain
434	Hiawatha,	73	S. H. Cowan,	Mount Vernon
435	Otseningo,	189	H. E. Allen,	Binghampton
436	Schroon Lake,	44	Robert Taylor,	Schroon Lake
437	Wamponamon,	96	Peter French,	Sag Harbor
438	Marathon,	66	Du Ray Hunt,	Marathon
439	Delhi,	113	Maurice Farrington,	Delhi
440	Vienna,	76	A. P. Chatfield,	Vienna
441	An. Landmark,	169	J. O. Monroe,	Buffalo
442	Windsor,	117	F. S. Smith,	Windsor
444	Sherburne,	107	John P. Dietz,	Sherburne
445	Cassia,	135	Isaac J. Greenhalgh,	Brooklyn, E. D.
446	Oltman's,	112	Geo. Zollinhoffer,	do
447	Franklin,	129	Barne H. Wolf,	New York City
448	Huguenot,	81	Walker T. Bell,	New Rochelle
449	Hiram,	105	Wm. E. Bishop,	New York City
450	Rising Star,	154	A. C. Mott,	Yonkers
451	Delta,	196	John R. Penfold,	Brooklyn
452	Ancient City,	125	James C. Wilsdon,	Albany
453	Clinton,	98	Geo. W. Bell,	Brooklyn, E. D.
454	Kane,	226	W. H. Simonson,	New York City
455	Newport,	115	Geo. H. Hurlbut,	Newport
456	Senate,	68	G. R. Harris,	Glen's Falls
457	Harlem,	159	Robert Ogilvy,	Harlem
458	Shukomeko,	125	Chas. H. Losee,	Mabbettsville
459	Urbana,	51	Chas. L. Brownell,	Hammondsport
461	Yew Tree,	159	J. C. Cabble,	Brooklyn, E. D.
462	Attica,	113	Jacob Algier,	Attica,
463	Weston,	84	Theo. M. Horton,	Weston
464	Downsville,	98	Chas. E. Radeker,	Colchester
465	Wilton,	69	D. Washburn,	Wilton
466	Oneonta,	94	Newton J. Ford,	Oneonta
467	Greenwich,	174	Wm. B. Shove,	New York City

No.	Name of Lodge.	Members.	Name of Sec'y.	Post Office.
468	Catskill,	152	Edgar Russell,	Catskill
470	Cortlandville,	153	Michael J. Grady,	Cortland
471	Tompkins,	83	A. W. Mullen,	Stapleton.
472	Dryden,	95	D. E. Bower,	Dryden.
473	White Plains,	72	D. Verplanck.	White Plains.
474	Belmont,	90	H. N. Gardiner,	Belmont
475	Batavia,	179	A. R. Warner,	Batavia.
476	Fairport,	63	W. A. Vance,	Fairport.
477	Wildwood,	86	Amos Newton,	Edwards.
478	Dansville.	43	L. K. Robinson,	Rogersville
479	Etolian,	123	Geo. M. Cole,	Spencerport.
480	Webotuck,	67	H. H. Walker.	North East
481	Cambridge Val.	103	W. A. Starbuck,	Cambridge.
482	Richfield Spr's,	85	Willard A. Smith,	Richfield Springs.
483	Zeradatha,	267	Hooper C. Packard,	Brooklyn
484	Columbian,	188	Geo. Mellish,	New York City.
485	Stella,	280	D. Grant,	Brooklyn
486	Ionic,	167	Louis Tucot,	New York City.
487	Tecumseh,	169	Saml. J. Hunt,	do
488	Corinthian,	234	Geo. F. Thornton,	do
489	Manahatta.	106	Wm. Byfield,	do
490	Pyramid,	286	Thos. G. Grounsell,	do
491	Schoharie Val.,	89	Wm. O. Root,	Schoharie.
492	Wyoming,	46	Isaac Butter,	Westchester
493	South Side,	96	G. F. Chicester,	Patchogue
494	Jeptha,	103	A. B. Gildersleeve,	Huntington
496	Groton,	80	E. A. Marsh,	Groton
497	Glendale,	39	Saml. C. Barnes,	Pottersville.
498	De Moley,	168	J. E. Barnard,	Buffalo
499	Deer River,	39		Lawrenceville.
500	Hermon,	87	J. J. Haile,	Hermon
501	Syracuse,	230	D. N. Lathrop,	Syracuse.
503	Old Ti,	60	John C. Fenton,	Ticonderoga
504	Montgomery,	98	P. Van Vechten,	Stillwater.
505	Northern Light,	67	Chas. H. Holbrook,	West Chazy.
506	Rodman,	137	A. C. Hughes,	Rodman
507	Genessee Falls,	323	D. T. Hunt.	Rochester
508	Herschel.	116	John Norton.	Hartford
509	Lindenwald,	107	Wm. S. Hollenbeck,	Kinderhook.
510	Liberty,	59	Chas. H. Beyer,	Cohocton
511	King's Co.,	69	R. S. Strong,	Flat Bush.
512	Humboldt,	131	M. Cahn,	New York City.
513	Massena,	73	H. S. Ransom,	Massena
514	Zion,	42	Geo. Abbott,	East Hamburg.
515	Butternuts,	72	L. H. Coye,	Butternuts
516	Park,	235	H. Sands,	New York City.

No.	Name of Lodge.	Members.	Name of Sec'y.	Post Office.
517	Frontier,	90	John M'Coy,	Chateaugay.
518	Coventry,	53	Jas. H. Phillips,	Coventry.
519	Architect,	190	Wm. A. Conklin,	New York City.
520	Salt Springs,	79	Henry H. Briggs,	Syracuse.
521	Callicoon,	95	A. E. Wenzel,	Callicoon.
522	Skaneateles,	123	C. L. Derby,	Skaneateles
523	Normal,	140	Robt. Stephensen,	New York City.
524	Morning Star,	85	Oscar J. Brown,	Marcellus.
525	Liverpool,	63	Geo. Baxter,	Liverpool
526	Henrietta,	73	James Dunn,	Henrietta.
527	Akron,	72	Perry P. Hart,	Akron.
528	Monitor,	154	T. F. Watson,	New York City.
529	Mountain,	67	D. C. Tibbals,	Windham Center.
530	Wash'ton H'ts,	41	Peregrine White,	New York City.
531	Fultonville,	104	Nicholas Wemple,	Fultonville
532	Monticello,	117		Monticello
533	Round Hill,	103	M. B. Robbins,	Union
534	Tioga,	87	Charles H. Miller,	Smithboro
535	Americus,	150	H. Clay Lanius,	New York City
536	Nassau,	191	Chas. D. Andrews,	Brooklyn.
537	Gramercy,	100	T. L. Graham,	New York City.
538	Webster,	67	Hugh M'Kay,	Webster.
539	Fayette,	71	J. B. Shiley,	Fayette
540	Hill Grove,	140	J. Henry Gifford,	Brooklyn.
541	Brasher,	68	L. C. Lang,	Brasher Falls
542	Garibaldi,	19	Erqui Macoggi,	New York City.
543	Triluminar,	78	C. R Adams,	Pike.
544	Warwick,	88	Louis D. Adams,	Warwick
545	Copernicus,	46	Geo. F. Gollmar,	Brooklyn. E. D.
546	Jamaica,	90	Sam. C. Aymar,	Jamaica
547	Cameron Mills,	82	John M. Sly,	Cameron Mills.
548	Laurens,	85	Albert S. Allen,	Laurens.
549	Warsaw,	95	L. N. Wilson,	Warsaw
550	Hannibal.	108	A. B. Bower,	Hannibal.
551	Ransomville,	100	Tomkins D. Miller,	Ransomville
552	Hancock,	171	Wm. H. Garritt,	Hancock
553	Farmers',	78	Wm. Talbott,	W. Burlington
554	Working,	77	Stephen J. Tyler,	Jefferson
555	Diamond,	81	Adolph Corduan,	Dobb's Ferry
556	North Bangor,	84	P. J. Stickle,	Bangor.
557	Jas. M. Austin,	117	T. James Rundle,	Greenville
558	Andover,	92	Geo. A. Green,	Andover.
559	Walton,	85	John T. Ames,	Walton.
560	Red Creek,	119	D. D. Becker,	Red Creek.
561	Delaware,	92	Leroy Bonesteel,	Cochecton
562	Franklin,	67	C. R. Bucher,	Franklin.

No.	Name of Lodge.	Members.	Name of Sec'y.	Post Office.
563	Cornucopia	119	W. H. D. Nimmio,	Flushing
564	Sandy Creek,	68	D. E. Wilds,.	Sandy Creek
565	Guiding Star,	42	Carey D. Stearns,	Tremont
566	Russell,	53	Darius Chapin,	Russell
567	Argyle.	53	T. R. Wade,	Argyle
568	St. Cecile,	89	David Graham.	New York City
569	Greenwood.	125	Harmanus Bennett,	Brooklyn
570	Avon Springs,	60	C W. M'Cown,	Avon Springs
571	Cœur de Leon,	75	Charles E. Graves,	Roxbury
572	Mount Hermon.	43	J. E. Schutt.	Ellenburg.
573	Depeyster,	67	A. Thornton,	Depeyster
574	Bedford,	89	Wm. H. Donnell,	Brooklyn.
575	Olive,	108	C. H. Corbett,	Sherman.
576	Fessler,	107	Chas. Rosenstedt,	New York City.
577	Elk,	45	Joseph T. Camfield,	Nicholasville
578	Fayetteville.	84	T. H. Mackham,	Fayetteville
579	Portville.	63	W. B. Archibald,	Portville
580	Glen Cove,	70	John Verney,	Glen Cove
581	Winfield,	102	Jas. B. Rafter,	West Winfield
582	Wawarsing,	188	E. D. Russell.	Ellenville.
583	Prattsburg,	87	F. R. Frost,	Prattsburg
584	Ashlar,	76	Nicholas M. Masters,	Greenwich
585	Cosmopolitan,	202	Hiram Bloomer,	Brooklyn
586	Island City,	107	J. R. Laws,	Long Island City
587	Ahwago,	156	Frank M. Baker,	Owego
588	Globe,	70	Wm. V. King,	New York City.
589	Ramapo,	80	E. E. Suffern,	Suffern
590	Rose,	77	James M. Horne,	Rose.
591	Ilion,	141	E. H. Bennett,	Ilion.
592	Shenevus Valley,	71	Nelson Lane,	Schenevus
593	Charlotte River,	45	John Turner,	Davenport
594	Alden,	73	Lorin Farnsworth,	Alden.
595	Socrates,	92	August Bans,	New York City.
596	Hopewell,	72	N. H. Strippel,	Fishkill Plains.
597	Western Light,	56	J. P. Lewis,	Lisle.
598	Tabernacle,	114	Geo. E. Glines,	New York City.
599	Kennyetto,	64	D. V. Cleveland,	Broadalbin
600	Evangelist,	136	Chas. H. Ackerman,	New York City.
601	Altair,	140	Rufus W. Powell,	Brooklyn.
602	Adirondack,	48	Amon Bosley,	Elizabethtown.
603	Astor,	68	A. B. Cory,	New York City.
604	Perfect Ashlar,	87	Wm. Sinclair,	do
605	Tienuderrah,	76	John Bowne,	Morris
606	Masonville.	46	Orrin A. Priest,	Masonville
607	Hudson River,	197	Louis H. Blackman,	Newburgh
608	Lessing,	73	Chas. Lamber,	Brooklyn

No.	Name of Lodge.	Members.	Name of Sec'y.	Post Office.
609	Rensselaer,	46	J. H. Evans,	Rensselaerville.
610	Ivanhoe,	115	Wm. Chave,	New York City.
611	St. Johnsville,	75	Morris Klock,	St. Johnsville
612	Hillsdale.	80	Benj. House,	Hillsdale
613	Cleveland,	71	James W. Deans,	Cleveland
614	Newark Valley,	54	W. A. Howard,	Newark Valley.
615	Stissing,	58	A. B. Vedder,	Pine Plains.
616	Cazenovia,	60	John E. Tapping,	Cazenovia
617	Teutonia,	96	Wm. Heyenga,	New York City.
618	Tyrian,	94	Louis J. Witte,	East New York.
619	Eagle,	54	Oliver B. Brown,	Richmond
620	Clinton F. Paige,	75	John T. Newman,	Otto
621	Orange,	70	Abram Barkley,	Orange
622	Central Square,	46	D. D. Drake,	Central Square.
623	Sayles,	46	I. G. Childs,	Bridgeport
624	Sharon Springs,	63	W. Swift,	Sharon Springs.
625	Fraternal,	53	Saml. R. Saunders,	White's Corners.
626	Franklinville,	74	Chas. Phillips,	Franklinville.
627	Walkill,	55	L. M. Mason,	Montgomery
628	Citizen's,	70	Geo. W. Weed,	New York City.
629	Goethe,	99	John Asche,	do.
630	Gilboa,	70	Geo. A. Wallace,	Gilboa
631	Girard,	43	C. L. Uhrbach,	New York City.
632	Prudence,	59	J. G. Fitzgerald,	do.
633	Richville,	44	Geo. W. Hurd,	Richville
634	Scotia,	168	W. M. Robinson,	New York City.
635	Advance,	62	Martin Welles,	Astoria.
636	Manuel,	122	J. E. Rhodes,	Brooklyn, E. D.
637	Rising Light,	90	N. B. Scott,	Belleville.
638	Crystal Wave,	200	Benj. Cromwell,	Brooklyn.
639	Somerset,	66	Geo. A. Perkins,	Somerset Corner.
640	Adytum,	46	Jos. Hartley,	Brooklyn.
641	Copestone,	160	H. T. Gibson,	New York City.
642	Knickerbocker,	82	John Millar,	do.
643	Dan. Carpenter,	189	M. Chappell,	do.
645	Riverhead,	98	A. S. Hait,	Riverhead
646	Red Jacket,	77	C. Stacy Mack,	Lockport.
647	Mistletoe,	50	E. G. Williams,	Brooklyn.
648	Centreville,	36	Granville Baum,	Centreville.
649	M'Clellan,	26	W. N. Greggs,	Troupsburg.
650	Amboy,	51	W. S. Cole,	West Amboy.
651	True Cr'ftsman's,	70	B. Brooks,	New York City.
652	Perseverance,	109	Alfred J. Murray,	do.
653	Marmaro,	38	W. T. Cornell,	Mamaroneck.
654	Emanuel,	71	Alfred J. Murray,	New York City.
655	Bunting,	51	Ira B. Read,	Harlem.

No.	Name of Lodge.	Members.	Name of Sec'y.	Post Office.
656	Euclid,	76	A. S. Rawley,	Brooklyn
657	Livingston,	100	Edward Foley,	New York City
658	Morrisville,	75	J. S. Stewart,	Morrisville
659	South Otselic,	80	H· S. Wheeler,	Otselic
660	Rochester,	190	Chas. A. Brady,	Rochester
661	Beethoven,	101	Gustavus Levy,	New York City
662	Cambridge,	52	Hooper C. Packard,	Brooklyn
663	Middlebury,	79	J. L. Stanton,	Middlebury
664	Amicable,	65	Marshall Sackett,	Washington Mills
665	Macedon,	46	Robert P. Magee,	Macedon
666	Dover,	113	C. F. Segelken,	Dover Plains
667	Churchville,	70	Chas. W. Craig,	Chuchville
668	Jersey,	59	Chas.'D. Walters,	Bradford
669	Port Leyden,	59	John Gibson,	Port Leyden
670	Star,	63	W. H. Reynolds,	Petersburg
671	Wappinger's,	82	John Halfpenny,	Wappinger's
672	Amenia,	52	J. A. Davis,	Amenia
673	Avoca,	64	John E. Storms,	Avoca
674	Gratitude,	71	Daniel Smith,	Nassau
675	Yates,	69	E. R. Barrett,	Yates
676	Schuyler,	49	E. Doolittle,	Schuylersville
677	Remsen,	72	Geo. H. Worden,	Remsen
678	Seawanhaka,	207	Ethan S. Blank,	Brooklyn, E. D.
679	Aeonian,	54	E. A. Van Horne,	Oswego
680	Victor,	142	Chas. Minor,	Hart's Falls
681	Caroline,	75	Chas. L. Davis,	Slatersville
682	Nunda Station,	42	D. C. Grunder,	Nunda Station
683	Corinth,	56	D. B. Ide,	Corinth
684	Berne,	105	A. J. Lobdell,	East Berne
685	Aquahonga,	29	Willis Burton,	Richmond
686	Jasper,	30	M. M. Taft,	Jasper
687	Oswegatchie,	32	F. L. Whittier,	Fine
688	Depauville,	49	L. E. Frume,	Depauville
689	What Cheer,	33	F. Foord,	Norfolk
690	Republic,	135	J. W. Stopford,	New York City
691	Meridian,	44	James Baylis,	Islip
692	De Ruyter,	57	E. B. Parsons,	De Ruyter
693	Kedemah,	54	Edwin E. Darly,	Cairo
694	Blazing Star,	61	John P. Bartlett,	East Aurora
695	Alcyone,	37	Chas. M. Sammis,	Northport
696	Peacock,	50	J. Frank Bly,	Mayville
697	Faxton,	72	John Peattie,	Utica
698	Herder,	68	Fred. Hagendorf,	Brooklyn, E. D.
699	Harmonic,	39	Fred. Traenkle,	Buffalo
700	Aquila,	56	Edgar Remington,	Hudson
701	Beacon Light,	26	John M. Hawkins,	New Brighton

No.	Name of Lodge.	Members.	Name of Sec'y.	Post Office.
702	Marble,	27	Alex. Smith,	Tuckahoe
703	Gavel,	45	Geo. A. J. Norman,	Mott Haven
704	Tuscan,	38	F. C. Conrady,	Brooklyn.
705	Acacian,	27	A. E. Smith,	Ogdensburg
706	Cincinnatus,	26	Jeff. Kingman,	Cincinnatus.
707	Mount Horeb,	33	J. M. Corleins,	Moore's Forks
708	Kisco,	42		Mount Kisco
709	Merchants,	42	Wm. H. Burt,	New York City
710	Ridgewood,	26	A. G. Merwin,	Brooklyn.
711	Standard,	18		Chester.
712	Pelham,	21	Benj. Hegeman,	Pelham
713	Social,	47	Sumner Austin,	Kendall

North Carolina.

According to the best information obtainable, the first independent grand lodge in this State was organized in 1787 by a convention of brethren, in manner somewhat like the movement in New Jersey the previous year, to the extent at least that the members of this convention were not appointed by any lodge for the work they performed at Hillsborough, except, it may be, those who represented the lodge at that place. Indeed the movement may be considered as. mainly, the act of that lodge. The Hon. Samuel Johnson, President of the State, was elected the first grand master — an act which was of itself, at the time, sufficient to legalize the performance, and neutralize any opposition that might be met. There is no evidence, however, that any such was offered. In those days Masonic grand lodges did not spring up in a night armed for battle ; they excited little attention or question as to the legal or illegal manner of their organization, as they had exercised but little consequence in the spread of Masonry. It is but in our own day that nice shades of regularity are striven for in this matter, and their attainment regarded necessary.

This grand lodge holds its annual communication in the City of Raleigh in December. In Dec. 1870 there were holding under its charters 199, lodges, with 10,204 members. To this the Gr. Sec'y adds 905, as " obtained from the last returns of lodges failing to make returns in 1870," and thus obtains a " total membership and resident Masons not members of lodges " of 11,109. This grand lodge pays neither mileage nor per diem. Its revenue in 1870 was $2,986.48, and after the necessary payments were made the G. T. reported a balance in hand of $779.68. This grand lodge owns the wreck of a property, located in the town of Oxford, known as " Saint John's College." and which is in its present valueless condition incumbered with claims amounting to about $4,000. The latest decision of the grand lodge concerning it is to sell it if possible—a matter that previous efforts renders doubtful.

The executive grand officers elected (the D. G. M. is appointed,) in 1870 were—

CHARLES G. CLARK, of New Berne, Grand Master.
JOSEPH B. BATCHELOR, of Raleigh, Deputy Gr. Master.
WM. E. ANDERSON, of Raleigh. Grand Treasurer.
DONALD W. BAIN, of Raleigh, Grand Secretary.

The following list is obtained from the printed Proceedings of the G. L. for 1870, exclusively, no circulars having been sent to the lodges in this State.

No.	Name of Lodge.	Members.	Name of Sec'y.	Post Office.
..1..	St. John's,	120	Wm. M. Poisson,	Wilmington.
..2..	Royal Wh. Hart,	54	John T. Gregory,	Halifax
..3..	St. John's,	89	E. B. Roberts,	New Berne
..5..	Charity	55	R. W. Askew,	Windsor
..7..	Unanimity,	39	Wm. R. Skinner,	Edenton
..8..	Phœnix	83	J. B. Troy,	Fayetteville
.10..	Johnson Caswell.	19	John C. M'Craw,	Warrenton
.17..	American George.	41	A. M. Darden,	Murfreesboro
.31..	Phalanx,	55	E. H. White,	Charlotte
.32..	Stokes	67	David F. Cameron,	Concord
.37..	Wm. R. Davie,	78	Thomas Symons,	Lexington
.40..	Hiram	71	James C. Marcom,	Raleigh
.56..	King Solomon,	68	G. W. Cook,	Jackson
.58..	Concord,	71	Benjamin T. Hart,	Tarboro
.59..	Perseverance,	27	John M. Foote.	Plymouth
.64..	Kilwinning,	118	J. H. Horton,	Wadesboro
.71..	Eagle,	100	John L. Finch,	Hillsboro
.75..	Widow's Son,	88	P. G. Morrisett,	Camden C. H.
.76..	Greensboro,	50	S. C. Dodson,	Greensboro
.81..	Zion,	47	Joseph Kinsey,	Trenton
.82..	Mount Moriah,	36	P. C. Carlton,	Statesville.
.83..	Lafayette,	—		Jacksonville.
.84..	Fellowship,	45	Charles S. Powell,	Smithfield
.85	Morning Star,	88	Wm. T. Griffin,	Nashville.
.90..	Skewarkey,	38		Williamston.
.91..	Western Star,	27	H. H. Mitchell,	Rutherfordton
.92..	Joseph Warren,	46	J. H. Applewhite,	Stantonsburg
.95..	Jerusalem,	49	Dr. F. M. Rountree,	Hookerton
.96..	St. John's	67	Alex. Nicol,	Kinston
.97..	Wake Forest,	23	W. W. Wynne,	Raleigh
.98..	Hiram,	86	J. W. Lane,	Clinton
.99..	Fulton,	58	J. K. Burke,	Salisbury
101..	Warren,	58	Thomas S. Watson,	Kenansville
102..	Columbus,	60	W. F. Barry,	Pittsboro

No.	Name of Lodge.	Members.	Name of Sec'y.	Post Office.
104	Orr,	59	O. W. Telfair,	Washington ....
106	Perquimans,	29	G. W. Hudgins,	Hertford ....
107	Clinton,	108	L. L. M. Totten,	Yanceyville.....
108	Belmont,	35	R. R. Bell,	Bear Swamp....
109	Franklin,	87	W. C. King,	Beaufort........
112	Wayne,	52	John H. Powell,	Goldsboro......
113	Person,	127	S. W. Glenn,	Roxboro ....
115	Holly Springs,	50	W. H. Stinson,	Holly Springs...
117	Mt. Lebanon,	50	James E. Shepherd,	Wilson ....
118	Mt. Hermon,	118	J. M. Israel,	Asheville.......
121	Logan,	57	W. G. Sapp,	Jamestown .....
122	Tuscarora,	55	J. M Matthews,	Oxford.........
123	Franklinton,	68	J. A. Winston,	Franklinton.....
124	Clinton,	30	B. P. Clifton,	Louisburg......
125	Mill Creek,	42	H. N. Bizzell,	Mill Creek Ch...
126	Gatesville,	27	Geo. J. Costen,	Gatesville ......
127	Blackmer,	100	A. J. Burton,	Zion ....
128	Hanks,	60	J. W. Bean,	Franklinville ...
129	Dan. River,	81	J. A. Vernon,	Madison........
131	Conoho,	20	R. E. Wethersbee,	Hamilton.......
132	Radiance,	59	J. H. Allbritton,	Snow Hill......
133	Alamance,	65	W. A. Albright,	Graham ....
134	Mocksville,	73	C. U. Rich,	Mocksville......
135	Black Rock,	33	James F. Oliver,	Marlville ......
136	Leakesville,	63	Wm. S. Martin,	Leakesville. ....
137	Lincoln,	68	John M. Lawing,	Lincolnton ....
138	King Solomon,	42	W. S. Larkins,	Long Creek.....
140	Mount Energy,	45	Wm. C. Bullock,	Tranquillity....
141	Carolina,	68	W. A. Smith,	Ansonville .....
142	Cane Creek,	42	Thomas Parrott,	Clover Or. Fact'y
143	Mount Vernon,	67	W. H. Dark,	Mt. Vernon Spr'g
145	Junaluskee,	56	Chas. E. Wiggins,	Franklin ....
146	Cherokee,	46	Wm. Beal,	Murphy ....
147	Palmyra,	55	N. S. Stewart,	Averasboro.....
149	Adoniram,	31	C. F. Clack,	Young's X Roads
151	Chalmers,	35	A. McLeod,	Carbonton ......
154	Scotch Ireland,	28	John Graham,	Rowan Mills....
155	White Stone,	56	Wm. B. Chamblee,	Wakefield. ......
156	Rolesville,	25	Wm. K. Hunter,	Rolesville.......
157	Mt. Pleasant,	64	D. Killoove,	Roger's Store....
158	Knap of Reeds,	72	F. J. Tilley,	Knap of Reeds..
160	Beaumont,	30	J. N. Green,	Beaumont.......
161	Rock Rest,	54	J. B. West,	Hadley's Mills...
162	Yadkin,	74	John D. Johnson,	Yadkinville.....
165	Archer,	34	D. L. Barnes,	Creechville .....
166	St. Paul's,	24	A. J. Barnhill,	Beatty's Bridge..

No.	Name of Lodge.	Members.	Name of Sec'y.	Post Office.
167	Winston,	74	M. J. Bodenhamer,	Winston
170	Blackmer,	54	W. M. Weaver,	Reem's Creek
171	Delk,	26	D. A. Watford,	Coleraine.
172	Buffalo,	76	J. B. Cole.	Jonesboro
174	G. Washington,	62	J. E. Johnson,	Lasater's X Roads
176	Mecklenburg,	14	G. A. Andrew,	Davidson College
178	Siloam,	31	W. L. Johnson,	Harrell's Store
179	Lafayette,	24	Wm. Paylor, jr.,	Leasburg
180	Caldwell,	46	Andrew Mickle.	Chapel Hill
181	Carthage,	95	C. P. Jenkins,	Carthage
182	Townsville,	43	Thos. H. Morrow,	Townsville.
183	Center Grove,	77	Saml. Whitt,	Hillsdale
184	Jordan,	24	J. F. Howell,	Reynoldson.
185	Sandy Creek,	68	E. T. Swanson,	Laurel
186	Pine Forest,	57	J. M. L. Harrington,	Harrington
187	Central Cross,	66	H. A. Hines,	Peach Tree Grove
190	Fair Bluff,	51	E. D. Meares,	Fair Bluff.
191	Granite,	25	J. M. White,	Clayton
192	Burnsville.	53	W. A. M'Clenan,	Burnsville
195	Mount Olivet,	47	John L. Stuart,	Cross Roads.
196	Falkland,	24	P. H. Mayo,	Falkland
197	Cherokee,	43	J. R. Smith,	Cherokee.
198	Carey,	30	W. M. Sorrell,	Carey
201	Eagle Rock.	30	L. W. Hood,	Eagle Rock
202	Cleaveland,	35	Lee M. McAfee,	Shelby
203	Roanoke,	31	Jordan Stone,	Weldon
204	Berea,	37	Thos. D. Clement,	Tar Riv. Academ.
205	Long Creek,	54	D. F. Dixon,	Hopewell
206	Mingo,	43	Wm. Daughtrey,	Mingo Must. Gr'd
207	Lebanon,	60	A. J. Butner,	Whiteville
208	Mount Olive,	28	Wm. Vernon,	Mt. Olive.
209	New Salem,	69	J. E. Walker,	New Salem
210	Enoe,	53	John L. Markham,	Durham
211	Ashland,	91	J. W. Shepherd,	Mount Airy
212	Industrial,	36	J. C. Holt,	Company Shops
214	Richland.	67	J. D. Paylor,	Thomasville.
217	Catawba Valley,	43	J. W. Happoldt,	Morgantown
218	W. G. Hill,	63	James H. Alford,	Raleigh.
219	Jefferson.	101	J. E. Foster,	Jefferson
220	Stokesburg,	70	R. H. Massey,	Stokesburg.
222	Webster,	21	Abraham Dixon,	Elevation.
223	Tabernacle,	27	W. D. Hardin,	Tabernacle Ch.
225	Haw River,	42	W. W. Ragsdale,	Haw River.
226	Wilson,	38	H. A. Mowbray,	Olin.
227	Jonesville,	97	E. T. Thompson,	Jonesville
228	M'Cormick,	32	S. H. Lawrence,	Jonesboro

No.	Name of Lodge.	Members.	Name of Sec'y.	Post Office.
229	Henderson,	30	Sam. J. Parham,	Henderson
230	Corinthian,	27	W. B. Jordan,	Rocky Mount
231	Wm. T. Bain,	18	C. H. Stephenson,	Hollands
232	Gunter,	36	James H. Mann,	Haywood
233	Lenoir,	33	A. J. McIntire,	La Grange
234	Anchor,	18	L. H. Poole,	Auburn
235	Cokesburg,	30	W. A. Dewar,	Chalk Level
236	Mount Zion,	13	Geo. Kirkman,	Silk Hope
238	Atlantic,	57	W. D. Barnard,	Currituck C. H.
239	Nohunta,	40	S. R. Steel, jr.,	Nohunta
242	Loch Lomond,	21	Robert Lilly,	Floral College
243	Rountree,	39	Fred. Harding,	Contentnea Neck.
244	Monroe,	33	T. E. Winchester,	Monroe
245	New Berne.	47	Thomas Powers,	New Berne
246	Elmwood,	36	R. P. Troy,	Greensboro
247	Mount Hermon,	32	Jasper N. Wood,	Mt. Hermon Ch.
248	Catawba,	24	E. A. Warlick.	Newton
249	Pythagoras,	23	Thomas G. Drew,	Smithville
250	Shiloh,	13	Adam C. Harris,	Sassafras Fork
251	Rockford.	22	J. D. Hamlin,	Rockford
252	Holly Grove,	20	John R. Hill,	Holly Grove
253	Lee,	38	Alfred Carson,	Taylorsville
254	Mt. Bethel,	16	D. T. Deanes,	Lomaxville
255	Oaks,	37	S. S. Webb,	Oaks
257	J. B. Person,	24	Ray Phillips,	Beulah
258	Harnett,	14	R. H. Smith,	Harnett Chapel
259	Waynesville,	33	M. H. Love,	Waynesville
260	Center Hill,	25	Rich. Dillard,	Center Hill
261	Excelsior,	20	C. A. Mason,	Charlotte
262	High Brighton,	51	A. A. Scroggs,	Lenoir
263	Gaston,	32	John G. Lewis,	Dallas
264	Coble.	16	E. S. Euliss,	Brick Church
265	Farmington,	39	C. F. Bahnson,	Farmington
266	Dublin,	22	J. L. Autry,	Blockersville
267	Dunn's Rock,	28	A. A. England,	Brevard
268	Unaka,	36	Rich. M. Wilson,	Webster.
269	East Bend,	41	A. Horn,	East Bend
270	Builders,	13	D. P. Sink,	Friendship
271	Tabasco,	23	Joel Allen,	Gibsonville
272	Mebaneville,	19	Wm. B. Lynch,	Mebaneville
273	Watauga,	35	W. L. Bryan,	Boone
276	Beaver Dam,	23	J. A. Marsh,	Beaver Dam
277	Green Level,	25	G. A. Upchurch,	Green Level
278	Colesville,	37	Rufus J. Woolwine,	Colesville
279	Rehoboth,	27	D. H. Williams,	Teachey's
280	Sapona,	21	John W. Lee,	Asbury

No.	Name of Lodge.	Members.	Name of Sec'y.	Post Office.
281	Rich. Watt York,	15	J. H. Farrell,	Hanks Chapel. ..
282	Forestville,	16	S. M. Stone,	Forestville......
283	Eureka,	20	S. G. Patterson,	China Grove ....
284	Greenville,	27	W. A. Cherry,	Greenville......
285	Flat Creek	39	S. E. Teague,	Moffitt's Mills ...
286	Castalia,	20	W. H. Watson. M. D	Castalia ....
287	Blue,	17	A. A. Campbell,	Carthage ....
288	Eureka,	23	J. H. Simpson,	Company Shops..
289	Salem,	30	A. F. Pfohl,	Salem ....
290	Germanton,	14	Wm. Campbell,	Germanton......
291	Richland Creek,	24	J. A. Scott,	Moffitt's Mills....
292	French Broad,	24	R. S. Gage,	Marshall........
293	Vance,	20	J. D. Barnard,	Democrat. ......
294	Atlantic,	26	Jos. M. Watson,	Swan Quarter. ..
295	Bladen,	20	R. S. Gillespie,	Elizabethtown...
296	Stonewall,	22	John A. Manning,	Robesonville....
297	Little River,	16	C. Parker,	L. R. Academy..
298	Edgecombe,	19	P. S. Petway,	Joyner's Depot..
299	Hunting Creek,	16	J. L. Nicholson	Eagle Mills .....
300	Pamlico,	19	J. B. Bonner,	Aurora. ....
301	Clay,	41	W. A Curtis,	Hayesville......
302	Lillington,	12	B. F. Shaw,	Harnett C. H. ...
303	Evergreen,	8	D. Morrison,	Johnsonville....
305	Laurinburg,	23	Jas. J. M'Callum,	Laurinburg .....
306	Galatia,	15	Mathew Morgan	Fayettsville. ....
307	Patterson,	15	H. T. J. Ludwick,	Mt. Pleasant ....
308	Randolph,	28	P. B. Saunders,	Lassiter's Mills..

Ohio.

The following account of the organization of the Grand Lodge in this State, copied from the *American Freemason* for April, 1870, is worthy of a place in this connection, as being quite exact :

" On the 4th of January 1808, it was decided by the representatives of five of the six lodges then existing in this State, who had met in convention for that purpose in Chillicothe, then the capital of the State, to organize a grand lodge. Those lodges were located, respectively, at Marietta, Cincinnati, Chillicothe, Warren and Zanesville. The sixth lodge, located at Worthington, was also represented, but the credentials of its representative being pronounced informal, a seat in the convention was refused him. Four days were occupied with the proceedings of this convention, and, at their close, eleven brethren, constituting the total representation, subscribed their names to the proceedings, after electing nine of their number officers of the proposed grand lodge, and a tenth, not present, Gen. Rufus Putnam, then resident at Marietta, grand master. On the succeeding 2d of January, representatives from four of those lodges eleven in number, met at the same place, and being in doubt whether there were a sufficient number of lodges represented to organize a grand lodge—Dermott's *Ahiman Rezon* being their guide, and it requiring five—finally concluded to organize, and, having done so, they prepared a circular letter to the other grand lodges in the United States, announcing their organization ; then, after adopting for the time being the constitution of the Grand Lodge of Kentucky, a Past Masters' Lodge was opened, and the Deputy Gr. Master elect, Thomas Henderson, of Cincinnati Lodge was introduced by the Sen'r Gr. Warden elect, and by him duly installed. The Past Masters' Lodge was then closed, and a Master's lodge opened, when " the several subordinate officers elected by the convention" the previous January " were, by the Deputy G. M. regularly installed.'' In a letter very creditable to the old hero, Gen. Putnam resigned, and the grand lodge thereupon went into election of officers for the year 1809. But ten delegates being present, they were all elected and installed, with Samuel Huntington, of Erie Lodge, at Warren in Trumbull County, as Grand Master, and who was, therefore, the first actual grand master the brethren in Ohio ever had ; while Gen. Lewis Cass, then representing Amity Lodge, at Zanesville, was the first actual deputy grand master.

" A precedent established by necessity was exercised, it will be observed, in the fact that the brethren did not look beyond their own assembly for a grand officer to install them. The Senior Gr. Warden elect, George Tod, did, on this occasion, install the Dep. Gr. Mr. Thomas Henderson, before he was installed himself, and thereupon the Dep. G. M. Henderson installed Tod and all the other officers elect, including the grand master.''

This grand lodge has no stated place of meeting : its annual communications are held at the place elected at the previous meeting in October. In 1870 there were 403 lodges, with a total membership of 24,087. The annual revenue of this grand lodge is sufficient to pay mileage and per diem, the current expenses, and generally leaves a surplus which, in 1870, the grand treasurer reported had accumulated in his hands to the sum of $11,805.96. Compared with the constituency, the expenses of the grand secretary's office is the least known to any grand lodge, being for salaries, postage, and office rent, fuel, light, and stationery, about $3 for each lodge in the jurisdiction.

The executive grand officers, all re-elected in 1870, were—

ALEX. H. NEWCOMB, of Toledo, Grand Master.
PHILIP M. WAGENHALLS, of Lancaster, Dep. Gr. Master.
FLAVIUS J. PHILLIPS, of Georgetown, Grand Treasurer.
JOHN D. CALDWELL, of Cincinnati, Grand Secretary.

From the Proceedings of the G. L. for 1870, with omissions courteously supplied by the grand Sec'y, the following information has been arranged.

No.	Name of Lodge.	Members.	Name of Sec'y.	Post Office.
1	Amer. Union,	100	S. A. Cooper,	Marietta.
2	N. C. Harmony,	119	Charles Folger,	Cincinnati
3	Old Erie,	153	R. A. Baldwin,	Warren.
4	New England,	44	Walter Foss,	Worthington
5	Amity,	159	G. L. Phillips,	Zanesville
6	Scioto,	124	Geo. L. Wolfe,	Chillicothe.
7	Morning Dawn,	86	S. D. Cowden,	Gallipolis.
8	Harmony,	108	Kersey Roberts,	Urbana.
9	Mount Zion,	115	O. G. Daniels,	Mt. Vernon
11	Center Star,	76	Harvey Gates,	Granville
12	Unity,	117	G. P. Reed,	Ravenna.
13	St. John's,	130	Val. Schaeffer,	Dayton
14	Franklin,	87	James Nesbitt,	Troy
15	Cleveland City,	217	J. C. Wagner,	Cleveland.
16	Belmont,	73	J. B. Ryan,	St. Clairville
17	Washington,	114	David W. Davies,	Hamilton.
18	Hiram,	147	Harvey Pumphrey,	Delaware.
19	Jerusalem,	81	G. A. Clark,	Hartford.
20	Magnolia,	182	Henry O'Kane,	Columbus
21	Western Star,	151	Eli B. Walker,	Youngstown
22	Rising Sun,	86	Richard Radford,	Ashtabula
23	Pickaway,	98	T. K. Wittich,	Circleville

No.	Name of Lodge.	Members.	Name of Sec'y.	Post Office.
.24.	. Warren,	...... 64.	. . John S. Patterson,	. . Piqua ....
.25.	. Paramuthea,	.... 79.	. . Henry J. Topky,	.... Athens ....
.26.	. Lebanon,	.... 109.	. . Geo. W. Carey,	.... Lebanon.... ......
.28.	. Temple,	...... 146.	. . A. T. Tuttle,	...... Painesville......
.29.	. Clermont Social,	74.	. . S. N. Ferguson,	.... Williamsburg ...
.30.	. Columbus,	.... 81.	. . Horatio J. Cox,	.... Columbus.......
.33.	. Ebenezer,	.... 122.	. . J. DeWitt,	...... Wooster ......
.35.	. Mansfield,	.... 118.	. . Ed. B. Christmas,	.... Mansfield. ......
.37.	. Mount Moriah,	. . 65.	. . Chas. W. Reynolds,	. . Beverly ....
.38.	. Highland,	...... 47.	. . J. L. Hill,	.... Hillsboro. ......
.40.	. Northern Light,	. 44	. . E. H. Koch,	...... Maumee City....
.43.	. West Union,	.... 39.	. . John K. Billings,	.... West Union. ....
.44.	. Columbia,	...... 41.	. . G. W. Arnold,	...... Miamitown......
.45.	. Steubenville,	... 67.	. . E. G. McFeely,	.... Steubenville ....
.46.	. Miami,	.... 122.	. . J. C. Campbell,	.... Cincinnati .....
.47.	. Clinton,	.... 132.	. . Thornton Briggs,	..... Massillon. ......
.48.	. Aurora,	.... 109.	. . Francis Cleveland,	. . Portsmouth .....
.49.	. Xenia,	.... 112.	. . J. A. Harned,	...... Xenia ....
.50.	. Science,	...... 155.	. . Voltaire Scott,	...... Sandusky. ......
.52.	. Wilmington,	.... 69.	. . W. B. Wolf,	..... Wilmington. ....
.54.	. Milford,	.... 52.	. . Robert Kemehan,	... Milford. ....
.55.	. Eastern Star,	... 42.	. . Martin V. Dickey,	..'. Franklin........
.56.	. King Solomon,	. 119.	. . Laertes B. Smith,	... Elyra...........
.57.	. Lancaster,	..... 102.	. . John B. Townsley,	. . Lancaster.......
.58.	. Medina,	.... 138.	. . R. R. Rood,	.... Medina. ....
.59.	. Tuscarawas,	.... 52.	. . Geo. W. Crites,	.... Canal Dover ....
.60.	. Canton,	.... 118.	. . John Krause,	.... Canton.........
.61.	. Bethel,	.... 35.	. . R. M. Griffith,	.... Bethel ....
.64.	. Mount Vernon,	108.	. . Chester W. Flinn,	... Norwalk........
.65.	. New Lisbon,	.... 63.	. . G. W. Brown,	..... New Lisbon.....
.66.	. Cambridge,	.... 80.	. . Chas. E. Mitchener,	. . Cambridge......
.67.	. Oxford,	.... 61.	. . Adrian Beaugurea,	.. Oxford ..' ....
.70.	. Marion,	.... 79.	. . F. C. Ruehrmund,	... Marion ....
.71.	. Union,	.... 100.	. . A. K. Williams,	..... Ripley..........
.72.	. Georgetown,	... 62.	. . W. Jesse Thompson,	. . Georgetown. ....
.73.	. Temperance,	... 63.	. . J. S. Reed,	.... Sydney. ....
.74.	. Seville,	.... 33.	. . John N. High,	...... Seville ....
.76.	. Somerset,	...... 54.	. . J. W. Shirley,	...... Somerset ....
.77.	. Sandusky,	...... 84.	. . Charles Martin,	.... Tiffin ....
.78.	. Leesburg,	...... 42.	. . C. G. Starr,	.... Leesburg. ......
.79.	. Lafayette,	.... 117.	. . Edgar W. Allen,	.. Zanesville ......
.80.	. Libanus,	.... 27.	. . Wm. T. Kelly,	...... Lewisburg......
.81.	. Lafayette,	..... 202.	. . B. D. Stevenson,	.... Cincinnati ......
.82.	. Bolivar,	.... 52.	. . Robt. W. Quinn,	... Eaton ....
.83.	. Akron,	.... 219.	. . John McGregor,	.... Akron..........
.85.	. Jackson,	.... 29.	. . M. C. Hamilton,	.... Brownsville....

No.	Name of Lodge.	Members.	Name of Sec'y.	Post Office.
.87.	.Salem,.........	65..	.Tunis McNaughten,.	.New Salem......
.88.	.King Hiram,	...39..	.Michael Aiken,......	West Alexandria.
.89.	.Friendship,....	.97..	.Benj. Mackall,.....	.Barnesville ....
.90.	.Jefferson, ...	.55..	.Frank B. Erwin, ...	.Middletown. ....
.91.	.Western Sun,..	.60..	.John P. Merrill,.....	Wheelersburg...
.93.	.Chardon,......	.123..	.O. N. McGonigal, ...	Chardon........
.94.	.Montgomery,..	.52..	.Wm. H. Morrison, .	.Montgomery ....
.96.	.Coshocton, ...	.76...	....	...Coshocton......
.97.	.Newark.	136..	.J. D. Williams,......	Newark ....
.98.	.Minerva,.......	.53..	.J. H. Grove,........	Miamisburg. ....
100.	.New Carlisle,...	.—..	.H. H. Young, ...	New Carlisle ....
101.	.Clark, ...	143..	.Luther Brown......	Springfield .....
102.	.Felicity	49..	.Moses S. Dimmitt, .	.Felicity ....
103.	.Dresden, ...	.44..	.David Jones, ...	Dresden ....
105.	.Moriah, ...	.42..	.Peter Giffin,......	Powhatan ......
106.	.Fellowship, ...	.50..	.C. J. Whitridge, ...	.New Paris ......
107.	.Fayette, ...	120..	.B. H. Milliken,......	Washington C.H.
108.	.Wakatonika,....	.25..	.Patrick Thompson,.	.West Bedford...
109.	.Batavia,........	.70..	.Samuel F. Dowdney,	Batavia ....
111.	.Corinthian,.....	.62..	.Sam. E. Jones,......	M'Connellsville..
112.	.Wood County, .	.70..	.James Bloom, ...	Bowling Green..
113.	.Mechanicsburg..	66..	.Joseph W. Davis,....	.Mechanicsburg..
115.	.Hanover,.......	.64..	.John C. Campbell, .	.Loudonville ...
116.	.Hebron,........	.36..	.John Yost, ...	.Hebron.........
118.	.Malta, ...	.93..	.Henry Timms,......	Norwich........
119.	.Goshen,........	.43..	.William Haight, ...	.Goshen.........
120.	.McMakin, ...	.41..	.S. L. Wykoff,......	.Mount Healthy..
121.	.Mercer,........	.79..	.John Keller,........	Saint Mary .....
122.	.Moscow, ...	.37..	.J. W. Penn,........	Moscow.........
123.	.Phœnix, ...	.90..	.F. J. Oblinger, ...	Perrysburg .....
124.	.Carroll, ...	.66..	.Absalom Karns, ...	.Carrollton ......
126.	.Sparta, ...	.38..	.Robert Justice, ...	.Millersburg ....
127.	.Wellington, ...	.92..	.T. P. Hamlin,......	.Wellington .....
131.	.Vinton,........	.32..	.Wm. S. Matthews,..	.Vinton ....
132.	.Trowel,........	.64..	.Tim. S. Matthews, .	.Jackson ....
133.	.Cincinnati, ...	128..	.William H. Shober,.	.Cincinnati ......
134.	.Columbiana,...	104..	.Russell Bethel, ...	Cumberland ....
135.	.Butlerville,.....	.40..	.Henry Runyan,.....	Butlerville.....
136.	.Sharon,........	.91..	.Rich'd Burlingame,	.Sharon ....
137.	.Harrisville,.....	.87..	.David Rumbaugh,..	.Harrisville .....
138.	.Chandler, ...	.90..	.Wm. H. Chandler, .	.London ....
139.	.Bucyrus, ...	.62..	.George Keller, ...	Bucyrus........
140.	.Cheviot, ...	.48..	.A. J. Applegate ...	.Cheviot ......
141.	.McMillan,.....	180..	.Wm. G. Gale, ...	Cincinnati ......
143.	.Greenville,.....	.81..	.Aaron W. Arnold, .	.Greenville......
144.	.Toledo, ...	.—..	.(*No Returns*.)......	....

No.	Name of Lodge.	Members.	Name of Sec'y.	Post Office.
145	Valley,	59	Albert L. Miller,	Malta
147	Dayton,	105	Isaac H. Kneisly,	Dayton
148	Mount Olive,	39		Chesterfield
149	Aberdeen,	43	Robt. G. Campbell,	Aberdeen.
150	Buckeye,	64	Ezra Towner,	New Richmond.
151	Ashland,	113	Alfred O. Long,	Ashland
152	Venus,	91	M. B. Finfrock,	Mansfield
153	Farmer's,	45	Silas O. Preston,	Fredonia
154	Latham,	79	R. F. M'Connell,	Kenton
155	Cynthia,	133	Joshua Wadsworth,	Cincinnati
156	Albany,	43	W. W. Blake,	Albany
157	Philodorian,	54	W. C. Hickman,	Nelsonville
158	Palestine,	122	Orson B. Williams,	Marysville
159	Camden,	37	J. H. L. Bohn,	Camden
160	New Vienna,	44	George W. Mory,	New Vienna
161	Mad River,	58	L. M. Jones,	West Liberty
162	Yeatman,	66	Thos. S. Dewar,	Columbia.
163	Waynesville,	69	E. S. Shewalter,	Waynesville.
164	Pomeroy,	95	Leonidas H. Lee,	Pomeroy
165	Hildreth,	47	D. M. Neikirk,	Republic
166	Russellville,	36	W. P. Williams,	Russellville
167	Hamer,	52	R. McMurray, jr.,	Wapakonetta.
168	Covington,	—	(No returns,)	
169	Lithopolis,	71	Geo. S. Courtright,	Lithopolis
170	Thrall,	—	C. D. Hyler,	Fredericktown .
171	Mingo,	125	Wm. F. James,	Logan
172	Doric,	31	John M. French,	Deavertown
174	Tippecanoe,	67	Peter Fair,	Tippecanoe City.
175	Lone Star,	54	J. B. White,	New Comerstown
176	Warpole,	70	R. N. M'Connell,	Upper Sandusky.
177	New Philadelphia,	93	Oliver H, Hoover,	New Philadelphia
178	Lynchburg,	49	Edward A. Ubrey,	Lynchburg.
179	Superior,	72	W. Gardner,	West Unity.
180	Wellsville,	97	Wm. G. Foster,	Wellsville.
181	Bridgeport,	44	Henry C. Crawford,	Bridgeport
182	Smithfield,	81	Saml. Johnson,	Smithfield.
184	Irville,	59	C. H. Baker,	Nashport
185	Perry.	98	Eli Sturgeon,	Salem
186	Glendale,	24	Saml. M'Cune,	Glendale
187	Star,	90	H. Packard,	Cuyahoga Falls.
189	Monroe,	44	Jerry Williams,	Woodsfield
191	Blanchester,	30	E. M. Mulford,	Blanchester.
192	Fielding,	46	W. M. Ernst.	South Charleston.
193	Snow,	45	Richard White,	Harrison
194	Mystic Tie,	88	L. A. Conwell,	Uhrichville
195	Tu-en-da-wie,	67	Geo. W. Bechel,	Defiance

No.	Name of Lodge.	Members.	Name of Sec'y.	Post Office.
196	Bainbridge,		(*No returns.*)	
197	Kreider,	36	Isaac Putnam,	Quincy
198	Lawrence,	101	Edwin Bixby,	Ironton
199	Ohio,	39	Alex. S. Kerr,	Bladensburg
200	Venice,	35	Daniel Brown, jr.	Ross
201	Richland,	76	T. B. Tucker,	Plymouth
202	Port Washington,	51	Geo. D. Hill,	Port Washington.
203	Marathon,	29	Wm. H. Hartmann,	Marathon
204	Sharonville,	37	Peter R. Tortney,	Sharonville.
205	Lima,	153	Geo. W. Overmyer,	Lima
206	Mount Gilead,	76	W. W. M'Cracken,	Mount Gilead
207	Delta,	75	Geo. Lentz,	McArthur.
208	Hanselmann,	126	F. G. Warner,	Cincinnati.
209	Bellefontaine,	116	Geo. H. Allen,	Bellefontaine.
210	Olive,	68	Jonas Danford,	Sarahsville.
211	Rushville,	65	Albert B. Mortal,	Rushville
213	Summit,	103	Cassius O. Baldwin,	Twinsburg
214	Hope,	72	W. G. Davies,	Delphos.
215	Bryan,	98	Jefferson Miller,	Bryan.
216	Mount Pleasant,	58	Jno. F. Mitchell,	Mount Pleasant.
217	Social,	44	Thos. Wilgus,	Lena.
218	Van Wert,	88	G. M. Hall,	Van Wert.
219	Harrison,	99	Julius Brilles,	Cadiz.
220	Hubbard,	45	Jno. B. Spellman,	Adamsville.
221	Madison,	29	Jacob McNeil,	West Jefferson.
222	Evergreen,	96	Wilbur F. Stanley,	Conneaut.
224	Plainfield,	26	S. M. Bosset,	East Plainfield.
225	Fort Stevenson,	37	Jno. G. Spicher,	Fremont.
226	Mount Olivet,	38	Geo. McCullough,	Christianburgh.
227	Findlay,	53	Ben. F. Hyatt,	Findlay.
228	Hamer,	48	A. D. Daugherty,	Owensville.
229	Iris,	264	Isaac D. Faxon,	Cleveland.
231	New Birmingham.	49	Geo. N. Meredith,	New Birmingham
232	Lockbourne,	47	Isaac Miller,	Lockbourne.
233	Eureka.	87	S. B. Lawrence,	Washington.
234	Meridian,	88	Jackson H. Dawson,	Steubenville.
235	Brown,	87	Sylvester S. West,	Minerva.
236	Winchester,	37	Frank G. de Druin,	Winchester
237	Rubicon,	161	Don A. Pease,	Toledo.
238	Chester,	57	Washington Strong,	Chesterville
239	Erie,	71	Darwin Fay,	Milan.
240	Groveport,	23	Wm. Chandler,	Groveport.
241	Celina,	81	J. W. De Ford,	Selina.
243	Bigelow,	220	Wm. A. Madison,	Cleveland.
244	Monticello,	66	Mathias Benner,	Clyde.
245	Golden Gate,	101	E. C. Blackman,	Chagrin Falls.

No.	Name of Lodge.	Members.	Name of Sec'y.	Post Office.
246	Garrettsville,	97		Garrettsville.
247	East Liberty,	58	Oliver S. Balinger,	East Liberty.
248	Fulton,	64	Wm. H. Brinkman,	Delta
249	Newton,	25	Geo. W. Baxley,	Newton.
250	New Lexington,	54	Geo. A. Granger,	New Lexington.
251	Hazen,	55	Jenkinson Wright,	Belmont.
252	Webb,	42	Jason Roberts,	Stockport.
253	Hoffner,	61	M. S. Turrill.	Cumminsville
254	Buford,	59	Sanford Bradley.	Buford
256	Napoleon,	86	H. B. Lantzenheiser,	Napoleon
257	Germantown,	47	Elias L. Bone,	Germantown
258	Emory,	51	N. P. Turner,	Loveland
259	Mineral,	50	S. Lantz.	Hamden
260	Floral,	103	Gilb. E. Washburn,	New London.
261	Fairfield,	50	Henry W. Owen.	North Fairfield.
262	Naphtali,	40	Michael Heistand,	Carroll.
263	Clarington,	47	Jacob Roemer,	Clarington
264	Paddy's Run,	26	John L. Evans,	New London.
265	Morrow,	49	Oliver H. Smith,	Morrow.
266	Meridian Sun,	99	N. S. Brittan,	Richfield.
267	Bellair,	96	Frank J. Smith,	Bellair.
268	Blazing Star,	60	E. B. Kirk,	North Lewisburg
269	Mount Sterling,	75	C. H. Hanawalt,	Mt. Sterling
270	Union City,	88	John Parent,	Union City
271	Alliance,	146	Joseph Barnaby.	Alliance
272	Arcana,	97	Benj. Eaton.	Crestline
273	Bellevue,	63	Henry H. Moore,	Bellevue
274	Village,	80	E. L. Ford.	Burton
275	Orphan's Friend,	42	Hazen E. Soule.	Wilkesville
276	Allen,	53	John F. Sturgeon,	Columbiana.
277	Rock Creek,	63	C. R. Meigs,	Morgan.
278	Amesville,	69	Wm. H. Curfman,	Amesville
280	Kalida,	28	Harrison G. Lee,	Kalida
281	Ward,	56	Saml. Zollinger,	Piqua
282	Pleasant Ridge,	26	A. W. Schenck.	Pleasant Ridge.
283	Anchor,	67	John C. Wilhelm,	Duncan's Falls.
284	Relief.	52	F. H. Follett,	Pierpont.
285	Clement Amitie.	28	J. W. Barkhurst,	Unionville
287	Sylvania,	45	G. W. L. Probert,	Sylvania.
288	Fostoria,	56	B. L. Caples,	Fostoria
289	Gilead,	47		Gilead.
290	Versailles,	50	Jacob Lehman	Versailles.
291	Licking,	48	R. S. Fulton,	Utica.
292	Boggs,	58	Danl. W. Koch,	De Graff.
293	Bartlett,	42	Alex. U. Brill,	Plymouth.
295	Ithaca,	58	Abel T. Cloyd,	Ithaca.

No.	Name of Lodge.	Members.	Name of Sec'y.	Post Office.
296	West'n Phœnix,	54	C. T. Brown,	Parkman
297	Grand River,	51	L. F. Brakeman,	Harpersfield
298	Flushing,	39	Jesse B. Kirk,	Flushing
300	Stafford,	63	Wm. Gibson,	Stafford
301	Gibson,	45	Geo. W. Clary,	Birmingham.
302	Willoughby,	109	Saml. Phipp	Willoughby.
303	Mount Carmel,	103	B. L. Talmage,	Richwood
304	Rose,	47	A. S. Skilton,	Monroeville
305	Stokes,	50	John F. Rice,	Port Jefferson
306	Acadia,	17	H. M. Hill,	Spencerville
307	Lake Shore,	73	Ozro Hoskin,	Madison
308	Aurelius,	69	Henry Ahrendts,	Middlebury
309	Frankfort,	75	Marion J. Timmons,	Frankfort.
310	Eden,	25	J. W. Barrack,	Melmore.
311	Urania,	37	J. P. Winger,	Pleasant Valley.
312	Harveysburg,	53	J. B. Nickerson,	Harveysburg.
313	Sullivan,	60	Lafayette Boller,	Sullivan
314	Wyandott,	49	Geo. W. Sampson,	M'Cutchenville.
315	Riddle,	86	John M. Cook,	East Liverpool.
316	Rockton,	102	B. F. Keller,	Kent.
317	Manchester,	52	David Dunbar,	Manchester
318	Greenfield,	57	F. G. Waddell,	Greenfield
319	Osborn,	81	Geo. Williams,	Osborn.
322	East Townsend,	87	M. M. Perkins,	Townsend
323	Clarksville,	31	W. H. Gardiner,	Clarksville
324	Sabina,	38	S. A. Christy,	Sabina
325	Ottawa,	82	Alex. Williamson,	Ottawa.
326	Centre,	78	D. K. Trowbridge,	Johnstown.
327	Fidelity,	43	T. H. B. Beale,	Galion
328	Rural,	131	H. B. Hammon,	North Bloomfield.
329	Perseverance,	48	Chas. Brumm,	Sandusky
330	Caldwell,	40	J. G. Manne.	Bolivar
331	Golden Rule,	80	Jos. W. Linsley,	Cherry Valley.
333	Unionport,	53	C. B. Templeton,	Unionport
334	Geneva,	59	Daniel W. Wells,	Geneva.
335	Antwerp,	60	Thos. B. Harris,	Antwerp.
336	Brainard,	119	W. J. Norton,	Fremont.
337	Coolville,	107	A. S. Tidd,	Coolville
338	New Home,	45	A. F. Hall,	Hanover.
339	Blendon,	42	H. T. Sibell,	Westerville
340	Reynoldsburg,	78	Hiram Dysart,	Reynoldsburg.
342	Tuscan,	82	Jos. C. Howard,	Jefferson
343	Nevada,	36	V. C. Pease,	Nevada.
344	Ada,	70	Lewis F. Stumm,	Ada.
345	Concordia,	81	Wm. Wagner,	Cleveland.
346	North Bend,	40	W. G. Riggin,	Cleves

8²

No.	Name of Lodge.	Members.	Name of Sec'y.	Post Office.
347	Belle Center,	35	J. H. Morton,	Belle Center ....
348	Salineville,	57	Francis Rogers,	Salineville ......
349	Wauseon,	111	Jason R. Hibbard,	Wauseon ....
350	Shelby,	71	R. D. Stobert,	Shelby ....
351	Pottage,	54	G. Zeiger.	Elmore. ....
352	Jamestown,	40	C. K. Marshall,	Jamestown......
353	Orion,	66	Gaylor G. Viets,	Kingville ....
354	Somerton,	45	W. H. Helpbringer,	Somerton. ......
355	Pharos,	34	Emerson Gault,	St. Paris........
356	Kilwinning,	93	Geo. D. Martin,	Cincinnati ......
357	Edgarton,	40	R. R. Gillespie,	Edgarton ......
358	Swan,	88	E. E. Parish,	Mt. Pleasant ....
359	Marks,	54	J. L. Brooks.	Huron..........
360	Point Pleasant,	40	Wm. T. Larrick,	Point Pleasant ..
361	Pleasant Hill,	50	Jacob Reiber,	Pleasantville. ...
362	Sunburg,	29	Alex. L. Griffith,	Beallsville ......
363	Middleport,	82	Eli S. Branch,	Middleport .....
364	Rufus Putman,	38	Henry H. Gessells,	Columbus Grove.
366	Portland,	56	John W. Jones,	Portland........
367	Attica,	63	Simon A. Ringle,	Attica. ....
368	Muskingum,	46	Ezekiel Vanatta,	Fultonham......
369	Excelsior,	89	D. A. Mitchell,	Cincinnati ......
370	Tyrian,	65	C. E. Dustin,	Cleveland.......
371	Centerville,	31	R. W. Thomas,	Centerville.....
372	Goodale,	62	Henry E. Bryan,	Columbus.......
373	Higginsport,	29	W. L. Shinkle,	Higginsport.....
374	Metamoras,	40	A. W. Hutchison,	Matamoras ......
375	Bedford,	68	I. M. Harrington,	Bedford........
376	Belleville,	35	Solomon Wagner,	Belleville. ......
377	Shanes,	26	Levi L. Dysert,	Shanes' Crossing.
378	Senate,	33	R. C. Wiley,	Forest..........
379	Newburg,	63	Geo. E. Dunbar,	Newburg ......
380	Oberlin,	57	P. R. Tobin.....	Oberlin. ....
381	Litchfield,	36	Geo. F. Hutchings,	Litchfield. ......
382	Berea,	39	J. E. Cecil,	Berea ....
383	Waynesburg,	21	Robert Jones,	Waynesburg ....
384	Cardington,	55	D. A. Stark,	Cardington ....
385	Wadsworth,	54	J. G. Caskey,	Wadsworth. .....
386	Vattier,	107	Wm. Steele,	Cincinnati ......
387	Gorham.	57	J. S. Moffett,	Fayette.........
388	Forest City,	83	Frank Brewster,	Cleveland.......
389	King's Creek,	29	Simon E. Morgan,	Kingston ....
390	Harmer,	37	Henry Chapin,	Harmer. ....
391	Martinsville,	29	Edwin C. Ellis,	Martinsville.....
392	New Holland,	45	W. W. Blandin,	New Holland....
393	Miami Valley,	16	Wm. Longsdon,	Springsboro.....

No.	Name of Lodge.	Members.	Name of Sec'y.	Post Office.
394	Mahoning,	61	Geo. W. Mawby,	Niles
395	Portsmouth,	51	John S. Munn,	Portsmouth
396	S. L. Collins,	64	Marcus Kyle,	Toledo
397	Hart's Grove,	46	Rodney Marsh,	Hart's Grove
398	West Salem,	63	F. L. Parsons,	West Salem
399	Lagrange,	43	H. Bartholemew,	Lagrange
400	Sparrow,	66	Marshall Smith,	Sunbury
401	Leetonia,	39	M. F. Forney,	Leetonia
402	Willshire,	35	Geo. A. Dettmer,	Willshire
403	Blanchard,	33	F. W. Firmin,	Finlay
404	Pataskala,	27	Edwd. D. Clark,	Pataskala
405	Mystic,	50	D. C. Wogaman,	Dayton
406	Orange,	49	Bas. W. Price,	Leesburg
407	Ashley,	24	Elias Cole,	Ashley
408	Sandy Valley,	34	Wm. L. Parthe,	Hanover
409	Hamilton,	32	Adolph Schmidt,	Hamilton
410	Warren,	29	R. B. Poore,	Xenia
411	Harrisonville,	33	Gilman Riggs,	Paigeville
412	Painesville,	36	John S. Morell,	Painesville
413	Fort Black,	38	Jas. W. Broderick,	New Madison
414	Galion,	43	H. A. Cooper,	Galion
415	Freeport,	28	Jas. C. Carver,	Freeport
416	Caledonia,	24	Dennis B. Strail,	New Albany
417	East Palestine,	36	Hugh Laughlin,	East Palestine
418	Benton,	30	David Corner,	Benton Ridge
419	Madisonville,	26	John H. Crugar,	Madisonville
420	Carey,	25	Robert Gregg,	Carey
421	Yellow Springs,	36	Wm. M. Haffner,	Yellow Springs
422	Boomfield,	44	C. Gunsaulus,	Sparta
423	Deersville,	26	S. S. Welsh,	Deersville
424	Ely,	33	Jos. Hayes,	Vermillion
425	Summerfield,	42	W. Sparling,	Summerfield
426	Green Springs,	45	H. D. Parmenter,	Green Springs
427	Constitution,	33	M. L. Griswold,	Marshfield
428	Gerard,	18	E. F Jewett,	Newtown
429	Masterton,	23	F. A. Barnes,	Masterton
430	Cedar,	24	J. C. Grabill,	Orrville
431	Eagle,	31	A. W. Heldenbrand,	Canton
432	Bluffton,	18	Ahdrew Hauenstein,	Bluffton
433	Genoa,	28	L. D. Gregg,	Genoa
434	Royalton,	39	Darwin Bickford,	Royalton
435	New Harmony,	22	Wm. Sammons,	New Harmony
436	Lowell,	24	Joseph Cox,	Lowell
437	J. B. Covert,	24	Jas. H. Whitaker,	Withamsville
438	Ionic,	23	J. T. Mercer,	Bellaire
439	Thatcher,	18	Wilbur F. Sorter,	Nottingham

No.	Name of Lodge.	Members.	Name of Sec'y.	Post Office.
440	Union,	18	W. Frankwood,	New Bremen....
441	Pioneer,	17	C. G. Sweet.	Pioneer ....
442	Gustavus,	37	John C. Smith,	Gustavus ....
443	Crawford,	11	Geo. C. Gormley,	Bucyrus........
444	Prospect,	19	Henry Hain,	Middleton......
445	Monitor,	11	David E. Adams,	Delhi ....
446	Fairview,	20	Arch. M. Morrell,	Fairview ....
447	Oliver	11	Ernest Cauzler,	Caledonia.......
448	Gage & Gavel,	15	O. H. P. Crumbaker,	Chandlersville ..
449	Bloomingburg	10	D. M. Hays,	Bloomingburg ..
450	Mt. Washington.	—	S. Morse.	Mt. Washington .
451	Tontogany,	24	John S. Skinner,	Tontogany......
UD	New Lyme,	16	Frank E. Crosby,	New Lyme......

Oregon.

The Grand Lodge in this State was organized at Oregon City on the 16th August, 1851, by three lodges, two of which held charters from the G. L. of California, and Berryman Jennings was elected the first grand master. The annual communications are held in June at such place as may at the preceding meeting be elected. In 1870 there were at work 39 lodges, with 1441 members. This grand lodge has chartered in all 50 lodges. Of those the charters of six were surrendered for sufficient cause ; four became constituents of the G. L. in Washington Territory, and three of that in Idaho Territory. This grand lodge pays mileage and per diem to its members. Its cash revenue is moderate, being in 1870 reported at about $2,000, the same being insufficient to pay the matter of mileage and per diem for that year—two representatives having over 800 miles to travel, and one nearly 900, and all paid at the rate of 15 cents a mile. This grand lodge, it would seem, does much of its business on time payments, taking and giving promissory notes. It has an " Educational Fund," loaned on bond and mortgage—a matter of voluntary subscription authorized by resolution of the grand lodge in 1854, and in 1869 by same declared to be irreducible, but that it be allowed to accumulate for five years, by adding interest to principal. In 1870 this fund amounted to $10,400, and the ultimate disposition of it is yet to be determined. There is also a Relief Fund, of uncertain amount, contributed by a minor part of the lodges, and the disposition of which seems to be limited annually to a few beneficiaries.

The executive grand officers, all re-elected in 1870, were—

D. G. CLARK, of Corvallis, Grand Master.

T. McF. PATTON, of Salem, Dep. Gr. Master.

B. F. BROWN, of Salem, Grand Treasurer.

J. E. HURFORD, of Portland, Grand Secretary.

From the Proceedings of the G. L. for 1870 the following list is compiled.

No.	Name of Lodge.	Members.	Name of Sec'y.	Post Office.
∴1	Multnomah,	72	J. T. Apperson,	Oregon City
2	Willamette,	61	Sylvester Pennoyer,	Portland
3	Lafayette,	25	H. H. Snow,	Lafayette.
4	Salem,	75	E. N. Gillingham.	Salem
6	Tuality,	39	W. D. Pittenger,	Hillsborough
7	Temple,	43	H. S. Aikin.	Astoria.
9	Jennings.	35	J. H. Lewis,	Dallas
10	Warren,	69	Max Mueller,	Jacksonville
11	Eugene City,	69	E. W. Whipple,	Eugene City
12	Harmony,	102	Geo. H. Himes,	Portland
13	Laurel,	56	G. Webster,	Roseburg.
14	Corvallis,	52	B. W. Wilson,	Corvallis
15	Wasco,	53	Geo. H. Knaggs,	Dalles City
16	Oakland,	34	Wm. D. McGee,	Oakland
17	Corinthian,	40	A. Carothers,	Albany
18	Belt,	24	Chas. Hughes,	Kirbyville
20	Amity,	36	W. W. Brown.	Amity.
27	Champoeg,	27	J. D. Crawford.	Butteville.
28	Thurston,	47	Jas. W. Brassfield,	Harrisburg
29	Lyon,	24	H. Crone,	Independence.
30	Holbrook,	47	G. M. Raymond,	Forest Grove.
32	St. Helen's,	36	Thos. Elrington.	St. Helens
33	Jefferson.	24	Jacob Conser,	Jefferson
34	Canyon City,	46	E. J. W. Stemme,	Canyon City
36	Brownsville,	38	Almon Wheeler,	Brownsville.
39	Scio,	39	E. E. Wheeler,	Scio
40	Umatilla,	33	J. S. Schenk,	Umatilla.
41	La Grange,	41	S. M. Black,	La Grange
42	Columbia,	26	A. Pullen.	Columbia Bottom
43	Union,	25	Thos. Pettigrew,	McMinnville
44	Lebanon,	38	J. B. Calloway,	Lebanon
45	Silverton,	24	L. J. Wolford,	Silverton
46	Washington,	21	J. L. Shute,	East Portland
47	Baker,	18	Dudley Nichols.	Baker City
48	Blanco,	30	M. N. North, M. D.,	Empire City
49	Monroe,	14	J. M. Wells,	Monroe.
50	Pacific,	12	T. H. Cox,	Salem
UD	Cottage Grove,	—	A. H. Spare,	Cottage Grove
UD	Pendleton,	—	Geo. A. La Dow,	Pendleton

Pennsylvania.

───

ⲧⲛe Grand Lodge in this State waꞩ organized at Philadelphia by the representatives of about one half of the lodges in the State on the 26th of September, 1786, or three months previous to the New Jersey movement, and three years subsequent to the evacuation of the United States by the British forces. It holds quarterly communications, and, on the 27th of December, a grand annual communication in Philadelphia, when the election of officers takes place. In 1871 there were 315 lodges in the jurisdiction, and, up to 27th Dec. 1870, there were reported 30.488 members as belonging to but 269 of those lodges, leaving the true membership of 46 lodges unknown to the reader of G. L. Proceedings for that year, but estimated by the grand master in his address at 2,470. The principal business of this grand lodge is the construction of the New Temple in Philadelphia, upon which, for the purchase of the site and construction accounts to Dec. 1870, there had been expended $619.614. To raise a great part of this money, and continue the construction to completion every resource and asset is pressed into the service. A bonded loan has been put on the market from which there had been realized up to the above date $514,325. In this the Grand Charity Fund of $50,000, the Girard Fund of $50.000, with their unexpended interest acccumulations in addition, have been invested, while the balance realized from the loan up to that date had been taken by the Grand Chapter of Pennsylvania, 52 lodges, 14 Mark Lodges, Chapters and Encampments, principally in Philadelphia, "25 lodges, etc., of kindred societies, such as Odd Fellows, Knights of Pythias, United Americans, &c. and 172 individuals." All fees. including charter fees and fees for the degrees, have been raised, the former to $200, and the latter in Philadelphia city and county lodges to $75, and in all others to $40. It is expected that these extraordinary measures, and the continued sale of the bonded loan. will enable the building committee to complete the New Temple. The financial affairs of the grand lodge are in keep ing of men of ability, and who will, its believed, conduct them to a successful issue.

The jurisdiction is divided into 28 districts, each in charge of a a District D. G. M. appointed by the G. M. elect. If they report, such reports do not appear in the G. L. Proceedings — these for 1871 being mainly occupied with For. Cor. and Building Committees and Charity Funds reports, and the address of the grand master, and contain little if any information of a statistical character concerning the condition of the lodges.

The executive grand officers re-elected for 1871 were—

ROBERT A. LAMBERTON, of Harrisburg, Grand Master.
SAMUEL C. PERKINS, of Philadelphia, Deputy Gr. Master.
PETER WILLIAMSON, of Philadelphia. Grand Treasurer
JOHN THOMPSON, of Phildelphia. Grand Secretary.

For the following information we are indebted to the Proceedings of the grand lodge for 1869-'70-'71, Manning's Masonic Register for 1871, and the returns received from the Secretaries, in reply to our circulars addressed to them.

No.	Name of Lodge.	Members.	Name of Sec'y.	Post Office.
..2	...No Name,	...206	...John Winterbottom,	.Phildelphia.....
..3	......do........	245	...A. Nelson Batten,	.......do........
..9	......do.......	195.	..S. M. Duffield,	..........do........
.19	..Montgomery,	..301	...Charles Tiel,.........	.do.......
.21	..Perseverance,	.226	...Levi Wolfinger,.....	Harrisburg .....
.22	....No Name,	...142	...James Kershner,....	Sunbury........
.25	..Bristol.	134	...Levi M. Wharton,...	Bristol ....
.43	....No Name,	..350	...Hugh S. Gara,......	Lancaster ......
.45	......do...	..216	...Thos. W. Wright,	...Pittsburg.......
.51	......do.......	202	...Wm. L. Marshall,..	.Philadelphia ....
.52	..Harmony,.....	191	...George E. Wagner,.....	.do.........
.59	..Washington,...	368..	..Wm. B. Reed,..........	.do.........
.60	..Brownsville,....	88	...Geo. W. Lenhart,	...Brownsville ....
.61	... No Name,...	153	...Geo. Urquhart, M. D.	Wilkesbarre.....
.62	......do.......	325	...Wm. Briner,........	Reading ....
.67	..Concordia. ...	230	...Robt. Hutchinson,	..Athens.........
.70	..Rural Amity,...—..		.Font. T. Sage, ...	Philadelphia..
.71	..Lafayette.	275	...Chas. Carroll Burns,.....	do.........
.72	.Philadelphia, ..	236..	.Edw'd H. Ogden, ...	do........
.75	..Phœnix,.......	139	...Jas. W. Pennypacker,	Phœnixville....
.81	..Hiram,.......	133	...David B. Morrell,	...Chesnut Hill....
.91	..Columbia,.....	203	...Geo. S. Mustin,	.....Philadelphia....

No.	Name of Lodge.	Members.	Name of Sec'y.	Post Office.
106	...No Name,	...210	...Wm. R. Prior,	......Williamsport....
108	..Union,	170	...A. D. Harding,	......Towanda. ......
114	..Solomon's,	245	...Chas. H. Kingston,	..Philadelphia ....
115	..St. John's,	259	...John Q. Adams,	.........do.........
121	..Union,	256	...Alph. C. Ireland,	........do.........
125	..Hermann's,	...215	...Fred. Philipp,	.........do.........
126	..Rising Star,	...202	...Michael Nisbet.	.........do.........
130	..Phœnix,	215	...Edwd. P. Lescure,	......do.........
131	..Industry,	100	...Jas. B. Alvord,	..........do.........
134	..Franklin,	186	...Geo. J. Becker,	..........do.........
135	..Roxborough,	..211	...Thos. M'Cully,	......Cabinet.. ......
138	..Schuylkill,	56	...Sam. H. Madder.	....Orwigsburg. ....
143	..G. Washington,	.98	...A. C. McGrath,	.....Chambersburg ..
144	..Charity,	83	...Geo. E. Long,	.....Lewisburg......
152	..Easton.	275	...Dan. H. Neimann,	...Easton ....
153	..Waynesburg,	...80	...Jas. R. Rinebart,	...Waynesburg ....
155	..Mount Moriah,	.401	...Thos. E. Woodbury,	..Philadelphia ....
156	..Washington,	...198	...E. Ambler,..	......Liberty Square..
158	..Meridian Sun,	.408	...Wm. D. Shubert,	..∴..Philadelphia ....
163	..Evergreen,	67	...A. G. Cranmer,	.....Monroeton......
164	..Washington,	...113	...Wm. Wolf.	.........Washington. ....
186	..Eastern Star,	..411	...Geo. P. Little,	......Philadelphia ....
187	..Integrity,	266	...David Rittenhouse,	......do.... ....
190	..Charity,	177	...Sam. Brown. jr.,	.....Norristown .....
194	..La Fayette.	...165	...Aug. M. Carey,	.....Selin's Grove....
197	..Cumberl'd Star,	109	...Theo. Cornman,	.....Carlisle.........
199	..La Fayette,	...218	...Wm. H. Smith,	......Lock Haven ...
203	..Lewistown,	105	...D. E. Robeson,	......Lewistown......
211	..Kensington,	...354	...Chas. K. Neisser,	....Kensington .....
216	.Pulaski,.⟨....	.220	...John M. Miller,	....Pottsville. ......
218	..Honesdale,	157	...Jas. W. Kesler,	......Honesdale ......
219	..St. John's,	256	...Jos. Eichbaum,	....Pittsburg ....
220	..Portage,	120	...L. Q. Hoover.	......Hollidaysburg ..
221	..Franklin,	235	...Henry P. Ford,	.....Pittsburg ....
222	...No Name,	96	...Frank Heisler,	......Minersville .....
223	..Allegheny,	145	...Jacob Colmer,	......Allegheny City..
224	.Danville,	103	...Edw. G Hoffman,	...Danville........
225	..Philanthropy.	..36	...J. H. Highberger,..	Greensburg. ....
226	..Mt. Lebanon,	.147	...Wm. G. Ward.	......Lebanon........
227	..Chandler,	350	...Henry A. Tyson,	....Reading ....
228	..Fayette,	..:....—	...W. E. Beall,........	...Uniontown......
229	..Rochester,	128	...John Conway.	......Rochester ......
230	.Richmond,	256	...Henry Z. Ziegler,..	.Philadelphia ....
231	..Solomon's.	84	...G. W. Schluderburg.	Pittsburg. ......
232	..La Belle Valle,	.57	...Jas. S. Allen,	.......Jersey Shore....
233	..St. John's,	173	...Samuel Fear,	.......Pittston. ....

No.	Name of Lodge.	Members.	Name of Sec'y.	Post Office.
234	Crawford,	160	J. H. Lenhart,	Meadville.
236	Chester,	183	Wm. Hinckson,	Chester.
237	Chandler,	65	H. H. Young,	Bealsville.
238	Tamaqua.	122	Wm. Priser,	Tamaqua
239	Armstrong,	51	W. D Louther,	Freeport.
240	Warren,	191	Wm. L. Cox,	Montrose
241	North Star,	88	Rufus B. Smith,	Warren
242	Carbon,	127	James Houston.	Mauch Chunk
243	Mahoning,	104	Aaron L. Hazen,	New Castle
244	Kittanning,	107	Geo. T. Crawford,	Kittanning
245	Doylestown,	166	Hiram Lukens,	Doylestown.
246	Shekinah.	366	Alfred T. Jones,	Philadelphia
247	Friendship,	79	Mart. King,	Mansfield.
248	Temple.	141	Chas. J. Henry,	Tunkhannock
249	Carbondale,	128	N. P. Cramer,	Carbondale.
250	Sharon,	86		Sharon.
251	Hebron,	77	S. R. Thompson,	Mercer.
252	Gummert,	65	Hugh.H. Conelly,	Fayette City
253	Washington,	126	A. G. Lucas,	Pittsburg
254	Stichter.	167	Alex. Malsberger,	Pottstown
255	Shamokin,	67	John B. Savidge,	Shamokin
256	Milton,	104	R. L. Hatfield,	Milton.
258	West'n Crawford,	100	John Barr,	Conneautville.
259	Union,	95	Geo. L Lang,	New Brighton
260	St. John's,	98	M. C. Herman,	Carlisle.
261	Hiram,	114	Dr. H. Hollister,	Providence
262	Orrstown,	45	Max Kennedy, M.D.	Orrstown.
263	Franklin,	93	Samuel Neal,	Laceyville
264	Columbus,	87	W. H. Muzzy,	Columbus.
265	Washington,	161	C. F. Knapp,	Bloomsburg
266	York,	197	Fitzjames Evans,	York.
267	Swatara.	95	Wm. Schwenk,	Tremont.
268	Bellefonte,	132	Geo. B. Weaver,	Bellefonte
269	Monongahela,	171	Fred. Tyhurst,	Birmingham
270	Page,	61	Henry C. Voute,	Schuylkill Haven
271	Keystone,	213	Cornelius Baker,	Philadelphia
272	Butler,	80	Thos. S. McNair,	Butler.
273	Cassia,	99	J. L. Stadelman,	Athensville
274	Hamilton,	182	Wm. Smiley,	West Philadelphia.
275	Loyalhanna,	90	Sam. Singleton,	Latrobe
276	Hobah,	147	W. D. J Marlin,	Brookville.
277	Clarion,	115	Thos. B. Barber,	Clarion
278	Cambria,	98	Irvine Rutledge,	Johnstown
279	Newcomb,	37		Carmichaels.
281	Mountain,	125	Henry B. Kendig,	Altoona
282	Juniata,	78	John R. McFarlane,	Holidaysburg

No.	Name of Lodge.	Members.	Name of Sec'y.	Post Office.
283	Bethlehem,	160	B. A. Lehman	Bethlehem
284	Porter	115	Wm. H. Laubach,	Catasauqua
285	Anthracite,	74	Thos. A. Nichols,	St. Clair
286	Columbia,	127	Jacob G. Pence,	Columbia
287	Milnor	287	Peter C. Shidle,	Pittsburg
288	Jefferson,	89	Wm. Miller,	Allegheny City
289	Orient,		Thos. B. Simpson,	Philadelphia
290	Eureka,	108	D. A. Thalimer,	Greenville
291	Union	135	Geo. Parton,	Scranton
292	Frankford,	270	Thad. Stearn,	Frankford
294	Ashland,	130	Geo. H. Helfrich,	Ashland
295	Melita,	203	Dennis F. Dealy,	Philadelphia
296	Mitchell,	322	Wm. Mottram,	Germantown
297	Chartiers.		J. B. Musser,	Cannonsburg
298	G. W. Bartram,	83	Joseph G. Cummins,	Media
299	Muncie	81	Rev. Geo. C. Drake,	Muncie
300	Mount Moriah,	137	J. C. Africa,	Huntington
301	Waverly,	90	N. B. Hills,	Waverly
302	Eureka,	150	S. N. Eminger,	Mechanicsburg
303	Oil Creek	260	Robert Lyman	Titusville
304	Western Star,	110	Geo. Van Riper,	Albion
305	Hawley.	67	M. K. Bishop,	Hawley
306	Trojan.	150	R. C. Kendall,	Troy
307	Williamson,	98	Wm. M. Salladé,	Womelsdorf
308	Fort Washingt'n,	81	Alf. E. Smith,	Fort Washington
309	Williamson,	117	Rich. D. Wells,	Downington
310	Warren,	57	Henry W. Kratz,	Trappe
311	Mount Bethel,	78	Benj. Raesler,	Mount Bethel
312	Summit,	89	Geo. A. Kinkead,	Ebensburg
313	Indiana,	56	A. L. M'Clusky,	Indiana
314	Clearfield,	77	D. F. Etzweiler,	Clearfield
315	Cumberl'd Val.,	66	D. K. Wagner,	Shippensburg
316	Myrtle,	112	Marcus E. Hawkins,	Franklin
317	Ossea,	77	Hugh Young,	Wellsboro
318	M'Kinley,	160	James Brown.	Allegheny City
319	Adams,	68	Wm. N. Seibert,	New Bloomfield
320	Bedford,	128	Thos. R. Gettys,	Bedford
321	Hallman,	88	Sam. Davis,	East Liberty
322	West Chester,	132	E. B. Lamborn,	West Chester
323	P. Williamson,	137	A. Miner Renshaw,	Scranton
324	Union,	78	John E. Hallobaugh,	Mifflintown
325	Barger,	110	B. S. Jacoby,	Stroudsburg
326	Lehigh,	133	James D. Schall,	Trexlertown
327	Hazel,	126	Thos. Daugherty	Hazleton
328	Freedom,	60	H. D. Tennant,	Jackson
329	Craft,	49		Greensboro

No.	Name of Lodge.	Members.	Name of Sec'y.	Post Office.
330	Salem	93	Angelo Brown,	Hamlinton
331	Fort Ligonier,	—	John G. Albright,	Ligonier
332	Plymouth,	41	Fred. Schneider,	Plymouth
333	Barger	149	Ed. D. Lawall,	Allentown
334	No Name,	69	Aug. W. Newell,	Bradford
335	Eureka,	50	John A. Buck,	Montourville
336	Good Samaritan,	99	H. S. Benner,	Gettysburg
337	H. M. Phillips,	—	J. G. Farquahar,	Monongahela
338	Great Bend	110	David C. Bronson,	Great Bend
339	Hyde Park,	133	Chas. Corliss,	Hyde Park
340	Thomson	99	Sam. Fetters,	Garrett's Siding
341	Factoryville,	75	E. C. Browning,	Factoryville
342	Eulalia,	80	D. C. Larrabee,	Coudersport
343	Skerrett,	142	Dr. R L. M'Clellan,	Cockransville
344	Milford,	63	James H. Dorry	Milford
345	Schiller	87	Leopold Schimpff,	Scranton
346	King Solomon's,	62	Jos. T. M'Cormick,	Connellsville
347	Lake Erie,	80	David E. Day,	Girard
348	Patmos,	46	W. F. Stair,	Hanover
349	Catawissa,	101	Clinton Ellis	Catawissa
350	Bloss	113	Jas. H. Bannerman,	Blossburg
351	Cowanesque,	32	J. P. Biles,	Knoxville
352	L. H. Scott,	60	Alfred Taylor,	Chester
353	Oxford,	81	Eli M'Kessick,	Oxford
354	Sylvania,	48	Bernard D. Coons,	Shickshinny
355	Acacia,	40	Wm. P. Stratton,	Blairsville
356	Ten Mile,	56	John F. Miller,	Ten Mile Bridge.
357	Mahanoy,	96	Daniel Krebs,	Mahanoy City
358	Somerset,	63	Frank Stutzman,	Somerset
359	Humboldt	95	Wm. Sprungk,	Philadelphia
360	Canawacta,	92	Chas. O. Vedder,	Susq. Depot
361	Big Spring,	65	Stacy G. Glauser,	Newville
362	Tyrian,	123	R. M. Moore,	Erie
363	Petrolia,	108	J. N. Pratt,	Oil City
364	Susquehanna,	65	Simon S. Bowman,	Millersburg
365	Corry,	109	E. N. Gifford,	Corry
366	Eureka,	56	A. S. Tillottson	Union Mills
367	Teutonia,	45	T. L. Knéchler,	Reading
368	Corinthian,	49	Silas W. Pettit,	Philadelphia
369	Williamson,	202	Geo. Bertram,	do
370	Mifflinburg,	66	H. C. Steadman, M.D.	Mifflinburg
371	Lamberton,	40	Wm. C. Logan,	Thomsontown
372	Spartan,	36	Moses Higgins,	Spartansburg
373	Tioga,	47	J. Schiefflin. jr.,	Tioga
374	Davage,	79	Matt. G. Clark,	Manchester
375	Alliquippa,	60	Bichri Wilson,	M'Keesport

No.	Name of Lodge.	Members.	Name of Sec'y.	Post Office.
376	McVeytown,	50	Sam M Troxell,	McVeytown
377	Huguenot.	—	Lewis Fisher,	Kurtztown.
378	Mt Carmel,	50	Joseph Gould,	Mount Carmel
379	Elk.	85	G. L. M'Cracken,	Ridgeway.
380	Pennsylvania,	79	J Eldon Salter,	Philadelphia
381	Newport,	35	Wm S. Millegan,	Newport.
382	Emporium,	101	S. H. Storrs.	Emporium
383	Goddard	65	Clayton Taggart,	Coatesville
384	Richard Vaux	80	Joseph Boucher,	Philadelphia.
385	Oriental,	104	Wm. D. Atmore,	W. Philadelphia.
386	Apollo.	242	Jarvis W. Tindall,	Philadelphia.
387	Drushore.	50	Wm. K. Taylor,	Drushore
388	M'Kean.	60	E. H. Bard,	Smithport.
389	Kedron	29	Frank M. Powell,	West Middlesex.
390	M'Candless,	82	Wm. King,	Lawrenceville
391	Moshannon.	81	O. Perry Jones.	Philipsb'g Centre
391	Perry,	84	F. P. Longstreet,	Erie
393	Vaux.	199	Wm. S. Bailey,	Philadelphia.
395	Kingston,	65	P. B. Reynolds,	Kingston
396	Dallas,	75	Wm. W. Cottingham,	Easton
397	Ivy,	61	James Goodlander,	Williamsport.
398	Ashara,	42	Geo. H. Ettla,	Marietta.
399	No Name,	60		Northeast.
400	Friendship,	50	Sam. C. Conard,	Jenkintown
401	Watsontown,	74	James W. Bowman	Watsontown
402	Perkins.	124	Frank M. Highiey,	Philadelphia.
403	Clarkesville,	32	U. W. Teegarden,	Clarksville.
404	Eureka,	49	Dr. F. M. Thomas,	Northumberland.
405	Howell,	38	Geo. N. Shaffner,	Honey Brook.
406	Vaux.	44	Chas. A. Seidel,	Hamburg.
407	Geo. Connell,	40		Jacksonville
408	No Name,	41	Jos. Shippen,	Meadville.
409	Pine Grove,	34	Ezra J. Haak,	Pine Grove
410	W. K. Bray,	34	W. H. Stoker,	Hatboro
411	Meridian.	41	Saml. W. Reed,	Darlington
412	Temple,	35	J. C. Long,	Tidioute.
413	Manoquesy,	54	W. H. Seip.	Bath.
414	Elysburg,	—	Simon Wright,	Elysburg
415	Canton,	63	N. Van Namee,	Canton
416	Oasis,	41	O. W. Irish,	Edinboro.
417	Coleraine,	23	B. S. Patterson,	Kirkwood
418	Roman.	44	Frank Vaught,	Rome.
419	W. B. Schnyder,	166	Wm H. H. Davis,	Philadelphia
420	Fritz,	30	Joseph Chrislett,	Conshohocken
421	Osceola,	23	R. K. Skinner,	Osceola.
422	No Name,			Newton.

No.	Name of Lodge.	Members.	Name of Sec'y.	Post Office.
423	Shrewsbury,	44	Wm. F. Meyers,	Shrewsbury.
424	Adelphic.	32	H. M. Troutman,	Jamestown
425	Waterford,	52	A. D. Johnson,	Waterford
426	Cressona,	35	John M'Collin,	Cressona
427	Newtown,	31	O. W. Worstall,	Newtown.
428	Smithfield,	53	J. O. Gerould,	East Smithfield
429	Harmony,	37	Amos Lusk,	Zelienople
430	Stuckrath,	80	Jos. D. Long,	Allegheny City
431	Williamson.	19	Jas. L. Crawford,	Saltzburg
432	Price I. Patton,	57	Theo. Warner,	Philadelphia
433	Of the Craft,	65	Wm. R. Johnston,	Newcastle
434	Lake,	25	Heman Tolcott,	Sandy Lake
435	St. John's,	103	W. G. M'Gowan,	Reading
436	Mozart,	100	Jas. S. Woodward,	Philadelphia
437	Apollo,	27	W. G. Hunter,	Apollo
438	Nicholson,	40	N. P. Wilcox,	Nicholson.
439	Clifford,	30	Jas. C. Decker,	Clifford Corner
440	Slatington,	20	Lewis C. Smith,	Slatington
441	Potter,	128	Robert Mackey,	Philadelphia
442	Landmark,	28	D. P. Ayers,	Wilkesbarre
443	Mount Pisgah.	32	J. A. Davison,	Greencastle
444	Philo,	29	Alex W. Nutt,	Philadelphia
445	Harford,	17	J. C. Edwards,	Harford
446	Mt. Pickering,	15	M. S. Chrisman,	Upper Uwchlan
447	Claysville,	18	Simon White,	Claysville.
448	Zaradatha,	12	John D. Hirber,	Sharpsburg
449	Ivanhoe,	31	Chas. C. Hall,	Philadelphia
450	Stephen Girard,	14	F. W. Fisk,	do
451	Zeradatha.	19	J. W. Buckingham,	York.
452	Sewickley,			Sewickley
453	Welcome,		Dr. Wm. Taylor,	Philadelphia
454	Richard Vaux,		Lewis J. Able,	Burgettstown
455	Keystone,		M. H. Taylor,	Erie
456	Covenant,		Chas. W. Carns,	Philadelphia
457	St. James,		J. Morton Hall,	Beaver
458	Perry,	31	J. L. Weaver,	Marysville.
459	Valley,			Masontown
460	Oriental,			Orangeville
461	Monongahela,		Jacob G. Huggins,	Greenfield
462	Knapp,	33	A. B. M'Crea,	Berwick
463	Shepherd,	60	Thos. J. Young, M.D.	Titusville.
464	Robert Burns,		John T. Wilson,	Harrisburg
465	Hebron,		J. L. Worley,	York Springs.
466	Kingsbury,		Josiah H. Trine,	Olyphant
467	Laurel,		Daniel Heimbach,	White Haven.
468	Wyoming,			Wyoming.

No.	Name of Lodge.	Members.	Name of Sec'y.	Post Office.
470	Palestine		Joseph Evans,	Falls of Schuylkill.
471	Le Raysville,	17	Stephen W. Buck,	Le Raysville ....
472	Mount Hebron,		Jas. W. Fowler,	Pleasant Mount..
473	Covenant,	25	Horace Mann,	Cambridgeboro..
474	Coalville,	50	J. C. Wells,	Coalville ....
475	Kennett,		Josiah Jackson,	Kennett Square .
476	Lamberton,		H. B. Fahnestock,	Lancaster.......
477	Westfield,			Westfield ....
478	Beaver Valley			Beaver Valley ..
480	Noble,	27	James Innis,	New Washington.
481	St. Pauls,		Jos. R. Lonabough,	Philadelphia .....
482	Athelstan,		Wm. C. Probasco,	Kensington .....
483	Knapp,			Rouseville ......
484	Pittsburg,			Pittsburg ....
485	Glasgow,			Smith's Ferry ...
487	Robt. A. Lamberton,		James B. Shaw,	Philadelphia ....
491	Excelsior,			do.........

Rhode Island.

The Grand Lodge in this State was organized at Providence, on the 6th of April, 1791. by the only two lodges then in the State, and which had been both chartered by the Provincial grand lodge of Massachusetts. Christopher Champlin was elected the first grand master. Not until 1799 did a third lodge exist in Rhode Island, such third lodge being chartered by this grand lodge. The masonic year ends in March, and the annual communication in December. In 1870 there were 25 lodges, with 3.335 members of all grades. By this grand lodge no dues are exacted from the lodges except $4 per capita for new "makings," consequently the revenue is but sufficient to meet current expenses. There being no dues exacted by the grand lodge, the same rule prevails among the lodges, hence there is no discipline for nonpayment of dues. Masonry in this State, as in Connecticut adjoining, is not a joint stock monied corporation, but a fraternity. under the direction of a master.

The executive grand officers elected for 1871 were—

THOMAS A. DOYLE, of Providence, Grand Master.
LLOYD MORTON. of Pawtucket, Deputy Gr. Master.
GARDNER T. SWARTS. of Providence, Grand Treasurer.
EDWARD B. KNIGHT. of Providence. Grand Secretary.

From the Proceedings of the G. L. for 1870 the following list is compiled. Where it differs the information has been supplied by the lodge secretary.

No.	Name of Lodge.	Members.	Name of Sec'y.	Post Office.
..1	..St. John's,	242	...Wm. G. Stevens,	....Newport........
..1	. St. John's,	410	...Edwd. B. Knight,	...Providence .....
..3	. Washington,	...139	...Alfred Barton,	......Warren. ....
..4	..Mt. Vernon,	... 389	...Charles D. Greene,	..Providence......
..5	..Washington,	52	...Emory C. Tucker,	...Wickford. ......
..6	..St. Albans,	151	...John H Gladding.	..Bristol..........
..7	..Friendship,	130	...John Perkins,	......Mapleville......
..8	..Mount Moriah,	..68	...Simon A. Sayles,	....Woonsocket. ....
..9	..Harmony,	78	...Chas. H. Peck,	......Pawtuxet.......
.10	..Union,	296	...O. H. Briggs,	.......Central Falls....

No.	Name of Lodge.	Members.	Name of Sec'y.	Post Office.
11	King Solomon's,	63	Lowell H. Kenyon,	East Greenwich
12	Manchester,	136	Dwight R. Adams,	Quidnick.
13	Morning Star	174	Geo. C. Wilder,	Woonsocket.
15	Hamilton,	94	Geo. K. Tyler,	Mount Vernon
16	Warwick,	97	Vernum A. Bailey,	Phœnix
18	Temple	80	Henry Lomas,	North Scituate
20	Franklin,	140	Isaac F. Burdick.	Westerly
21	What Cheer,	323	Joshua M. Addeman.	Providence
22	Eureka,	95	Con. C. Chase,	Portsmouth
23	Charity	79	G. E. Greene	Hope Valley
24	Jenks,	80	Fred. A. Horton,	Central Falls
25	Hope	52	James F. Mowry,	Narragansett Pier
26	Granite	35	Sam. O. Griffin.	Pascoag
27	Corinthian,	36	Z. C. Rennie.	Providence
28	Ionic,	17	Leonard Tillinghast.	Greene

South Carolina.

The Grand Lodge in this State was organized in 1817 for the last time by the final union of the two grand lodges which, for some years previously had, together and separately, exercised equal jurisdiction, the one known as the Grand Lodge of South Carolina, and the other as the Grand Lodge of Ancient York Masons. The first derived its authority through appointments by G. M's of Grand Lodge of England, and the second through charters granted by Laurence Dermott's grand lodge ; and not until four years after the union in England of those grand lodges did a union in South Carolina of their offspring take place. The annual communication of this grand lodge convenes at Charleston in November. In 1870 there were 146 lodges, with 6,200 members, in the jurisdiction. The report of a committee on G. T's books made it apparent that in Nov., 1870, this grand lodge was about $4,000 short. It pays mileage and per diem, and has a Grand Hall in the City of Charleston, which it is proposed to sell and ·build a new one that will be a more profitable investment.

The executive grand officers elected in 1870 were—

WM. K. BLAKE, of Spartanburg, Grand Master.

R. S. BRUNS, of Charleston, Deputy Grand Master.

W. H. SCHROEDER, of Charleston, Grand Treasurer.

B. RUSH CAMPBELL, of Charleston, Grand Secretary.

Repeated applications to the grand secretary, continued up to the last day the preparation of these plates could be delayed, having failed in eliciting from him any response, either with or without a list of the lodge secretaries' names, we are unable to present them more completely than we here do—those given being supplied us directly in response to our circulars.

No.	Name of Lodge.	Members.	Name of Sec'y.	Post Office.
..1..	Solomon,	117		Charleston ......
..3..	Clinton,	37		Abbeville C.H...
..4..	Union Kilwin'g,	99	Adam E. Gibson,	Charleston ......
..5..	Washington,	126		do.
..9..	Friendship,	63	Levi Loeb,	do.
.10..	St. Andrew's,	41		do.
.11..	Winnsboro,	37		Winnsboro. ......
.14..	Orange,	102		Charleston ......

No.	Name of Lodge.	Members.	Name of Sec'y.	Post Office.
.15.	.Cheraw,	46		Cheraw
.17.	.Harmony,	—	(*Revived in* 1870.)	Barnwell C.H.
.18.	.Chester,	67		Chester C.H.
.19.	.Palmetto,	70		Laurens C.H.
.21.	.Pythagorean,	75		Charleston
.22.	.Harmony,	58		Beaufort
.23.	.Independent,	42		Due West.
.24.	.Williamston,	52		Williamston
.25.	.Friendship,	64		Kirksey's X Ro'ds
.26.	.Benton.	66		Timmonsville.
.27.	.Buford.	41		Buford's Bridge .
.28.	.Shibboleth,	—	(*Revived in* 1870.)	Orangeburg C.H.
.29.	.Kershaw,	69		Camden
.30.	.Ridgeway,	21		Ridgeway.
.31.	.Recovery,	92	W. L. Mauldin,	Greenville C.H.
.33.	.Aurora,	50		Clio
.34.	.Pendleton,	72		Pendleton.
.36.	.La Candeur,	50		Charleston
.37.	.Centre,	36		Honea Path.
.38.	.Allen,	34		Bamberg.
.39.	.Richland,	69		Columbia
.40.	.Winyah,	37		Georgetown.
.43.	.Eureka,	55	John D. Pearson,	Bennettsville.
.44.	.Campbell,	46	Wm. B. Bell,	Clinton.
.45.	.Effingham,	37		Effingham.
.46.	.Kingstree,	47		Kingstree.
.47	.Eureka,	36	John M. Gambell,	96, G. & C. R. R.
.48	.Lebanon,	58		Leesville
.49.	.Wallace.	54		Young's Store.
.50.	.Concordia,	48		Edgefield C.H.
.52.	.Grove,	38		Hickory Grove.
.53.	.Jackson,	33		Lancaster C.H.
.54.	.St. Peter's,	97		Manning.
.56.	.Catawba.	54	A. B. Banks,	Fort Mills.
.57.	.Mt. Willing,	21		Mount Willing ..
.58.	.Mt. Moriah,	43		White Plains.
.59.	.Butler,	50		Claryton.
.60.	.Clinton,	74		Marion C.H.
.61.	.Harmony,	33		George's Station.
.62.	.Charity,	31		White Cane
.63.	.Blackville,	48		Blackville
.64.	.Claremont,	83		Sumter
.65.	.Horry,	43		Conwayboro
.66	.Walhalla,	68		Charleston
.67.	.Harmony,	23		Hamburg.
.68.	.Hiram,	121	J. Baylis Lewis,	Anderson C.H.

No.	Name of Lodge.	Members.	Name of Sec'y.	Post Office.
.69.	.Ornan,	.53		Cedar Falls .....
.70.	.Spartan,	.82		Spartanburg C.H.
.71.	.Egeria,	.31		Rockville.......
.72.	.St. David.	.34		Darlington C.H..
.73.	.Str't Obs'vance,	.95.	.Clarence Wagner,	..Charleston ......
.74.	.Washington,	.13		Long Cane......
.75.	.Union.	.57		Union C.H......
.76.	.Landmark,	.72		Charleston ......
.77.	.Mackey,	.36		Harleesville.....
.78.	.Philanthropic,	.72		Yorkville. ......
.79.	.Keowee,	.41		New Pickens C.H.
.80.	.Bascom,	.40		Cokesbury ......
.81.	.Calhoun,	.55		Glenn Springs...
.82.	.Caldwell,	.60		Liberty Hill. ...
.83.	.Little Pee Dee,	.43		Nichol's Depôt ..
.84.	.True Brotherh'd,	25		Columbia ....
.85.	.Flint Hill,	.12		Gladden's Grove.
.86.	.Roslin,	.38		Lowndesville....
.87.	.Amity,	.75		Newberry C.H...
.88.	.Marlboro.	.34		Bennettsville....
.89.	.Bascomville.	.48	.J. G. Backstrom,...	Rich Hill X Ro'ds
.91.	.Greenwood,	.33		Gr'nw'd, G. & C. R.
.92.	.Blue Ridge,	.60		Walhalla........
.94.	.Acacia,	.38	.F. M. Drennan, jr.,	..Columbia. ......
.95.	.Etiwan.	.28		Mt. Pleasant ....
.96.	.Franklin,	.60		Charleston ......
.97.	.Coleman,	.12		Feasterville. ....
.98.	.American,	.15	.Jno. S. Overstreer..	.Grahamville ....
.99.	.Starr,	.68	.Tilman Faulkner,..	.Graniteville.....
101.	.Ebenezer,	.65	.Jno. W. Bolling,...	.Marietta ....
102.	.Reidville,	.39		Reidville ....
103.	.Saluda,	.44	.J. B. Etbridge,	......Leesville ....
104.	.Bishopville,	.58		Bishopville .....
105.	.Summerville,	.20	.R. K. Rutledge,	....Wright's Bluff ...
106.	.Barnett,	.50	.J. W. Carpentet,	....Piercetown .....
107.	.Gowansville,	.40		Gowansville. ....
108.	.Columbia,	.23		Columbia. ......
109.	.Allendale.	.33		Allendale.......
110.	.Branchville,	.29		Branchville .....
111.	.Rock Hill,	.53		Rock Hill.......
112.	.Bethel,	.26	.S. S. Robuck,	......Woodruff's......
113.	.Skull Shoals,	.36	.Jno. R. Crocker,	....Gowdeysville ...
114.	.Faust,	.36		Graham's, S. C. R.
115.	.Prosperity,	.55		Frog Level......
116.	.Hermon,	.39		Millford's. ......
117.	**.Mine,**	**.18**	**.....**	**Dorn's Mines ....**

No.	Name of Lodge.	Members.	Name of Sec'y.	Post Office.
118	Bruns	27		Parnassus
119	Livingston	24	H. F. Sally,	Orangeburg C.H.
120	Sumter	25	Wm. H. Cutteno,	Sumter C.H.
121	Amity	56		Florence
122	Hope	62		Kinnard's Mills
123	Boylston	39		St. John's
124	Stonewall	22		Millway
125	Pine Grove	26		Pine Grove
126	Hope	52		Williston
127	Hopewell	22		E. L. Patterson
128	Mount Hope	15		Mt. Hope
129	Tumbling Shoal	39	Dr. T. A. Perritt,	Tumbling Shoal
130	Belton	58		Belton
131	Watson	28		L. J. Watson's
132	Fair Play	29		Fair Play
133	Oliver	23		Rucker's
134	Hampton	15		Bethel Church
135	Cherokee	48		Cherokee Springs
136	Tyre	22		Charleston
137	Crosskeys	64		Gregory's Store
138	Batesvile	23		Batesville
139	Prudence	22		Jonesville
140	Lydia	52		Lydia
141	Salem	27		Maycoville
142	Blue	16		Gaddey's Mills
143	New Prospect	45		New Prospect
144	Schroeder	20		Fountain Inn
145	St. Matthew's	32		Wash'ton Sem'y
146	Bailey	23		Bailey's X Roads
147	Society Hill	25		Society Hill
148	Edisto	20		L. P. Rutland's
149	Pleasant Cross	16		Pleasant Cross
150	Pacolet	27		Pacolet Depôt
151	Pomaria	35		Pomaria
152	Lexington	16		Lexington C.H.
153	Evergreen	36		Hickory Hill
154	Sinclair	19		Pine Ridge
155	Savannah River	26		Four Mile Branch
156	Aiken	33		Aiken
157	Bethlehem	11		Bethlehem Acad.
158	Flintville	15		McNeill's Store
159	Cross Hill	13		Cross Hill
160	Dalcho	11		Oak Grove
161	Damascus	13		Mullin's Point
162	Jefferson	14		Mount Carmel
163	Little River	16		

Tennessee.

The Grand Lodge in this State was organized at Knoxville, on 27th December. 1813, by representatives of the several lodges in the State which held charters from the G. L. of No. Carolina, and Thomas Claiborne was elected the first grand master. The annual communication occurs at Nashville in October. In 1870 there were 338 lodges, with 18,601 members. This grand lodge pays mileage and per diem. At the 1870 annual session, after $13,856.60 was disbursed by him, the balance in G. Tr's hands was $219.85. The annual revenue is about $10.000. A very effective effort is being made in this jurisdiction to have a fund equal to $1000 from each lodge in it raised to endow an Orphans' Home. Up to 1870 about $80,000 had been pledged by about as many lodges. An Act of the Tennessee legislature passed on the 30th Nov., 1869, incorporates the "Masonic Orphans' Home, and for other purposes," of which Thomas Anderson is president. The "other purposes," covers life insurance privileges, giving the corporators power to go into that business in aid of the endowment. This feature may be regarded as the hodiernal substitute for the lottery incorporations of other days ; and while. in the event of failure to suitably endow the "home," the subscriptions are returnable to the subscribers, the money derived from this feature is liable and excepted. This privilege, up to 1870. had not been put into operation, and probably will not be, as the subscriptions have been liberal, and it is deemed best not to hazard the success of the "home" project by speculating in human life assurance.

The executive grand officers elected in 1870 were—

JOHN C. BROWN, of Pulaski, Grand Master.
TOWNSEND A. THOMAS, of Clarksville, Dep. Gr. Master.
JOHN M'CLELLAND, of Nashville. Grand Treasurer.
JOHN FRIZZELL, of Nashville, Grand Secretary.

From the G. L. Proceedings for 1870 we arrange the following information, in which the names of Secretaries not received in reply to our request have been courteously supplied by the grand secretary, Bro. John Frizzell.

No.	Name of Lodge.	Members.	Name of Sec'y.	Post Office.
..5	Overton,	54	W. N. Clarkson,	Rogersville
..7	Hiram,	60	James L. Parkes,	Franklin.
..8	Cumberland,	211	Jos. S Carels,	Nashville
..9	Western Star,	98	W. B. Lowe.	Springfield.
.13	Whitesides,	94	W. G. Taylor,	Blountville.
.14	Carthage,	77	Wm. B. Pickering,	Carthage
.18	Mount Moriah,	125	R. T. Tompkins,	Murfreesboro.
.84	Elkton.	32	James A. Bowers,	Elkton.
.31	Columbia,	66	James L. Guest,	Columbia.
.38	Union,	65	B. G. Lowery,	Kingston
.44	Rising Star,	62	B. K. Cunningham,	Rutledge,
.45	Jackson,	95	A. B. Jones,	Jackson.
.47	Rhea.	123	Chas. W. Meek,	Jonesboro
.50	Meridian Sun,	81	T. J. Cate,	Athens.
.54	Clinton.	91	W. V. Robertson,	Bolivar.
.57	Mount Pleasant,	45	J. W. Hagan,	Mount Pleasant.
.58	Brownsville,	156	W. W. Rutledge,	Brownsville
.64	Constantine,	84	John M. Taylor,	Lexington
.68	Jackson,	70	Lucius P. Bright,	Fayetteville.
.73	Somerville,	67	Thos. G. M'Clellan,	Somerville
.77	Liberty,	50	Thos. B. Potter,	Smithville
.80	Tellico,	77	E. E. Griffith,	Madisonville
.81	La Grange,	60	T. H. Webb,	La Grange
.86	Trenton,	72	P. D. M'Culloch,	Trenton
.88	Western Sun,	63	Ira Percy Clark,	Troy
.89	Clarksville,	131	Wm. J. Ely,	Clarksville
.90	Dresden,	73	W. J. Reavis,	Dresden
.93	Hess,	95	Wm. C. Doyle,	Dyersburg
.94	King Solomon,	78	Jesse Cage.	Gallatin
.95	Germantown,	26	M. P. Webb,	Germantown
.96	Caledonia,	86	W. S. Stephens,	M'Kenzie
.97	Charlotte,	72	J. A. Dodson,	Charlotte
.98	Lebanon,	120	R. Swain,	Lebanon.
.99	Sparta.	65	E. A. Defrees,	Sparta.
100	Ripley,	42	B. S. Fisher,	Durhamville
101	Pulaski.	81	W. R. Garrett,	Pulaski
102	Savannah,	65	H. R. Hinkle,	Savannah
104	Union,	77	G. M. Whitthorne,	Mason
105	St. James,	72	W. S. M'Bride,	Williamsport
106	Huntingdon,	95	Jas. P. Priestley,	Huntingdon
107	Lawrenceburg.	53	Wm. A. Gilmore,	Lawrenceburg
108	Paris,	83	John M. Clark,	Paris.
109	Marshall,	65	J. Wade Barton,	Cottage Grove.
111	Benton,	61	J. T. Younger,	Santa Fé.
112	Dillahunty,	52		Lewisburg
113	Union,	57	J. W. Johnson,	Hartsville.

No.	Name of Lodge.	Members.	Name of Sec'y.	Post Office.
114	Harrison,	65	S. A M'Kenzie,	Harrison
115	Yorkville,	83	H. J. Thomas,	Yorkville
117	McLemoresville.	55	R. H. Carter.	McLemoresville
118	So. Memphis,	145	Benj. K. Pullen,	Memphis
119	Greenville,	108	W. T. Jones,	Greenville
120	Macon.	68	R. A. Donoho,	Macon
121	Boydville.	50	J. Wes. Cook,	Boydsville
122	Shelbyville,	147	Tom E. Cowan,	Shelbyville.
123	Petersburg,	87	Rufus Harris,	Petersburg
124	Spring Hill,	93	Jim Blair,	Spring Hill.
125	Warren,	49	I. I. Womack,	McMinnville.
126	Cornersville,	68	A. E. Blackburn,	Cornersville
127	Waynesboro.	38	W. H Shields,	Waynesboro
128	New Providence,	85	J. P. Dean,	Marysville
129	Mars Hill.	69	S. G. Thompson.	Middleton
130	Sandy Hill,	81	R. B. Foster.	Sandy Hill
131	Phœnix,	117	John W. Barry,	Nashville
132	Purdy.	77	John M. Harris,	Purdy
133	Tannahill,	71	J. B. Anderson,	Gainesboro
134	Cleveland,	105	C. L. Hardwick,	Cleveland.
135	Triune.	30	Chas. R. Donoho,	Triune
136	Oakland,	48	Jas. A. Flippin,	Oakland.
137	Hampton,	75	J. W. Fort.	Port Royal
138	Pleasant Grove,	50	A. M. Davis,	Pleasant Grove.
140	Union,	38	J. H. Fry,	Mifflin
141	Martin.	87	O. L. Ewing.	Rome.
144	Morning Sun,	61	D. A. Hanell,	Fisherville
145	Conyersville,	61	John W. Martin,	Conyersville
146	Holly Springs,	37	John Dillahunty,	Macedonia
147	And'w Jackson,	60	Owen W. Miles,	Jordan Sta'n, Ky
148	Whiteville,	44	J. G. Johnson,	Whiteville
149	Lafayette,	50	James M. Marshall.	Lafayette
150	Dunham,	52	John W. Calhoun,	Covington
151	Hatchie,	26	Saml. T. Arent,	Midddleburgh
152	Collierville,	41	A. Young,	Collierville
153	Cotton Grove,	51	J. C. Potts,	Cotton Grove.
154	Denmark,	100	John H. Jones,	Denmark
157	Acacia,	41	Berry Lyle,	New Providence.
158	Cumberland,	85	Jesse T. Merritt,	Winchester
159	Washington,	94	B. Ray.	Washington.
160	Chapel Hill,	95	E. Williams,	Chapel Hill
161	Boon's Hill.	70	Jas. M. McAfee,	Boon's Hill
163	Mason's Grove,	64	W. H. Williams,	Gadsden
164	Cageville,	74	R. W. Fleming,	Cageville.
165	Danceyville,	65	H. G. D. Collins,	Danceyville.
166	Medon,	70	J. A. Thomas,	Medon.

No.	Name of Lodge.	Members.	Name of Sec'y.	Post Office.
167	Bigbyville,	58	W. L. Henderson,	Bigbyville
168	Angerona,	121	John Beamish,	Memphis
169	Dukedom,	86	W. P. Taylor,	Dukedom
170	Berlin,	70	G. W. Prewitt,	Salisbury.
172	Owen Hill,	71	W. R. Hazelwood,	College Grove
173	Clifton,	75	J. G. Witherspoon,	Clifton
174	Lavinia.	99	N. H. Childress,	Lavinia
175	Alexandria,	73	S. W. M'Clellan,	Alexandria
176	Limestone,	57	G. A. Matthews,	Georgetown.
177	Mount Pelia,	62	Wm. Taylor,	Mount Pelia.
178	Como,	64	I. I. Steel,	Como.
179	Camden,	110	W. F. Mayden,	Camden
180	Evening Star,	51	E. E. Eppes,	Tazewell
181	Washington,	38	A. R. James.	Louisville
182	Nolensville,	81	Rob't M. Howell,	Nolensville
183	Polk,	46	H. Clagett.	Centreville.
184	Harmony,	45	D. L. Tipton,	Tiptonville
185	Lynnville.	37	Geo. T. McLaurine,	Lynnville.
186	Morning Star,	75	T. N. Hughes,	Sulphur Wells.
188	Hiwassee.	96	James H. Darr,	Calhoun
189	M'Culloch,	53	W. J. Powers,	Palmyra.
190	Brazelton.	92	Joseph C. French,	Dandridge
191	Shady Grove,	97	W. H. Algee,	Milan
192	Merriwether,	35	W. J. Strayhorn,	Hampshire
193	Spring Creek,	89	G. W. Donnell,	Spring Creek.
194	Bethel,	54	Alonzo Gilbert,	Prospect Station.
195	Roche.	58	A. J. Armstrong,	Columbia.
197	Mountain Star,	64	M. J. Graham,	Sevierville.
198	Moscow,	45	J. S. Hill.	Moscow
199	Chattanooga,	107	Elbert F. Sevier,	Chattanooga
200	Pearl,	71	I. H. M'Knight,	Troy.
201	Bethesda,	65	P. D. Scales,	Bethesda
202	Humboldt,	149	Jas. B. Gillespie,	Humboldt
203	Milton,	83	A. W. Rhodes,	Milton
204	Tennessee,	83	W. H. Browning,	London
206	Eaton,	65	T. C. Patterson,	Eaton.
207	Lineport,	46	L. D. Hargis,	Dover.
208	Bethlehem,	44	C. S. Summers,	Tenn. Riv. Stati'n
209	Baker,	56	W. M. Carson,	Shiloh.
210	Linden.	62	H. Rice.	Linden.
211	Woodlawn,	45	H. L. Priddy,	Bartlett.
212	Ocoee,	44	Wm. A. Bible,	Benton
213	Meigs.	63	W. R. Senty,	Decatur
214	Harmony,	52	C. M'Crary,	Manchester
215	Sulphur Wells,	49	G. R. Thompson,	Paris.
216	Green Mount,	50	James J. Davis,	Green Mount

No.	Name of Lodge.	Members.	Name of Sec'y.	Post Office.
217	Pinewood,	53	Jesse James,	Pinewood
218	Decaturville,	77	David M. Scott,	Decaturville
220	Hamburg,	62	James A. Reeder,	Pebble Hill
221	Smyrna,	58	E. W. Owen,	Smyrna
222	Pinson,	54	A. S. Rogers,	Pinson
223	St. James,	50	John W. Kittenbury,	Henryville
224	Lanefield,	34	W. W. Whitaker,	Lanefield
225	Fredonia,	59	S. H. R. Wilson,	Clarksville
226	Tipton,	77	W. A. Bowers,	Mount Zion
227	Cherry Mound,	58	W. N. Warren,	Cherry Mound
228	Valley Forge,	42	E. S. Winn,	Oak Wood
229	Friendship,	43	John A. M'Culley,	Jack's Creek
230	Cuba,	60	T. W. Hines,	Cuba.
231	Morristown,	81	H. C. Witt,	Morristown
232	Gravel Hill,	81	L. M. Huggins,	Gravel Hill
233	Salem,	69	I. W. Powers,	Salem
234	Newport,	65	W. W. Langhorne,	Newport
235	Woodbury,	82	J. A. Jones,	Woodbury
236	Washington,	65	H. A. Crawford,	Washington.
237	La Guardo,	92	J. B. Wright,	La Guardo
238	Dashiell,	86	Wm. C. Emmert,	Elizabethtown
239	Hermon,	47	Jas. W. Keele,	Beech Grove
240	Beech,	72	F. K. Taylor,	Beech Church
241	Ducktown,	88	Henry Jory,	Mine City
242	Thyatira,	53	R. A. Moore,	Bradyville
243	Taylorsville,	65	Robt. E. Berry,	Taylorsville
244	Masters',	220	C. C. Nelson,	Knoxville
245	Woodville,	51	J. M. Anderson,	Woodville
246	New Market,	34	W. H. Moffett,	New Market
247	John Hart,	17	A. B. Williams,	Peucher's Mill
248	Vesper,	65	A. D. Norris,	Taylorsville
249	New Middleton,	64	Thos. Fuller,	New Middleton
250	Centre Point,	61	H. M. Sears,	Center Point
251	Friendship,	53	J. H. Davis,	Friendship
252	Bone,	82	A. J. Fletcher,	Rutherford
253	Chota,	71	W. D. Rodgers,	Concord
254	Edgefield,	88	Geo. W. Jenkins,	Edgefield.
255	Sycamore,	55	Isaac N. Clifton,	Sycamore Mills
256	Bradshaw,	47	Willie Willeford,	Bradshaw
259	Livingston,	25	A. L. Wendle,	Livingston
260	Clarksburg,	77	L. R. Clark,	Clarksburg
261	Mountain,	33	Harman Yuh,	Spencer.
262	Tullahoma,	76	John H. Lasater,	Tullahoma.
263	Ellen,	49	S. D. Pillow,	Double Bridges
264	Adam's,	46	A. H. Thornton,	Middleton Station
265	Farmville,	51	John K. Clark,	Farmville

No.	Name of Lodge.	Members.	Name of Sec'y.	Post Office.
266	Cookeville,	28	E. H. Stone,	Cookville
267	Saltillo,	52	A. B. Hanna,	Saltillo.
268	Reliance,	77	Wm. J. Peacock,	Bellbuckle
269	Fuller,	79	W. H. Wardlaw,	Ripley
270	Phœnix.	29	Jas. P. Flood,	Dover
271	Goodlettsville,	87	J. M. Shivers,	Goodlettsville
272	Burton.	52	Stokely Cook,	Cross Plains
273	Caldwell,	45	J. B. Wilkerson,	Johnsonville
274	Johnson,	67	Wm. S. White,	Fall Branch.
275	Newcastle,	42	R. H. Baird,	Newcastle
276	Turley,	52	N. Ailar,	Maynardville
277	Sneedville,	22	J. F. McNeill,	Sneedville
278	Tyre,	79	H. W. Hickman,	Union City
279	West Point,	66	C. Rhodes,	West Point
280	Sale Creek,	47	J. A. W. Patterson,	Sale Creek
281	Jamestown,	18	J. W. Gandin,	Jamestown.
282	Crystal Fount,	53	J. E. Moore,	Black Jack
283	Union Chapel,	40	T. T. Turner,	Union Chapel
284	Felix Grundy,	46	M. Gilliam,	Pelham
285	Newbern,	90	R. P. M'Cracken,	Newbern
286	Lewis,	26	Wm. Harder,	Palestine
287	Farmington,	52	R. T. Mount,	Farmington
288	Marlboro.	44	N. T. Leiles,	Marlboro
289	Leila Scott,	71	S. Sturm,	Memphis
290	Pleasant Ridge,	27	M. A. Clarke,	Big Sandy
291	Pleasant Green,	43	J. H. Smith,	Trazevant
292	Sweetwater,	80	J. H. Patton,	Sweetwater
293	Claiborne,	85	Jno. G. Hailey,	Nashville
294	Union City,	95	J. C. Foster,	Union City
295	Unitia,	45	Wm. E. Sheddon,	Unitia.
296	Palestine,	52	J. M. Harris,	Kenton
297	Olive Branch,	60	W. Byrne,	Jasper
298	Lowreyville,	26	A. H. Kendel,	Boyd's Landing
299	De Soto,	114	R. W. Shelton,	Memphis,
300	Wisdom.	38	R. C. Rushing,	Dover
301	Moriah Grove,	63	E. G. Sexton,	do
302	Thos. M'Culloch,	65	A. L. Bartlett.	Cedar Hill
303	Indian Mound,	52	Wm. J. Atkins,	Indian Mound
304	Waverly,	53	Z. Drummond,	Waverly
305	Pleasant Plains,	66	W. A. Rhodes,	Blanche
306	Forked Deer,	55	L. W. Daniels.	Belleville.
307	Anderson,	45	G. B. McPeak,	Gladeville
308	Libanus,	57	Jos. B. Muse.	Wartrace
309	Mount Moriah,	36	J. M. Matthews,	Whiteville
310	Rhea Springs,	71	R. B. Shirley,	Sulphur Springs.
311	Chas. A. Fuller,	17	J. C. Harrell,	Rossville

No.	Name of Lodge.	Members.	Name of Sec'y.	Post Office.
312	Manley	44	J. L. Cobler,	Tenn. River P. O.
313	Rock Springs	41	John F Dowell,	Columbia
314	Western Valley	17	S. M. Glenn,	Ripley
315	Mount Tabor	49	W. F. Clary,	Unionville
316	Ten Mile Valley	72	S. H. Baker	Ten Mile Stand
317	T. A. Hamilton	56	Dr. Chas. J. Dupont,	Riceville
318	Lynchburg	51	J. N. Taylor.	Lynchburg
319	Yellow Creek	33	W. T. Nesbitt,	Danielsville
320	Barren Plains	21	J. B. Taylor,	Lynchburg
321	Snoderly	47	J. R. Snipe,	Graveston
322	Jacksboro	30	W. C. Hall	Jacksboro
323	Nolachucky	42	J. A. Johnson,	Rheatown
324	Verona	30	Milo Scott,	Cranesville
325	Perry	33	A. J. M'Collum,	Lobelville
326	Fountain Head	76	W. G. Pond,	Fountain Head
327	Ashland City	38	G. W. M'Quarry,	Ashland City
328	Mooresville	27	P. D. Houston,	Mooresville
329	Buffalo	44	L. R. Meredith	Ashland
330	Oakwood	54	J. M. Finch	Gleason
331	Gilbert	60	John M. Dixon,	Trazevant
332	St. John's	42	George G. Hughes,	Jackson
333	Mount Carmel	38	Samuel Williams,	Mount Carmel
334	Sevier	21	John A. Watson,	Trundle's X R'ds
335	Statesville	40	N. Oakley.	Statesville
336	Marble Plains	39	Geo. W. Byrom.	Marble Plains
337	Peytonsville	38	W. H. Williams,	Peytonsville
338	Adamsville	62	J. W. Roach,	Adamsville
339	Sequatchie	69	D. B. Rankin,	Walnut Valley
340	Gibson Wells	44	A. G. Blake,	Trenton
341	Kilwinning	25	Louis Czapski,	Memphis
342	Granville	42	D. G. Shepberd,	Granville
343	Johnsonville	23	R. A. Vaughn,	Johnsonville
344	Mount Hebron	44	N. D. Crawford,	Mount Hebron
345	Cotton Valley	34	M. M. Massey,	Cotton Valley
346	Snow Creek	53	W. W. Vaden,	Snow Creek
347	Kelly's Chapel	35	W. G. Weatherly	Red Clay, Ga.
348	Greenwood	34	A. M. Reaves,	Little Lot
349	Mount Vernon	43	E. T. Hollis,	Dresden
350	M'Callum	28	James P. Dobbins	Appleton
351	Dyer	58	Jno. D. McLin,	Dyer Station
352	Smith's Fork	37	J. G. Reynolds	Temperance Hall
353	Mossy Creek	55	M. N. Garrett,	Mossy Creek
354	Fulton	14		Fulton
355	Germania	31	G. Schiff. M.D.	Nashville
356	Pleasant Hill	20	P. S. Faulk,	Troy
357	Cedar Springs	19	J. L. McAuley,	Cedar Springs

No.	Name of Lodge.	Members.	Name of Sec'y.	Post Office.
358	De Kalb,	41	W. D. G. Carnes,	Liberty
359	Saundersville,	28	R. J. Lyles,	Saundersville.
360	Pleasant Plains,	29	Willis Moore,	Pleasant Plains.
361	Campbellsville,	36	J. H. Cook,	Campbellsville
362	Park Avenue,	21	J. C. Gee	Park Avenue
363	Albert Pike,	25	John McBrooks,	White's Station
364	Hender'n Stat'n,	29	T. A. Smith,	Henderson Stat'n.
365	Pleasant.♦	30	Wm. Gambill,	Fulton Stat'n, Ky
366	Beaver Ridge,	33	S. W. Collier,	Beaver Ridge
367	Stockton Valley,	27	Jas. A. Mifflin,	Stockton Valley
368	Chestnut Bluff,	27	J. B. Parker,	Chestnut Bluff
369	Pocahontas,	36	H. R. Dorris,	Pocahontas
370	Charity,	35	T. W. Nichols,	Cumberland City.
371	Mansfield,	30	E. B. Hawkins,	Mansfield
372	Marshall,	35	Thos. B. McGahey,	Crockett's Corner
373	Short Mountain,	17	S. E. Jones,	Mechanicsville
374	Jerusalem,	34	B. Randolph,	Murfreesboro
375	McWhirtersville,	36	Robert Bee,	McWhirtersville
376	Alpha,	37	C. J. Sawyer,	Clinton.
377	Emerald,	20	W. R. Williams,	Wartburg.
378	Unity,	14	Peter P. Fugate,	Rob Camp
379	Mount Juliet,	34	S. Jarmon,	Mount Juliet
380	Center,	40	L. Sparks,	Swallow Bluff
381	Ezel,	41	W. D. Wallace,	Vervilla.
382	Hillsboro,	23	D. E. Mend,	Hillsboro
383	Valley,	40	W. W. Weaver,	Wallace's X R'ds
384	Flat Creek,	23	A. M. Kieth,.	Flat Creek
385	Henry,	33	J. B. Jones,	Henry Station
386	Clay,	19	F. L. Phipps,	New Canton
387	White Bluff,	30	J. C. Harris,	White Bluff.
388	Pilgrim Rest,	29	W. F. Scates,	Pilgrim Rest.
389	Gardner,	34	J. F. Gardner,	Gardner
390	Leadvale.	23	Harris E. Dewitt.	Leadvale
391	W. A. Nelson,	38	George P. Wells,	Ooltewah
392	Kenton,	22	Harvey Eckley,	Kenton
393	Stanton,	33	L. D. Price,	Stanton
394	Palmersville,	43	R. F. Bostick,	Dresden
395	Anderson,	10	W B. Parish,	Butler's Creek
396	Comasauga,	33	W. W. Dodd,	Cleveland
397	Bledsoe,	24	John P. Swofford,	Orme's Store
398	Selina,		T. T. Halsell,	Selina
399	Zion.		James M. Cartwell,	Humboldt
400	Sulphur Springs,	25	Wm. W. Parker,	Oregon
401	Confidence,	27	G. C. Dromgoole,	Fostersville
402	McAllister,	16	Sid. C. Batson,	McAl'r's X Roads
403	Rockwood,	11	J. A. Shadden,	Rockwood

No.	Name of Lodge.	Members.	Name of Sec'y.	Post Office.
404	Mulberry,	7	W. Y. Nix,	Mulberry.
405	Sewonnee,	22	E. O. Nathurst,	Tracy City
406	Cawood,	22	Aaron Lewis,	Tryon
407	Bethelhem,	16	E. O. Watson,	Memphis.
408	Mountain,	7	B. W. Woodward,	Flag Pond
409	Centre Star,	29	F. P. White,	White's Creek
410	Rowellen,	22	M. J. Hart,	Rowellen.
411	Joppa,	12	J. A. Williams,	Lebanon
412	Chas. Fuller,	12	C. B. Wooten,	Carlockville
413	Rock Vale,	21	A. J. Whitehead,	Versailles.
414	Corinthian,	25	A. C. Ross,	Nashville
415	Richmond,		W. R. Looing,	Richmond
416	Peabody,	24	J. A. Turley,	Cog Hill.
417	Comer,		(No returns,)	Cherry Valley
418	Soddy		do	Soddy
419	Chatata,		do	Cleveland.

Texas.

The Grand Lodge in this State was organized at Houston, on the 20th December, 1837, by representatives from the three lodges then in the State, holding charters from the G. L. of Louisiana, and Anson Jones was elected the first grand master. Its annual communication takes place at Houston in June. In 1870 there were 263 lodges with 11,500 members. This grand lodge is constructing a Masonic Temple at Houston. Its revenue for year ending in June 1870, was about $10,000. Of this $1,147 was contributed to the Grand Charity Fund—a fund that, like nearly all of the kind, is a Charity Fund but in name, and, also like them, sunk in a new temple. This immense State is at present divided into thirty-five Masonic Districts, for each of which a Dist. Deputy G. M. is appointed, and whose expenses of visiting the lodges are paid by the grand lodge, unless provided for by the lodges visited. Neither mileage nor per diem are paid by this grand lodge, and the attendance, consequently, of members is sparse, the lodges being represented in great part by proxy.

The executive grand officers elected in 1870 were—

CLINTON M. WINKLER, of Corsicana, Grand Master.
T. J. H. ANDERSON, of Port Sullivan, Dep. Gr. Master.
BENJ. A. BOTTS, of Houston, Grand Treasurer.
GEO. H. BRINGHURST, of Houston, Grand Secretary.

From the Proceedings of the G. L. for 1870 the following list is compiled. Where it differs the information has been supplied by the lodge secretary.

No.	Name of Lodge.	Members.	Name of Sec'y.	Post Office.
..1..	Holland,	......151...	Geo. H. Bringhurst,.	Houston ....
..2..	Milam,........:..49...		Edwin J. Fry, ...	Nacogdoches....
..3..:	San Augustine..50...		Geo. F. Crockett, ...	San Augustine ..
..5..	St. John's,......56...		W. F. Swain, ...	Columbia...-....
..6..	Harmony, ...179...		Chas. N. Eley,......	Galveston.......
.11..	Milam,........:.30...		J. L. Hallum, ...	Independence...
.12..	Austin..........79...		W. J. Oliphant.....	City of Austin ...
.13..	Constantine, ...94...		Jas. K. Blair,......	Bonham ....

No.	Name of Lodge.	Members.	Name of Sec'y.	Post Office.
.14.	Trinity	33	Theo. F. Meece,	Livingston
.16.	Friendship,	.66	Tom A. Carter,	Clarksville
.17.	Orphan's Friend,	49	Franklin Brigance,	Anderson
.18.	Washington,	31	B F. Wilson,	Washington
.19.	Forest	52	J. H. Banton,	Huntsville
.20.	Graham,	83	J. L Compton,	Brenham
.21.	Lothrop.	63	Rich'd Duglass,	Crockett
.22.	Marshall,	108	W. T. Smith,	Marshall
.23.	Clinton,	57	A. D. Stroud,	Henderson
.25.	Montgomery,	38	Joseph Boone	Montgomery
.27.	Paris,	93	Jas D. Wortham,	Paris.
.29.	DeWitt Clinton,	39	D J. Henderson,	Jasper
.30.	Gonzales,	83	H. L. Qualls	Gonzales
.31.	Palestine,	54	Jesse H. Woodard,	Palestine
.34.	La Grange,	63	R. S. Shepherd,	La Grange
.36.	Port Lavaca,	32	C. B. Kibbe,	Port Lavaca
.37.	Mount Moriah,	24	A. W. Harrell,	Cold Springs
.38.	Jefferson,	106	T. H. Durr,	Jefferson
.39.	Leona Union,	53	W. G. Edwards,	Leona
.43.	Douglass,	27	Fliel Rowe,	Douglass
.44.	Alamo,	108	W. T. Marshall.	San Antonio
.45.	Euclid,	66	Geo. T. Neely,	Rusk
.46.	Florida,	30	L. Schlottmann,	Round Top
.48.	Liberty,	31	B. F. Cameron,	Liberty
.51.	Saint John,	68	James P. Nenney,	M'Kinney
.52.	Tannehill,	86	Z. E. Combes,	Dallas
.53.	St. John's,	75	Geo. M. Johnson,	Tyler
.54.	Grand Bluff,	43	David M. Vawter	Grand Bluff
.56.	Warren,	45	E. B. Bell,	Caldwell
.57.	Larissa,	33	J. A. Shamblin,	Larissa.
.60.	Mt. Enterprise,	31	Chas. Barthold,	Mt. Enterprise
.62.	Woodville,	59	John W. Stewart,	Woodville
.63.	Rocky Mount,	58	J. B. Hollingsworth,	Bunker Hill
.65.	Joppa,	50	Martin Jernigen,	Elysian Fields
66.	Cherino,	29	Matt. W. Burke,	Cherino
.67.	Hurbert,	51	J W. Stone,	Chappell Hill
.68.	Caledonia,	69	H. M. Ehrenwerth,	Columbus
.69.	Boston	46	Lewis Alexander,	Boston
.70.	Temple,	33	John L. Riddle,	Mt. Pleasant
.71.	Mount Vernon,	65	Geo. F. Yates,	Mt. Vernon
.72.	Morton,	40	P. E. Pearson,	Richmond
.74.	Springfield,	79	H. C. Smith,	Smithfield.
.76.	Cameron,	20	L. W. Miller,	Clinton
.77.	Concord,			Jonesville
.79.	Oasis,	44	J. T. Turrentine,	Dangerfield
.80	Murchison,	54	Sam. Devall,	Hallettsville

No.	Name of Lodge.	Members.	Name of Sec'y.	Post Office.
.81.	Rio Grande,	81	F. Siebert,	Brownsville....
.83.	Ferrell,	56	S. B. Findley,	Alto. ....
.84.	Indianola,	33	C. R. Geyor,	Indianola. ......
.85.	Pine Bluff,	12	J. M. Day,	Troy ....
.86	Tuscaüm,	31	W. H. Payne,	Pine Tree Church.
.87.	New Salem,	57	James Lowe,	New Salem .....
.88.	And'w Jackson,	40	J. P. Wood,	Linden ....
.89.	San Gabriel,	38	W. P. Beall,	Georgetown... .
.90.	Waxahachie,	105	J. H. Bullard,	Waxahachie.....
.91.	Tarrant,	48	Z. G. Matthews,	Tarrant. ....
.92	Waco,	104	Thos. F. Skidmore,	Waco......,....
.93.	Augusta,	31	John C. Douglass,	Augusta ....
.94.	Goliad,	50	Jas. A. Burke,	Goliad ....
.95.	Sharon,	81	Wm. F. Nelson,	Sharon ....
.96.	Colorado,	59	R. E. Flaniken,	Webberville ....
.97.	Newbern,	35	P. N. Bentley,	Buena Vista ....
.98.	Canton,	61	R. R. Collier,	Canton ....
101.	Danville,	101	P. A. Pegues,	New Danville...
102.	Unity,	45	R. T. Walker,	Moscow ....
103.	Fairfield,	53	John T. Murray,	Fairfield........
105.	Kickapoo,	33	A. A. Gillian.	Kickapoo.......
106.	San Jacinto,	19	J. M. Westmorland,	Danville . ....
108.	Jacksonville,	39	H. I. Morris,	Jacksonville ....
109.	Guadalupe,	68	A. B Moore.	Seguin ....
111.	Burleson,	13	P. B. Curry,	Navarro ....
112.	Bloomfield,	61	J. T. Ayres,	Kaufman ....
114.	Prairie Lea	65	W. B. Walker,	Prairie Lea .....
115.	Kaufman,			Iron Mountain ..
116.	Red River,	35	H. B. Holloway,	Pine Creek Ch...
117.	Travis,	56	G. A. Dickerman,	Sherman ....
118.	Starr,	69	Thos. L. Myrick,	Starrville.......
119.	Flora,	56	E. G. Carter,	Quitman........
120.	McDonald,	30	A. W. Rogers,	Linn Flat.......
121.	Mount Hope,			Mount Hope ....
122.	Quitman,	39	John C. Baird,	Chatfield........
123.	Texana,	42	John T. White,	Texana.........
124.	Colletto,	42	L. Schumaker,	Yorktown.......
125.	Baylor,	31	W. E. Copeland	Gay Hill........
126.	Madison,	37	F. A. Davis,	Orange.........
129.	Brazos Union,	94	S. M. Hunter,	Bryan. ....
130.	El Paso,	15	B S. Dowell,	El Paso.........
131.	Belmont,	36	C. C. Littlefield,	Belmont........
133.	Retreat,	34	W. S. Callaway,	Courtney ....
134.	Bethel,	61	W. F. Eaton,	Ladonia ....
135.	Camden,	25	F. H. Garrison.	Camden ....
136.	Newton,	42	T. K. Seastrunk,	Burkville......

No.	Name of Lodge.	Members.	Name of Sec'y.	Post Office.
137	Mount Horeb,	50	A. M. Ramsay,	Mahomet
138	Lexington,	51	W. H. Koffman,	Lexington
139	Herschell,	42	E. J. Glover,	Coffeeville
140	Keechi,	54	Wm. M. Johnson,	Centreville
141	Castilian,			Canton
142	Bethesda,	61	J. M. Whitehead,	Gilmer.
143	Ochiltree,			Melrose
144	Pierce,	37	George Randolph,	Calvert
145	Walnut Creek,			San Anders
146	Winnsboro,	47	James B. Estes.	Winnsboro.
147	Planters.	18	A. B. Easeley.	Plantersville.
148	Fort Worth.	93	Geo. W. Newman,	Fort Worth
149	Sam Sanford,	61	John Holt,	Center
152	Marlin,	76	Sam. E. Watters,	Marlin.
153	Eclectic.	73	J. H. Scruggs,	Eclectic Grove.
154	Cotton Gin.	45	Fred R. Shipman,	Cotton Gin.
155	Spring Hill.	36	J. M. Berry,	Spring Hill
156	Hickory Hill,	30	H. J. Avinger,	Hickory Hill.
157	East Trinity.	36	J. D. Parsons,	Rock Wall.
158	Wm. M. Taylor,	26	R. P. Thweatt,	Carmel,
159	M'Clellan,	50	D. J. Morris,	Union Hill
160	Lancaster,	48	C. H. Patrick,	Lancaster
162	Murival.	35	Wm. Walton.	Murival.
164	Honey Grove,			Honey Grove
165	Athens,	51	L. H. Bryant.	Athens.
166	Belton,	85	Joseph Cater,	Belton
167	Kentucky,	55	H. B. Lindsay,	Kentuckytown.
168	Monroe.	73	J. T. Class,	Madisonville
169	James F. Taylor,	35	D. A. Dickard,	Hallville
170	San Anders,	57	R. Sterrett,	Cameron
173	Mound Prairie,	40	W. J. Duval,	Plenitude.
174	Corsicana,	57	Sam. R. Frost,	Corsicana.
175	Valley,	35	E. Sampson,	Burnett
177	St. Paul's,	52	Thomas Martin,	Port Sullivan
179	Hardiman.	29	P. M. Kellar,	Plum Creek
181	Post Oak,	67	J. S. Smith,	Post Oak Island.
182	Concrete,	38	J. C Woodworth,	Concrete
183	Hopkinsville,	70	E. W. Walker,	Hopkinsville.
184	Hickory Grove,	42	B. W. Thompson,	Seven Leagues.
185	White Oak,	37	J. P. Orr,	White Oak,
186	Decatur,	34	A. B. Foster,	Decatur
187	Tyrian.	38	F. C. McReynolds,	Sabine Pass
189	Corpus Christi,	46	R. J. Denny,	Corpus Christi
190	Refugio,	35	R. P. Clarkson,	Refugio
191	Havana,	41	A. C. Smith.	Havana
192	Cusseta,	32	J. N. Yateman,	Cusseta.

No.	Name of Lodge.	Members.	Name of Sec'y.	Post Office.
193	Leon	48	James B. Allen,	Aiken
194	Jack Titus,	29	J. B. Scroggins,	Red Oak Grove.
195	Lyons,	42	Chas. A. Kessler,	Lyons
196	Aquila.	49	W. B. Tarver,	Hillsboro.
197	Gatesville,	45	James R. Raby,	Gatesville
198	Tyre.	34	T. H. Vannoy,	Tenn. Colony.
201	Denton.	38	R. H. Donald,	Louisville
202	J. A. Baker,	38	S. P. Montgomery,	Eben. Church
203	Pine,	58	G. L. Malone,	Edom
204	Mount Calm,	33	W. T. Westmorland,	Montcalm
205	Walnut Creek,	62	S. D. Stout,	Veal's Station
206	Frank Sexton,	44	D. Puckett,	Pittsburg
208	McMahan,	96	A. A. Ellison,	Lockhart
209	Mantua.	83	J. L. Green,	Mantua.
210	Gainesville.	59	F. L. Cleaves.	Gainesville
211	Science Hill,	27	Isaac Allen.	Science Hill
214	Farmersville,	52	Dan. D. Graham,	Farmersville
216	Twin Sisters,	27	R. C. Traweek,	Blanco
218	Dresden,	78	B. F. Carroll,	Dresden
219	Millville,	33	J. L. Findley.	Millville.
220	Onion Creek,	43	D. A. Todd.	Onion Creek
221	Bright Star,	79	Wm. M. Ewing,	Sulphur Springs.
222	Parsons,	44	T. C. Bittle.	Parsons Sem'y.
223	Bellville,	16	L. L. Prouty,	Bellville.
224	Butler,	26	H. Manning,	Butler
224	Miller,	28	E. B. Shoemaker,	White Rock
225	San Saba,	53	D. S. Hanna.	San Saba
226	Brahan.	27	Jas. M. Trainer,	Concrete
227	Round Rock.	52	John B. Walker,	Round Rock
228	Newport,	25	P. S. Leigh,	Newport
229	Randolph,	17	S. J. Collins.	Pleasant Grove.
231	Sampson.	30	Robt. Blalock,	San Jacinto
232	Lampasas,	21	J. P. Gibson.	Lampasas
233	Eutaw,	77	J. A. Harrington,	Eutaw
234	White Rock,	35	R. P. Thompson,	Trinity Mills.
235	Plano.	65	C. C. Patton,	Plano
236	Relief.	21	B. M. Berry,	Rush Creek.
237	Lively.	26	J. R. Harper.	Masonic Hall.
239	San Felipe.	18	A. F. Silliman,	San Felipe
240	Fayetteville,	41	B. F. Dunn,	Fayetteville.
241	Forbert,	26	E. T. Gentry,	Turner's Pt.
242	Llano.	23	Wm. Haynie,	Llano
244	Gamble.	73	Jos. D. Sayers,	Bastrop
245	Gray Rock.	40	E. W. Giles,	Gray Rock
246	Sulphur Bluff,	41	J. P. Hargrave,	Sulphur Bluff.
247	Adah Zillah,	39	W. L. Abbott,	Millican

No.	Name of Lodge.	Members.	Name of Sec'y.	Post Office.
248	Ruthven,	28	John H. Brantley,	Llano
249	A. Jackson.	30	Wm. M. Perdue,	Pine Town
250	Black Point,	23	T. M. Dorsett,	St. Mary's
251	Sexton,	24	Wm. Gallatly,	Sexton
252	Hondo,	40	J. W. Rowland.	New Fontaine
254	Homer,	38	John Granberry,	Homer
257	J. A. Lawrence,	34	M. Schamburger,	Antioch
258	Oakland,	44	P. H. Hargon,	Oakland
261	Beeville,	37	T. J. Smith,	Beeville
262	Milford,	31	Champe Carter, sr.,	Milford
263	Whitesboro,	62	John W. Truett,	Whitesboro
264	Carthage,	50	N. W. Gillaspie,	Carthage
265	Grayson,	49	M. C. Fuller,	Piersonville
266	Grand View,	56	J. M. Watt,	Grand View
267	Stephensville,	47	E. J. Belcher,	Stephensville
268	Meridian,	23	W. L. Jones,	Meridian
269	Pleasant Hill,	25	A. M. Tucker,	Pleasant Hill
270	Pilot Point,	68	J. M. Elmore,	Pilot Point
272	Dixie,	34	F. R. Gilbert,	Knoxville
275	Phœnix,	75	B. L. Richey,	Weatherford
276	Comal,	32	T. L. Lyons,	New Braunfels
277	Mountain,	25	J. W. Hodges,	Burlison Springs.
278	Henry Thomas,	17	Herman L. Hensel,	Burton's
281	Hempstead,	46	Henry L. Rankin,	Hempstead
282	Winchester,	37	James H. Hall,	Winchester
283	Pleasanton,	69	Jas. C. Carr,	Pleasanton
284	Eastern Star,	30	J. T. Deaton,	Nogarlus
285	Acton,	47	P. H. Thrash,	Acton.
286	Beaumont,	23	Wm. Wiess,	Beaumont
287	Stonewall,	30	T. B Murphy,	Stonewall
288	Grapevine,	39	Jas. S. Chapman,	Grapevine
289	Harmony Hill,	26	S. W. Chamness,	Harmony Hill
290	Tyler Prairie,	43	W. A. Nelmes,	Pennington
291	John Armstrong,	36	J. T. Vaughn,	Hog Creek
292	Kimball,	40	A. Wellingham,	Kimball
293	Mars Hill,	49	Thos. W. Allred,	Mars Hill
294	Nathan Corley,	32	D. B. Haynes,	Magnolia Springs
295	Scyene,	30	Henry C. Sweet,	Scyene
296	Salado,	35	J. H. Barbee,	Salado
297	Tucker,	77	N. B. Sligh,	Galveston
298	Moulton,	24	R. J. Carr,	Moulton
299	Navaseta,	46	P. B. Perry,	Navaseta
300	Cedar Creek,	50	J. P. Lloyd,	Tryon Church
301	Osage,	36	Rowan Green,	Osage
302	Blackwell,	17	M. G. Settle,	Charleston
303	Starkville,	44	H. Fernandez,	Starkville

No.	Name of Lodge.	Members.	Name of Sec'y.	Post Office.
304	Live Oak,	21	J. B. Ratliffe,	Live Oak.
305	Littleton Fowler.	24	E. M. Sweet,	Hemphill.
306	G. W. Foster,	34	J. W. Lott.	Nelsonville
307	Shiloh	47	John A. Schenck,	Shiloh
308	Cedar Grove,	38	T. C. Saddler.	Cedar Grove
309	Hull's Store,	21	W. F. Walker,	Hull's Store
310	Red Rock.	36	B. D. Rhodes,	Red Rock.
311	Bryan's Station,	28	W. B. Sparks,	Bryan's Station.
312	Wm. Foster,	30	G. W. Barber,	Fosterville
313	Zion,	17	John Vernon.	Davistown
314	Alvarado,	59	H. E Chambers,	Alvarado.
315	Cleburne,	43	Wm. O. Menifee,	Cleburne
317	Shuler.	22	G. W. Betts,	Mount Thalia.
319	Palo Pinto,	16	J. H. Baker,	Stribling
320	Fort Richardson,	25	H. B. Verner.	Fort Richardson.
321	Cedar Bayou,	12	H. F. Gillette,	Cedar Bayou.
322	Prairieville,	11	J. H. Rierson	Prairieville
323	Rockport,	19	H. O. Ives,	Rockport.
324	Bandera,	18	W. H. Davenport.	Bandera.
325	Evergreen,	16	Elisha Lawley.	Oakville
326	Victoria,	17	N. A. Thomson,	Victoria.
327	Brazoria,	18	C. R. Cox,	Brazoria.
328	Perryville,	21	S. W. Biggs.	Perryville
329	Gray.	—	Robert C. Files,	Houston.
330	Carolina,	24	Isnad D. Wright.	Carolina Church.

Vermont.

The Grand Lodge in this State was organized by the represent-atives of the lodges in the State on the 19th of October, 1794. The number of those lodges we,have been unable to ascertain. In the early provincial times Vermont was claimed as a part of N. York; but whether this fact led brethren to apply to any Prov. G. M. in the latter for a lodge charter, and receive the same, or not, we are at present unable to determine. Not previous to 1781 does there appear to have been a lodge in Vt. In that year one was chartered by the Boston 1777 grand lodge, and it subsequently was known as Vermont Lodge, No. 1. Four years afterward another lodge was chartered by the same authority, and there is no evidence at our command. nor can we ascertain from any record,that more than those two lodges existed in that State when the grand lodge was organized in 1794, nor at any previous time. We are thus parti-cular in the expression of this matter, as the fact that *two* lodges, if they compose the whole number within a grand lodge jurisdic-tion, are as competent.to organize a grand lodge as any greater number has been established by the action of such a number, re-spectively, in the States of Rhode Island and Vermont.

In 1870 there were 91 lodges with a total membership of 7.747 within the jurisdiction of this grand lodge. Paying mileage and per diem, with a revenue of about $1,000, necessarily leaves a low treasury. With an accumulated Charity Fund of less than $500, its total assets in 1870 were about $3,500. There are 14 Dist. Dep. G. M's in charge each of a Masonic District, after the manner in other States.

The executive grand officers elected in 1870 were—

> GEORGE M. HALL, of Swanton, Grand Master.
> PARK DAVIS, of St. Alban's, Dep. Gr. Master.
> CHAS. W. WOODHOUSE. of Burlington, Grand Treasurer.
> HENRY CLARK, of Rutland, Grand Secretary.

From the Proceedings of the G. L. for 1870 the following list is compiled. Where it differs the information has been supplied by the lodge secretary.

[222]

No.	Name of Lodge.	Members.	Name of Sec'y.	Post Office.
..1	.Dorchester,	97	...Ezra A. Scovel	......Vergennes ......
..2	.Union	175	...Henry L. Sheldon,	..Middlebury. ....
..3	..Washington,	...171	...W. H. S. Whitcomb,	.Burlington ......
..4	..Franklin.	157	...Chas. A. French,	....St. Alban's......
..5	..Morning Sun,	..103	...John H. Witherell,	..Bridport........
. 6	..Lamoille.	78	...A. B. Beeman,	......Fairfax. ....
..7	..Rising Sun,	...132	...Jno. W. Metcalf,	....Royalton ......
..8	..Mount Vernon,	151	...G. W. Doty,	........Morristown .....
..9	..Missisquoi,	88	...Lester Rounds	......Richford........
.10	..Independence,	..69	...L H. Jennings,	.....Orwell ....
.11	..Columbus.	47	...H. G. Stearns,	......Alburgh. ....
.12	..North Star,	140	...W. K. Christan,	.....Richmond ......
.13	..Mt. Anthony,	..125	...Buel N. Walker,	... Bennington .....
.14	..Seventy-six,	63	...S. S. Morey,	........Swanton........
.15	..De Witt Clinton,	162	...W. C. Johnson,	....Northfield ......
.16	..Masonic Union,	97	...C. H. Benton,	.......Troy. ....
.17	..Isle of Patmos,	.47	...A. B. Conro,	.......North Hero. ....
.18	..Vermont,	 160	...L. N. Ferris,	.......Windsor. ....
.20	..Meridian Sun.	..83	...Nelson Rand,	.......Craftsbury ......
.21	..United Brethren,	57	...N. W. White	.......Hartford........
.22	..Aurora,	202	...James T. Sabin,	....Mt. Pelier ......
.23	..Blazing Star,	...78	...Lucius H. Cathan,	..East Townshend.
.24	..Friendship	90	...H. D. Edgerton,	....Charlotte ....
25	..St. Paul's	132	...Alva F. Smith,	......Brandon........
26	..McDonough,	85	...Albert A. Slater,	....Essex ....
.27	..Passumpsic,	256	...L. B. Heald,	......St Johnsbury. ..
.28	..Phœnix.	102	...E. O. Wires.	.......West Randolph..
.29	..Rural,	80	...Julius G. Fassett.	...Rochester.......
.30	..Lee.	108	...W. Henry Northrop,	Castleton. ......
.31	..Woodstock,	...137	...O. D. Randall,	......Woodstock......
.32	..Golden Rule,	...80	...Alexis B. Hewitt,	....Putney ....
.33	..Patriot,	116	...Stephen W. Palmer,	..Hinesburgh. ....
.34	..Center,	162	...James H. Dyer,	.....Rutland ....
.35	..Granite,	104	...Clark Holden,	.....Barre. ....
.36	.Columbian,	154	...E. F. Brooks,	......Brattleboro ....
.37	..Morning Star,	.131	...Henry Ruggles,	.....Poultney ....
.38	..Social,	65	...C. M. Russell,	.....Wilmington.....
.39	..Haswell,	43	...A. H. Keith,	........Sheldon ....
.40	..Seneca,	46	...Henry O. Clark,	....Milton ....
.41	..St. John's,	115	... A. M. Titus,	......Springfield......
.42	..Adoniram,	107	...James P. Black,	....Manchester ......
.43	..Charity,	83	... J. B. W. Prichard,	..Bradford........
.44	..Island Pond,	68	...Geo. S Robinson,	..Island Pond.....
.45	..King Solomon's,	92	...Chas. E Holbrook,	..Bellows Falls ...
.46	..Mt. Lebanon,	...47	...H. J. Livermore,	....Jamaica ....
.47	..Libanus,	113	...L. Munson,	.........Bristol ....

No.	Name of Lodge.	Members.	Name of Sec'y.	Post Office.
.48..	Tucker,	........76...	L. B. Newton,	.....North Bennington
.49..	Winooski,	......75...	Edgar C. Smith	......Waterbury......
.50..	Warner,	........75...	Clinton S. Kinsley,	..Cambridge......
.51..	G. Washington,	.57...	Albert Dodge,	......Chelsea.... ....
.52..	Chipman,	......87...	D. H. Sabin	........Wallingford.....
.53..	Lafayette,	86	..Silas E. Wright,	......Cavendish ......
.54..	Temple,	........55...	Ira P. Morrill,	.....South Stafford...
.55..	Orleans,	.......97...	Chas. H. Dwinell,	...Barton ....
.56..	Mystic,	........85...	Warren J. Atkins,	.. Stowe ....
.57..	West River,	....80...	Mark H. Farnsworth.	Londonderry....
.58..	Pulaski,	........55...	Ira T. Bronson,	.... Newberry......
.59..	Simonds,	......65...	H. M. Atwood,	.....Shoreham.......
.60..	Jackson,	......113...	Wm. Pollard,	.......West Fairlee....
.61..	Webster,	......64...	E. H. Blossom,	......Winooski Falls ..
.62..	Central,	........73..	L. S. Thompson,	...Irasburgh.......
.63.	Red Mountain,	..74...	John B. Lathrop,	...Arlington.......
.64	.Olive Branch,	.108...	D. W. Davis,	.......Chester.........
.65..	Memphremagog,	93..	Henry Hoskins,	.....Newport.........
.66..	Crescent,	.......92...	Ira W. Cunningham,	.Lyndon.........
.67..	Eagle,	....65...	L. M. Hull,	........Bakersfield......
.68..	Green Mountain,	94...	Geo. M. Webster,	...Cabot ....
.69..	Mount Norris,	..47...	L. E. Harrington,	...Eden Mills......
.70..	Otter Creek,	.... 28...	Rollin C. Smith,	...Pittsford.......
.71..	Morning Flower,	54...	H. N. Bradley,	.....West Rupert ....
.72..	Sherman,	......85...	R. M. Harvey,	......West Topsham ..
.73..	Clyde,	.........45...	B. F. D. Carpenter,	..West Charleston.
.74..	Frontier,	......52...	Jacob E. Toof,	......Franklin........
.75..	Eureka,	........89...	I. W. Parkhurst,	....Fairhaven ......
.76..	Marble,	.......51...	Austin S. Baker,	.....Danby..........
.77	Mad River,	......44...	T. J. Deavitt,	.......Moretown ......
.78..	Lincoln,	......42...	R. E. Welch,	......Enosburg Falls..
.79..	Rutland,	56	..A. H. Cobb,	...Rutland.........
.80..	Wyoming,	......53...	W. R. Gove,	........Plainfield.......
.81..	Isle la Motte,	...32...	Elisha R. Goodsell,	.Isle la Motte....
.82..	Moose River,	...43...	J. H. Walbridge,	....West Concord...
.83	.Waterman,	......31...	Geo. Dallingham,	...Johnson.......
.84..	Englesby,	......45...	H. P. Aldrich,	.......St. Albans......
.85..	Black River,	....46...	Rufus S. Warner,	...Ludlow.........
.86..	Minerva,	........38...	Victor Richardson,	..Corinth ....
.87..	Caspian Lake,	..66...	W. W. Goss,	.......Greensboro.....
.88..	Oriental,	......24...	A. S. Samson,	.......Montgomery.....
.89..	Unity,	.........28...	E. H. Stetson,	.....Jacksonville....
.90..	White River,	....46...	C. T. Odiorne,	......Bethel ....
.91..	Acacia,	........38...	F. G. Halstead,	.....Benson.........
.92..	Washburn,	....37...	A. S. Babbitt,	......Danville.......

Virginia.

According to the most reliable information, viz. that contained in an address of the veteran grand secretary Bro. John Dove, M. D., of Richmond, Va. on the history of the G. L. of Va., four of the lodges in the State did, on the 13th of October, 1778, organize the Grand Lodge in this State by the election of John Blair as the first grand master. At the time there were in this State lodges holding charters respectively from grand lodges in England, Scotland, and Ireland, and a Prov. G. M. in Pennsylvania. No other organization of a grand lodge subsequently took place—the lodges of the various registers gradually, after the ratification of peace between Great Britain and America, submitting to the organization of 1778 above mentioned. In 1870 there were 173 lodges and 8,555 members. The revenue is about $5.000 a year, and as this grand lodge pays neither mileage nor per diem, it is sufficient to meet all necessary current expenses. This grand lodge has funded property to the value in 1870 of $26.600, the principal part of which comprises the capital stock of the Masonic Temple Association, the object of which is the erection of the New Masonic Temple in the City of Richmond The State is divided into 29 districts, each in charge of a Dist. D. G. M. appointed by the G. M. elect. This grand lodge has no Deputy G. M.—the duties of that officer being administered by a Grand Lecturer. The ann. com. is in December.

The executive grand officers elected in 1870 were—

> THOMAS F. OWENS, of Richmond. Grand Master.
> JOHN DOVE, of Richmond. Grand Secretary.
> WM. B. ISAACS, of Richmond, Deputy Gr. Secretary.
> THOS. U. DUDLEY, of Richmond, Grand Treasurer.
> JAMES EVANS, of Richmond, Grand Lecturer.

From the well-printed Proceedings of this grand lodge for 1870 we present the following list of the lodges in this State. Wherein it differs the information has been more recently supplied by the lodge secretaries, in response to our circulars.

No.	Name of Lodge.	Members.	Name of Sec'y.	Post Office.
..1..	Norfolk........	127	...Walter R. Russell,..	Norfolk.........
..2..	Atlantic.......	93	...John J. Sturdivant,	...do ....
..3..	Blandford, ...	128	...Thos. C. Parrack,..	.Petersburg ....
..4..	Fredericksburg,	91	...Isaac Hirsch,.......	Fredericksburg..
..5..	St. Tammany, ..	43	...E. K. Peek, ...	Hampton ......
..6 ..	Williamsburg, ..	26	...Friend Tuttle.......	Williamsburg...
..7..	Botetourt,.....	26	...Wm. E. Waitt,......	Gloucester ....
..8..	Roanoke,........		.......No Returns....................
..9..	Temple,........	43	...R. E. Tyler,........	Richmond ......
.10..	Richmond.	137	...James E. Riddick, ..	...do.........
.11..	Metropolitan,..	100	...S. B. Jacobs,.........	...do.........
.13..	Staunton.	130	...Jas. F. Patterson,..	Staunton........
.14..	Manchester,....	67	...L. S. Clarke, ...	Manchester ....
.15..	Petersburg,....	128	...Geo. W. Hall......	Petersburg ....
.17..	Chesnut Grove,.	49	...C. H. Tompkins,....	Whitwell ......
.18..	Smithfield Union,	34	...John R. Purdie.	Smithfield ......
.19..	Randolph,.....	120	...Wm. J. Riddick.....	Richmond ......
.20..	Oriental,.......	21	...Wm. Horatio Brown,	Westville.......
.21..	Hiram,........	106	...C. A. B. Coffroth,..	Winchester ....
.22..	Washington....	130	...James S. Douglas, ..	Alexandria ....
.23..	Taylor, ...	56	...Wm. M. Barnitz,....	Salem..........
.24..	Pittsylvania,....	44	...F. B. Watson, ...	Pittsylvania....
.26..	Sussex, ...	17	...R. T. Marable,......	Newville ....
.27..	Rock'm Union,	118	..J. T. Logan,........	Harrisonburg ...
.30..	Suffolk, ...	46	..J. P. Hall. jr.......	Suffolk ....
.31..	Marion, ...	48	.. H. C. Stevens, ...	Marion.........
.32..	George,........	36	...A. M. Pamplin,....	Howardsville ...
.33..	Warren,........	54	...Chas. L. Ellis.	Pedlar Mills....
.34..	Solomon,......	23	...H. D. Cowper,......	Suffolk ....
.35..	Catlett, ...	80	...E. F. Tiller.........	Estillville.......
.36..	St. John's,.....	88	...James R. Fisher,....	Richmond ......
.37..	Hamilton,......	46	...Gabriel V. Braden,..	Hamilton.......
.38..	Central,.......	31	...Geo. W. Murphy,..	New Market ....
.39..	Marshall,......	215	...Henry F. Bocock....	Lynchburg ....
.40..	Joppa,........	118	...Wm. J. Riddick.	Richmond ......
.41..	Farmville,......	44	...Z. A. Blanton,.....	Farmville ......
.42..	Berlin,........	19	...W. G. Holmes,.....	Berlin..........
.43 .	Fairfax,........	58	...J. F. Pendleton,.....	Culpepper C. H..
.44..	Prudence,......	24	...C. T. Andrews.......	New London....
.45..	Scottsville,.....	34	...John A. Doll,......	Scottsville......
.46..	Worthington,...	19	..Dr James T. Clark, .	Mount Solon....
.47..	Preston,.......	43	...G. K. Turner, ...	Jonesville ......
.48..	Abingdon, ...	51	...P. C. Landrum,.....	Abingdon ......
.49..	Greenbrier,.....	79	...Geo. H. Lewis,.....	Lewisburg, W. V.
.50..	Piedmont,......	45	...James L. Dunn,....	Stanardsville ...
.51..	**Dove,**........	**70**	...**Aug. Arsell, jr**......	**Richmond** ......

No.	Name of Lodge.	Members.	Name of Sec'y.	Post Office.
.52.	Brunswick,	23	John A. Michael,	Lawrenceville ..
.53.	Loge Français,	102	Peterfield Trent,	Richmond
.54.	Excelsior,	31	Charles Sturkey,	Mill Creek
.55.	Withers,	14		Columbia
.56.	Seaboard,	65	August Buff.	Portsmouth
.57.	Henry,	33	Geo. H. Williams,	Fairfax C. H.
.58.	Day,	66	Jesse J. Porter,	Louisa C. H.
.59.	Mecklenburg,	16	Wm. H. Harris.	St. Tammany
.60.	Widow's Son,	117	Wm. L. Cochran.	Charlottesville ..
.61.	Polk.	42	Sam. S. Thomson.	Riceville
.62.	Tazewell.	49	Henry C. Alderson,	Tazewell C. H...
.64.	Natural Bridge,	29	John K. Watkins.	Balcony Falls...
.66.	Friendship.	89	B. M. Allen,	Fincastle.
.67.	Mountain City,	54	W. T. Chapin,	Lexington,
.69.	Mackey,	35	Wm. A. Clement,	Campbell C. H..
.70.	Boonsboro,	27	Robert W. Coffee,	Forest Depôt....
.72.	James Evans.	32	John W. Haney,	Buchanan
.73.	Clinton.	37	James M. Thompson,	Amherst C. H. ..
.74.	Blue Ridge,	35	John S. Browning,	Flint Hill
.75.	Lone Star,	32	James H. Binford,	Rocky Mount...
.77.	Chuckatuck,	29	T. H. Urquhart,	Chuckatuck
.78.	Washington.	73	James Green,	Washington
.79.	Seven Mile Ford,	18	J. H. Baker,	Seven Mile Ford.
.80.	Malta.	50	Samuel Walton,	Charlestown
.81.	Salem,	32	W. H. Adams,	Middleburg
.82.	W. Fraternal,	51	Joseph C. Sexton,	Wytheville
.84.	Mt. Pleasant,	24	B. L. Taliaferro,	Tye River Depôt
.85.	Astræa.	45	W. S. Thornton,	Sussex C. H.
.86.	McDaniel.	60	Henry W. Cox,	Christianburg...
.87.	Vincent Witcher.	29	Wm. T. Mitchell,	Calland's.
.88.	Union,	50	H. W. Harding,	Lancaster C. H..
.89.	Ruth,	37	T. F. Rogers,	Norfolk,
.91.	Mount Nebo.	48	Geo. M. Beltzhoover,	Shepherdstown..
.92.	Fleetwood Har.,	28	Willis P. Wills,	Massey's Mills .
.93.	Elk Branch.	24	John M. Engle,	Duffield's Depôt .
.95.	Liberty,	55	W. W. Berry,	Liberty
.96.	Halifax,	35	A. R. Green.	Halifax C. H....
.97.	Frankford,	35	Wm. B. Reid,	Frankford
.98.	Spurmont.	23	C. M. Borum,	Strasburg
.99.	Somerton,	19	J. C. Goodman,	Suffolk
100.	Portsm'th Nav.,	106	Chas. T. Myers,	Portsmouth
101.	Valley.	15	J. F. Kagey,	Mount Jackson ..
102.	Arlington,	19	S. P. Latane,	Miller's Tavern..
103.	Goose C'k Val.,	18	J. S. Slicer,	Buford's Depôt.
104.	John Dove,	24	L. F. Clark,	Peterstown. W.V.
105.	Rockfish Harm'y,	15	J. W. Robertson,	Afton Depôt ....

No.	Name of Lodge.	Members.	Name of Sec'y.	Post Office.
106	Giles,	30	H. B. Barbor,	Giles, C. H.
110	Highland,	44	A. J. Hobson	Newhampden
111	Charity,	23	A. M. Kitzmiller,	Harper's Ferry
112	Laurel,	35	C. W. Harvey,	Red House
113	Leesville,	25	R. A. Lee.	Leesville.
114	Olive Branch,	48	J. J. Stansberry,	Leesburg.
115	Prince George,	47	M. W. Raney,	Pr. George C. H.
116	Ocean,	23	S. T. Ross,	Accomac C. H.
117	Triluminar,	64	Wm. M'Coughtry,	Middleway
120	And'w Jackson,	123	Wm. M. Reardon,	Alexandria
121	Temp'ranceville.	28	W. J. Bayley,	Temperanceville.
122	Roman Eagle,	71	A. G. Taylor,	Danville
123	Blue Stone Un.,	27	J. J. Barnes,	Barnesville
125	Shenandoah,	28	Robt. H. Spindle,	Shenand'h I. Wk's
129	Independence,	60	F. J. Lundy,	Independence
130	Henrico Union,	61	Wm. Wilson,	Richmond
131	Leitch,	47	B. P. Elliott,	Floyd C. H.
132	Dallas,	49	R. M. Jobe,	Wadesville
133	Mount Carmel,	47	T. N. Fletcher	Warrenton
134	Blackwater,	35	L. B. Edwards,	Smithfield
136	Equality,	113	J. S. Haldeman,	Martinsville
137	Lafayette,	49	W. T. Young,	Luray.
138	Indep. Orange,	52	P. B. Hiden,	Orange C. H.
141	Dewitt Clinton,	41	B. M. England,	Cartersville
142	Cassia,	45	Wm. H. Haas,	Woodstock
144	St. John's,	35	Thos. J. Moore,	Charlotte C. H.
145	Indian Creek,	26	John W. Francis,	Indian Creek.
149	Harmony,	30	J. W. Ames,	Suffolk
150	Widow's Son,	27	J. W. Potts.	Hicksford
151	Franklin,	23	A. W. Norfleet,	Franklin Depôt.
152	Fitzwhylsonn,	31	A. S. Boyd,	Boydton.
153	Dan River,	27	John W. Tuck,	Buck Shoal
155	Staunton River,	31	Saml. H. Hudnall,	Brook Neal
156	Hunter,	38	W. W. Ballard,	Blacksburg
157	Prospect Hill,	39	A. C. Page,	Millwood.
159	Snowville,	19	J. B. Buckingham,	Snowville.
161	Chesterfield,	34	Dr. S. L. Ingraham,	Chesterfield
162	Shelby,	80	W. P. Brewer,	Bristol. Tenn.
164	Owens,	66	A. F. Santos,	Norfolk
165	Henry Clay,	38	E. S. Johnston,	Newbern
166	Mount Vernon,	58	J. H. Clements,	Portsmouth.
171	Covington,	30	J. F. Jordan,	Covington
177	Virginia,	32	C. O. Higgins,	Cabin Point
183	Hill City,	99	Thos. N. Davis,	Lynchburg
187	Rye Cove,	47	J. P. Horton,	Rye Cove.
188	Martin Station,	33	Thos. A. Bacon,	Rose Hill.

No.	Name of Lodge.	Members.	Name of Sec'y.	Post Office.
189	Patmos,	23	J. W. Hough,	Upperville
193	Fulton.	47	W. J. Woltz,	Hillsville
194	King Solomons,	28	W. T. Rea,	Mechanics' River
195	Eureka,	58	P. Hening,	Bridgewater
196	Stuart.	30	Dent King.	Willow Springs.
197	Monitor.	52	Wm. E. Prescott,	Old P't Comfort.
198	Wakefield,	38	Jno. C. White,	Wakefield Station
199	Freedom,	31	Peter A. Fry,	Lovettsville
200	Stonewall,	60	G. B. Hanes,	Gold Hill.
201	Johnson,	24		Stickleyville.
202	Bailey,	22	Thos. S. Rector,	Marysville
203	Reedy Spring,	26	B. W. Babcock,	Concord Depôt.
204	Warm Springs,	34	B. F. Hopkins,	Bath C. H.
205	Fancy Hill,	20	J. J. Moore,	Fancy Hill
206	Bland,	23	F. F. Repass,	Bland C. H.
207	Meadsville,	15	C. T. C. Carr.	Republican Grove
208	Linville.	22	J. A. Alexander,	Broadway
210	Maratock,	32	B. F. Farley,	Danville.
211	Midlothian,	18	J. Baach,	Midlothian.
212	Tower Hill,	29	Henry S. Layne,	Tower Hill.
213	Treadwell,	46	S. S. Neill.	Berryville
214	Stella,	22	B. Herndon,	Ruckersville.
215	Lebanon,	48	T. C. M. Alderson,	Lebanon
216	Cove Creek.	25	J. H. Fleenor,	Bristol
217	Grayson.	36	E. H. Livesay,	Elk Creek
218	Sinking Creek,	35	F. P. Payne,	Newport
219	Waterman,	55	Geo. R. Barr,	Abingdon
220	Mount Moriah,	25	Thos. D. Spindle,	Sperryville
221	Silentia.	22	O. Gresham,	Aytell's
224	Virginia.	25	Jesse M. M'Call,	Liberty Hill
225	King William,	14	W. W. Dabney,	Hanover C. H.
226	Woltz,	20	A. Aunfield,	Lambsburg
227	William King,	21	A. T. Starrett,	Saltville.
228	Waddell.	36	H. C. Baker,	Gordonsville.
229	Glade Spring,	35	D. E. Bentley,	Glade Spring
230	Big Island,	32	Barnet M. Page,	Big Island
231	Old Dominion,	34	George Guard,	N. T. Stephensburg

Washington.

The Grand Lodge in this Territory was organized by the representatives of four lodges, all chartered by the G. L. of Oregon, meeting in convention at Olympia on the 6th of December, 1858, and who, on the 7th, elected their officers, with T. F. McElroy as the first grand master. The annual communication occurs in September at Olympia City. In 1870 there were 13 lodges with 417 members—one of those lodges being at Sitka, in Alaska Territory. The revenue for 1870 was $991.50 of which $387 was appropriated to pay mileage and per diem.

The executive grand officers elected in 1870 were—

JOHN T. JORDAN, of Seattle, Grand Master.
JAMES H. BLEWETT, of Walla Walla, Dep. Gr. Master.
BENJ. HARNED, of Olympia, Grand Treasurer.
THOS. M. REED, of Olympia, Grand Secretary.

From the Proceedings of the G. L. for 1870 the following list is compiled. Where it differs the information has been supplied by the lodge secretary.

No.	Name of Lodge.	Members.	Name of Sec'y.	Post Office.
1	Olympia,	51	P. E. Hyland,	Olympia
2	Steilacoom,	32	H. D. Montgomery,	Steilacoom
4	Washington,	45	August A. Schaeben,	Vancouver
5	Franklin,	42	Amasa S. Miller,	Port Gamble
6	Port Townsend,	51	Wm. L. Chalmers,	Port Townsend
7	Walla Walla,	29	Chas. W. Frush,	Walla Walla
8	Kane,	33	Irving M. Guindon,	Port Madison
9	St. Johns,	50	S. P. Andrews,	Seattle
11	Mount Moriah,	18	Alex. F. Chapman,	Oakland
13	Blue Mountain,	23	R. Guichard,	Walla Walla
14	Alaska,	14	David Flannery,	Sitka, Alaska
15	Whidby Island,	20	Thomas Cranney,	Coupville
16	Waittsburg,	9	Platt A. Preston,	Waittsburg

West Virginia.

The Grand Lodge in this State was organized on the 10th of May, 1865, by delegates from nine lodges, who met for that purpose at Fairmont, and W. J. Bates was the first grand master. The annual communication takes place at Wheeling in November. In 1870 there were 43 lodges, with 2,140 members, and three lodges in the State holding the charters of and subject only to the G. L. of Virginia, under which they were organized. No difficulty has followed this arrangement. At the annual communication for 1870 it was resoved to thereafter pay mileage and per diem to the representatives. The revenue up to that year had been sufficient to meet current expenses, and leave a balance of $545 in the treasury.

The executive grand officers elected in 1870 were—

WM. J. BATES, of Wheeling. Grand Master.
ROBERT WHITE, of Romney, Deputy Grand Master.
WM. P. WILSON, of Wheeling. Grand Treasurer.
THOS. LOGAN. of Wheeling, Grand Secretary.

From the well-printed Proceedings of this grand lodge for 1870 we present the following list of the lodges in this State. Wherein it differs the information has been more recently supplied by the lodge secretaries, in response to our circulars.

No.	Name of Lodge.	Members.	Name of Sec'y.	Post Office.
..1..	Ohio,	166...	Alex. II. Forgey,...	Wheeling. ......
..2..	Wellsburg,	75...	Thos. M. Lloyd.	Wellsburg ......
..3..	Mount Olivet.	97...	F. B. Toothaker,....	Parkersburg ....
..4..	Morg'nt'n Union,	91...	John J. Brown, ...	Morgantown ....
..5..	Wheeling,	94...	John C. Hervey.....	Wheeling. ......
..6	Hermon.	61 ...	Evan F Lowther,...	Clarksburg .....
..7..	Franklin,	34...	J. II. Rohrbough,...	Buckhannon ....
..8..	Marshall Union.	44...	W. II. II. Showacre,.	Moundsville.....
..9..	Fairmont,	109...	Robt. C. Dunnington.	Fairmont ....
.10..	Weston.	30...	Geo. W. Strickler, .	Weston.........
.11..	Western Star,	36...	Thos. J. Hayslip,....	Guyandotte.....
.12..	Ashton,	36...	J. T. Smith.......	Ravenswood ....
.13..	Minerva,	42...	Thos. Thornburg,...	Cabell C. H.....

No.	Name of Lodge.	Members.	Name of Sec'y.	Post Office.
.14.	.Preston,	31	J. W. Parks,	Kingwood
.15.	.Grafton,	84	Lee Swearengen,	Grafton
.16.	.Ripley,	57	Wm. T. Greer,	Jackson C. H.
.17.	.Cameron,	68	D. M. Burley	Cameron.
.18.	.Wayne.	75	Chas. W. Ferguson,	Wayne C. H.
.19.	.Minturn,	55	B. Franklin,	Point Pleasant
.20.	.Kanawha,	42	W. B. Clarkson,	Charleston
.21.	.Clinton.	35	C. S. White.	Romney
.22.	.New Cumberl'd.	51	Geo. H. Daniels,	New Cumberland
.23.	.Clifton,	34	Allen C. Mason,	Clifton
.24.	.St John's,	30	John W. Monroe,	Shinnston
.25.	.Eureka,	24	H. V. Daniels,	Harper's Ferry
.26.	.Liberty,	48	S. S. Jacob,	West Liberty
.27.	.Salina,	48	R. A. Colman,	Malden.
.28.	.Piedmont,	27	John Brown,	Piedmont.
.29.	.Moorfield,	45	E M. Williams,	Moorfield
.30.	.Nelson.	58	Alfred Caldwell,	Wheeling
.31.	.Mannington,	42	William Hall,	Mannington
.32.	.Crescent,	28	Chas. B. Webb,	Ceredo.
.33.	.Bates,	41	Sam'l Adams,	Wheeling.
.34.	.Middlebourne,	49	David Hickman.	Middlebourne
.35.	.Jackson.	31	John S. McWhorter,	Jane Lew.
.36.	.Kanawha Valley.	19	Sam. T. Alexander,	Buffalo.
.37.	.Berkeley,	15	G. A. Chrisman.	Hedgesville.
.38.	.Moriah.	57	John G. Schilling,	Spencer
39.	.Wetzel,	35	Geo. E. Boyd,	New Martinsville.
.40.	.Fairview,	20	Jas. E. Morrow,	Fairview.
.41.	.St. Mary's,	31	James M Gallaher,	St. Marys
.42.	.Fort Union,	22	J. W. A. Ford,	Lewisburg
.43.	.Aurora,	19	Evans Rush,	Fellowsville

Wisconsin.

The Grand Lodge in this State was organized at Madison on the 18th of December, 1843, by representatives from the three lodges then in the State, and which at present stand first on the list. all chartered originally by the G. .L. of Mo., and B. T. Kavanaugh, then W. M. of Melody Lodge, of Platteville, although not present, was elected the first grand master. The annual communication takes place at Milwaukee in June. ·In June, 1870, there were 160 lodges, with 8,944 members in the State. Although this grand lodge pays mileage and per diem, the revenue is sufficient to meet current expenses, and there was a balance on hand and invested at the above date of $10,065.96.

The executive grand officers elected in 1870 were—

> GABRIEL BOUCK, of Oshkosh, Grand Master.
> J. HAMILTON, of Milwaukee, Deputy Gr. Master,
> WM. H. HINER, of Fond du Lac, Grand Treasurer.
> WM. T. PALMER, of Milwaukee, Grand Secretary.

For the following information we are indebted to the Proceedings for 1870. Where it differs the correction has been made by the lodge secretary.

No.	Name of Lodge.	Members.	Name of Sec'y.	Post Office.
1	Mineral Point,	84	Orrin E. Minor,	Mineral Point
2	Melody,	95	J. H. Evans,	Platteville
3	Kilburne,	168	Wm. B. Brown,	Milwaukee
4	Warren,	48	Henry B. Coons,	Potosi
5	Madison	91	David H. Wright,	Madison
9	Jefferson.	55	Warren H. Potter,	Jefferson
10	Morning Star,	146	W. P. Frost,	Beloit
11	Sheboygan,	31	F. Walther.	Sheboygan
13	Wisconsin.	222	Chas. A. Smith,	Milwaukee
14	Western Star,	129	E. J. Foster,	Janesville
16	Franklin,	44	George Parr,	Avoca
17	Ozaukee,	45	L Towsley,	Ozaukee
18	Racine,	163	S. C. Yout,	Racine
20	Lancaster,	44	Joseph Bock,	Lancaster
21	Washington,	90	Wm. H. Norris, jr.,	Green Bay

10²

No.	Name of Lodge.	Members.	Name of Sec'y.	Post Office.
.24.	St. John's.	....56...	Charles A. Mueller,	..Sheboygan Falls.
.25.	Amicitia,	....76...	Fred. C. Frebel,	....Shullsburg......
.26.	Fountain,	....25...	J. C. Waterbury,	....Fon du Lac ....
.27.	Oshkosh,	...119...	L. W. Holsey.	......Oshkosh ....
.28.	Burlington,	...:.44...	John Reynolds,	....Burlington......
.30.	Aurora,	....72...	Jacob Wahl,	........Milwaukee*......
.31.	Smith,	....86..	Wm. Chadwick,	....Monroe........
.32.	Union,	...89...	R. C. Pierce,	.......Evansville ......
.33.	Ft. Winnebago.	105..	E. S. Baker,	.... Portage.........
.34.	Baraboo,	....67...	M. Pointon,	........Baraboo ....
.36	.Albany,	....37...	J. H. Ludington,	....Albany........
.37.	Waukesha,	....94...	Van H. Bugbee,	....Waukesha ......
.38.	Berlin,	....98...:	John Megran,	......Berlin ....
.40.	Horicon.	49...	Hiram Lake,	......Horicon.......
.41.	St. James,	....30...	Wash. S. Keats,	......East Troy......
.43.	Hazel Green,	...52...	T. W. Summersides,	.Hazel Green ....
.44.	Geneva.	....65...	Judson G. Sherman,	.Geneva.........
.45.	Frontier.	....94...	J. W. Jones,	......La Cross........
.46.	Lake Mills,	....42...	Geo. Clapp,	....Lake Mills......
.47.	Kenosha,	...122...	S. C. Johnson,	......Kenosha........
.48.	Waupun.	....78...	A. A. Greenman,	:..Waupun ....
.49.	Watertown,	...126...	A. J. Œheling,	......Watertown......
.50.	Hiram.	....68...	E. P. Henika.	........Madison ....
.51.	Waverly.	....75...	Thos. W. Briggs,	...Appleton. ......
.52.	Rio.	....45...	P. M. Pool,	........Rio ....
.55.	Janesville,	...135...	F. M. Davis,	........Janesville.......
.56.	St. Croix.	....37...	G. R. Hughes,	......Hudson.........
.57.	St. John's,	....65...	Byron Brown,	......Whitewater .....
/59.	Markesan,	....50...	A. Nichols.	......Markesan. ......
.60.	Valley,	...'..94...	H. E. Kelley,	......Sparta...........
.61.	Kane.	....44...	W. B. M. Torry,	....Neenah..........
.62.	Vesper.			........Mayville........
.63.	Waterloo.	....73...	A. Weiner,	........Waterloo ....
.64.	Evening Star,	...72...	Edwin Dain,	........Darlington......
.65.	Manitowoc,	....59...	E. B. Treat.	........Manitowoc.....
.66.	Richland,	....72...	A. W. Stockton,	....Richland Center.
.67.	Fox Lake,	....52...	Thos. R. Daniels,	...Fox Lake.......
.68.	Palmyra,	....53...	W. F. M'Cord,	......Palmyra........
.69.	Fulton,	....53...	S. S. Lord;	.........Edgarton ....
.70.	Orion.	....16...	John Kraus.	......Orion...........
.71.	Quincy,	....46...	Albert F. Hill,	.....Friendship......
.72.	Dodge Co.,	....106 ..	John H. Barrett.	....Beaver Dam ....
.73.	Kegonsa,	....54...	Albert P. Lusk.	.....Stoughton ......
.74.	Black River,	....80...	C. R. Johnson,	......Black Riv. Falls.
.75.	Columbus,	....86...	N. A. Robinson,	.....Columbus. ......
.76.	Plover,	....44...	W. R. Alban,	.......Plover..........

No.	Name of Lodge.	Members.	Name of Sec'y.	Post Office.
.77..	Elkhorn,	......44..	.J. C. M. Kehlor,	....Elkhorn . ...
.78..	Dells,	......29..	.Sylv. H Todd,	.....Delton ....
.79..	Ironton	......42..	.E. Blakesley,	......Ironton.........
.80	Independence,	.126...	C. S. Kitchel,	.....Milwaukee......
.81..	Northern Light,	.62...B. F.	Parker,	.......Manston........
.82..	Weyauwega,	...37...W.	C. Potter,	.......Weyauwega.....
.83.	.Concordia, ..	..47...	Charles Hinrichs,	...Madison........
.84..	La Belle,	......57...R.	C. Bierce.	.......Viroqua ....
.85..	Des l`ères,	.....35...H.	F. Tucker.	......Depère ....
.86..	Solomon,	......19...A.	B. Hitchcock,	....Juneau. ....
.89..	Pepin`,	......21...	Virgil D. Carruth,	..Pepin ....
.90..	Waucoma,	.....40...J.	Savage	...........Cooksville. .....
.91..	Oxford,	......53...	Frank Abbott,	......Oxford ....
.92..	Belle City,	....85...	Jas. A. Beaugrand,	..Racine........
.93..	Evergreen,	.....49...	Henry Hoeffler,	.....Steven's Point ..
.94..	Bicknell,	......65...A.	Wood,	...........Broadhead......
.95..	Ripon,	........94...	W. Workman,	.....Ripon. ....
.96..	Temple,	........65...N.	H. Palmer.	......Waterford ......
.97..	Crescent,	......55...	John Darby	........Mazomanie .....
.98..	Bryan,	........61...C.	V. Donaldson,	...Menasha ....
.99..	Lodi Valley,	...63...Horace	M. Ayer,	...Lodi .. . .
100..	Fairfield,	......30...A.	W. Maxon,	......Fairfield........
102..	Marquette,	.....18...Jas.	J. Barrett,	......Marquette ......
103..	Juneau,	......42...Geo.	P. Kenyon,	....New Lisbon ....
104..	Astrea.	......30...Hugo	Boclo.	....Cedarburg......
105..	North Western,	.45...Chas.	Cook,	........Prescott. ....
106..	Prairie du Chien,	76...T.	A. Mathews.	.....Prairie du Chien.
108..	Neosho,	......44..	Stephen L. Brown,	...Neosho.........
109..	River Falls,	...50...	Osborn Strahl,	.....River Falls.....
110..	Lowell,	........35...	James Lowth,	......Lowell.........
111	.Rosendale,	....53...J.	C. Le Fevre,	.....Rosendale ......
112..	Eau Claire,	.....85...	Geo. E. Groutt,	...Eau Claire......
113..	Eureka,	........92...G.	T. Moore,	.......Prairie du Sac ..
114..	Palestine,	......49...A.	G. Burnham,	....Lone Rock .....
115..	Robert Morris,	..46...Wm.	McWilliams.	....Eagle ....
116..	Sharon,	......34...Wm.	S. McDougall,	.Sharon ....
117..	Trempeleau,	. 41...L.	C. Huntley,	......Trempeleau.....
118..	Warden,	......44...Simon	G. Beebe,	....Wiota..........
119..	Dodgeville,	.....46...Chas.	Bishop,	......Dodgeville......
120..	Hartford,	......51...H.	W. Sawyer,	......Hartford ....
121..	Delavan,	......70...F.	L. Von Snessmilch,	Delavan........
122..	Back River,	....39...James	Rea,	........Hartland ....
123..	Waupaca,	......68...Myron	Reed,	.......Waupaca ....
124..	Columbia,	......51...W.	J. Weber,	........Kilbourn City...
125	.Salem,	........66...Daniel	Schell,	......West Salem.....
126..	Darien,	........59...E.	H. Knapp,	.......Darien ....

No.	Name of Lodge.	Members.	Name of Sec'y.	Post Office.
127	Lebanon,	40	John Swan,	Judah
128	Grand Rapids,	58	E. Mennet,	Grand Rapids
130	Forest,	40	J. A. Farnham,	Wausau
131	New London,	40	Aug. H. Pape,	New London
132	Tomah,	47	E. N. Palmer,	Tomah
133	Ellsworth,	58	D. B. Smith,	Oconomowoc
134	Osceola,	47	Dugald Kennedy,	Osceola
135	Good Samaritan,	68	G. C. Babcock,	Clinton
136	Springfield,	48	D. J. Sheffield	Springfield
137	Footeville,	34	Henry C. M'Coy,	Footeville
138	West Bend,	48	C. Gray	West Bend
139	Billings,	70	Rev. J. Britton,	Fort Atkinson
140	Fond du Lac,	74	Lucius D. Hurd,	Fond du Lac
141	Montello,	44	John Barry,	Montello
142	Harmony,	83	Wm. Hatzenstein,	Milwaukee
143	Sun Prairie,	51	Cyrus C. La Bore,	Sun Prairie
144	Brandon,	59	A. O. Kelly,	Brandon
145	Washburn,	45	Geo. Curtis,	Bristol
146	Beetown,	43	D. B. Arthur,	Beetown
147	Green Lake,	31	J. D. Sherwood,	Dartford
148	Wautoma,	45	A. H. Walker.	Wautoma
149	Durand,	28	Christian Bruen,	Durand
150	Burnet,	25	J. B. Cole,	Burnett
151	Oregon,	53		Oregon.
152	Cambria,	43	Robert King,	Cambria
153	Mifflin,	45	Samuel Clayton,	Mifflin
154	Chilton,	34	A. H. Hammond,	Chilton
155	M'ticello Union,	24	F. Pierce	Monticello
156	Corinthian,	30	J. S. Putnam,	Union Grove
157	Reedsburg,	40	A. P. Ellinwood,	Reedsburg
158	Oakfield,	50	Henry A. Ripley,	Oakfield
159	Zerah,	43	T. A. Rice,	Necedah
160	Bloomfield,	30	George Ballard,	Bloomfield
161	Milton,	26	Carl Gifford,	Milton
162	West Eau Claire,	70	H. M. Culbertson,	West Eau Claire.
163	Neillsville,	13	S. C. Boardman,	Neillsville
164	Menomonee,	31	Philetus Bogue,	Menomonee
165	Ferrin,	24	E. Sylvester,	Montford
166	Princeton,	25	Thos. M'Connell,	Princeton
167	Cassia,	16	Geo. Higgins,	Greenbush
168	Omro,	46	W. W. Race,	Omro
169	Grant,	57	B. W. Colt,	Boscobel
170	Shawano,	13	C. M. Upham,	Shawano
171	Pardee,	23	Chas. J. Pardee,	Pardeeville
172	New Holstein,	11	R. Buchner,	New Holstein
173	Poynett,	23	W. J. Robinson,	Poynett

No.	Name of Lodge.	Members.	Name of Sec'y.	Post Office.
174	Key,	26	W. N. Perry,	Ahnapee
175	Excelsior.	96	S. R. Smith.	Milwaukee
176	Chippewa Falls,	25	Henry Coleman.	Chippewa Falls.
177	Decora,	21	Edward F. Wade,	Galesville
178	Argyle.	10	A. Anderson,	Argyle
179	Black Earth,	18	Geo. C. Howard,	Black Earth
180	Middleton,	19	R. E. Davis,	Middleton

British Columbia.

A Grand Lodge for this Province was organized on the 24th of Dec., 1867, at Victoria, Vancouver's Island, by representatives from the four lodges in the Colony, and Isa. W. Powell was elected the first grand master. No information later than 1869 has been received from there, and hence our register of this body must be and remain imperfect. Four lodges with 142 members, so far as known, are all which were in the province in May, 1869. Of these lodges three were originally chartered by the G. L. of Scotland, and one by the G. L. of England. H. F. HEISTERMAN, of Victoria, is the present grand Secretary.

Canada.

The grand lodge which has jurisdiction in the upper or western province of the British Dominion of Canada, at present known as Ontario, is styled the Grand Lodge of Canada, and which name, since the organization and general recognition of a grand lodge in the lower or eastern province known as Quebec, is regarded a misnomer. In 1855 the first earnest movement took place toward the organization of a grand lodge for those interior provinces, formerly known as Upper and Lower, and then as Western and Eastern Canada, and in October of that year such a grand lodge was erected, with Wm. M. Wilson as the first grand master. But this grand lodge, though claiming such, did not exercise jurisdiction to any extent in the now province of Quebec until the year 1857, when the differences between this grand lodge and the lodges yet adhering to the British provincial grand masters being in great measure reconciled, one grand lodge was erected under the name and style of the Grand Lodge of Canada, and of which Sir Allan N. McNab, the senior Provincial, was elected the first grand master. Not being for some time afterwards recognized or acknowledged by the Grand Lodge of England, several lodges were, notwithstanding the rightful claim of the new grand lodge, allowed to remain in obedience to the British grand lodge from which they held their charters, and, in 1859, by arrangement of the respective grand masters of the G. Lodges of England and Canada, such lodges were not required to transfer their allegiance to the latter. This was the condition when the grand lodge was organized in 1869 at Quebec, and a majority of those lodges entered into that organization.

The Grand Lodge of Canada holds its annual communication in July, at that place which may at the previous ann. com. be elected. In 1870 there were carried on its register 229 lodges, with 9,991 members, of which numbers 21 lodges with 990 members (as per their reports for 1869,) did not report in 1870 to the G. L. of C., having transferred their allegiance to the G. L. of Quebec. The

[239]

additions to the register of 1870--the 21 lodges above mentioned being dropped from it by us to appear in the Quebec register—have been courteously made by the grand secretary, in response to our request, and is, therefore, correct to July, 1871. This grand lodge is arranged upon the model of the G. L. of England, and with a Board of General Purposes. allows similar latitude of lodge representation. It pays neither mileage nor per diem. After the same model, its treasury is divided into various "funds," which, in 1870, amounted in the aggregate to over $40,000.

The principal grand officers elected in 1871 were—

JAMES SEYMOUR, of St. Catharine's, Grand Master.
THOS. WHITE, of Montreal, Deputy Gr. Master,
HENRY GROFF, of Simcoe. Grand Treasurer.
THOS. B. HARRIS, of Hamilton. Grand Secretary.

No.	Name of Lodge.	Members.	Name of Sec'y.	Post Office.
..0.	Antiquity,	54	Richard Rowe,	Montreal
..2.	Niagara.	:42	John Best.	Niagara
..3.	St. John's.	128	John M. Horsey,	Kingston
..4	Dorchester,	21	W. A. Osgood.	St. Johns.
..5.	Sussex,	61	W. A. Schofield,	Brockville
..6.	Barton,	113	R. Kennedy,	Hamilton
..7.	Union,	39	J. N. Kitchen,	Grimsby
..9.	Union.	84	Charles James.	Napanee.
.10.	Norfolk,	64	Amos A. Merrill,	Simcoe.
.11.	Moira,	53	James Peard,	Belleville.
.14.	True Briton's,	25		Perth.
.15.	St. George's,	90	Thos. E. Dudley,	St. Catherines.
.17.	St. John's,	36	George Pringle.	Coburg.
.18.	Prince Edward's,	83	Thos. Shannon,	Picton.
.20.	St. John's	70	John H. Bell,	London.
.22.	King Solomon's,	142	R. W. Purvis,	Toronto
.23.	Richmond,	40	R. E. Law,	Richmond Hill
.24.	St. Francis,	12	Stewart Moag,	Smith's Falls.
.25.	Ionic.	80	W. M. Ross,	Toronto
.26.	Ontario.	34	S. C. B. Dean,	Port Hope.
.27.	Strict Obser'nce,	89	J. M. Gibson,	Hamilton
.28.	Mount Zion,	38	W. R. Anderson,	Kemptville.
.29.	United,	39	W. A. Mayhew,	Brighton.
.30.	Composite.	49	A. Borrowman,	Whitby.
.31.	Jerusalem,	40	Richard Reid,	Bowmanville.
.32.	Amity.	84	C. S. E. Black,	Dunnville.
.33.	Goderich,	19	Wm. Dickson,	Goderich
.34.	Thistle, ,	25	John Conroy,	Amherstburg.

No.	Name of Lodge.	Members.	Name of Sec'y.	Post Office.
.35.	St. John's,	26	Jos. Hurssell,	Cayuga
.36.	Welland,	40	J. C. Page,	Fonthill
.37.	King Hiram,	64	Alex. Reid	Ingersoll
.38.	Trent,	38	A. H. Wright,	Trenton
.39.	Mount Zion,	29	James A. Maybee,	Brooklyn
.40.	St. John's,	38	A. Rutherford,	Hamilton
.41.	St. George's,	63	Jas. Greaves,	Kingsville
.42.	St. George's,	50	J. M. Lougan,	London.
.43.	King Solomon's,	64	R. McWhinnie,	Woodstock
.44.	St. Thomas,	40	Albert Hutson,	St. Thomas
.45.	Brant,	77	W. C. Trumble,	Brantford.
.46.	Wellington,	79	Chas. Dunlop,	Chatham
.47.	Great Western,	78	Thos. Burnie,	Windsor
.48.	Madoc,	52	Jas. O'Hara, jr.,	Madoc
.50.	Consecon,	31	Levi C. Bailey.	Consecon.
.51.	Corinthian,	19	C. Burrell,	Grahamville
.53.	Shefford,	56	Jno. Blackwood.	Waterloo
.54.	Vaughan,	53	Henry Hurst,	Maple
.55.	Mirickville,	36	P. Y. Merrick,	Mirickville
.56.	Victoria,	80	Wm. Taylor,	Sarnia.
.57.	Harmony,	19	Robert H. Biggar,	Binbrook
.58.	Doric.	84	D. P. Williams,	Ottawa.
.59.	Corinthian,	49	Geo. L. Orme.	do
.61.	Acacia.	84	R. McN. Smith.	Hamilton
.62.	St. Andrews,	53	Thos. B. Howell,	Caledonia.
.64.	Kilwinning.	70	C. T. Campbell.	London.
.65.	Rehoboam,	7	Daniel Spry, *W. M.*	Toronto
.66.	Durham,	39	M. W. Bailey,	New Castle
.68.	St. John's,	67	I. B. Crawford,	Ingersoll
.69.	Stirling,	62	R. Finch.	Stirling
.72.	Alma.	66	John Cavers.	Galt
.73.	St. James',	54	C. L. Von Guntern,	St. Mary's
.74.	St. James',	33	S. A. Horton,	Maitland
.75.	St. John's,	129	John Erskine,	Toronto
.76.	Oxford,	39	Chas. L. Beard,	Woodstock,
.77.	Faith'l Brethren,	28	Thos. Beall,	Lindsey
.78.	King Hiram,	47	Thos. Ledus,	Tilsonburgh
.79.	Simcoe,	37	S. H. Dewart,	Bradford
.80.	Albion,	39	Andrew Wilson,	Newberry
.81.	St. John's,	44	E. Handy,	Mount Bridge
.82.	St. John's,	60	D. N. Mitchell,	Paris.
.83.	Beaver,	54	Richard Baker,	Strathroy.
.84.	Clinton.	30	George Chidley.	Clinton.
85.	Rising Sun,	30	J. H. Blackburn,	Farmersville.
86.	Wilson,	122	James B. Nixon,	Toronto
87.	Markham Union,	39	H. R. Corson,	Markham

No.	Name of Lodge.	Members.	Name of Sec'y.	Post Office.
.88.	St. George's,	...55	James Caton,	Owen Sound....
.90.	Manito.	79	Arthur Moberly,	Collingwood....
.91.	Colborne,	59	A. Vars,	Colborne
.92.	Cataraqui,	104	H. S. Minnes,	Kingston
.93.	Northern Light,	.40	James LeGear,	Kincardine
.94.	St. Marks,	32	Wm. Hemphill,	Port Stanley....
.95.	Ridout,	26	M. Durkee,	Otterville
.96.	Corinthian,	48	A. B. McPhee,	Barry
.97.	Sharon,	40	A. H. Wilson.	Sharon
.98.	True Blue.	21	James Roberts,	Albion
.99.	Tuscan.	35	P. S. Caldwell,	Newmarket
100.	Valley,	37	J. S. Baillie,	Dundas
101.	Corinthian,	41	W. N. Kennedy,	Peterboro
103.	Maple Leaf,	...98	J. A. Alexander,	St. Catharine's..
104.	St. John's,	28	Wm. Topham,	Norwichville
105.	St. Mark's,	65	T. W. Woodruff,	Drummondville .
106.	Burford,	28	John Findlay,	Burford
107.	St. Paul's,	34	D. B. Burch,	Lambeth
108.	Blenheim,	29	Rob. J. Mann,	Drumbo
103.	Albion,	30	Schuyler Shibley	Harrowsmith
110.	Central,	79	C. Moore,	Prescott
112.	Maitland,	72	Horace Horton,	Goderich
113.	Wilson,	36	J. W. Green,	Waterford
114.	Hope,	44	A. W. Pringle,	Port Hope
115.	Ivy.	26	Rob't Thompson,	Smithville
116.	Cassia,	43	Tho's Canlan,	Widder
118.	Union,	20	John R. Bond,	Schomberg
119.	Maple Leaf,	30	John Balfour,	Bath
120.	Warren,	34	George Glasgow,	Fingal
121.	Doric,	69	James P. Excell,	Brantford
122.	Renfrew,	14	John Burns,	Renfrew
123.	The Belleville,	.76	John P. Thomas,	Belleville
125.	Cornwall,	43	Charles Pool,	Cornwall
126.	Golden Rule,	.32	James Archer,	Campbellsford ..
127.	Franck,	59	Reuben W. Scott,	Frankford
128.	Pembroke,	27	Asher Ansell,	Pembroke
129.	Rising Sun,	35	James Watson,	Aurora
130.	Yamaska,	19	George Vittie,	Granby
131.	St. Lawrence.	25	John Eastwood,	Southampton
133.	Lebanon Forest,	52	A. D. Freeman,	Franceston
134.	Shawenegam,	.38	John Goodwin,	Three Rivers....
135.	St. Clair,	54	J. D. Matheson,	Milton
136.	Richardson,	42	G. Pingle,	Stouffville
137.	Pythagoras,	34	Rob't R. Fulton,	Meaford
138.	Aylmer,	31	C. W. Deegan,	Aylmer, Quebec.
139.	Lebanon,	65	C. W. Smith,	Oshawa

No.	Name of Lodge.	Members.	Name of Sec'y.	Post Office.
140	Malahide,	52	Wm. Campbell,	Aylmer, Ontario
141	Tudor,	35	D. H. Stewart,	Mitchell.
142	Excelsior.	64	Hiram Carman,	Morrisburg
143	Friendly Bro's,	43	John N Tuttle.	Iroquois
144	Tecumseh.	71	A. R. McFarlane,	Stratford
145	J. B. Hall.	27	Jacob Atkins.	Millbrook
146	Prince of Wales,	54	W. A Hope,	Newburgh
147	Mississippi.	24	O. E. Henderson,	Almonte
148	Civil Service.	37	John Welsh,	Seat of Gov'ment
149	Erie,	37	H. H. Sovereign,	Port Dover
150	Hastings,	50	John Peters.	Hastings.
151	Grand River,	62	J. S. Hoffman,	Berlin
153	Burns,	36	H. G. Taylor,	Wyoming.
154	Irving,	28	Wm. Frank.	Lucan
155	Peterborough,	38	Geo. Burnham. jr.	Peterboro
156	York.	40	J. Fitzallen Ellis,	Eglinton
157	Simpson,	39	A. W. Bell,	Newboro
158	Alexandra,	37	Henry Brown,	Oil Springs
159	Goodwood.	20	John McLaren,	Richmond, Ont.
160	Quebec Gar'son,	30	H. G. Mead,	Quebec.
161	Percy,	33	R. P. Hurlbut.	Warkworth
162	Forest,	31	A. Worthington,	Wroxeter.
164	Star in the East,	40	Nathaniel Gordon,	Wellington
165	Burlington.	28	Robert Halson,	Wellington Sq.
166	Wentworth,	27	E. B. Smith,	Stony Creek
168	Merritt.	38	John J. Sidey,	Welland
169	McNab,	43	C. B. Nimmo,	Port Colborne.
170	Britannia,	41	W. R. Counter,	Seaforth.
171	Prince of Wales,	55	Duncan Sinclair,	Iona.
172	Ayr,	36	J. M. K. Anderson,	Ayr
174	Walsingham,	52	Wm. Ross,	Port Rowan
176	Spartan.	26	F. A. Henderson,	Sparta.
177	The Builders,	63	Wm. Rea,	Ottawa
178	Plattsville,	35	R. J. Bourchier,	Plattsville.
179	Bothwell,	41	N. H. Avery,	Bothwell.
180	Speed,	85	J. B. Thornton,	Guelph.
181	Oriental,	55	G. W. Hare,	Port Burwell.
183	Prince Albert,	40	W. H. Browne,	Prince Albert.
184	Old Light.	32	Wm. Kennedy,	Lucknow.
185	Ennis Killen,	29	Asa K. Atkinson,	York
186	Plantagenet.	20	J. Vanbridge,	Plantagenet.
187	Royal Canadian,	33	Curtis S. Boright.	Sweetburgh.
189	Filius Viduae,	21	J. J. Watson.	Adolphustown
190	Belmont.	38	Wm. D. Eckert,	Belmont
192	Orillia,	28	G. M. Wilson,	Orillia.
193	Scotland,	27	J. D. Eddy,	Scotland.

No.	Name of Lodge.	Members.	Name of Sec'y.	Post Office.
194	Petrolia,	44	Octavius Prince,	Petrolia
195	The Tuscan,	17	S. Blackburn,	London
196	Madawaska,	21	A. Garrioch,	Arnprior
197	Saugeen,	42	Hugh Davidson,	Walker
198	White Oak,	44	E. R. Skilley,	Oakville
200	St. Alban's,	40	John McLaren,	Mount Forest
201	Leeds,	44	W. B. Carroll,	Gananoque,
202	Mount Royal,	35	John Robson,	Montreal
203	Irvine,	25	Andrew Connell,	Ellora
205	New Dominion,	39	Jacob Leyler,	New Hamburg
206	North Gower,	12		North Gower
207	Lancaster,	28	Jno. S. Bowden,	Lancaster
209	Evergreen,	15	A. G. Dobbie,	Lanark.
210	Hawksbury,	18	W. Earle Hayes,	Hawksbury
211	Brome Lake,	17	W. H. O'Reagan,	Knowlton
212	Elysian,	32	G. F. Charles,	Garden Island
213	Dominion,	25	Robert Balfour,	Ridgeway
214	Craig,	22	Wm. McIntosh,	Ailsie Craig
215	Lake,	45	John N. Sprague,	Ameliasburg
216	Harris,	39	R. J. M'Kittrick,	Orangeville.
217	Frederick	13	G. W. Wood,	Delhi
218	Stevenson,	37	Thomas Drewry,	Toronto
219	Credit,	39	J. S. Harley,	Georgetown
220	Zeradatha,	16		Uxbridge
221	Mountain,	35	Hugh James,	Thorald
222	Marmora,	16	David Fitchell,	Marmora
223	Norwood,	19	J. A. Butterfield,	Norwood
224	Zurich,	11	Robert Brown,	Zurich
225	Bernard,	14	J. H. Halstead,	Listowel
226	Mount Moriah,	22	James Reid,	Montreal
227	Sutton,	17	E. Dyer,	Sutton Flat
228	Prince Arthur,	14	John K. Booth,	Odessa
229	Ionic,	21	J. P. Clark,	Brampton
230	Kerr,	24	G. P. Mackay,	Bell Ewart
231	Fidelity,	22	G. Levin,	Ottawa
232	Cameron,	26	W. H. Loud,	Wallacetown
233	Doric,	24	R. Porte,	Park Hill
234	Beaver,	16	Joseph Rourke,	Clarksburg
235	Aldworth,	8	George Sherwood,	Paisley
236	Manitoba,	21	Ira Doane,	Bondhead
237	Vienna,	24	Rob't L. M'Cally,	Vienna
238	Havelock,	20	Alex. L. Leitch,	Watford
239	Tweed,	16	Wm. Wray,	Tweed
240	Prince Rupert's,	40	H. T. Champion,	Winnipeg
241	Quinte,	26	R. A. Fullerton,	Shannonville, On.
242	Macoy,	20	J. A. Bradley,	Escott Front.

No.	Name of Lodge.	Members.	Name of Sec'y.	Post Office.
243	St. George,	20	Benj'n Bell,	St. George
244	Lisgar,	13	Sam'l L. Bedson,	Lower F'rt Garry
245	Tecumseh,	19	E. C. Decow,	Thamesville
246	Union of St. Obs.,	31	Joseph Mitchell,	Montreal
247	Ashlar,	34	Wm. C. Pridham,	Yorkville
248	Eureka,	16	Henry Drummond,	Pakenham
249	Caledonian,	23	Thos. F. Chapin,	Angus
250	Thistle,	7	John Patterson,	Embro
251	Assiniboine,	7	Charles Curtis,	Portage la Prair.
252	International,	9	Fred'k T. Bradley,	North Pembina
253	Minden,	9	Patrick Geraghty,	Kingston
254	Clifton,	19	Sam'l Smith,	Clifton
255	Sydenham,	10	Thos. C. McNab,	Dresden
256	Farran's Point,	12	A. G. McDonell,	Farran's Point
257	Galt,	26	James M. Hood,	Galt
258	Guelph,	21	Edmund Harvey,	Guelph
259	Springfield,	16	Rev. E. Lounsbury,	Springfield
260	Washington,	16	Daniel Trotter,	Petrolia

New Brunswick.

The Grand Lodge in this Province was organized at St. John in September, 1867. by a majority of the lodges in the province, and B. Lester Peters was elected the first grand master. Its annual communication takes place in September at the City of St. John, and there were at that meeting in 1870 the representatives of a majority of 26 lodges. with 1593 contributing members. The manner of the G. L. of England is followed as nearly as is possible in the management of this grand lodge. An elective officer in the other American grand lodges, in this the grand secretary is subject to appointment of the grand master elect, although paid by the grand lodge. The grand master also appoints a Board of General Purposes, consisting of ten members of the grand lodge, selected from among the senior and past grand officers, such Board being completed by the accession of the six principal grand officers, as *ex-officio* members. At its first meeting this Board is organized by the election of a chairman, and thereupon it becomes the executive of and reports its operations to this grand lodge, at the next subsequent annual meeting. The report of the grand treasurer exhibited a balance in bank of $1,039.35.

The principal grand officers elected in 1870 were—

WILLIAM WEDDERBURN, of Hampton, Grand Master.
JOHN V. ELLIS, of Carleton, Deputy Gr. Master,
BLISS BOTSFORD, of Monckton, Sen. Grand Warden.
WM. F. DIBBLEE, of Woodstock, Jun. Grand Warden.
WM. H. A. KEANS, of St. John, Grand Treasurer.
WM. F. BUNTING, of St. John, Grand Secretary (app'ted).

For the following information we are indebted to the Proceedings for 1870.

No.	Name of Lodge.	Members.	Name of Sec'y.	Post Office.
..1..	Albion,	.......170...	Wm. S. Marvin,	.....St. John ....
..2..	Saint John's,	...104...	Edward Manning,	......do...........
..3..	Hibernia,	.....129...	David S. Stewart,	......do...........

No.	Name of Lodge.	Members.	Name of Sec'y.	Post Office.
..4..	Sussex,	45	Jno. W. Dealy,	Dorchester.
..5.	Saint Mark's,	54	Geo. F. Stickney,	St. Andrews
..6..	Solomon's,	72	A. G. Beckwith,	Fredericton
..7..	Sussex,	64	John H. Rose,	Saint Stephen.
..8..	Carleton Union,	98	Chas. Ketchum,	Carleton
..9..	Midian,	25	Rev. D. J. Wetmore,	Clifton
.10..	Portland Union,	132	Chas. Hillman,	St. John
.11..	Woodstock,	59	Isaiah J. M'Coy,	Woodstock
.12..	St. George,	49	L. B. Messenett,	St. George
.13..	Corinthian,	21	Henry Hallett,	Hampton
.14..	Alley,	76	James D. Woodcock,	Upper Mills
.15..	Howard,	53	Benj. Williams,	Hillsborough
.16..	St. Andrew,	75	Thos. W. Bliss,	Richibucto
.17..	Northumberland,	51	Kirk W. Hobart,	Newcastle
.18..	Miramichi,	54	Sam. U. M'Cully,	Chatham
.19..	Leinster,	48	Jos. E. N. Holder,	Saint John
.20..	Salisbury,	24	John S. Colpitts.	Salisbury.
.21..	Zion.	34	Fred'k L. Smith,	Sussex
.22..	New Brunswick,	65	Alex. Morrison,	Saint John
.23..	Keith.	32	Ebenezer Oliver,	Monckton
.24..	Zetland,	32	A. R. Weldon.	Shediac
.25..	Restigouche,	27	Henry A. Johnson,	Dalhousie
.26..	Victoria,	—	David Main, (*W.M.*)	Milltown

Nova Scotia.

A grand lodge was organized for this Province in June 1866, and the same was generally recognized by the United States grand lodges, but it could not properly be termed the G. Lodge of Nova Scotia, for the reason that none of the lodges in the Province holding charters from the G. L. of Scotland acknowledged it. Not until June 24, 1869, was the Grand Lodge of Nova Scotia organized by the complete union of all the lodges then in the Province, fifty-one in number, and holding originally their charters from the several British grand lodges of the past century. The Hon. Alex. Keith, who had for many years, under Scottish appointment, filled the office of Provincial grand master, was elected the first grand master of the united grand lodge, and which in October, 1870, had on its register 57 lodges with 1811 subscribing members—several of the lodges making no return of membership. By the adoption, at the annual meeting that year, of a new constitution this grand lodge will hold two regular communications each year : the annual in June and the semi-annual in December, both at Halifax. The assets of this grand lodge were, in October 1870, reported at nearly $4000 in cash and invested, and it was resolved to pay the reasonable expenses of one representative from each lodge, situate more than twenty miles from Halifax, to attend those communications. Except in the matter of lodge representation, otherwise, this grand lodge in the manner of its organization resembles that of those bodies in the United States.

The executive grand officers elected in 1870 were—

> Hon. ALEX. KEITH, of Halifax, Grand Master.
> WM. TAYLOR, of Halifax, Deputy Grand Master
> ANDREW MACKINLAY, of Halifax, Grand Treasurer
> BENJAMIN CURREN, of Halifax, Grand Secretary.

From the Proceedings of the G. L. for 1870, courteously correc ted by the grand secretary, the following list is arranged.

No.	Name of Lodge.	Members.	Name of Sec'y.	Post Office.
..1..	St. Andrew's,	..31...	N. L. Herbert,......	Halifax.......
..2..	St John's,......	35...	Dr. Thos. Milsom, ...	do...........
..3..	Virgin, ...	47...	Wm. Daking,..........	do...........
..4..	Unity.	26...	Wm. M. B. Lawson,.	Lunenburg ....
..5..	Albion.........	90...	Rob't Walker, ...	New Glasgow ...
..6..	Royal Sussex, ..	74...	Geo. Gordon,......	Halifax.........
..7..	St. Andrew's,..	36...	Rob. I. Ingraham,..	Sydney, C. B....
..8..	Acacia, ...	34..| George Deery,......	Amherst........
..9..	Zetland, ...	84...	W. McG. Scott, ...	Liverpool......
.10..	Burns..........	71...	Wm. Taylor,'......	Halifax.........
.11..	New Caledonia.	124...	J. W. H. Cameron,.	Pictou... ....
.12..	Hiram.........	54...	A. W. Homer,......	Yarmouth.......
.13..	Acadia,.............		:Donald Macaulay, ..	Pugwash........
.14..	Acadia, ...	42...	Jas. G. Smith, ...	Halifax.........
.15..	Athole.........	45...	Wm. S. McDonald, ...	do...........
.16..	Keith, ...	50 ..	E. G. Miller,.......	Hillsburg......
.17..	Keith, ...	57...	G. McMann,........	Halifax........
.18..	Union,.........	27...	Wm. B. Thomas, ...	do.........:
.19..	Royal Albert, ..	28...	Chas. A. Robertson,.	Nor. Sydney, C.B.
.20..	St. George,.........		Jas. W. Bigelow,...	Wolfville ......
.21..	Davies, ...	28...	Chas. Jaques,......	Wilmot. ....
.22..	Scotia,.........	41...	A. S. Sutherland,...	Halifax........
.23..	Keith, ...	49...	Jas. Mitchell,......	Albion Mines....
.24..	Concord,............		(No returns,)......	Barrington......
.25..	Westport,.............		do...........	Westport, Brier I.
.26..	Welsford, ...	59...	Chas. W. Payzant, .	Windsor........
.27..	Widow's Friend,......		(No returns.)	Weymouth......
.28..	Scotia,........	29...	C. F. Eaton,.......	Canning ....
.29..	Prince of Wales,	57...	L. S. Ford, ...	Milton..........
.30..	Albert, ...		Dr. J. A. Purney, ...	Shelburne ......
.31..	Scotia,........	38...	Geo. W. Tooker,....	Yarmouth.......
.32..	El Dorado,..........		(No returns,)......	Wine Harbor....
.33..	Annapolis, ...	39...	John Tobias.........	Annapolis ......
.34..	Queen's, ...	41...	Edw. Williams, ...	Sherbrooke. ....
.35..	St. Mark's, ...	37...	Donald McRae, ...	Baddeck, C. B...
.36..	Thistle.........	45'...	Nathan Martell, ...	Cow Bay ....
.37..	Cobequid,......	41...	John K. Andrews....	Truro ....
.38..	Of St. Mark,....	39...	W. S. McDonald,....	Halifax.........
.39..	Acacia, ...	52...	P. M. Morrison,....	Bridgewater ..
.41..	Rothsay, ...	64...	Benj. Starratt, ...	Bridgetown ....
.42..	Eureka,........	37...	Benj. Tupper, ...	Sheet Harbor ...
.43..	Truro, ...	27...	Chas. E. Perry,......	Truro ....
.44..	Poyntz, ...	23...	J. W. Lawrence,....	Hantsport ......
.45..	Tyrian, ...	9...	Francis Lewis,......	Little Glace Bay.
.46..	Solomon,......	26...	Peter Grant,.......	Port Hawksbury
.47..	Philadelphia, ...	26...	Israel K. Wilson,....	Barrington ....

No.	Name of Lodge.	Members.	Name of Sec'y.	Post Office.
.48.	Widow's Son,.	.11.	O. B. Davidson,	River Philip .
.49.	Orient,.	24.	David Pottinger,	Richmond .
.50.	Western Star,.	19.	Thos. Johnstone,	Westville.
.51.	Eastern Star, .	33.	J. Hollis,	Dartmouth.
.52.	Harmony,.	40.	Geo. W. Sandford,	Aylesford.
.53.	Hiram, .	22.	Marshall Sinclair,	Goldenville
.54.	King Solomon,.	—.	T. M. Quirk,	Digby.
55.	Morien,.	—.	Isaac Archibald,	Cow Bay, C. B.
.56.	Harmony,.	—.	Thos. S. Perry.	Shelburne
.57.	Temple,.	—.	John A. McMillen,	Port Mulgrave .
.58.	Kentville,.	—.	Dr. J. Struthers.	Kentville .
.59.	Manitoba, .	—.	*Chartered Dec.* 2, '70,	New Glasgow.
.60.	Leman, .	—.	do.... *Mar.* 1,'71,	Petite Rivière.
.61.	Clarke, .	—.	do.......do	Chester.

☞ Note.—In the *General History*, &c., published by Robert Macoy at New York in 1869 and since, it is stated that " the first " lodge in Quebec was organized by authority of a warrant from " St. John's Grand Lodge, of Boston, Mass." This statement is entirely incorrect, and unsupported by any evidence. *Albion* Lodge, No. 0, on the page following this, ranks as No. 17 on the register of the United Grand Lodge of England. It was organized in 1722—*eleven* years before a Masonic lodge existed in Boston, or elsewhere in those colonies which subsequently became the United States. This is, outside of the city of London, the eldest lodge of those which have been chartered by the first grand lodge of Free and Accepted Masons ever organized.

Quebec.

The Grand Lodge in this Province was organized on the 20th of October, 1869, by the representatives of a majority of the lodges at that time in the Province convened for that purpose at Montreal, and John H. Graham was elected the first grand master. Its first annual communication was held in that city on the 19th and 20th days of October, 1870, at which time there were on its register 31 lodges, with 1279 contributing members. In its Proceedings of that date we find no reference to its finances. Being, so to say, but lately organized and, as yet, denied recognition by the Grand Lodge of Canada, with which, when so recognized, it should share to extent of a *pro rata* division the funds of the latter, the subject of finances has not, as it appears, been yet arranged or regarded with the degree of interest usual in such bodies. Like that of New Brunswick, this grand lodge is organized with the appointment of a Board of General Purposes, which, with the principal elective grand officers, constitute the executive between each ann. com., and at which such Board reports. Lodge representation in this grand lodge is unlimited as in those of the other provinces, being in all alike modeled on that of England.

The principal grand officers elected in 1870 were—

JOHN HAMILTON GRAHAM, of Richmond, Grand Master.

H. J. PRATTEN, of Quebec, Dep. Gr. Master.

H. M. ALEXANDER, of Montreal, Grand Treasurer.

JOHN H. ISAACSON, of Montreal, Grand Secretary.

From the well-printed Proceedings of this grand lodge for 1870 we present the following list of the lodges in this Province then acknowledging allegiance to the G. L. of Quebec.

No.	Name of Lodge.	Members.	Name of Sec'y.	Post Office.
0	Albion.	40	Wm. Miller,	Quebec
1	St. John's,	55	Peter Brady,	do
2	Prevost,	55	F. F. Wood,	Durham
3	Nelson,	28	P. E. Luke,	Philipsburg
4	Golden Rule,	132	H. C. Hyalt,	Stanstead.

No.	Name of Lodge.	Members.	Name of Sec'y.	Post Office.
..5	St. Andrew's,	..63	Joseph Bates,	Quebec.....'...
..6	St. George,	93	G. A. Sargison,	Montreal ....
..7	Zetland,	...32	Jas. G. Cleghorn,	do...........
..8	Harington,	36	Wm. Jacques,	Quebec.........
..9	Hoyle.	22	Jas. A. Hume,	Lacolle.........
:10	St. Francis,	46	Edwin Cleveland,	Richmond ......
.11	Victoria,	66	A. D. Bostwick,.	Sherbrooke .....
.12	Stanbridge,	56	M. V. Bryan,	Stanbridge......
.13	Kilwinning,	...162	W. H. Hall,	Montreal........
.14	Brown,	28	Hy. Bowker,	West Farnham...
.15	Royal Albert,	..55	Jno. S. Ferguson,	Montreal........
.16	Victoria,	20	Alex. Murray,	do...........
.17	St. John's,	51	D. A. Manson,	Masonville......
.18	Ascot,	40	W. H. Leranet,	Lenoxville......
.19	Ashler,	53	W. H. Thomas,	Cooticook.......
.20	Tuscan,	30	Moses Cass,	Levis ....
.21	Clarenceville,	..21	W. L. Simpson,	Clarenceville....
.22	Frelighsburg,	..21	E. E. Spencer..	Frelighsburg....
.23	Doric.	45	Wm. Boutelle,	Danville ....
.24	Chateaugay,	50	Stuart McDonald,	Huntingdon.....
.25	Milton,	31	Aug. F. Holt,	Three Rivers....
.26	Abercorn,	15	Benj. Seaton,	Abercorn.......
.27	Corner Stone,	..23	E. H. Goff,	Cowansville.....
.28	Clarke,	10	Jos. Patenaude,	Ormstown ......
.29	St. Charles,	....	H. T. Loomis,	Pt. St. Charles...
.30	Des Cœurs Unis,	.....	A. Bolté,	Montreal ....

In the British Provinces of Prince Edward Island, Newfound-
land, and the West India Islands the lodges hold their charters
from the Grand Lodges of England or Scotland. According to the
Registers of those grand lodges there are in the colonies named
the following lodges :—

PRINCE EDWARD ISLAND.

.397	Eng. Reg.	St. John's, Charlotte Town,	Chartered in 1829
.821	.... do	King Hiram, St. Eleanor's,	........do.... 1860
.866	.... do	St. George's, Georgetown,	........do.... 1861
.983	.... do	Alexandra, Port Hill,	...do.... 1863
984	.... do	Mt. Lebanon, Summerside,	........do.... 1863
1200	.... do	Zetland, Alberton,	........do.... 1867 .
1251	.... do	True Brothers, Tryon,	........do.... 1869
.383	Scot. Reg.	Victoria, Charlotte Town,	........do.... 1858

NEWFOUNDLAND.

```
.579..Eng Reg...St. John's, City of St. John,........do.....  1850
.776.... do......Avalon, ....... do..............do....  1859
1281.... do......Hiram, Burin, ...................do....  1869
.431..Scot. Reg..St. John, City of St. John, ........do....  1864
.454.... do......Tasker,....... do.................do....  1866
.476.... do......St. John's, Harbor Grace,........do....  1867
```

WEST INDIA ISLANDS.
ANTIGUA.

```
.492..Eng. Reg...St. John's, at St. John,............do....  1843
.669.... do......Star in the West, at St. John,......do....  1856
```

BARBADOES.

```
.196.... do......Albion, at Bridgetown,...........do....  1770
.340..Scot. Reg..Scotia,........do................do....  1843
```

BERMUDA.

```
.224..Eng. Reg...Atlantic Phœnix, at Hamilton, ....do....  1774
.233.... do......Prince Alfred, at Somerset, .......do....  1776
.358.... do......Loyalty, at Ireland Island,........do....  1819
.200..Scot. Reg..St. George, at St. George,.........do.....  1797
```

JAMAICA.

```
.207..Eng. Reg...Royal, at the City of Kingston,....do....  1772
.239.... do......Friendly, ......do......do.......do....  1777
.354.... do......Sussex,........do......do.......do....  1817
.383.... do......Friendly, at Montego Bay,.........do....  1825
.513.... do......Union & Concord, at Kingston,....do....  1845
.805.... do......Hamilton, at Spanish Town, ......do....  1859
.914.... do......Phœnix, at Port Royal,...........do....  1862
.344..Scot. Reg..Elgin, at the City of Kingston,.....do....  1844
.346.... do......Glenlyon,...do.........do........do....  1844
.359.... do......Union, .....do....... do........do....  1851
.367.... do.....Athol Union. at Falmouth,........do....  1853
.369.... do......St. Andrew Kilw'g, St. Andrews,...do...,  1855
.402.... do......Victoria, at Port Royal,..........do....  1860
```

TRINIDAD.

```
.405..Eng. Reg...Royal Philanthropic, Port of Spain, do....  1831
.572.... do......Royal Trinity, San Fernando, .....do....  1850
.867.... do...'...Prince of Wales, Port of Spain,....do....  1861
.911.... do......Royal Phœnix, .....do...........do....  1862
.251..Scot. Reg..United Brothers,....do..........do....  1813
.368.... do......Eastern Star.........do..........do....  1854
.438.... do......Athole, at San Fernando,.........do....  1864
.488.... do......Scarboro, Island of Tobago, ......do....  1869
```

BAHAMA ISLANDS.

.443..Eng. Reg...Royal Victoria, Nassau. N. P.,   Charte'd in 1837
1277.... do......Britannia, Harbor Island..........do.... 1869
.647.... do......Turk's Island, Grand Turk, T. I....do.... 1856

IN the Island of Cuba, under the old regime of Spain, Masonic lodges are prohibited ; nevertheless such do exist, but nothing of a reliable character concerning them is known to us, or can be recorded with propriety.

WE here close our presentation of as full and correct a register of the lodges and grand lodges of Freemasons in North America which recognize each other, or correspond to any extent, as it is possible, we believe, at this time to produce. To these might be added about three hundred lodges of colored men. more or less, but which are not to any extent, from political and social causes, recognized by United States lodges or grand lodges the names of which we have given ; nor are we enabled to record that, taking their orders from their Mother grand lodges of Great Britain, do the lodges or grand lodges in any part of North America recognize them. However much, in view of the truly catholic and universal character that is claimed for Freemasonry, this fact may be deprecated by those of the Fraternity who *in paternitatem Dei crederem, et fraternitatem magnam Hominis,* nevertheless those very men, while they may not cease to work and hope for the early realization of this their belief, must be content also to believe that majorities will rule while *voluntas populi lex suprema est.*

Advertisements.

IN books of this character a few select advertisements, especially those of brethren dealers in the necessary outfit and equipments for any of the various Masonic bodies, may not be regarded out of place. but, as reference, be useful to the brethren in whose hands this little book may rest. Each of the advertisements here presented may be relied upon as representing an entirely responsible party or firm. Were we so disposed we could extend this department largely, but we prefer to confine it mainly to the advertisements of Manufacturers and Dealers in Masonic and other Society Furnishing Goods, and have, therefore, refused to insert in it several advertisements offered of a miscellaneous character, and which might be regarded as objectionable and improper to appear in a book of this kind.

www.ingramcontent.com/pod-product-compliance
Lightning Source LLC
Chambersburg PA
CBHW021616270326
41931CB00008B/721